The End of Engagement

The End of Engagement

*America's China and Russia Experts and
U.S. Strategy since 1989*

DAVID M. McCOURT

OXFORD
UNIVERSITY PRESS

Oxford University Press is a department of the University of Oxford.
It furthers the University's objective of excellence in research, scholarship,
and education by publishing worldwide. Oxford is a registered trade mark of
Oxford University Press in the UK and in certain other countries.

Published in the United States of America by Oxford University Press
198 Madison Avenue, New York, NY 10016, United States of America.

© Oxford University Press 2024

All rights reserved. No part of this publication may be reproduced, stored
in a retrieval system, or transmitted, in any form or by any means, without the
prior permission in writing of Oxford University Press, or as expressly permitted
by law, by license or under terms agreed with the appropriate reprographics
rights organization. Inquiries concerning reproduction outside the scope of the
above should be sent to the Rights Department, Oxford University Press, at the
address above.

You must not circulate this work in any other form
and you must impose this same condition on any acquirer

Library of Congress Cataloging-in-Publication Data
Names: McCourt, David M., author.
Title: The end of engagement : America's China and Russia experts and
U.S. strategy since 1989 / David M. McCourt.
Description: New York, NY : Oxford University Press, 2024. |
Includes bibliographical references and index.
Identifiers: LCCN 2024017098 (print) | LCCN 2024017099 (ebook) |
ISBN 9780197765210 (paperback) | ISBN 9780197765203 (hardback) |
ISBN 9780197765234 (epub)
Subjects: LCSH: National security—United States. | World politics—1989– |
United States—Foreign relations—China. |
United States—Foreign relations—2017-2021. |
China—Foreign relations—United States. |
United States—Foreign relations—Russia (Federation) |
Russia (Federation)—Foreign relations—United States.
Classification: LCC JZ1480 .M347 2024 (print) | LCC JZ1480 (ebook) |
DDC 355/.033073—dc23/eng/20240508
LC record available at https://lccn.loc.gov/2024017098
LC ebook record available at https://lccn.loc.gov/2024017099

DOI: 10.1093/9780197765241.001.0001

Paperback printed by Marquis Book Printing, Canada
Hardback printed by Bridgeport National Bindery, Inc., United States of America

For Stephanie, always

Contents

Preface ... ix

Introduction: Engaging China and Russia since 1989 ... 1

PART I RETHINKING ENGAGEMENT

1. What Was Engagement? ... 31
2. From Engagement to Strategic Competition ... 60

PART II THE END OF ENGAGEMENT WITH CHINA

3. Beyond Hawks and Doves: Polarization in the U.S. China Field ... 115
4. Professional Status Oppositions and the Wisdom of Engagement ... 139
5. Engagement Is Personal ... 163

PART III ENDING ENGAGEMENT WITH RUSSIA

6. The Russia-We-Have, or the Russia-We-Want? Polarization in the Russia Field ... 193
7. The Politics of U.S. Russia Expertise ... 221
8. Engagement with Russia Is Personal ... 240

Conclusion: After Engagement ... 260

Methodological Appendix ... 281
Bibliography ... 287
Index ... 295

Preface

In an open letter to the *Washington Post* in July 2019, a group of distinguished U.S.-based China experts expressed concern at the "growing deterioration in U.S.-China relations" under Donald Trump.[1] "China is not an enemy," the writers urged, pushing back against a "new consensus" in Washington. The authors, which included prominent political scientist Taylor Fravel,[2] think tanker Michael Swaine,[3] and former diplomats Stapleton Roy[4] and Susan Thornton,[5] collected the signatures of over 100 national security specialists opposed to Trump's anti-China rhetoric and trade war. While China's growing authoritarianism and aggressive external behavior required a strong response, the writers acknowledged, policymakers should not view Beijing as an existential threat but rather base policy on "a realistic appraisal of Chinese perceptions, interests, goals and behavior ... and a rededication of U.S. efforts to strengthen its own capacity to serve as a model for others."

Open letters often come in multiples, and so did this one. Journalist John Pomfret[6] was first to the punch with a case against a gentler approach.[7] "Treat China as an enemy, the tired chestnut goes, and China will become one," Pomfret warned. "Treat China as a friend, and China will become a friend. It's as if China has no role to play in this drama whatsoever. Can't we bury that notion once and for all?" An organized response came, meanwhile, not in the *Post* but in the more obscure *Journal of Political Risk*, where a group of strident China critics urged the Trump administration to "stay the course of countering

---

[1] M. Taylor Fravel, J. Stapleton Roy, Michael D. Swaine, Susan A. Thornton, and Ezra Vogel, "Opinion: China Is Not an Enemy," *Washington Post*, 3 July 2019, https://www.washingtonpost.com/opinions/making-china-a-us-enemy-is-counterproductive/2019/07/02/647d49d0-9bfa-11e9-b27f-ed2942f73d70_story.html. All online sources accessed August 2023 unless otherwise stated.

[2] Throughout the book I focus on the critical role played by individual members of America's China and Russia expert communities in the making and remaking of U.S. strategy. When I introduce new people, I will provide a brief biographical description denoting key positions and roles (current as of August 2023). M. Taylor Fravel is the Arthur and Ruth Sloan Professor of Political Science at the Massachusetts Institute of Technology.

[3] Senior research fellow at the Quincy Institute for Responsible Statecraft, previously a senior associate in the Asia Program at the Carnegie Endowment for International Peace.

[4] Former diplomat, including as ambassador to China (1991–1995).

[5] Former diplomat, including acting assistant secretary of state for East Asian and Pacific affairs.

[6] Writer and journalist for the *Washington Post*.

[7] John Pomfret, "Why the United States Does Not Need a Return to a Gentler China Policy," *Washington Post*, 9 July 2019, https://www.washingtonpost.com/opinions/2019/07/09/why-united-states-doesnt-need-return-gentler-china-policy/.

communist China."[8] Echoing Pomfret, for the over 100 former military officers, academics, commentators, and officials—whom I will term in this book the "anti-Engagers"—"No amount of U.S. diplomatic, economic, or military 'engagement' will disrupt the . . . PRC's global ambitions to suppress freedom and liberty."[9]

The following summer another flurry of open-letter activity emerged in a different corner of the U.S. foreign policy community: America's Russia watchers.[10] Here too the opening call was for a more cooperative policy. Rallying to the cry to "deal with Russia as it is, not as we wish it to be," over 100 experts agreed with the letter's authors—including arms controller Rose Gottemoeller,[11] former National Security Council Russia director Thomas Graham,[12] and think tanker Fiona Hill[13]—for whom policymakers were sleepwalking into dangerous relations with Moscow.[14] "We are drifting toward a fraught nuclear arms race, with our foreign policy arsenal reduced mainly to sanctions, public shaming, and congressional resolutions." The authors called for a foreign policy "open eyed" about the challenges of dealing with Russia, but one that includes diplomacy and a flexible sanctions regime.

This time, not one but three responses appeared. Six days later, 33 experts joined former assistant secretary of state for democracy, human rights, and Labor David Kramer[15] in expressing horror at the proposition of a "new Russia reset."[16] Acknowledging some U.S. responsibility for poor relations, Kramer and company laid blame squarely at the door of Vladimir Putin. "Since President George H.W. Bush, every American administration has tried to establish good relations. . . . But since Putin came to power, the Russian side has not reciprocated." No amount of diplomacy could avoid the reality that "Putin is more interested in portraying the United States as Russia's greatest enemy—to justify his repressive

---

[8] http://www.jpolrisk.com/stay-the-course-on-china-an-open-letter-to-president-trump/.

[9] http://www.jpolrisk.com/stay-the-course-on-china-an-open-letter-to-president-trump/.

[10] Throughout I use the terms China and Russia "experts" and "watchers" as shorthand, always aware of the contested nature of the terms themselves, of which more later.

[11] Former diplomat, including as undersecretary of state for arms control and international security (2012–2016), and deputy secretary general of the North Atlantic Treaty Organization (NATO) (2016–2019).

[12] Graham served in the role from 2002 to 2004. He previously served as associate director of the Policy Planning Staff at the Department of State. He is now Distinguished Fellow at the Council on Foreign Relations.

[13] Distinguished Fellow at the Brookings Institution, formerly senior director for Europe and Russia at the National Security Council (2017–2019).

[14] Rose Gottemoeller, Thomas Graham, Fiona Hill, Jon Huntsman Jr., Robert Legvold, and Thomas R. Pickering, "It's Time to Rethink Our Russia Policy," Politico, 5 August 2020, https://www.politico.com/news/magazine/2020/08/05/open-letter-russia-policy-391434. Curiously, unlike the letter's responses, the link to the original letter seems to no longer work.

[15] Assistant secretary of state for democracy, human rights, and labor (2008–2009).

[16] David J. Kramer, "Opinion: No, Now Is Not the Time for Another Russia Reset," Politico, 11 August 2020, https://www.politico.com/news/magazine/2020/08/11/russia-reset-response-open-letter-393176.

control at home." For the writers of two further letters penned by representatives of the Eastern European diaspora, "Now is not the time to go soft on Russia."[17]

Open letters are a common feature of life "inside the Beltway." They are also a sociologist's dream. They trace the boundaries of what is sayable and doable in the contentious DC foreign policy space. Open letters must be handled with care—as important as who signs is who doesn't, or who wasn't invited. Nonetheless, by their existence they highlight the main issues that divide the policy elite, while identifying the thought leaders and the stakes of their bureaucratic turf wars. In short, open letters lay bare all the fault lines and factions, not to mention drama, behind the making of policy, as people jostle for notoriety, prestige, and that prized job in government.

This book is about the fault lines and factions, disputes and personalities, and very much the drama, in two such parts of Washington—America's China and Russia experts—in a time of tumultuous policymaking toward Beijing and Moscow. I show that the demise of America's long-standing approach toward the People's Republic (PRC), often labeled "Engagement," was made possible by a paradigmatic turnover within the U.S. China expert community prior to and during the Trump administration (2017–2020). Through Engagement, generations of U.S. foreign policymakers hoped to realize the benefits of integrating Beijing into the Western-led international order while avoiding the perils of dealing with a more powerful China. Against common wisdom that accounts for Engagement's demise as a straightforward response to the failure of this rose-tinted vision,[18] the book shows the more contingent and contested path to Engagement's end.

The book demonstrates how a combative and China-skeptical set of views emerged as a coherent, powerful, and crucially *legitimate* alternative among America's China experts prior to 2016. The election of Donald Trump as president brought into positions of power and authority a set of advisors from what I call the "anti-Engager" camp in the China field. Once in government, anti-Engagers set about reorienting America's approach to Beijing, designing and implementing an approach known as Strategic Competition to orient the making of policy toward China across the U.S. government. Rather than return to Engagement, Trump's successor, Joseph Biden, doubled down on Strategic Competition. The Biden team did not return to Engagement, I show, because

---

[17] Sławomir Dębski, James Sherr, and Jakub Janda, "Take It from Eastern Europe: Now Is Not the Time to Go Soft on Russia," *Politico*, 31 August 2020, https://www.politico.com/news/magazine/2020/08/31/open-letter-not-time-to-go-soft-on-russia-405266; Ariana Gic, Hanna Hopko, and Roman Sohn, "Appeasing Vladimir Putin's Russia Will Only Embolden It," *Politico*, 25 September 2020, https://www.politico.com/news/magazine/2020/09/25/open-letter-russia-ukraine-421519.

[18] For example, Rogin 2021; Friedberg 2022.

the center of gravity in the China field—from which they staffed their key China positions—had shifted firmly against Engagement.

I develop this argument via a comparison with the dynamics of America's Russia-watching community and its relationship to U.S. policy toward Moscow. Despite opposed understandings of how best to deal with Putin's Russia on display in the 2020 open letters, the Russia community has not experienced the sort of paradigmatic turnover witnessed among America's China watchers. The Russia community is smaller, more collegial, and less polarized than the China field—the inverse of how things were during the Cold War—limiting the urgency to reframe America's understandings of Moscow. Official relations between Washington and Moscow were also already at a low ebb by 2016, rendering a pro-cooperation framing unrealistic and a threat-focused framing unnecessary. The result was policy stasis, with a ratcheting sanctions regime overtaken by the Russian invasion of Ukraine in February 2022. The absence of struggle among America's Russia watchers to reframe Russia, highlights its centrality to the end of Engagement with the PRC.

Knowledge communities like America's China and Russia watchers rarely feature as central objects in analyses of U.S. foreign policy. The reason is simple: the activity of researchers, think tankers, academics, pundits, and self-styled intellectuals and experts is only indirectly connected to policy. Each monograph, article, op-ed, tweet, report, or podcast is a single grain of sand in the hourglass of policymaking, a vast machine shaped by powerful forces, from the whims of Congress to the lobbying of U.S. multinationals and labor, from public opinion to the shifting balance of global power. From time to time a work makes its way onto everyone's reading list—hopefully soon including this one. Even then, it does not *cause* policy or strategy. Policy reflects the beliefs, agendas, and biases of top-level policymakers, the outcomes of the bureaucratic struggles they wage and their bargaining with foreign governments.

Why then concern ourselves with the role of America's China and Russia experts in the demise of Engagement with Beijing and in worsening relations with Moscow since the Cold War? Let us return to the open letters of 2020. The signatories were not just anyone: they included former ambassadors, National Security Council directors, deputies, assistants, and acting officials. In short, the letters' signatories were *both* members of the China and Russia professional communities *and* former and possible future policymakers and officials. There is no neat divide between policymakers and knowledge communities. The two are intertwined—most obviously when knowledge communities supply the credentialed individuals who staff administrations and help formulate and implement policy. America's knowledge communities do not determine policy, therefore, but they are a crucial conduit between the government and broader societal views of the U.S. national interest.

Common-sense accounts of U.S. foreign policymaking make scant reference to America's knowledge communities, however. The standard explanation for the downward trajectory of U.S.-China and U.S.-Russia relations since the Cold War tells of a rational response to a changing world: deepening authoritarianism in Russia and China; the rapid growth of Chinese relative power and the lack of the same in Russia; and the growing assertiveness of each on the world stage. This common sense is powerful in U.S. foreign policy circles, especially after Russia's invasion of Ukraine in February 2022, with China siding with Moscow. As an account of why engagement failed, however, it is also partial at best.

In this book, I trace the intense personal, professional, and policy struggles over China and Russia in U.S. strategy since 1989. Based on over 150 original interviews with members of the China- and Russia-watching communities—former policymakers and diplomats, prominent think tankers and academics, and aspiring experts—the book chronicles the ongoing contests among America's national security exerts over the virtues, vices, even *existence* of something called "engagement" with Moscow and Beijing. The book paints a unique picture of the end of engagement, with crucial implications for what comes next.

It is a pleasure difficult to capture in words to acknowledge the people and institutions without whose help the research and writing for this book would have been impossible.

First, and most important, this book would not exist were it not for the dozens of interviewees who kindly gave their time and shared their insights—busy people willing to respond to emails and to arrange time to meet and chat, which often necessitated finding alternative times and venues at the last minute. They did so based solely on my promise to faithfully reflect their views. I hope to have fulfilled that promise. While I have my own opinions about U.S. policy toward China and Russia, past and present, my aim here has been to describe my interviewees' views as objectively as possible. The debates I chronicle will not stop if I have succeeded, nor should they. But if I have kept my promise, interviewees should find their world and their worldviews accurately represented in these pages.

At the University of California, Davis, my sociology colleagues deserve thanks for strong support of my endeavors while making working life a pleasure. Drew Halfmann, Stephanie Mudge, Ori Tamir, and members of the Power and Inequalities workshops where I presented draft versions of the work offered important feedback. Eddy U has been a consistent supporter as well as insightful reader. Colleague and friend Jenny Kaminer offered insights and made much-needed connections to America's Russia expert community. I received generous funding from the East Asian Studies program, with thanks to Xiaoling Shu and Eddy U (again), the UC Davis Senate, the Hellman Family Fellows program, and the Davis Humanities Institute. Together, this support allowed me to find sufficient calm among the disruptions of the Covid pandemic, not to mention everyday life, to complete the research and writing for the book. Also at Davis, Robert Taylor and Yvonne Chiu recognized my residual political science credentials, while sampling a certain Northern Californian beverage.

The book benefited from comments provided by audiences at Brown University, kindly arranged by the incomparable Mark Blyth, as well as at many panels at annual conferences of the International Studies Association, International Studies Association West region, American Sociological Association, and the Social Science History Association. Important individuals here include in international relations circles Jonathan Acuff, Jack Amoureux, Alex Barder, Dave Blagden, Mauro Caraciolli, Frank Foley, Jamie Frueh, Jamie Gaskarth, Andrew Glencross, Harry Gould, Inanna Hamati-Ataya, Jarrod Hayes, Eric Heinze, Patrick Thaddeus Jackson, Daniel Levine, Dan Nexon, Mark Raymond, Garrett Ruley, Len Seabrooke, Ty Solomon, Brent J. Steele, Michael Struett, Stephanie Winkler, and Ayse Zarakol; and in sociology Zach Griffen, Ho-Fung Hung, Lyn Spillman, and Yang Zhang. Richard Lachmann provided early encouragement and is much missed.

Gregoire Mallard deserves special thanks for his prescience in suggesting, in early 2015 if I remember rightly, that I narrow down my interest in the institutional architecture of American hegemony to relations with China. A big thank you goes to roving China watcher Kaiser Kuo, who generously brought me on to his *Sinica* podcast in January 2022. Both Bob Kapp and David Shambaugh were kind enough to read a draft of the manuscript, catching far more errors than I'd like to admit and offering critical feedback at a crucial time. My sincere thanks.

The book benefited greatly from the following support: first, I am proud to be among the second cohort of Wilson Center China Fellows. Lucas Myers and Robert Daly took a gamble on a sociological fly-on-the-wall. I hope to have offered an insightful perspective a little out of the ordinary. Second, I gratefully acknowledge the support of the Charles Koch Foundation and especially Andrew Byers, Ted Tyler, and David Snyder, who each saw potential in the book project very early. Third, the Institute for Humane Studies provided generous support facilitating a trip to Washington, DC, in spring 2023. A big thank you in particular to Maria Rogacheva for her interest in my ongoing research. Finally, I am proud to be a nonresident fellow at Defense Priorities. Thanks to Ed King, Ben Friedman, Tucker Kass, Ryan Nuckles, Natalie Armbruster, and Cameron Wilkie for making me feel a welcome part of the team. I hope this book contributes to the organization's aim to promote realism and restraint in Washington, while grappling with the profound challenge posed by a risen China.

Several sets of friends across the country deserve thanks. Jenny and Dave Ware are owed a special note for allowing me to impose myself on their Alexandria home while visiting DC over the last nine years(!). I simply would not have been able to complete the book without them. Getting to see their beautiful girls Charlotte and Julia grow up into the fine young women they are has been a delightful bonus. Davis friends Paul and Liz Ashwood, Christoph Gumb and Jenny Kaminer, and Molly McCarthy and their wonderful families made Covid a time of fun as well as struggle. To our Covid podmates Siobhan Brady and Jeremy, Ciaran, and Shia Koch, I will never be able to say thank you enough for helping us through.

My mum, dad, sister Clare, her husband Scott, and my super niece Alice are a constant source of support, care, and laughter. Thank you.

To my boys Leighton and Julian, this is the second book mostly written in the parking lot at your soccer practices. Please don't give it up or I'll never make Full.

The book is dedicated to Stephanie. As always.

In haste to complete the manuscript, I am certain there will be those I've missed. To you, my apologies. I will thank you in person, I promise.

Introduction

Engaging China and Russia since 1989

The End of the Post–Cold War Era

Russia's invasion of Ukraine in February 2022 proved to many commentators on U.S. foreign policy that world politics had entered a new era.[1] Think tanker Emma Ashford summed up the feeling: "The post-Cold War Era is over."[2] Fallout from the wars in Iraq and Afghanistan, and a shift in global power away from America, had long portended the end of the post-1989 "unipolar moment."[3] For Robert Kagan, the geopolitical "jungle" has grown back.[4] For Fareed Zakaria, the world is increasingly post-American.[5] The 2022 National Security Strategy (NSS) made it official, stating "the post-Cold War era is definitively over."[6]

Most striking about such pronouncements is their target: Moscow. For most of the five years prior to the 2022 NSS, Russia was not Washington's focus, *China* was. During its tenure (January 2017–January 2021), the Trump administration oversaw a transformation in America's approach to the People's Republic. Out went Engagement, which sought to incorporate a growing China into the U.S.-led international order, and in came Strategic Competition, which seeks to confront a Beijing that hopes "to shape a world antithetical to U.S. values and interests."[7] The Biden administration deepened America's commitment to competition with China, most notably via the AUKUS (Australia–United

---

[1] See Mary Else Sarotte, "I'm a Cold War Historian. We're in a Frightening New Era," *New York Times*, 1 March 2022, https://www.nytimes.com/2022/03/01/opinion/russia-ukraine-cold-war.html.

[2] Emma Ashford, "It's Official: The Post-Cold War Era Is Over," *New York Times*, 24 February 2022, https://www.nytimes.com/2022/02/24/opinion/ukraine-russia-biden.html.

[3] See Layne 2012.

[4] Kagan 2019.

[5] Zakaria 2012.

[6] *National Security Strategy*, October 2022, https://www.whitehouse.gov/wp-content/uploads/2022/10/Biden-Harris-Administrations-National-Security-Strategy-10.2022.pdf, 6.

[7] *United States Strategic Approach to the People's Republic of China*, May 2020, https://trumpwhitehouse.archives.gov/wp-content/uploads/2020/05/U.S.-Strategic-Approach-to-The-Peoples-Republic-of-China-Report-5.24v1.pdf; *National Security Strategy of the United States*, December 2017, https://trumpwhitehouse.archives.gov/wp-content/uploads/2017/12/NSS-Final-12-18-2017-0905.pdf, 25.

The End of Engagement. David M. McCourt, Oxford University Press. Oxford University Press 2024.
DOI: 10.1093/9780197765241.003.0001

Kingdom–United States) defense agreement with Australia and the UK.[8] While a domestic headache because of its election meddling, prior to February 2022 Russia remained a secondary strategic problem. If relations with any rival was likely to signal an end to the post–Cold War era, it was not Russia. It was the PRC.

Worries over what Russia's invasion of Ukraine meant for U.S.-China relations thus surfaced early in the conflict.[9] Did China green-light the invasion?[10] What did it mean for American policy over Taiwan? Was there a new Beijing-Moscow axis? Was Xi Jinping looking for signs of weakness?

Concerns over a Beijing-Moscow entente betray how the invasion was read through a novel frame for international affairs at the end of the post–Cold War era. As the 2017 NSS stated, "China and Russia challenge American power, influence, and interests, attempting to erode American security and prosperity. They are determined to make economies less free and less fair, to grow their militaries, and to control information and data to repress their societies and expand their influence."[11] The new era is marked by a return of geopolitics, and an entanglement of domestic and international affairs: authoritarianism is not only a foreign threat but one able to reach inside Western, liberal states. As the 2021 Interim NSS made plain, "Today, more than ever, America's fate is inextricably linked to events beyond our shores. We confront a global pandemic, a crushing economic downturn … a world of rising nationalism, receding democracy, [and] growing rivalry with China and Russia."[12]

Announcements that the post–Cold War world is over should not be dismissed. They have a powerful performative quality—making true what they seem merely to reflect, especially when made from positions of authority like the U.S. government. The 2021 Interim National Security Guidance termed the current moment "an inflection point,"[13] the December 2017 NSS a new era of "great power competition."[14] The ability to perform or make the world means if the NSS says the current moment is an inflection point, it becomes an inflection point.[15]

---

[8] "Biden Announces Defense Deal with Australia in Bid to Counter China," *New York Times*, 11 October 2021, https://www.nytimes.com/2021/09/15/us/politics/biden-australia-britain-china.html.

[9] "Biden Sending Mission to Taiwan to Reaffirm Commitment Amid Russia's Invasion of Ukraine," *Washington Post*, 28 February 2022, https://www.washingtonpost.com/politics/2022/02/28/biden-delegation-taiwan-commitment-russia-invasion-ukraine/.

[10] "China Asked Russia to Delay Invasion until after Winter Olympics, U.S. Official Says," *New York Times*, 2 March 2022, https://www.nytimes.com/2022/03/02/us/politics/russia-ukraine-china.html.

[11] *National Security Strategy of the United States*, December 2017, 2. Homing in on the PRC, the October 2022 NSS states that "the People's Republic of China harbors the intention and, increasingly, the capacity to reshape the international order in favor of one that tilts the global playing field to its benefit," President Biden's opening comments.

[12] *National Security Strategy of the United States*, December 2017, 2.

[13] *Interim National Security Strategic Guidance*, March 2021, https://www.whitehouse.gov/wp-content/uploads/2021/03/NSC-1v2.pdf.

[14] *National Security Strategy of the United States*, December 2017.

[15] *National Security Strategy*, October 2022, 12.

If it says we are in an era of great power competition, the U.S. government acts on the assumption that America is in a great power competition. While critics might object, the post–Cold War world *is* over. Russia's invasion underlined the point.

This book is about how we got here.

The Argument in Brief

For readers eager to get to the main argument, it is as follows: the demise of engagement with China and Russia was not simply a response by U.S. policymakers to a changed world—a return of authoritarianism and aggressive foreign policy on the part of Beijing and Moscow. The demise of engagement with China and with Russia respectively were not the same thing at all, with crucial implications for how we should understand U.S. policy toward each since the Cold War.

Engagement with China—what I will call Engagement with a capital *E*—was more than a policy or strategy. Engagement was a paradigmatic view of China held across the government and China professional community in America: a perspective that saw close contact with a Beijing integrated into the international system as in the U.S. national interest. The end of Engagement was therefore a shift away from such an optimistic paradigm, one effected, I show, under the Trump administration.[16] Although there are those in Washington who still see Engagement as the best way to deal with China, the U.S. government now works under the assumption that America is locked in a decades-long struggle, that is, "Strategic Competition," with Beijing.

No such paradigmatic turnover has taken place among America's Russia experts, by contrast. Especially after the Putin's return to power in 2012 and the failure of the attempted "reset" of relations under Obama, the center of gravity among the Russia professional field in America concluded engagement—with a small *e*—was an inappropriate way to deal with an intransigent leadership in Moscow. The result has been a more gradual slide into frozen relations and policy stasis, absent the paradigmatic shift witnessed in relation to China.

I make this argument in two steps. The first is to define engagement with China and Russia, which in much popular commentary and analysis remains vague. What, *precisely*, is or was "engagement?"

As I explore in the next chapter, Engagement with China had three aspects: *policy*, *frame*, and *community*. Engagement as policy refers to the concrete decisions and processes of U.S.-China relations—from high-level dialogues to extensive people-to-people exchanges below the governmental

---

[16] The notion of paradigmatic nature of Engagement emerged from discussion with several interviewees. See also Harding 2023.

level. Engagement as frame refers to a predominant narrative about China, which justified specific Engagement policies. Engagement as community, finally, refers to those China experts who supported and continue to support Engagement as policy and frame, a group I term "the Engagers." U.S. China policy is now no longer backed by tight connections between the government and pro-Engagement China professionals, nor by an optimistic framing of China's rise for America. The Engagers, who occupied the mainstream view on China in Washington up through the second Obama administration, and who staffed many important Asia-focused roles in government until that point, now find themselves at the margins of the U.S. China expert field.

The second step in the argument is to show how Strategic Competition as an alternative frame and community emerged within America's China field, which I trace to three key processes: *polarization, professional status competition,* and *personalization.*

Polarization is the formation of distinct groups within professional communities like the China and Russia fields. On China, I label these groups the "Engagers" and the "anti-Engagers." I show that anti-Engagers had long maintained a presence in the U.S. China community, but Trump's election was a critical juncture leading to the development of an alternative frame and policy for China: Strategic Competition. As it did so, the Trump administration's China frame- and policymaking posed a challenge to the broader China segments of the U.S. national security community: adapt to the new world of China as competitor or stake out another perspective, whether "Engagement" or something else. Trump's election thus forced Engagers onto the intellectual and political defensive, weakening the Engager position by fragmenting between those willing and unwilling to adapt to the new reality of Strategic Competition.

In the Russia space, I trace a more fluid distinction between those seeking to deal with Russia "as it is" and those seeking to mold a "Russia we want." The effect of Trump's election on America's Russia watchers was different, both opening a window of opportunity for a possible reset with Moscow given the new president's positive opinions of Putin, and closing down any serious attempt to recast Russia as an opportunity for the United States, on account of allegations of Russian influence on Trump's own victory. In the context of the tumultuous Trump presidency, Russia policy thus remained in stasis, as national security frame- and policymaking moved decisively to the Indo-Pacific.

Realist IR theory has long held the struggle for power among opposed groups as the primary social dynamic—in domestic as in international life. Yet realism famously fails to account for why groups differ in what they want, what they struggle *over.* In the case of America's China and Russia communities, why do different foreign policy professionals interpret the national interest in sharply opposed ways? In the case of both China and Russia policy, I show, the struggle for policymaking control is inseparable from a second key process—*professional status competition*—through which the groups themselves are formed and the stakes they struggle over are defined. In professional contests, participants struggle for cultural rewards such as status and prestige. In particular, they struggle over recognition as knowledgeable and insightful on China and Russia—over being *right*.

I trace the incorporation of Engagement with China into professional struggles for intellectual prestige and employment opportunities, and contrast these with struggles among America's Russia watchers. A primary division in the China professional community separates the holders of intellectual prestige and credibility from those without such status, outsiders nevertheless seeking to influence the conversation on China. The division manifests itself as arguments for "nuance" and deep country knowledge, over calls for bolder political action against a Beijing understood as a clear challenger or threat to the United States. The vehemence with which anti-Engagers criticized the views of their Engager colleagues can only be explained by resentment at the former's professional marginalization over time, as much as the two groups' policy prescriptions.

In the following chapters, then, I interpret the end of Engagement with the PRC and its replacement with Strategic Competition as the outcome of politicization and professional status struggle in America's China expert community. I contrast the story with the case of a Russia community that, absent a set of outsiders—resentful of the reigning paradigm—uploaded a new set of policies under a new foreign policy frame.

The account I develop would be incomplete, however, without a final, *personal* form of contestation. Engagement with China, like Russia policy, was tied to the hopes, views, and career achievements of real individuals. No account of the end of Engagement is complete without attention to personal competition—the interpersonal dynamics driving often-intense emotional and affective ties to certain policies, decisions, and ambitions. While it goes against the desire for more neutral, objective analysis, in the end the story of the end of engagement with China and Russia is a personal one, of America's China and Russia watchers' ongoing attempts to grapple with the United States' two most intractable 21st-century foreign policy problems.

America's China and Russia Experts

Accounts of U.S. foreign policy toward China and Russia since the Cold War that ignore their respective professional communities are partial at best. Again, the signatories of the open letters of 2019 and 2020 were not just anyone: they were former ambassadors, NSC directors, and all shades of deputies, assistants, and acting officers across the U.S. government. In short, the letters' signatories were prominent members of the U.S. national security community and its China and Russia sub-fields. Many were formerly in positions of power or are poised to assume such positions in future administrations. Far from peripheral, the China and Russia communities lie at the heart of the U.S. foreign policymaking system. They supply the credentialed individuals who staff administrations. Indirect influence over policy is still influence. This book takes the reader into a world too often obscured in writing on U.S. foreign policy.[17]

China- and Russia-watching fields are part of America's vast national security community. Composed of federally funded research and development centers like the Rand Corporation and the Center for Naval Analyses (CNA), university research centers, and think tanks like the Carnegie Endowment for International Peace and the Center for Strategic and International Studies, the community is a vibrant mass of knowledge production, contestation, and dissemination: a "permanent conference" on U.S. national security.[18] Centered on Washington, DC, the U.S. national security community has offshoots across the country, from the New York think tanks like the Council on Foreign Relations (CFR) and Asia Society, to the "Beltway Bandits" outside DC, to the military-security firms in the Raleigh-Durham triangle. America's far-flung national laboratories extend its geographical reach, as do universities and research organizations up and down the West Coast. Home to the U.S. Indo-Pacific Command, Hawaii is another important hub.

At one time, the concept of an "establishment" made sense to describe this elite foreign policy tribe.[19] No longer. For one thing, the community's borders do not stop at America's own. Experts in Europe, East Asia, Australia, and beyond are key participants: in London, for example, at Chatham House, the Institute for International Security Studies, and the Royal United Services Institute; in Australia, the Lowy Institute and the Australian Strategic Policy Institute; in Brussels, the European Council on Foreign Relations, and many others besides. U.S. foreign policy is a global enterprise.

For another, the community is more diverse than the notion of a homogenous, liberal, internationalist blob—in the words of Barack Obama's former

---

[17] Exceptions, of course, abound, most notably in the work of reflexively inclined historians and when members of America's knowledge communities reflect on the state of their own fields. On China, see Mertha 2021 and especially Shambaugh 2023 for a more exhaustive set of references. On U.S. relations with Russia, see Engerman 2009. Other important exceptions include Flibbert 2006 and Oren 2003. The study of experts was more commonplace during the Cold War, including of China's own Americanist and Soviet China specialists. See respectively Shambaugh 1991 and Gates 1974, Rozman 1983 and 1984, Schwartz 1978, and Sandles 1981.

[18] See Ash, Shambaugh, and Takagi 2007 on America's scholarly watchers of China. For an analysis of the formation of policy more specifically, see Sapolsky, Gholz, and Talmadge 2017: 117–39.

[19] Roberts 1992.

speechwriter, Ben Rhodes—allows.[20] While typical Left-right divisions apply less clearly to foreign than domestic politics, organizations like the American Enterprise Institute and Heritage Foundation are ideologically distinct from Brookings and the CFR, for example. Defense Department–funded organizations such as the Center for Strategic and Budgetary Assessments and CNA, meanwhile, specialize more narrowly on national security, which organizations with regional affiliations, again like the Center for European Policy Analysis in the case of Russia, or the Global Taiwan Institute and the Sasakawa Peace Foundation in the case of China, further the community's heterogeneity. The presence of new media outlets, from newsletters to podcasts, and for-profit consulting firms—from Booz Allen Hamilton to public relations firms like APCO Worldwide, to the Eurasia Group—deepen the sense that the establishment is no more.

However we choose to characterize what has evolved in its place—the military-industrial-academic complex,[21] the foreign policy "ideas industry"[22]—national security knowledge production is quite different today than 30, much less 70, years ago. The China and Russia communities form part of an institutional architecture that employs tens, if not hundreds, of thousands, a far cry from the handful of former diplomats, professors, and businesspeople who had any real knowledge of China and Russia as late as the 1970s.

Although they overlap, the China and Russia communities are not the same. For one thing, the China community is far larger. Forged in America's rise to globalism after the end World War II,[23] the community suffered more than most from the effects of McCarthyism, as a leading scholars such as Owen Lattimore saw their careers ruined by charges of communist sympathizing.[24] Lattimore was born in China, a trait he shared with many of America's best Sinologists and China hands for more than one generation after the war, including John Paton Davies and J. Stapleton Roy.[25] McCarthyism decimated China scholarship in the United States, leaving peering beyond the "Bamboo Curtain" into China from the Universities Service Centre for Chinese Studies in the British-controlled Hong Kong (founded 1962) as America's China watchers' only chance at firsthand knowledge of China.[26] Against this background, the vast cultural and economic exchanges made possible by the opening to China in 1972 and the subsequent

---

[20] David Samuels, "The Aspiring Novelist Who Became Obama's Foreign Policy Guru," *New York Times Magazine*, 5 May 2016, https://www.nytimes.com/2016/05/08/magazine/the-aspiring-novelist-who-became-obamas-foreign-policy-guru.html. See also McCourt and Ruley 2023.
[21] Leslie 1994.
[22] Drezner 2017.
[23] Wertheim 2020.
[24] Newman 1992.
[25] Davies 2012.
[26] See Austin and Clurman 1969; Bernstein 2015.

normalization of diplomatic relations in 1979 brought with them a sense of optimism and opportunity.[27] The feeling held sway into the 21st century, as the U.S. China field spread from early hubs at the universities of Michigan, Columbia, Harvard, Stanford, California-Berkeley, and the University of Washington.

America's Russia community suffered at the hands of McCarthyism too. But with the exigencies of Cold War, Sovietology was a necessary evil—the need to "know your enemy," in historian David Engerman's words.[28] In a field then-populated by many émigrés from the Soviet Union, a popular saying was "to study Russia, is to hate it." In this, the Russia and China communities are quite dissimilar. In the latter, residual romanticism remains a marked feature. Nonetheless, until 1989 Russia was a better career bet than China—indeed, some of today's leading China specialists, Kurt Campbell,[29] Elizabeth Economy,[30] Susan Thornton, and Michael Pillsbury[31] among them started out by focusing on Russia. After the demise of the Soviet Union, however, the Russia community's raison d'être vanished. Current scrambling for recognized Russia expertise reflects the community's shrinkage, which only began to turn around after the capture of Crimea in 2014. Compared to the China watchers, Russia watchers remain relatively few in number.

The Usual Story: Engagement's Rise and Fall

By centering America's China- and Russia-watching communities and their shifting relations to the U.S. government, the story I tell in this book is very different from the usual one about the end of the post–Cold War era, which goes something like this:

The post–Cold War era began with high hopes. The end of the Cold War meant a "New World Order."[32] History, political theorist Francis Fukuyama was misunderstood as saying, was over.[33] On distinct timelines, a wave of optimism about engaging Russia and China free from the strictures imposed by the

---

[27] Li 2005; Lampton, Madancy, and Williams 1986.
[28] Engerman 2009.
[29] Appointed National Security Council coordinator for the Indo-Pacific, 20 January 2021. Previously assistant secretary of state for East Asian and Pacific affairs 2009–2013.
[30] Senior fellow at the Hoover Institution at Stanford University, previously C.V. Starr Senior Fellow and director of Asia Studies at the CFR. At the time of writing, Economy was senior foreign advisor (China) in the U.S. Commerce Department.
[31] Assistant undersecretary for policy planning at the U.S. Defense Department (1984–1986) and special assistant to director of the Office of Net Assessment (1992–1993).
[32] See "Bush 'Out of These Troubled Times . . . a New World Order," *Washington Post*, 11 September 1990, https://www.washingtonpost.com/archive/politics/1990/09/12/bush-out-of-these-troubled-times-a-new-world-order/b93b5cf1-e389-4e6a-84b0-85f71bf4c946/.
[33] Fukuyama 1992.

Cold War gave way to bumps in respective bilateral roads.[34] Points of opposing interest created friction as the 1990s unfolded. After the millennium, a United States preoccupied by the war on terror, together with the emergence of populist authoritarian leaders in Vladimir Putin and Xi Jinping, led to the collapse of relations as the 2010s progressed.[35] The war in Ukraine, and the possibility of a Beijing-Moscow axis, is the seemingly inevitable endpoint.

Post–Cold War U.S.-China relations began on a sour note. A Congress outraged by the events of 4 June 1989 in Tiananmen Square pushed hard for the Chinese regime to face real consequences.[36] The H. W. Bush administration's decision to send emissaries Brent Scowcroft and Lawrence Eagleburger, national security advisor and deputy secretary of state respectively, to Beijing soon after the crackdown to maintain calm in the relationship, however, indicated diplomatic ties would be prioritized.[37] Similarly, while the Clinton administration criticized the Bush government over its genuflection toward the "Butchers of Beijing" during the 1992 election campaign, it followed suit once in office, supporting big-business lobbying for the annual extension of Most Favored Nation (MFN) status for China in the late 1990s.[38] Clinton's backing for permanent MFN status and Chinese membership of the World Trade Organization amid significant domestic opposition, including accusations of China-linked corruption,[39] represented the peak of optimism about what engaging Beijing could achieve.

The beginning of the 1990s also featured optimism about Russia, especially after the collapse of the Soviet Union in December 1991. America's experts poured into the country to assist the expected "transition" from autocracy to democracy, and to ensure the former superpower's vast military stockpiles did not fall into the wrong hands. At the same time, U.S. interest and attention quickly waned, and state decay in Eastern Europe, East Africa, and the Middle East took the place of the "Evil Empire" as Washington's geostrategic priority. As historian Mary Eloise Sarotte has examined, the close personal relationship struck between Clinton and Russian president Boris Yeltsin withstood the interventions against Serbia in Bosnia (1995) and Kosovo (1999) and the expansion of

---

[34] Optimism about China's trajectory lasted longer, well past the millennium. See, for example, Hutton 2007; Jacques 2009. Also Kissinger 2011; Paulson 2016.

[35] For a powerful account along these lines, including the development of illiberal trends in Europe and the United States, see Snyder 2022. On Putin, see Hill and Gaddy 2015; Short 2022. On Xi, see Brown 2017, 2022.

[36] See Suettinger 2003.

[37] "2 U.S. Officials Went Secretly to Beijing in July," *New York Times*, 19 December 1989, https://www.nytimes.com/1989/12/19/world/2-us-officials-went-to-beijing-secretly-in-july.html.

[38] "American Presidents Have a Long History of Walking Back Tough Talk on China," *Washington Post* 6 December 2016, https://www.washingtonpost.com/news/wonk/wp/2016/12/06/american-presidents-have-a-long-history-of-walking-back-tough-talk-on-china/.

[39] See Gertz 2000; Timperlake and Triplett 1998.

NATO.[40] Yeltsin's retirement in 1999, however, left control of Russia to former KGB agent Vladimir Putin. He was cut from a different cloth than his predecessor,[41] and commentators soon questioned how relations would fair, especially in light of NATO expansion in 1999 to include much of Moscow's former sphere of influence.

The election of George W. Bush in November 2000 heralded, for a moment, a hardening of U.S. foreign policy both toward Beijing and Moscow. In relation to China, Nina Silove has traced what she terms a "pivot before the pivot"—a stalled attempt to reorient U.S. security policy toward East Asia, well before the better-known "Asian pivot" of 2010.[42] Then came the attacks of 11 September 2001, pushing great power politics off America's national security radar for the better part of the next 15 years. Heightened suspicions between Putin and U.S. policymakers vanished as the Russian leader expressed sympathy with Washington, before—in a surprising move—offering permission to use Russian airspace for operations against al-Qaeda in Afghanistan.[43]

Here respective histories diverge, U.S.-Russia relations declining faster than those between Washington and Beijing. Tightening his grip on power at home, Putin expressed greater alarm than his Chinese counterparts as the global war on terror spilled over from Afghanistan to Iraq. In a 2007 speech at the Munich Security Conference, the Russian leader shocked delegates with a scathing critique of American arrogance.[44] The following year, Russia engaged in a brief but intense war with the former Soviet republic of Georgia. A short-lived "reset" following Obama's election in 2008 did little to restore relations, as Putin returned to power in 2012, initiating the capture of the Crimea in 2014,[45] in what now appears a first move toward the 2022 invasion.

The slow but inexorable decline in U.S.-Russia relations was not mirrored in the rapid downfall in Sino-U.S. diplomacy beginning in 2017. Up through the second Obama administration disagreements in the relationship were isolated from top-level rhetoric, once again facilitated by priorities elsewhere—including Libya (2011–), Syria (2011–), piracy off East Africa, Russia's incursions in Ukraine (2014–), and ISIS (2014–2015).[46] Military planners at the Defense Department were not unaware of the growing power of the Chinese military. The 2017 NSS named China a "great power competitor," reflecting language

---

[40] Sarotte 2021.
[41] Hill and Gaddy 2015.
[42] Silove 2016: 46.
[43] See Michael McFaul, "U.S.-Russia Relations after September 11, 2001," Carnegie Endowment for International Peace, 24 October 2021, https://carnegieendowment.org/2001/10/24/u.s.-russia-relations-after-september-11-2001-pub-840.
[44] http://en.kremlin.ru/events/president/transcripts/24034.
[45] McFaul 2018.
[46] On Obama's foreign policy, see Chollet 2016. Criticisms were made of Obama similar to those of Clinton. See, for example, Decker and Triplett 2011.

gaining ground in Defense Department strategic thinking at the time—thinking reflected in the so-called Third Offset Strategy, announced in November 2014, which aimed to enable the United States to compete with peer competitors—notably China—via continued technological superiority in key areas.[47] Yet it was not until Trump's election that diplomatic relations took an unmistakable downturn. Candidate Trump railed against China's economic policies, explicitly casting Beijing as an enemy that has "destroyed entire industries."[48] Playing on economic resentment proved successful on Trump's road to the White House. Once there, his administration began the replacement of Engagement with a new approach, which by mid-2020 had crystallized as Strategic Competition.

No single account can capture the events of the last three decades, much as we might want to imagine a unity to the post–Cold War era. Attempts to tell a singular story tell us more about contemporary disputes than the motivations and interests driving policy in previous years. They assign blame and identify or deny paths not taken. Why did China fail to become a "responsible international stakeholder," as Deputy Secretary of State Robert Zoellick urged in 2005?[49] Why couldn't NATO and Russia engender a taken-for-granted form of cooperation?[50] What could America have done differently? We should be skeptical of neat stories.

Nevertheless, commonalities abound in the usual story of post–Cold War U.S.-China and U.S.-Russia relations: bad men, shifting power balances, arrogant or absent-minded Americans. In short, we tried to engage China and Russia, to bring them into the rules-based international order. *We failed.*

Readers already convinced of the virtues of taking a different tack can at this stage skip forward with confidence to my presentation of the sociological approach employed, the plan of the book, or even go straight to the reassessment of E/engagement in Part I of the book. For those sticking with me, next I press on by showing how existing scholarly explanations echo common understandings. Most center changes in China and Russia, alongside objective shifts in the balance of power. Some critical approaches reverse the lens to focus on what the United States could and should have done differently.

---

[47] Chuck Hagel, "Reagan National Defense Keynote," 15 November 2014, https://www.defense.gov/Newsroom/Speeches/Speech/Article/606635/.

[48] See https://archive.org/details/WMUR_20151103_120000_Good_Morning_America; Trump 2015: 43.

[49] "Robert Zoellick's Responsible Stakeholder Speech," https://www.ncuscr.org/fact/robert-zoellicks-responsible-stakeholder-speech/.

[50] Pouliot 2010.

Existing Explanations

The reasons behind the similar trajectories in U.S.-China and U.S.-Russia relations appear straightforward: the shifting balance of power and the seemingly inevitable return of great power rivalry; the rise of authoritarians Putin and Xi; and domestic political contestation in America leading to tougher responses. Taken together, these explanations form the common sense among many in Washington, especially in the China-watching community: the recent change in U.S. policy has been a rational response to the perception that the policy of engagement failed; it was undertaken largely by the Trump administration against the backdrop of shifts in the balance of power and an authoritarian turn in China. In the case of China, Americans—elites and public—are increasingly convinced that China's political development is heading in the wrong direction, with many strategists accepting what analyst Rush Doshi labels China's "long game" strategy to displace America as the world's leading power.[51] The most recent Pew poll shows that 83% of Americans have an unfavorable view of China, with 54% seeing it as an enemy.[52] The result is a new consensus in Washington. As one critic of engagement with China told me, "It's really been amazing to watch the... I hesitate to use the word consensus..., but for lack of a better word to watch the consensus shift in Washington just over the last four years, five years ... [It] moved to where I am and other colleagues elsewhere were."[53] Similarly, the invasion of Ukraine lays bare what many Russia experts have thought for a long time: there is no dealing with Putin.

All three explanations capture something of the truth. Yet each also contains important gaps, specifically relating to timing and the precise processes leading to changes in U.S. strategy, limiting the power of this common sense. Consequently, I suggest foregrounding the interpreters of Beijing and Moscow: America's China and Russia experts.

China, Russia, and the Failure of Engagement

A first explanation for the trajectory of America's post–Cold War China and Russia strategy is that U.S. policy failed. In the case of China, this explanation suggests Engagement was based on the false promise of influencing China to move in a more open, liberal direction. As the May 2020 *United States Strategic*

---

[51] Doshi 2021.
[52] See "U.S. Opinion of China Remains Negative," 11 April 2023, Pew Research, https://www.pewresearch.org/global/2023/04/12/americans-are-critical-of-chinas-global-role-as-well-as-its-relationship-with-russia/pg_2023-04-12_u-s-views-china_0-05/.
[53] China interview 097, 22 November 2021, via video call.

Approach to the People's Republic of China states, "United States policy toward the PRC was largely premised on a hope that deepening engagement would spur fundamental economic and political opening.... More than 40 years later, it has become evident that this approach underestimated the will of the Chinese Communist Party (CCP) to constrain the scope of economic and political reform."[54] Light years from opening, China's new authoritarianism represents a "third revolution" to a qualitatively new type of state from the one proclaimed by Deng Xiaoping[55]—a state featuring Orwellian social controls, face recognition technology, a censored internet, and a social credit system tying everything from job opportunities to romantic decisions to "good citizenship."[56] For Carl Minzner, the era of reform is over.[57] One analyst echoed a frequently cited explanation: the end of Engagement is "a recognition that China has changed and we can't expect the strategy we previously employed to get the outcomes we thought."[58]

A similar story can be told about relations with Russia, with distinct wrinkles. U.S. policy after 1991 was to stabilize the constituent parts of the former Soviet Union after its demise and to incorporate Moscow into the international system. As reported to Congress in 2007, the United States had provided some $28bn in assistance since 1992, with the aim of "facilitating the transition from authoritarianism to democracy, promoting the introduction and growth of free market economies, and fostering security by controlling the proliferation of nuclear, chemical, and biological weapons and expertise."[59] The gambit failed, however, as supposed westernizer Boris Yeltsin handed the reins of power to Putin as the 1990s closed, a Russia more authoritarian internally and hostile externally emerging by the mid-2000s. In short, we tried to engage, and it didn't work.

The strengths of the policy failure explanation are that it accords with the views of many of the major players behind policymaking. In the case of China in particular, Kurt Campbell and Ely Ratner's call in 2018 for a "China reckoning" in U.S. policymaking was something both subsequently continued after entering office with President Biden.[60] But therein lies the explanation's weakness: the policy-failed argument is American policymakers' rationale and justification for their actions. It is not an *explanation* of those actions.

In the case of China, the connection between the rejection of Engagement by U.S. policymakers after 2017 and its purported failure is less clear-cut than

---

[54] *United States Strategic Approach to the People's Republic of China*, May 2020.
[55] Economy 2019.
[56] See Chin and Lin 2022; Chiu 2021; Roberts 2018; Shum 2021.
[57] Minzner 2018.
[58] China interview 104, 11 May 2021, via video call.
[59] Curt Tarnoff, "U.S. Assistance to the Former Soviet Union," CRS Report for Congress, 1 March 2007, https://sgp.fas.org/crs/row/RL32866.pdf, 1.
[60] Campbell and Ratner 2018.

the policy failure explanation suggests. Put differently, did Engagement really fail? While high-level government rhetoric—especially aimed at securing changes to U.S. trade law to grant China Permanent Normal Trade relations[61]— explicitly linked Engagement and liberalization in the public's mind, everyday policymaking was not predicated on the expectation of liberal change in China.[62] In terms of Engagement's achievement, meanwhile, U.S.-China Engagement brought tangible diplomatic progress,[63] while in the economic realm, *Engagement did not so much fail as succeed too well, if only for a fraction of Americans.*

In the case of Russia, acknowledgment of America's role in the souring of bilateral diplomacy tends to be more prominent. Given the early and sharp fall in U.S.-Russia relations, Moscow's more evident bellicosity, and the strength of the "Engagement failed" argument among American China watchers, it is telling that many Russia experts suggest the United States engaged too little or in a counterproductive way. As Mary Sarotte has shown, the issue of NATO enlargement remains a salient point of contention.[64] For Russia, American policymakers promised to move NATO's borders "not one inch" after 1989. Despite the availability of alternative security architectures for Eastern Europe, such as the Partnership for Peace, Western leaders moved quickly toward NATO expansion, despite clear warnings of the likely consequences vis-à-vis Moscow.

Questioning the policy failure account is not to say that engaging China and Russia was irrational. Nor is it to say that rejecting engagement now is irrational or wrong. Rather, the point is that the claim of policy failure does not, by itself, explain how, why, and when engagement stopped making sense.

The Domestic Politics of Relations with China and Russia

A second, domestic politics, explanation can address the question of when and why engagement stopped making sense, at least in the case of China. From this perspective, the 2016 Trump election was a "critical juncture" that uploaded a skeptical view of China and the prospects for relations with Beijing to the highest echelons of U.S. policymaking. Candidate Trump criticized the "theft" of American jobs and reiterated long-standing criticisms of China's state-owned

---

[61] PTNR, renamed from Permanent Most Favored Nation (MFN).
[62] Neil Thomas, "Matters of Record: Relitigating Engagement with China," *Macropolo*, 3 September 2019, https://macropolo.org/analysis/china-us-engagement-policy/.
[63] https://www.ncafp.org/2016/wp-content/uploads/2021/09/NCAFP_China_Engagement_final_Sept-2021.pdf.
[64] Sarotte 2021.

enterprises and currency manipulation.⁶⁵ Trump's victory brought into positions of policymaking authority well-known China critics such as, on trade, Robert Lighthizer and Peter Navarro, the author of a "global call to action" on China.⁶⁶ Navarro's criticisms of China as a challenger to the United States over time morphed into the sort of geopolitical threat reminiscent of the warnings of Michael Pillsbury, Gordon Chang,⁶⁷ Newt Gingrich,⁶⁸ and others.⁶⁹ Once in office, the Trump administration launched a trade war with China in January 2018, while robust rhetoric contributed to diplomatic tensions.⁷⁰

U.S. policy toward Russia was not a significant political issue until, again, Trump. Lack of attention arguably facilitated the neglect of Russia's security interests during the 1990s and the elevation of those of former Soviet states eager for NATO expansion, especially in light of the breakdown of the former Yugoslavia. The latitude given to Obama officials Michael McFaul and Celeste Wallander to attempt a "reset" of relations in 2009 can equally be explained by the lack of domestic political resonance of Russia. With reputed reformer Dmitry Medvedev in the Kremlin, few voiced opposition to the attempt. Allegations of Russian meddling in the 2016 elections made relations with Moscow a wedge issue, however. In a striking turnaround from previous eras, Republicans are divided on Russia, with Trumpists attempting to push back on the demonization of Putin, while moderates line up alongside Democrats hostile to Moscow.

Yet important issues remain unexplained here too. Domestic politics does not determine the thinking of foreign policymakers who staff administrations. If Russia was not a salient domestic political issue in 2009, for example, why did Obama support the reset? In the case of China, what explains Trump's appointments? Unless these are to be seen as mere throughputs of Trump's own agenda, the domestic politics account fails to explain their understandings of China and U.S. policy, and why they—and not (pro-Engagement) others—were brought into the Trump administration. For example, Lighthizer's credentials for trade representative are unremarkable: a degree in law from Georgetown followed by private service in the prestigious firm of Covington and Burling.⁷¹

---

⁶⁵ id=46572567. https://abcnews.go.com/Politics/10-times-trump-attacked-china-trade-relations-us/story?id=46572567.

⁶⁶ Navarro and Autry 2011.

⁶⁷ Commentator and former lawyer in China for law firms Baker & McKenzie and Paul, Weiss, Rifkind, Wharton & Garrison.

⁶⁸ Republican representative for Georgia (1979–1999) and Speaker of the House of Representatives (1995–1999).

⁶⁹ Pillsbury 2015; Navarro 2008; Gingrich 2019. The warnings of Pillsbury and others echoed earlier books by so-called Blue Teamers—fierce critics of China—and those of a similar mindset. See, for example, Bernstein and Munro 1997; Gertz 2000, Menges 2005; Timperlake and Triplett 1998. On the Blue Team, see chapter 4 below.

⁷⁰ For example, "Pence's Speech Seen as a Portent of a 'New Cold War,'" *New York Times*, 5 October 2018, https://www.nytimes.com/2018/10/05/world/asia/pence-china-speech-cold-war.html.

⁷¹ In one interviewee's view, "Lighthizer's a pro. Lighthizer had an agenda." China interview 108, 20 August 2022, via video call.

By contrast, Navarro came out of left field. What explains his appointment? Moreover, the nature of the break with the second Obama administration is obscured by an account focused solely on Trump. Clear signals of a change in U.S. views, in fact, predate the 2016 election.[72] Thus, while domestic politics—particularly the Trump election—are critical to the final downfall of the post–Cold War era, key questions remain about the exact nature of the recent transformation of U.S. China and Russia strategy.

Rising Titans, Cornered Bears, and Falling Eagles: The Shifting Balance of Global Power

A third popular account, prominent especially in attempts to explain the breakdown in U.S.-China relations, centers the shift in the global balance of power away from the United States. This broad account draws from a family of perspectives rooted in materialist IR—realism on the one hand, power transition theory on the other.[73] In each, U.S. relative economic decline and the sense of threat engendered in Washington from rising challengers is deemed the key fact of contemporary international political life.[74] Together this view underpins frequently appearing books and articles that invoke the imagery of "rising titans,"[75] alongside hegemonic turnover,[76] the changing polarity of the international system,[77] and the timeless wisdom of Thucydides on the Peloponnesian War.[78]

The power of such accounts, indeed their self-evident nature, comes from the way they focus on material power—military force and the economic means to acquire it. The Trump administration's development of Strategic Competition with China, for example, demonstrated a noteworthy change in emphasis from the economic opportunity represented by China to military-security concern. From a balance-of-power perspective, the chief mechanism at play in the Trump administration's rejection of Engagement is the fear of a risen China, especially one displaying a turn to authoritarianism.

In the case of Russia, the Ukraine invasion brought realist argumentation back to the forefront. Longtime realist John Mearsheimer, for example, argued

---

[72] For example, a May 2016 speech by Secretary of Defense Ashton Carter, where he declared a new era of great power competition with Russia and China. More below. https://www.capitalgazette.com/education/naval-academy/cgnews-full-transcript-secretary-of-defense-ash-carter-s-naval-academy-commencement-address-20160527-story.html.

[73] Compare the realist perspective of Mearsheimer 2001 and power transition approach of Organski 1958; Tammen 2008. See also Beckley 2023.

[74] For example, Rachman 2017. Also Gill 2007; Meredith 2007.

[75] Shifrinson 2018. See earlier Shambaugh 2012 on the United States and China as "tangled titans."

[76] Montgomery 2016.

[77] Layne 2012.

[78] Allison 2017.

that America should have seen the resurgence of great power politics coming, and bears some of the responsibility for the war.[79] America only woke up to the challenge after the Kremlin recaptured Crimea, and only partially. Beyond stirring controversy, in so doing, Mearsheimer shows how the very strengths of the balance-of-power and China threat imagery are also a source of analytical weakness. *Why*, *how*, and *when*, is a potential challenger recognized as threatening by U.S. policymakers? Why did neither the 1996 Taiwan Straits Crisis nor the April 2001 Hainan Island incident—featuring the Chinese capture of 24 American aviators—lead to the sort of strategic rethink of 2015–2017? What explains America's response to the 2008 Russo-Georgian War, which now seems to foreshadow the war in Ukraine?

The signal story of the post–Cold War era is not a narrative of China's inexorable rise, Russian stagnation, and America's decline. The United States *is* declining relatively, but also becoming more powerful as America's population, economy, and military capabilities grow.[80] The balance-of-power explanation displays many of the flaws to which critics of realist theory point: a degree of determinism that downplays contingency and alternative possible outcomes; a macro or "30,000 feet" perspective with few real mechanisms of change; and a limited role for economics, domestic politics, and the interpretation of threats and interests. The key issue, therefore, is what China and Russian *mean* to which influential domestic actors in America.

Once again, taken together, changes in China and Russia, set against the shifting balance of global power, and U.S. domestic politics form a sort of a common sense in Washington about the rise and fall of America's policy of engaging Beijing and Moscow. Engagement failed. *Nothing could seem more obvious.*

Analytically, however, this common sense raises as many questions as it answers. It represents a Clue-type way of thinking. Who killed Engagement? Instead of Colonel Mustard, in the boardroom, with the candlestick, we have Trump facing up to authoritarian maniacs (Putin and Xi), with a new competitive frame for U.S. policy, in a now multipolar order. While the commons sense is rhetorically powerful, lingering questions remain: When, precisely, did engaging Russia and China stop making sense, for whom, and in response to which specific changes in Moscow and Beijing? Posing these questions suggests the need to take seriously two critical explanations.

---

[79] Mearsheimer 2014.
[80] Beckley 2018. Whether China will ultimately overtake America's economy remains an open question; see Hung 2015.

Cooperation Out of Reach: Why America Can't Get Along with Illiberal States

A first critical explanation suggests the United States has trouble getting along with illiberal regimes around the world, especially those as powerful as China. Developed in IR largely in relation to Russia, an explanation can be extrapolated to the PRC also.

Why did it prove impossible after 1991 to include Russia in what Emanuel Adler and Michael Barnett term the Western "security community"?[81] Looking at the long durée, IR scholars Iver Neumann and Ole Jacob Sending begin with a prior question: Why has Russia not been accepted as a great power? For them, Russia's exclusion from the great power club cannot be explained by the fact that it has never *been* a great power—Moscow has at times clearly been powerful enough—nor that Russia has not been *accepted* as a great power—many states in the unaligned world saw Moscow as a great power during the Cold War.[82] For Neumann and Sending, Russia's exclusion is due to its resistance to liberal governmentality, a historically specific mode of governing based on "an imperative whereby letting go of the state's direct control of society [is] becoming a necessity ... for reasons of conforming to a new ... standard of governance."[83] Russia, put simply, has not played by the rules dictating how Western, civilized, great powers are meant to conduct themselves internally. Moscow has not done what great powers *do*. Until it does, it will remain an outsider to the great power club and ineligible for membership of the liberal Western security community. The same could be said of China.

Ted Hopf offers an explanation of why Moscow did not adopt liberal governing practices, one that could also be extended to post-1989 China.[84] For Hopf, the Soviet Union was not essentially illiberal and uniformly threatening to the West during the Cold War. Instead, the degree of liberalism Moscow demonstrated in its foreign policy varied widely depending on how secure the Soviet regime felt domestically. When what Hopf terms a "discourse of danger" predominated at home, as in the immediate postwar years, leaders were more hostile abroad; when leaders felt secure at home, as during most of Khrushchev's tenure, a discourse of Soviet uniqueness lead to a ratcheting down of aggressive rhetoric and a thaw in relations with satellites. This relationship between domestic practices and foreign policy was frequently missed in the West, which tended to view the USSR as a monolith—again, as many in Washington do in relation to China.

---

[81] Adler and Barnett 1998.
[82] Neumann and Sending 2010: 93.
[83] Neumann and Sending 2010: 70–109.
[84] Hopf 2012.

From this perspective, Russia's recent actions are tied less to Putin's personality than to cyclical dynamics in Russia's historically fraught relationship with the West. As Ayşe Zarakol notes, Russia's actions "make sense only in a framework of status-seeking in a socially stratified international society of insiders and outsiders."[85] States like Russia manage the stigma associated with being outsiders to the West. Three options seem open to Russia: become Western, remain unique and isolationist, or adopt explicitly Slavic nationalist tendencies coupled with expansionism. Since returning to office in 2012, Putin clearly chose the latter, with a similar palette of options seemingly open to China's leaders.

This broad family of explanations offers insight into U.S. relations with China, recent and long term. Indeed, well before the collective handwringing among America's China experts over the failures of Engagement, sociologist Richard Madsen explored the moral meaning of China in the American imagination.[86] Showing how foreign policies rest on deeper societal understandings, understandings by which "we orient ourselves around common hopes and aspirations, expressed in stories about where we come from and where we are going,"[87] Madsen reflected on the shared story of liberal progress constructed since Nixon's opening to China in the 1970s. The events of June 1989 in Tiananmen Square punctured the positive views of China held by the American public and elites—including its businesses, religious leaders, and crucially social scientists[88]—many of whom had convinced themselves that China was following its own version of the American Dream. Madsen thus foreshadowed the insights of a critical IR explanation for Engagement's demise centered on the liberal or illiberal direction in which Beijing has headed in its domestic governance. A liberalizing great power China can be the object of cooperative policies justified to domestic audiences in the United States and the West. If sufficient evidence suggests illiberalism rules in Beijing, such engaged policies are off the table. The pendulum has swung, and an illiberal China must be contained.

Follow the Money: The Political Economy of Relations with China and Russia

If America's relations with China and Russia are in part explained by the dynamics of liberalism and its illiberal counterpoint, they are also in part explained by the dynamics of capitalism, and thus illuminated by political economy's imperative to "follow the money." As political scientists Lawrence Jacobs and

---

[85] Zarakol 2011: 202.
[86] Madsen 1995. For a related endeavor, see Cumings 1999.
[87] Madsen 1995: x.
[88] See especially Madsen 1995: 97–106.

Benjamin Page conclusively show, the interests of American business are, alongside the military, the crucial driver of U.S. foreign policy.[89] Business influence takes two forms: first via the activities of lobbyists; and second via the knowledge-producing activities of think tanks and research organizations paid for by business and nation-states.

The case is clearest in relation to China. Big-business interests initially pushed U.S. policy toward liberalization after the fallout from Tiananmen, culminating in support for Beijing's acceptance into the World Trade Organization in 2001.[90] As sociologist Ho-Fung Hung has explored, the Clinton administration entered office in early 1993 skeptical of free trade and critical of Bush Sr.'s China policy.[91] Clinton "honored the Democratic Party's campaign promise to organized labor, Southern manufacturers, and human rights advocates to put a brake on US–China trade liberalization by making Chinese access to the US market, under low tariffs, conditional on human rights progress."[92] Clinton reversed course the following year, however, as did most congressional Democrats, no longer linking trade liberalization to human rights. The reason, for Hung, was the lobbying activities of large multinationals strongly courted by the Chinese government—notably AT&T, Boeing, and Exxon Mobil.[93] Fast-forward two decades and many of the same firms had become disillusioned by doing business with China. Large multinationals frustrated with Chinese government policies aimed at supporting state-owned enterprises and keeping the renminbi cheap then began to push for U.S. government action toward protectionism.

The political economy of U.S.-Russia relations since the end of the Cold War is primarily one of absence when it comes to large MNCs. Whereas China offered seemingly limitless opportunity for growth, investment opportunities, and labor, after 1989 Russia represented marginal economic gains. Often termed disparagingly a "gas station with nukes," Russia's gas- and oil-dominated GDP stood at approximately $500bn in current U.S. dollars, less than a tenth of that of the United States.[94] Russia's economy warranted government aid assistance, and the transfer of knowledge in the form of "shock therapy" in the construction of a market economy, but not the sort of people-to-people and governmental exchanges seen in U.S.-China relations. As of 2020, the disparity between the two economies had grown—America's GDP at $20tn, Russia's at less than $1.5tn—a

---

[89] Jacobs and Page 2005.
[90] See Van Apeldoorn and de Graaff 2016.
[91] Hung 2021: 1003.
[92] Hung 2021: 1003.
[93] Hung 2021: 1012.
[94] More precisely $516bn for Russia, $5.96tn for the United States. See https://data.worldbank.org/indicator/NY.GDP.MKTP.CD?locations = RU; https://data.worldbank.org/indicator/NY.GDP.MKTP.CD?locations = US.

gap sowing disinterest in Russia above all, given the lack of a powerful business constituency pushing for cooperation at the top level of diplomatic ties.

The political economy of U.S.-Russia relations is not limited to multinationals, however. In the Washington, DC, national security community, a strong pro-Eastern Europe constituency remained skeptical of Russia, despite the Cold War's end, notably at the Atlantic Council and the Center for European Policy Analysis. Compared to those arguing for strong transatlantic ties, rooted in shared democratic and liberal values, few argued for close diplomatic and security engagement with Moscow.

U.S. national security policy does not simply reflect the balance of global power, the policy preferences of rotating administrations, or the rational analysis of policy failure. Yet critical accounts too leave questions unasked and unanswered. Why did illiberal China have to be countered? Why have the interests of U.S. businesses in good relations with China not trumped those of Beijing's critics?

The problem with all of these accounts is that they marginalize the activities of the very people through whom arguments about the balance of power, policy failure, changes in other countries' behavior, and their meanings in and for America are made and come to make sense—America's national security experts. To understand the shifting meaning of China and Russia in the United States, we must analyze the activities of the right people: America's China and Russia experts and their shifting relations with the U.S. bureaucracy.

In the following section, I draw on recent developments in the sociology of expertise to develop an approach to the role of knowledge communities in U.S. foreign policy that I contrast with three common alternatives in the IR literature. I show how Engagement with the PRC functioned as a paradigm within America's China-watching community, a paradigm increasingly opposed and subsequently overturned during the Trump administration. Non-sociologist readers nonetheless now convinced of the need to take knowledge communities seriously in the end of the post–Cold War era can move with confidence to the following chapters.

Ideas into Action: Knowledge Communities and U.S. Foreign Policy

What role do knowledge communities like the China and Russia fields play in the making of U.S. foreign policy? Three main literatures center ideas and expertise. A first foregrounds the role of intellectuals and "epistemic communities," from specific individuals like Henry Kissinger, to groups like the post–World War II defense intellectuals, climate scientists pivotal to 1980s U.S. environmental policy, and neoconservatives.[95] Impact tends to be fleeting, however—few overcome the gap between the government and the ivory tower with any longevity.[96] Again, lobbyists, policymakers, and the military typically drive policy, not experts.[97] As one interview for the project, a former diplomat now an academic, noted, "I don't know that the China-watching community has had a big impact. . . . I think the decline of engagement has been driven by larger macro forces. The China-watching community has been observers."[98] While individual China and Russia engagers have had influence, four decades is a long time to be explained by reference to single, supposedly coherent, groups.

Similar issues bedevil a second approach centered on how "groupthink" narrows strategic debate.[99] Patrick Porter, for instance, argues that liberal internationalist groupthink has repeatedly drawn America into foreign policy imbroglios.[100] As detailed throughout this book, however, Porter's diagnosis of a lack of contestation fails to square with the fractious debate among the China and Russia watchers. America may have entered foreign policy imbroglios, but it is not for a lack of dissenting voices within the U.S. foreign policy establishment. Whose ideas come to predominate in government is a theme throughout this book, not well grasped by the concept of groupthink.

Finally, a normatively inflected viewpoint focuses on the functioning of the "marketplace of ideas." Foreshadowed in John Milton's *Areopagitica* (1644) and usually traced to John Stuart Mill's defense of free speech in *On Liberty*,[101] the marketplace metaphor entered U.S. political discourse via Justice Oliver Wendell Holmes's dissent in the *Abrams* case of 1919, where Holmes argued that the "theory of our constitution" was one of "the free market competition of ideas."[102] The concept appears to have purchase on engagement's downfall, observed changes in first Russian and later Chinese behavior leading to the rejection of an outmoded set of ideas.

As noted above, however, the notion of a clear policy failure leading to changed opinions underplays continuing disagreement among China and Russia experts on the shifting rationale for engaging Beijing and Moscow, and the degree to which it can be said to have failed. The limitations of these approaches reflect a general issue with how to account for ideas and epistemic communities in policy formation. The assumption of neat causal arrows traveling from ideas generated in expert communities depicted as coherent entities, to receptive

---

[95] Kuklick 2007; Bessner 2018; Haas 1992.
[96] Desch 2019.
[97] Jacobs and Page 2005.
[98] China interview 081, 4 October 2021, via video call.
[99] Janis 1972.
[100] Porter 2018.
[101] Gordon 1997.
[102] Smolla 2019.

policymakers depicted as receptive to those ideas, poorly reflects reality. More often, dispersed and internally divided epistemic communities enjoy varied and changing connections with the government and thereby exhibit only indirect policy influence, if any at all.[103] Analytical tools sensitive to the contingency of connections between epistemic communities and policymaking processes are thereby required.

Insights from the Sociology of Expertise

The U.S. China and Russia fields are such dispersed communities, connected to the U.S. government but far from determining policy. Rather than a fixed commodity tied to a functional capacity, such as the skills of a surgeon or accountant, China and Russia expertise is the product of an ongoing professional competition to translate certain abilities into a reputation for policy-relevant knowledge. Recognized experts share some family resemblances, notably language ability, time spent in country, and notoriety gained through publication or government service. Members of the China- and Russia-watching communities engage in significant "boundary-work" or policing of the membership of the group along these two criteria.[104] Those who don't speak the language are considered useful interlocutors, who may impart skills and knowledge—like IR theory—but they are not "real" China or Russia "people."

In the words of sociologist Thomas Medvetz, the China and Russia fields are *interstitial*—they sit at the intersection of more bounded social spaces like the academy, business, and the government, which have distinct rules, incentive structures, and forms of power or capital that shape how individuals seek success within them.[105] Think tankers are thus pushed and pulled between often-contradictory goals: from notoriety gained via public prominence, to intellectual credibility gained via academic means like publishing, to funding gained from a variety of sources, tied to demonstrated public or policy impact. Viewing expert communities as the site of an ongoing struggle in an interstitial space follows recent work the aim of which is to produce a sociology of professional expertise that does not simply tell the story of the "necessary formation of a professional group nor by a presumed functional identity between profession and task."[106] Unlike doctors or accountants, one does not need a degree in Chinese or Russian studies to make U.S. policy. Recent work has thus moved from the consideration of experts as a distinct social type to a focus on the social conditions

---

[103] Cross 2013.
[104] Gieryn 1983.
[105] Medvetz 2013.
[106] Eyal 2013: 863–64; Abbott 1988.

enabling their expert interventions. Rather than posit the existence of some essential knowledge that constitutes expertise,[107] sociologist Gil Eyal, for example, focuses on expertise "analyzed as networks that link together objects, actors, techniques, devices, and institutional and spatial arrangements."[108]

Understood in this way, the sociology of expertise requires sensitivity to both experts and the effects of struggle over the performance of foreign policy expertise.[109] Taken together, the new sociology of expertise prioritizes struggle over expert competence over fixed meanings of expert status, displaying three tendencies that mark it off from older visions of the role of the expert and intellectual in policymaking.[110] First, agency is conceptualized as distributed rather than a singular attribute of an individual or group. In the case of foreign policy, agency is a function of a connection or relation between government officials seeking a new perspective or understanding of an issue, like China, and those with conceptualizations to offer. Second, in the place of singular truths uploaded to government by experts—China's "new authoritarianism," for instance—the new approach highlights truth effects—the convergence on new shared perspectives. And third, the approach foregrounds the dynamics of interstitial domains, such as the China community—rather than supposedly homogenous spaces of expertise. Individual experts and groups hold the potential for indirect influence, but such influence is not guaranteed.

In place of these images, I show that the principal role of knowledge communities in foreign policy is not to create, test, and transport ideas into government, but to take part in professional struggles over the construction, legitimation, and boundaries of national security frames, defining the parameters of mainstream views on a given issue, and what falls outside the mainstream, and to credential individuals available for consulting and government service. Contra critics of the U.S. foreign policy establishment, or "blob," such professional struggles are intense, at the same time as delimiting the scope of possible opinions and positions.[111] Drawing on the new sociology of expertise and interventions, the task is to interpret the varied processes by which those ideas, frames, and groups of allies cohere to make contingent expert interventions.

---

[107] Collins and Evans 2007.
[108] Eyal 2013: 864.
[109] Rohde 2013; Oren 2003. Beyond national security, see Hirschman and Berman 2014; Mudge 2018.
[110] Eyal and Buchholz 2010.
[111] Walt 2018; Porter 2018.

Plan of the Book

Drawing on a set of 170 original interviews with America's China and Russia experts, this book tracks an expert intervention made by a group of China experts skeptical of America's long-standing approach of engaging Beijing, juxtaposed to the lack of a similar intervention in relation to U.S. policy toward Russia. A full discussion of the data used for the book is contained in a methodological appendix.

Part I revisits Engagement and the birth of the paradigmatic alternative of Strategic Competition.

Chapter 1 asks, What *was* engagement? Is it really over? Separating E/engagement into its policy, community, and frame aspects, the chapter shows that large-E Engagement is a feature specifically of the China debate—a rationalization for a host of initiatives taken since the opening in the early 1970s, many constructed post hoc—now firmly in the rearview mirror. The makes clear that as an outsider to the end-of-Engagement debate, my role is not to adjudge Engagement's success or failure, but to offer an understanding of why it was overturned under Trump, an explanation rooted in three dynamics of Engagement among America's China community: *polarization, professional status competition,* and *personalization*.

Chapter 2 traces the emergence of Strategic Competition. Drawing on the disaggregation of Engagement as policy, frame, and community, I detail how the Trump administration brought in a set of officials opposed to the old approach, before demonstrating how Strategic Competition was retained under Biden as a paradigm for policymaking. The chapter finally explores continuity in U.S. Russia policy, absent a pro- or anti-engagement framing and community turnover.

Having set up the puzzle of Engagement's demise, the rest of the book moves from description to explanation. How was it possible for the Trump administration to import a set of advisors determined to overturn the Engagement paradigm? Why did the clock not turn back to Engagement with the shift from Trump to Biden? Parts II and III take the China and Russia cases in turn.

Chapter 3 begins by tracking the emergence of pro- versus anti-Engagement groups, and a shift in the center of gravity of the China-watching community away from Engagement. Here I note the importance of Trump's election, which furthered a latent polarization around Engagement.

Chapter 4 shows how, while at first blush the debate over Engagement with China is simply one over ideas, the Engagers/anti-Engagers are constituted via a struggle over professional investments, affiliations, and dispositions. I sketch a broad distinction between those defending the need for "nuance" versus those promoting conviction and a more black-and-white view of China's nature as a threat to the United States. These positions are traced to professional bases: former diplomats and academics, in the first place, military strategists, promoters of human rights, and those hoping to enter government, in the latter.

Chapter 5 explores Engagement's deeply personal aspects. Tracing the roots of anti-Engagement to the activities of the Blue Team in the late 1990s, Engagement's rejection meant the vindication of long-silenced China-skeptics. Consideration of the prominent Engagers demonstrates the stakes for those hoping to defend the old approach. A deeper analysis of Trump's leading China hand, Matthew Pottinger, furthers understanding of the personal nature of anti-Engagement, notably as a re-enacting of the early Cold War—this time with China as the enemy—on the part of the Strategic Competitors.

Part III then turns shifts the analytical lens to U.S. relations with Russia since the Cold War, highlighting points of similarity and difference to the China case.

Chapter 6 describes the formation of opposed groups in the American Russia community, groups who, respectively, want the United States to deal with Russia "as it is" and "as it could be." For the "Russia-we-havers," the United States should resist the temptation to change Russia in a more liberal democratic direction, in search of stability and Moscow's assistance in global governance, especially nuclear nonproliferation. The chapter finds the roots of the "Russia-we-have" and "Russia-we-want" camps in Cold War divisions among America's Russia specialists, some of whom saw the USSR as a totalitarian state unlikely to change without disintegrating, while others saw the Soviet Union as a more pluralistic polity, thereby capable of evolutionary change. The chapter finally explores the effects of the return of Vladimir Putin to the Russian presidency in 2012 on the Russia-we-have and Russia-we-want camps.

Chapter 7 traces a parallel yet distinct set of professional distinctions between America's Russia expert community when compared to America's China watchers. Revisiting the open letters of the summer of 2020, it describes the views of academics and former arms controllers in maintaining an understanding of Russia as an important international player, set against a broad group for whom Russia is a creator of global problems. Once again, America's Russia watchers police the boundaries of their field, using language ability and time in country to distinguish true experts from generalists and broader Eastern European specialists, and struggling over the virtues and vices of nuanced views of Russia.

Chapter 8 then dives into the personalization of U.S. Russia policy. A smaller and, in its self-understanding at least, a relatively collegial field, the Russia-we-have and Russia-we-want groups are nonetheless constituted by personal convictions, beliefs, and dispositions, not to mention often long-standing friendships and animosities. Assessment of the travails of Trump's chief Russia hand, Fiona Hill, subsequently provides a point of comparison to that of China hand Matthew Pottinger. Hill became enmeshed in palace struggles in the Trump administration, including Trump's eventual impeachment. As a critic of

Putin sitting in between the Russia-we-have and Russia-we-wanters, Hill was less interested in effecting a paradigmatic turnover of America's approach to Russia—as Pottinger was with China—than offering a steady, adult hand in the tumultuous Trump presidency. The case of Russia-we-haver Matthew Rojansky's failed nomination to the Biden White House offers a further case of the personal consequences of the polarization of U.S. Russia policy.

A final concluding chapter recaps the main argument before discussing implications for U.S. relations with China and Russia going forward. With pro-E/engagers in each field firmly on the margins, American policy toward Beijing and Moscow looks set for a long-frozen period, raising normative questions about what role, if any, America's China and Russia watchers can and should play in U.S. foreign policy.

PART I
RETHINKING ENGAGEMENT

1
What Was Engagement?

For 40 years we engaged [China]. We engaged on their advice, on their expert testimony, if you will. Guys like Ken Lieberthal,[1] Winston Lord,[2] guys like ... Stapleton Roy. Orville Schell,[3] all these people, they were all the intellectual foundation for advising every administration, Republican and Democrat, to engage, to engage, to engage. And some of them now recognize that they can't keep selling that because it's so patently false.
—China interview 072[4]

I was inside the government, deeply embedded for 25 years in China policy. We never had any fantasies about China becoming a liberal democracy. It was never a factor in a single policy decision that I was involved in.
—China interview 057[5]

A little over a year ago, President Obama and Secretary Clinton committed the United States to a policy of principled engagement [with Moscow].
—Daniel R. Russel, deputy assistant secretary of state for European and Eurasian affairs, 26 April 2010

The U.S. relationship with the Russian Federation, already among our most critical, complex, and difficult, remains severely strained.

---

[1] Senior fellow emeritus at the Brookings Institute. Formerly senior director for Asia on the National Security Council (1998–2000).

[2] Former diplomat, including as ambassador to China (1985–1989) and special assistant to the national security advisor (1970–1973). In the latter role Lord was the first American into the People's Republic and was present at all five meetings between Richard Nixon and Mao Zedong. See David Barboza, "Winston Lord on U.S.-China Cooperation during Covid-19," *The Wire China*, 12 April 2020, https://www.thewirechina.com/2020/04/12/winston-lord-qa/.

[3] Arthur Ross, director of the Center on U.S.-China Relations at the Asia Society and longtime journalist on China.

[4] China interview 072, 19 February 2019, via video call.

[5] China interview 057, 13 November 2018, Washington DC.

> ... In light of the current context and lack of mutual trust, engaging constructively with the Russian Federation is a challenge.
> —*Integrated Russia Strategy*, State Department, 11 March 2019, 2

The Era of Engagement Is Over

National Security Council Asia director Kurt Campbell's May 2021 proclamation that "the era of engagement with the PRC is over" came as a surprise only to those not paying attention.[6] After four years of deteriorating relations with China under Trump, the new Biden team had already signaled its intention to continue Strategic Competition as the operative mode of U.S. policymaking. At a tense meeting in Anchorage in March, Secretary of State Anthony Blinken expressed America's "deep concerns with actions by China, including in Xinjiang, Hong Kong, Taiwan, cyberattacks on the United States, and economic coercion toward our allies" that "threaten the rules-based order that maintains global stability."[7] Speaking to a virtual audience at Stanford University, Campbell and deputy Laura Rosenberger affirmed what everyone already knew.

A similar case might have been made about the end of America's attempts to engage Russia after the Cold War.[8] The February 2022 invasion of Ukraine put to bed any lingering hopes of moves away from ever-tightening sanctions. For many Russia watchers, the question became not how to engage Russia but how to deter it.[9] Yet the new Biden administration made no such pronouncement about U.S. relations with Moscow in spring 2021. Russia remained a secondary foreign policy issue until the fall troop buildup signaled possible trouble, which burst forth with Putin's announcement of Russia's "special military operation" in Ukraine. Evidently, "engaging" Putin's Russia was the horse so dead it did not need to be flogged.

Juxtaposition of the cases of America's engagement with China and Russia thus highlights a curious feature of each: the existence of a specific rhetorical framing of America's approach to China and its decline, a feature absent in relation to Russia policy except for the occasional incidental use of the word by officials. To capture this distinction, I capitalize "Engagement" in relation to China, but not Russia. Despite similarities, U.S. China policy is understood through the lens of

---

[6] https://www.bloomberg.com/news/articles/2021-05-26/biden-s-asia-czar-says-era-of-engagement-with-xi-s-china-is-over.
[7] https://www.brookings.edu/blog/order-from-chaos/2021/03/22/the-us-and-china-finally-get-real-with-each-other/.
[8] https://www.politico.com/news/magazine/2022/02/25/putin-russia-ukraine-invasion-endgame-experts-00011652.
[9] https://www.atlanticcouncil.org/blogs/ukrainealert/how-to-deter-russia-now/.

Engagement, not applicable to the debate over what to do about Russia, which remains just engagement. While they display important similarities, notably a relitigation of what happened in the 1990s—was it a mistake to expand NATO and facilitate China's accession to the World Trade Organization?—Russia policy over the period remains only that: Russia policy. China policy was, its critics assert and its defenders acknowledge, *Engagement*.

In this chapter, I demonstrate the significance of this framing of U.S.-China relations over the past four decades for how both policymakers and academics should seek to account for engagement's rise and fall. In short, the search for a clear account of engagement's demise faces an obstacle in the existence of the Engagement framing. With America's China watchers themselves in disagreement about what, precisely, Engagement *is,* or *was,* the analyst is cast into the role of adjudicator between different claims that properly reside in the policy realm. Was engaging China a reasonable strategy? At what point did it stop being a sensible approach? Was it even a strategy at all? While the analyst can adopt a longer temporal view or deploy novel theoretical perspectives, as an outsider to the policy debate, they have no special authority to say what, ultimately, Engagement was.

My aim, consequently, is not to act as another litigant over Engagement's virtues and vices. I cannot pass ultimate judgment on what Engagement was, or whether it worked. Critics of U.S. China policy prior to 2017—some were insiders to U.S. government decisions or close observers—are not likely to change their mind about what Engagement was and what its aims were. Supporters of Engagement, notably former policymakers and officials, by contrast, are equally unlikely to be convinced that "changing China" was the intention of U.S. policy all along. The groups differ, at times fundamentally, on what Engagement *was.*

To put the point differently, the relitigation of Engagement is a creature of the policy world. Questions over what Engagement was, and its aims, can only be settled there, not from my perspective from the ivory tower. What I can do is offer a way of thinking about American strategy toward China and Russia that takes into account Engagement, and its relitigation, as a specific and unique feature of U.S.-China relations.

I begin therefore by showing how "it"—Engagement with the PRC—is not a singular but a multifaceted object, part of the very thing we want to explain: America's approach to China since the Cold War. Differentiating capital-*E* Engagement with China from small-*e* engagement as a foreign policy applicable to Russia, shows how Engagement with China is in many ways a post hoc rationalization. I then disaggregate Engagement/engagement with China and Russia as *policy, frame, community,* drawing attention once again to the dynamics of the U.S. China- and Russia-watching communities as the key site of the formation, negotiation, and rejection of settled modes of knowing America's friends, rivals, and enemies.

Engagement with China Failed

In March 2018, two prominent China experts made a splash in U.S. national security circles by labeling the United States' long-standing policy toward Beijing an abject failure. In an article in *Foreign Affairs*, former assistant secretary of state for East Asian and Pacific affairs Kurt Campbell and Ely Ratner, then at the Center for a New American Security (CNAS), proclaimed America "got China wrong."[10] The decades-old policy of "Engaging" China in hopes of encouraging its leaders toward democracy and liberalism, they argued, was a bust. Economic development had not translated into political openness and a flourishing civil society, as Engagement's defenders had promised. Quite the opposite had happened: economic growth had proceeded hand in hand with authoritarianism, creating a communist state able to exert technologically sophisticated control over its population, while investing in the military and diplomatic capacity to spread influence internationally. For Ratner and Campbell, the lesson was clear: "America needs a China reckoning."

In striking contrast to Campbell and Ratner's impact is the deafening silence that followed a similar indictment of U.S. Russia policy not 18 months earlier. In an October 2016 article in *Foreign Policy*, two prominent Russia experts—Tom Graham, former special assistant to the president and senior director for Russia on the National Security Council (2004–2007), and the Wilson Center's Matthew Rojansky—declared "America's Russia Policy Has Failed."[11] Despite "suffering from diplomatic and economic isolation under a U.S.-led international sanctions regime," Graham and Rojansky stated, "Moscow has succeeded in challenging a wide range of America interests, most notably in Ukraine, Syria, and cyberspace." Graham and Rojansky assailed both presidential candidates—Hillary Clinton and Trump—for lacking a Russia policy capable of breaking out of "failed tropes of the past." For them, U.S. policy required accepting that "Russia is not a democracy, nor is it democratizing, and although Russia may be in secular decline, it is a major power on the world stage."

Whereas Graham and Rojansky's call would seem to have fallen on deaf ears,[12] the argument that a China reckoning was required was an idea whose time had come in Washington, tapping into pent-up frustrations among numerous

---

[10] Campbell and Ratner 2018.

[11] Thomas Graham and Matthew Rojansky, "America's Russia Policy Has Failed," *Foreign Policy*, 13 October 2016, https://foreignpolicy.com/2016/10/13/americas-russia-policy-has-failed-clinton-trump-putin-ukraine-syria-how-to-fix/.

[12] Measuring the impact of an attempted intervention is difficult if not impossible, rendered more difficult in the case of Trump's Russia policy due to the issue of election interference. Some evidence of the limited impact of Graham and Rojansky's call, however, is that none of their seven suggestions for improving relations were adopted: "1) understand that it's not just about Putin; 2) stop Ukraine from becoming a frozen conflict; 3) have an honest talk about Europe; 4) push for more arms control; 5) work with Russia in Asia; 6) recognize that Syria is about more than Syria."

China hands and grand strategists. Experts Robert Blackwill and Ashley Tellis had sounded the alarm three years earlier, stating, "China represents and will remain the most significant competitor to the United States for decades to come. As such, the need for a more coherent U.S. response to increasing Chinese power is long overdue."[13] No such sentiment existed in relation to Russia.

Even prominent China experts widely known to be in favor of Engagement, like David "Mike" Lampton, had recently signaled notes of caution in the direction of U.S.-China relations, proof that the center of gravity among the China expert community was shifting toward a far more concerned stance over changes in China and its implications for the United States.[14] By early 2018, the sense of gloom had moved beyond the small world of China watchers to the broader public, with journalist Evan Osnos capturing the mood in a January *New Yorker* article warning of Chinese premier Xi Jinping's growing ambitions.[15] By early 2019, the language used to describe U.S.-China relations had taken on explicit Cold War associations, with dragon-slaying imagery prominent.[16]

Of more consequence, Campbell and Ratner's clarion call appeared amid—and amplified—a shift in official rhetoric toward China effected by the Trump administration, which justified the need for a new approach for American policy toward the PRC by dismissing Engagement as naive and a failure. As Vice President Mike Pence told an audience at the Hudson Institute, the Trump administration sought to counter a China "applying [its] power in more proactive ways than ever before," including "exert[ing] influence and interfere[ing] in the domestic policy and politics of our country."[17] In response, the December 2017 NSS labeled China—alongside Russia—a "major competitor" of the United States.[18] Part of the rationale was that "America had hoped that economic liberalization would bring China into greater partnership with us and with the world. Instead, China has chosen economic aggression, which has in turn emboldened its growing military."[19]

The May 2020 document titled the *United States Strategic Approach to the People's Republic of China* made an unmistakable connection between the failure

---

[13] Blackwill and Tellis 2015.
[14] David Lampton, "A Tipping Point in U.S.-China Relations," Council on Pacific Affairs, 2 June 2015, https://www.councilpacificaffairs.org/news-media/security-defense/dr-david-lampton-on-a-tipping-point-in-u-s-china-relations/.
[15] Evan Osnos, "Making China Great Again," *New Yorker*, January 2018, https://www.newyorker.com/magazine/2018/01/08/making-china-great-again.
[16] For example, Westad 2019.
[17] "Vice President Mike Pence's Remarks on the Administration's Policy towards China," 4 October 2018, https://www.hudson.org/events/1610-vice-president-mike-pence-s-remarks-on-the-administration-s-policy-towards-china102018.
[18] *National Security Strategy of the United States*, December 2017, https://trumpwhitehouse.archives.gov/wp-content/uploads/2017/12/NSS-Final-12-18-2017-0905.pdf.
[19] *National Security Strategy of the United States*, December 2017.

of "engagement" and the need for a new U.S. policy toward China. "Since the United States and the People's Republic of China (PRC) established diplomatic relations in 1979," it stated, "United States policy toward the PRC was largely premised on a hope that deepening engagement would spur fundamental economic and political opening in the PRC and lead to its emergence as a constructive and responsible global stakeholder, with a more open society."[20] However, the document went on:

> More than 40 years later, it has become evident that this approach underestimated the will of the Chinese Communist Party (CCP) to constrain the scope of economic and political reform in China. Over the past two decades, reforms have slowed, stalled, or reversed. The PRC's rapid economic development and increased engagement with the world did not lead to convergence with the citizen-centric, free and open order as the United States had hoped. The CCP has chosen instead to exploit the free and open rules based order and attempt to reshape the international system in its favor. Beijing openly acknowledges that it seeks to transform the international order to align with CCP interests and ideology. The CCP's expanding use of economic, political, and military power to compel acquiescence from nation states harms vital American interests and undermines the sovereignty and dignity of countries and individuals around the world.[21]

Over the subsequent summer months, key Trump administration figures gave four coordinated speeches on different aspects of the "China challenge," which further cemented the connection between engagement's failings and the new approach.[22] After National Security Advisor Robert O'Brien spoke about the ideological dimensions, FBI director Christopher Wray detailed Chinese espionage activities, and Attorney General Bill Barr discussed economics, Pompeo tied the speeches together. Paying polite tribute to Richard Nixon's trip to China in 1972 in view of the location of the speech—the Nixon Presidential Library in Yorba Linda, California—Pompeo noted, "The world was much different then":[23]

> We imagined engagement with China would produce a future with bright promise of comity and cooperation. But today—today we're all still wearing

---

[20] *United States Strategic Approach to the People's Republic of China*, May 2020, https://trumpwhitehouse.archives.gov/wp-content/uploads/2020/05/U.S.-Strategic-Approach-to-The-Peoples-Republic-of-China-Report-5.24v1.pdf.
[21] *United States Strategic Approach to the People's Republic of China*, May 2020.
[22] Secretary Michael R. Pompeo Remarks at the Richard Nixon Presidential Library and Museum, "Communist China and the Free World's Future," 23 July 2020, https://mn.usembassy.gov/speech-secretary-pompeo-07-23-2020/.
[23] Pompeo, "Communist China and the Free World's Future."

masks and watching the pandemic's body count rise because the CCP failed in its promises to the world. We're reading every morning news headlines of repression in Hong Kong and in Xinjiang. We're seeing staggering statistics of Chinese trade abuses that cost American jobs and strike enormous blows to the economies all across America, including here in southern California. And we're watching a Chinese military that grows stronger and stronger, and indeed more menacing.... What do the American people have to show now 50 years on from engagement with China? Did the theories of our leaders that proposed a Chinese evolution towards freedom and democracy prove to be true?

For Pompeo, Americans had "to admit a hard truth..., that if we want to have a free 21st century, and not the Chinese century of which Xi Jinping dreams, the old paradigm of blind engagement with China simply won't get it done. We must not continue it and we must not return to it."[24]

The status of the "Engagement failed" framing of the need for a new approach was solidified, finally, in the breach, in a more neutral account of the *Elements of the China Challenge* put out by the State Department's Policy Planning Staff in November 2020, which repeated the new common sense. Locating the beginning of engagement after the "the Chinese Communist Party's massacre of civilians that ended the six-week Tiananmen Square protests of 1989 and Beijing's subsequent imposition of harsh restrictions on freedom of speech and press," the document described how "U.S. administrations of both parties doubled down on a China policy focused on engagement."[25] Admitting that the policy "had its justifications and brought its benefits," it was nonetheless apparent that China's "rapid modernization, prodigious economic growth and steady integration into the world economy, and the building of a world-class military have not inclined China to join, let alone play its part in maintaining, the community of nations dedicated to an international order grounded in freedom, democracy, national sovereignty, human rights, and the rule of law."[26] In other words, engagement failed.

Relitigating Engagement

Together, the effect of these Trump administration proclamations was to place the failure of Engagement at the heart of the justification for the development of

---

[24] Pompeo, "Communist China and the Free World's Future."
[25] *The Elements of the China Challenge*, by the Policy Planning Staff, Office of the Secretary of State, https://www.state.gov/wp-content/uploads/2020/11/20-02832-Elements-of-China-Challenge-508.pdf.
[26] *The Elements of the China Challenge*, 45.

a new approach labeled Strategic Competition. On its face, this is unsurprising. Yet it is noteworthy how the Trump administration and outside constituencies like Campbell and Ratner chose to justify the development of a new Strategic Competition framing for U.S.-China relations not on the back of changes in China or new calculations of the American national interest, but as a fundamental turn away from a failed prior approach. Here was a rhetorical tactic, not an objective fact.

The choice of "Engagement's failure," indeed, was not lost on legions of national security experts in Washington, DC, and beyond who pay close attention to subtle and no-so-subtle shifts in government rhetoric like these—as administrations signal valence of issues, with possible effects on the implementation of current policy and design of new ones. Opponents of the Trump administration's China policy quickly countered in the court of expert opinion. Neil Thomas refers to this ongoing feature of the U.S. China debate as the "relitigation" of Engagement.[27]

An early litigant was Stape Roy, former ambassador to Beijing (1991–1995), who attempted to reaffirm that "Engagement works."[28] Campbell and Ratner's critique, Roy asserted, fails "to distinguish between the way Washington publicly justifies its policies, by referring to values, and the way it actually formulates the, by putting national interests first."[29] From such a perspective, "Constructive engagement has served U.S. interests well," advancing American business ventures and facilitating China's accession to the nuclear nonproliferation treaty in 1992.[30] As Roy later told the nonpartisan Wilson Center, "The U.S. policy of engagement has been discredited by knowledgeable foreign policy specialists who claim engagement was based on wholly unrealistic expectations that it would produce positive change in China."[31] Pointing to the 1980s, Roy went on, "There is no question that engagement did facilitate Deng Xiaoping's reform and openness policies that produced several decades of rapid economic development in China, resulted in the globalization of its economy, and imbedded hundreds of thousands of western educated young Chinese in governing and educational institutions throughout the country."[32]

---

[27] Neil Thomas, "Matters of Record: Relitigating Engagement with China," *Macropolo*, 3 September 2019, https://macropolo.org/analysis/china-us-engagement-policy/.
[28] Roy 2018: 185–86.
[29] Roy 2018: 185.
[30] Roy 2018: 185.
[31] J. Stapleton Roy, "Keynote Remarks by Ambassador J. Stapleton Roy at the Wilson Center China Fellowship Conference 2021," Wilson Center, 3 February 2021, https://www.wilsoncenter.org/article/keynote-remarks-ambassador-j-stapleton-roy-wilson-center-china-fellowship-conference-2021.
[32] Roy, "Keynote Remarks." See Schell 1989 for one China hand's on-the-ground account of the period.

For one senior former national intelligence official, "I think it's historical nonsense that engagement failed because it was based on false premises. If you talk to people who were involved in the process, Charles Freeman, Stape Roy, others, it's simply historically inaccurate to claim that engagement was premised on the democratization of China."[33] Pointing to former president Richard Nixon's article "Asia after Vietnam," my interviewee went on, "I know that others have quoted this article ... about changing China.[34] [But] if you read the Nixon article, it's obvious that he's talking about changing China's external behavior, right? Not changing the way that it's governed internally."[35]

Political scientist Thomas Christensen[36] and the Brookings Institution's Patricia Kim too reject Campbell and Ratner's suggestion that Engagement was meant to change China's basic interests, to "abandon its political system and to curb its ambitions to become a great power."[37] Engagement was, rather, part of an effort to shape the choices of a rising China.[38] Given America's inability to fully dictate China's fate, it is unwise for them to abandon the limited leverage gained via engagement. Assessing the debate, political scientist Alastair Iain Johnston suggested that the "engagement failed" idea "rests on two empirical claims and one counterfactual claim": (1) that engagement "was designed to create a Chinese commitment to the U.S.-dominated liberal order, but basically failed to change China's preferences"; (2) that "engagement was designed to liberalize, even democratize, China's political system, and as such has failed"; and (3) that, had the United States never adopted the engagement strategy in the first place, the United States would be better off today because it would have been better prepared to compete with or contain China earlier.[39] Johnston dismisses the first and third. For him, the claim that engagement failed rests on an overly simplified view of the "rules-based international order," with China adhering to some aspects—especially sovereign integrity and noninterference in other states' domestic affairs—while opposing others, particularly those related to social and political rights.[40] The third, counterfactual, claim, meanwhile, ignores an equally plausible alternative history, one in which "the United States would have

---

[33] China interview 078, 27 September 2021, via video call.
[34] For example, Francis P. Sempa, "Richard Nixon's Asian Prophecy," *The Diplomat*, 20 December 2019, https://thediplomat.com/2019/12/richard-nixons-asian-prophecy/.
[35] China interview 078, 27 September 2021, via video call.
[36] James T. Shotwell, professor of international relations at the School of International and Public Affairs, Columbia University. Previously professor of world politics of peace and war at Princeton University. Christensen served as deputy assistant secretary of state for East Asian and Pacific Affairs between 2006 and 2008.
[37] Thomas Christensen and Patricia Kim, "Don't Abandon Ship," *Foreign Affairs* 97, 4 July–August 2018, 188–90.
[38] As former policymaker Christensen himself had laid out in 2015. Christensen 2015.
[39] Johnston 2019.
[40] Johnston 2019: 101.

faced a hostile, nuclear-armed China alienated from a range of international institutions and norms, kept out of global markets, and with limited societal/cultural exchanges."[41]

The more contested second claim is, Johnston recognized, the real crux of the debate: did U.S. policymakers and their advisors think of engagement as a way to "liberalize, even democratize, China's political system"? For Johnston the argument "is built on a straw person argument that is seemingly unquestioned in the current narrative."[42] Harvard academic William Overholt agrees, exploring public justifications and private motivations for American policy at crucial turning points in the U.S.-China relationship.[43] Taking as exemplary the case of Michel Oksenberg—political scientist and member of the National Security Council under President Jimmy Carter—a poster child for Engagement, Overholt describes Oksenberg's skepticism toward America's ability to "change China," rendering it an unlikely justification for America's policy of engaging China in the late 1970s.

> "America has only limited influence on China's internal affairs," [Oksenberg wrote] in a 1991 Foreign Affairs article. "The United States cannot create to its liking [even] small countries on its doorstep—Panama, Haiti, Cuba, El Salvador. And experiences in the Middle East and Southeast Asia demonstrate that Americans have no special talent for shaping the governance of countries further afield. Yet, for reasons that have fascinated successive generations of historians, America has sought to produce a China more to its liking. The efforts have always ended in a massive failure."[44]

For Overholt, while "multiple U.S. presidents dating to Ronald Reagan made occasional comments about liberalizing or democratizing China as a potential benefit of engagement,... this was in marketing moments or an informal expression of ideas, never pursued as a central thrust of policy."[45]

Reaching similar conclusions, for Neil Thomas the rejection of engagement is "premised on a selective historical record and risks oversimplifying what was a complex and multi-faceted approach to China across successive US administrations."[46] Thomas points particularly to a series of speeches made by

---

[41] Johnston 2019: 109.
[42] Johnston 2019: 103.
[43] William H. Overholt, "Was US-China Engagement Premised on Chinese Political Liberalization?," *The Hill*, 14 October 2021, https://www.google.com/search?q = overholt+china+engagement&rlz = 1C1GCEA_enUS963US963&oq = overholt+china+engagement&aqs = chrome.. 69i57j33i160.7897j0j4&sourceid = chrome&ie = UTF-8.
[44] Overholt, "US-China Engagement."
[45] Overholt, "US-China Engagement."
[46] Thomas, "Matters of Record."

Bill Clinton in the run-up to China's bid to join the WTO, which engagement's critics point to as strong evidence U.S. leaders explicitly tied the policy to political liberalization. While Clinton did use "soaring" rhetoric about how WTO accession meant China was "agreeing to import one of democracy's most cherished values: economic freedom" and how Beijing "will find that the genie of freedom will not go back into the bottle" as "liberty is the most contagious force in the world," together the speeches painted a "pragmatic" picture of what concrete national interests might be achieved via engagement with Beijing.[47] For Thomas, many of those U.S. interests remain over two decades later, including limiting nuclear proliferation, combating the trafficking of drugs, maintaining economic connections, and fighting climate change.[48]

Moving beyond Relitigation

Clarifying their aim as "to interrogate the old consensus and spark a debate about the assumptions that have guided U.S. China policy," and not to "assert that U.S. policymakers were naïve or ill informed," nor voice support for Trump's "American First" approach, the relitigation of engagement Campbell and Ratner's piece set in train nevertheless solidified the connection between the failings of something labeled Engagement and the need for a new approach. For Thomas, consequently, "What's missing from this debate is a more expansive and hence more accurate assessment of what engagement was—an account that does not simply cherry-pick the words proved most wrong by time."[49] However, attempts to nuance the debate over Engagement like those of Overholt, Johnston, and Thomas have not weakened the rhetorical power of the claim that Engagement failed. The connection has only grown stronger.

Princeton political scientist and noted China skeptic Aaron Friedberg, for example, connected the failure of engagement with China with that of Russia. Using almost identical language to Campbell and Ratner and the May 2020 *United States Strategic Approach to the People's Republic of China*, Friedberg claims that "for the past thirty years the Western strategy towards Russia and China was to try and incorporate them into the global, liberal, democratic order by developing deep economic ties with the two countries."[50] The strategy, Friedberg says, "has failed. Russia and China became richer, but they also became more authoritarian, imperialistic, and anti-Western. They are now using

---

[47] Thomas, "Matters of Record."
[48] Thomas, "Matters of Record."
[49] Thomas, "Matters of Record."
[50] Aaron Friedberg, "How the West Got China and Russia Wrong," *IAI News*, 5 April 2022, https://iai.tv/articles/how-the-west-got-russia-and-china-wrong-auid-2094.

the West's interdependence with their economies as a weapon, attempting to coerce their democratic trading partners. China and Russia seem ready for a new period of intense and aggressive rivalry with the West."[51]

Friedberg's case is shaky, if for no other reason that America's post-1989 policy toward Russia and the Soviet Union was not labeled "engagement."[52] There has been a significant amount of relitigation of U.S. *policy* toward Russia, to be sure, particularly NATO expansion. For Sarotte, for example, American policymakers too quickly dismissed the Partnership for Peace as a mechanism of post–Cold War European security, rushing instead toward NATO expansion.[53] Others, like Friedberg, suggest the historical record points in the opposite direction: against post-1989 U.S. policymakers who believed Russia and China could be brought into the rules-based international order. But nowhere does Friedberg quote U.S. policymakers describing or justifying their decisions as part of an overarching strategy of "engagement."

We should question why the distinction matters. Was U.S. policy toward Russia and China not, broadly speaking, the same? As a normative argument, perhaps not. Analytically, the difference certainly does matter.

The reason is that relitigations like that over Engagement rarely, by themselves, change the minds of commentators and policymakers, especially those with a hand in the events under scrutiny. Former policymakers normally double down on their aims and goals. Rather than change their ideas, their ideas fade away as they either retire or lose relevance from the political discussion through inactivity. And, sooner or later, they pass away and their convictions with them.

Thomas's idealistic call to more accurately plumb the historical record is thus admirable but misguided. Litigants cannot agree on what engagement was, never mind whether "it" failed or not—and whether, indeed, there was an "it" at all. Readers intimately involved in Engagement with China especially are almost certain to find my retelling here partial or incorrect in one direction or another.

What is required, therefore, is a different way of thinking about engagement itself, one that does not take "it" as necessarily having a single referent, especially not as a unified American approach toward China, the intentions of which can be proven or disproven with discovery of the correct quotation, memory, or assertion.

---

[51] Friedberg, "How the West Got China and Russia Wrong."
[52] Friedberg develops his analysis of Engagement with China in book form in Friedberg 2022.
[53] Sarotte 2021.

What *Was* E/engagement Again?

Typical accounts of Engagement display two tendencies that make it difficult to offer an alternative perspective, however. The first is the tendency to consider Engagement a unitary phenomenon that can begin and end in a definite way—typically a coherent strategy, policy, or approach. In James Steinberg's otherwise astute assessment, "Perhaps the answer to the question 'what went wrong?' [with Engagement] is not so much bad individual decisions, but rather a misguided overall strategy."[54] Or recall the authoritative statement of the May 2020 *United States Strategic Approach to the People's Republic of China*, which labels engagement a policy: "Since the United States and the People's Republic of China (PRC) established diplomatic relations in 1979, United States *policy* toward the PRC was largely premised on a hope that deepening engagement would spur fundamental economic and political opening in the PRC and lead to its emergence as a constructive and responsible global stakeholder, with a more open society."[55]

In typical accounts, the slippage between policy, strategy, and approach is significant. Which, *precisely*, is it? While some slippage might be desirable in the design and implementation of policy—for example, allowing officials to evade the specific usage of "strategy" in Department of Defense–speak as the rational alignment of national security means to ends—such slippage impedes scholarly analysis, for two reasons.

First, slippage between depicting Engagement as policy, strategy, and approach suggests a degree of coherence difficult to sustain over four decades. Can Nixon's way of dealing with China and Obama's pivot really be lumped together as the same kind of object? Second, it suggests a degree of concreteness typically lacking in international affairs. Has Engagement really ended? What about top-level climate change meetings? Are these not examples of engagement?[56] Indeed, despite the authority of Campbell's declaration of Engagement's passing, some supporters believe and opponents worry Engagement might not be dead after all. As one China law expert (obviously pro-engagement—that's not going to be a big surprise) noted, "Engagement is under a lot of new pressure, but I don't think it is dead."[57] For another pro-Engagement academic, "Engagement is changing,

---

[54] Steinberg 2019–2020: 128; https://tnsr.org/2020/01/what-went-wrong-u-s-china-relations-from-tiananmen-to-trump/.

[55] See *United States Strategic Approach to the People's Republic of China*, May 2020.

[56] Respectively, "Biden, Xi Meet in Virtual Summit," *Washington Post*, 16 November 2021, https://www.washingtonpost.com/politics/biden-to-meet-with-chinese-president-in-virtual-summit/2021/11/14/6f59b36c-45bb-11ec-973c-be864f938c72_story.html; "China Warns U.S. Strained Relations Could Sink Climate Cooperation," *New York Times*, 2 February 2021, https://www.nytimes.com/2021/09/02/world/asia/climate-china-us-kerry.html.

[57] China interview 080, 30 September 2021, via video call.

but I am not willing to throw the towel in just yet. [A] lot of the slowdown in engagement right now is just a product of Covid.... So I don't think engagement is over."[58] For a strong critic of Engagement and former congressional staffer for a prominent Republican, Biden's flirtation with the term "responsible competition"[59] was worrying: "I'm afraid engagement isn't really dead. I don't know. [Maybe] it's a zombie or was never dead in the first place."[60]

A further tendency compounds the confusion sown by seeing Engagement as a coherent object: the tendency to assess Engagement's record exclusively within the frame of U.S.-China relations.[61] China is only one aspect of U.S. policy, and its history cannot be told solely with reference to major events in Sino-U.S. relations. Most starkly, the primary rationale behind the opening to Beijing was to further confrontation with the Soviet Union. While China is a consistently prominent concern, it is rarely top priority—others, from elections to impeachments to pandemics, intervene. The global war on terror, for instance, reorganized U.S. foreign policy away from a nascent pivot to Asia for the better part of 15 years.[62]

Engaging the PRC in the Rearview Mirror

The first necessary step in countering these two obfuscatory tendencies is to recognize that as a political term of art "Engagement" is a relatively recent invention, emerging during the early 1990s and becoming more prominent in the run-up to China's WTO accession, before re-emerging in recent debates as a term of disparagement. While a somewhat crude measure, a Google Ngram of "Engagement with China" backs up these impressions.[63] Engagement with China was rarely used before the end of the Cold War, increasing exponentially over the 1990s, before declining again from 2000 until the end of the data in 2008. The lack of mention before 1989 equally suggests that use of the term to

---

[58] China interview 081, 4 October 2021, via video call.
[59] https://www.whitehouse.gov/briefing-room/statements-releases/2021/10/06/readout-of-national-security-advisor-jake-sullivans-meeting-with-politburo-member-yang-jiechi/. Also Patricia Kim, "Working toward Responsible Competition with China," Brookings, 8 October 2021, https://www.brookings.edu/blog/order-from-chaos/2021/10/08/working-toward-responsible-competition-with-china/.
[60] China interview 082, 8 October 2021, via video call.
[61] See, for example, Orville Schell, The Death of Engagement. *The Wire China* 7 June 2020, https://www.thewirechina.com/2020/06/07/the-birth-life-and-death-of-engagement/.
[62] See Silove 2016.
[63] This helps explain, in turn, why the term "Engagement" is absent from two prominent academic texts from the 1990s on U.S.-China relations by leading China scholars Harry Harding and Ezra Vogel. Harding 1992; Vogel 1997.

describe U.S. policy before the end of the Cold War lumps together two qualitatively different debates and political contexts.

Interviews back up the impression that Engagement is in many ways a retroactive, post hoc construction. "It seems like that came to be the fashion in the Trump [years]. I've heard it more since Trump than I ever heard it before Trump," one former diplomat noted.[64] As a senior think tanker explained, "Engagement was never really a strategy . . . it was sort of the keynote one, one of several in the relationship . . . [T]his notion that the era of engagement hit a wall and ended now is all, as you know, a reinterpretation. We never called it the era of engagement at the time. Yeah, we just called it U.S.-China relations."[65] As a longtime China hand explained, Engagement with China was not a special approach: "Maybe because I was in the State Department . . . I never really thought that we were doing something different with China than what we were doing with other countries."[66]

According to a former diplomat: "I do not recall any debate over 'engagement' per se with China; for that matter, the word 'engagement' rarely entered into the language of the seventies and eighties."[67] Finally, for a former trade diplomat, "As someone who worked inside the US government [from the 1990s] until 2018 . . . [n]o one I talked to had that view of, like, we are going to change China from the inside, right? . . . That's not a fair characterization."[68] As this interviewee elaborated: "The term 'engagement' only began to be heard frequently during the Bush administration, as President Bush, National Security Adviser Scowcroft and Secretary of State Baker sought to enunciate a new rationale for maintaining close ties with China—despite the Tiananmen Square atrocity, despite the halting of political 'reform,' despite the vanished Soviet threat."[69] Something called "Engagement" emerged Minerva-like after the fact: "No one called this the era of engagement when it was ongoing," a prominent think tanker explained. "If you look . . . you'll find it's only when it started to fade [that Engagement became prominent]."[70]

To be clear, the significance of the post hoc nature of the end-of-Engagement debate is *not* that Engagement did not exist. Rather, it is that Engagement is not a single thing, but an artifact of the ongoing struggle among America's China experts to shape U.S. policy. Interpretations of past and present are always *claims* to truth in search of future-oriented political projects. They are never settled. Events move on as the policy train "leaves the station." As one consultant

[64] China interview 085, 22 October 2021, via video call.
[65] China interview 083, 12 October 2021, Washington D.C.
[66] China interview 085, 22 October 2021, via video call.
[67] China interview 069, 7 February 2019, via e-mail correspondence.
[68] China interview 088, 28 October 2021, via telephone.
[69] China interview 069, 7 February 2019, via e-mail correspondence.
[70] China interview 083, 12 October 2021, Washington, DC.

and early litigator in the Engagement debate explained, "The debate [over Engagement] is basically over as far as the DC ... policymaking community is concerned.... I mean the debate about what engagement was [is] a historical debate at this point."[71]

The twin tendencies of adopting a perspective that isolates the history of U.S. relations with China and Russia from broader foreign policy concerns, alongside a fuzzy definition of E/engagement itself stands in the way of understanding what, *exactly*, has changed in each case and why. To gain a more accurate assessment, therefore, I first identify three distinct aspects of Engagement with China. I then show how engagement with Russia differs, with important implications for our attempts to understand why.

The Three Faces of E/engagement

Engagement with China had three aspects or "faces":[72] Engagement as *frame*, as *policy*, and as *community*. With its face turned toward the public, Engagement as frame justified Engagement as policy over time. After 2017, rejection of the Engagement frame was a vehicle for the development of a slate of new, competitive policies aimed at Beijing. The Engagement frame is distinct from policy, therefore. Facing the U.S. governmental apparatus, Engagement as policy covers a set of concrete decisions and processes of U.S.-China relations. As policy, Engagement is not to be confused with the presentation and justification of relations with Beijing via a constructed narrative about China and its meaning for the United States. Engagement as community, finally, refers to the group of China-oriented professionals with a stake in Engagement as policy and its predominant framing. As we will see, the rejection of Engagement under Trump, continued under his successor, has been in large part a rejection not just of the idea or rhetoric of engaging China, but also of the *bearers* of such a view—the Engagers themselves, as a community.

U.S. engagement with Russia shares only two of the aspects of Engagement with China: a set of policy manifestations and a community that has promoted engagement. Again, engagement with Russia has not been framed as a single thing, be it strategy, policy, or approach. The Obama administration aimed to "reset" the U.S.-Russia relationship—itself a manufactured foreign policy device. But neither it, nor other administrations, forged relations with Russia via a specific Engagement frame.

---

[71] China interview 104, 11 May 2021, via video call.
[72] For a similar analysis of the three faces of a complex social formation, see Mudge 2008.

Dissecting E/engagement into its policy, frame, and community faces does more than point out the unique language used to justify U.S. China policy. It identifies the questions that must be answered about each policy's rise and demise. Ultimately, we want to explain the changing policy manifestations of U.S.-China and U.S.-Russia relations. But to that end, we need to first account for why China policy was framed as Engagement, when Russia remained a mere policy area. In turn, we are drawn to the institutional pressures on E/engagement within the China and Russia communities and the broader national security architecture, a space that spans the government, think tanks, the academy, and beyond.

Engagement as Frame

Engagement with China as frame refers to what interviewees described as a "metanarrative" or "master narrative" on China in U.S. policy circles, one that provided the intellectual coherence and justification for specific actions, decisions, and initiatives relating to China over time.[73] Engagement centered on meeting the challenge of managing differences in Sino-U.S. relations, while realizing the enormous potential benefits of economic cooperation with a rapidly expanding Chinese market. Engagement as frame was most explicitly on display during the run-up to China's accession to the WTO, where the Clinton administration linked Chinese membership to the promise of change in Beijing in a broadly liberal direction, stating that Beijing "will find that the genie of freedom will not go back into the bottle" once the Chinese people experience it.[74]

Without re-entering the contested terrain of exactly what was promised, when, and by whom, Alastair Iain Johnston notes that the Engagement frame has recently re-emerged in a post hoc, caricatured, form, although "political liberalization and democratization were generally not the main criteria engagers used for judging the success of the policy. They believed that limited improvement in human rights performance was generally the most the United States could hope for, but even this goal was, in practice, a relatively low priority."[75]

A more concrete link between Engagement as frame and specific decisions and initiatives of successive U.S. administrations, then, can be forged less by what the Engagement frame urged American leaders to do than by what it urged them to *refrain from doing*. Namely, Engagement as frame justified their not engaging in actions potentially damaging to U.S.-China cooperation, such as, for

---

[73] China interview 035, 23 March 2018, Washington DC. See also Harding 2023.
[74] For a full analysis, see Thomas, "Matters of Record."
[75] Johnston 2019: 104.

example, labeling China a currency manipulator or signaling a change in the status quo on America's position on the status of Taiwan. In an indication of the changed policy frame and policy context of the Trump administration, both actions were undertaken before Trump left office in 2021, binding the hands of his successor.[76]

Critics of the Engagement frame point to its inertial effects as a key part of their opposition—what it prevented U.S. policymakers from doing over time. The 2012 Scarborough Shoal incident is a frequent reference point.[77] During the incident, Chinese fishermen appeared at the shoal and, when warned by Philippine navy, were supported by two unarmed Chinese marine surveillance vessels, leading to a protracted stand-off between vessels from each country. U.S. policymakers working under the Engagement frame, including Kurt Campbell, negotiated a solution that led to a Philippine withdrawal reneged upon by the Chinese, who remained in control of the shoal. For Engagement's critics, the effect of following Engagement's precepts was to give in to Beijing.

We should not conclude, however, as do Engagement's opponents, that Engagement as frame was uniform or uncontested prior to 2016. The George W. Bush administration entered office promising to develop a tougher policy for U.S.-China relations backed by more strident rhetoric. While this "pivot before the pivot" stalled after 9/11, the Asian Pivot under Obama was already moving in the direction of containment, rather than out-and-out engagement.[78] Nonetheless, Engagement remained the default framing of America's approach.[79] In the now much-maligned words of Deputy Secretary of State Robert Zoellick in 2005, the aim of U.S. policy was to urge China to become a "Responsible Stakeholder" in international society.[80]

Engaging the PRC as Policy

As a distinct aspect of Engagement, Engagement as policy is the decisions and actions taken by the U.S. government toward China, as well as ongoing diplomatic, military, and economic links between the two states, both bilateral

---

[76] See, for example, "Trump Upsets Decades of U.S. Policy on Taiwan, Leaving Thorny Questions for Biden," *Washington Post*, 13 January 2021, https://www.washingtonpost.com/world/asia_pacific/trump-biden-taiwan-china/2021/01/13/1bbadee0-53c0-11eb-acc5-92d2819a1ccb_story.html.
[77] https://amti.csis.org/counter-co-scarborough-standoff/.
[78] Campbell 2016.
[79] See Silove 2016: 46.
[80] "Robert Zoellick's Responsible Stakeholder Speech," https://www.ncuscr.org/content/robert-zoellicks-responsible-stakeholder-speech#:~:text = It%20was%20as%20National%20Committee,interestingly%2C%20had%20significant%20difficulty%20coming.

and as part of broader multilateral arrangements.[81] Engagement policy is not, to be clear, the intentions, justifications, or rhetorical connections used by policymakers—not what they thought, but what they actually did.

The Clinton administration's shift to supporting Most Favored Nation status for China, and then WTO membership are, from this perspective, unmistakably Engagement policies. Engagement policy also included military exchanges and joint exercises, and a series of high-level dialogues, including the U.S.-China Diplomatic and Security Dialogue, the Comprehensive Economic Dialogue, the Law Enforcement and Cybersecurity Dialogue, and U.S.-China Social and Cultural Dialogue. Engagement policy also included a host of exchanges across a range of issues between Washington and Beijing below the governmental level, so-called Track 2 dialogues—nongovernment to nongovernment—and "Track 1.5"—with some governmental involvement.[82] Such non- and semi-governmental contacts burgeoned after the end of the Cold War, from almost none in the early 1990s to some 269 Asia-Pacific Track 2s by 2008 by one count.[83] As one think tanker noted, while defending Engagement's policy record, "There were 100 dialogues thereabouts at the end of the Obama administration; there was deep engagement."[84] The final component is the many connections between prominent individuals associated with Engagement policy still active in consulting with parts of the U.S. government.[85]

As an expansive set of interconnections, Engagement as policy did not disappear after Trump took office, nor after he left it. But momentum in continuing old dialogues and developing new ones quickly stalled under the Trump administration,[86] overtaken by a series of actions aimed not at Engagement, but competition. Together, decisions such as the withdrawal of U.S. participation in the Trans-Pacific Partnership in January 2017, the introduction of tariffs on Chinese goods the following year, the imposition of sanctions on individuals involved in clamping down on political freedoms in Hong Kong, and recent decisions

---

[81] For a useful overview, see the Congressional Research Service's report *U.S.-China Relations*, at https://fas.org/sgp/crs/row/R45898.pdf.
[82] See Michael O. Wheeler, "Track 1.5/2 Security Dialogues with China: Nuclear Lessons Learned," Institute for Defense Analyses, September 2014, available at https://www.ida.org/-/media/feature/publications/t/tr/track-152-security-dialogues-with-china-nuclear-lessons-learned/p-5135.ashx. See also in general Jones 2015.
[83] Wheeler, "Track 1.5/2 Security Dialogues," 6.
[84] China interview 091, 9 November 2021, via telephone.
[85] While such behind-the-scenes links are difficult to detail with certainty, people like think tankers Scott Kennedy (Center for Strategic and International Studies), Evan Feigenbaum (Carnegie Endowment for International Peace), Kenneth Lieberthal, Evan Medeiros (Walsh School of Foreign Service at Georgetown University), Michael Swaine (Quincy Institute), and Robert Zoellick retain important connections to Beijing.
[86] The most recent high-level dialogues were Diplomatic and Security Dialogue, November 2018; Comprehensive Economic Dialogue, April 2017; Law Enforcement and Cybersecurity Dialogue, the first and only in October 2017; U.S.-China Social and Cultural Dialogue, 28 September 2017.

aimed at Huawei, TikTok, and WeChat, sum to a qualitatively different policy basis in U.S.-China relations.[87] As Pompeo explained in a speech in June 2020, the Trump administration's policy was to "distrust and verify" rather than engage for its own sake, leading to what others describe as a partial "decoupling" of the American and Chinese economies.[88] Thus, while there remains some remnants of Engagement viewed as policy—such as limited military exchanges like the Kowari U.S.-China-Australia survival training, joint antiterrorism drills, and defense policy coordination talks,[89] on balance a major policy shift away from Engagement has been effected since 2017.

Engagement as Community

The final aspect of Engagement with China obscured by a singular conceptualization is *Engagement as community*: the individuals and groups inside and outside the government whose work has served to define, justify, and execute Engagement with China as policy and frame across successive administrations. As a community, Engagement centered on a series of high-level advisors and political appointees. The list includes secretaries of state like Alexander Haig (1981–1982),[90] national security advisors like Sandy Berger (1993–1997),[91] and NSC Asia directors like Michel Oksenberg (1977–1980)[92] and Kenneth Lieberthal (1998–2000), in addition to many others across multiple government agencies.

As one interviewee—a leading think tank China expert, deeply involved in promoting U.S.-China relations since the late 1970s—explained, for the last eight administrations, some version of a group of colleagues and friends had been in a position of influence over the general direction of US-China relations, promoting Engagement with China: "Susan

---

[87] On U.S.-China competition in the technology space, see Brose 2020; Lee 2018; Wang 2020.

[88] See Pompeo's speech "Communist China and the Free World's Future"; and "TikTok Tussle Shows the Uneven Economic 'Decoupling' That Has Accelerated between the U.S. and China," *Washington Post*, 20 September 2020.

[89] See, respectively, "A Quiet Kawari: US, Australia, and China Trilateral Military Exercise, *The Diplomat*, 30 September 2019, https://thediplomat.com/2019/09/a-quiet-kawari-us-australia-and-china-trilateral-military-exercise/; and "China Hosts Largest Land-Based ADMM-Plus Joint Counter-terrorism drill," *Global Times*, 14 November 2019, http://en.people.cn/n3/2019/1114/c90 000-9632289.html, https://www.defense.gov/Newsroom/Releases/Release/Article/2058597/us-prc-defense-policy-coordination-talks/.

[90] Haig was previously a general in the U.S. Army, including supreme allied commander Europe (1974–1979), and assistant to Kissinger between 1969 and 1972.

[91] Sandy Berger served in the roles of deputy national security advisor (1993–1997) and advisor to President Clinton (1997–2001).

[92] University of Michigan political scientist who in 1977 joined President Jimmy Carter's National Security Council, Oksenberg frequently advised subsequent administrations on China until his death in 2001.

[Shirk][93] was in . . . [Ken] Lieberthal was in, Mike Oksenberg was in. Dick Solomon before was in.[94] Those were all in this group. . . . William Perry,[95] who's now out at Stanford, but was defense secretary, was in this group. Even at the beginning, Ashton Carter[96] was, and then, I think, he . . . began to migrate a bit on this topic. [Kurt] Campbell maybe a little bit."[97]

Engagement as community spanned the government and nongovernmental spheres, with institutional bases in an array of think tanks, university centers and departments, and cultural organizations in Washington, DC, and beyond, the work of which provided intellectual space and academic credibility to Engagement as an overarching frame. Indicative here are organizations such as the National Committee on U.S.-China Relations (NCUSCR) and business organizations like the U.S.-China Business Council and the American Chamber of Commerce. As economic connections deepened from normalization, expanding rapidly as outsourcing to China over the 1980s and 1990s increased exponentially, the business community became a crucial proponent mobilizing to forge and solidify Engagement, including providing funding for intellectual and lobbying efforts. Many Engagers shared intellectual lineages, including academic advisors and similar trajectories into their posts. Crucially, therefore, debate over Engagement's achievements and failings is tied to the careers and achievements and failures of specific people.

As the above chronicle of Engagement's relitigated demonstrates, remnants of Engagement as community survived the Trump administration and the handover to the Biden team.[98] Even inside the government, some key Trump administration figures like Treasury Secretary Steven Mnuchin voiced long-standings pro-Engagement concerns, notably possible negative adverse effects of the trade war.[99] Yet, since the Trump election, the

---

[93] Research professor and founding chair of the 21st Century China Center at the University of California, San Diego. Formerly deputy assistant secretary of state for East Asia (1997–2000).

[94] Richard Solomon was a diplomat and academic who served as assistant secretary of state for East Asian and Pacific affairs (1989–1992) and Director of policy planning (1986–1989).

[95] Deputy secretary (1993–1994) and secretary of defense (1994–1997).

[96] Secretary of defense (2011–2013). See Carter's later reflections in conversation with journalist Bob Davis. Davis, "Q&A: Ash Carter on the Pentagon's Lonely Pivot to Asia," *Wire China*, 2 October 2022, https://www.thewirechina.com/2022/10/02/ash-carter-on-the-pentagons-lonely-pivot-to-asia/.

[97] China interview 035, 23 March 2018, Washington, DC.

[98] See M. Taylor Fravel, J. Stapleton Roy, Michael D. Swaine, Susan A. Thornton, and Ezra Vogel, "China Is Not an Enemy," *Washington Post*, 3 July 2019, https://www.washingtonpost.com/opinions/making-china-a-us-enemy-is-counterproductive/2019/07/02/647d49d0-9bfa-11e9-b27f-ed2942f73d70_story.html. See also former deputy assistant secretary of state Susan Shirk's comments, "Overreaction to China Threat Could Turn into McCarthyite Red Scare," *South China Morning Post*, 31 March 2019, https://www.scmp.com/news/china/diplomacy/article/3003973/overreaction-china-threat-could-turn-mccarthyite-red-scare.

[99] See "How Mnuchin Keeps a Steady Grip in a Tug of War on Trade," *New York Times*, 3 June 2018, https://www.nytimes.com/2018/06/03/us/politics/mnuchin-trump-trade.html.

construction of China policy and the strategic competition frame underpinning it have no longer been under the control of the Engagement community. In the Engagement community's stead is a group of individuals and institutions opposed to Engagement for its own sake and in favor of a tougher line on relations with Beijing, from current and former advisors such as Peter Navarro and Steve Bannon, to administration figures like National Security Advisors H.R. McMaster (2017–2018) and Robert O'Brien (2019–), NSC deputy director Matt Pottinger (2017–), Trade Representative Robert Lighthizer (2017–), and Secretary of State Pompeo (2018–), again among others.

Analyzed in detail later, like the Engagement community, the new community extends beyond the government, to influential individuals, such as former Defense Department official Michael Pillsbury, and to a set of organizations in the broader national security community that take a more sanguine view of China's rise. Central here are two congressional commissions founded after China's WTO accession: the human rights-focused Congressional-Executive Commission on China and the economics and security-focused U.S.-China Economic and Security Review Commission. In addition, organizations with strong links to the Defense Department's Office of Net Assessments, such as the Center for Strategic and Budgetary Assessments and Project 2049, are key nodes of the strategic competition community. Also important are the longer-term origins of the opponents of Engagement, including a group of self-defined China hawks that emerged during the 1990s to oppose the Clinton administration's policies toward China. Styled the "Blue Team"—in contrast to the Red Teams formed in war gaming to test U.S. capacities—these individuals attacked Engagement as policy and frame and disparaged the community behind it.[100]

While far from having disappeared, with Trump's election the Engagement community was removed from the center of power. As consequentially, however, the rise of Strategic Competition—itself as policy, frame, and community—shifted the center of gravity in the national security community toward a harder line on China, prompted in part by former Engagers like Kurt Campbell. The question whether Engagement might return at some point in the future, therefore, turns on the types of individuals upcoming administrations might appoint to key foreign policy positions.

Russia Policy: Engagement amid Containment

Absent an engagement frame, the policy of engaging Russia centered on managing the transition from the conflictual relations of the Cold War to something resembling cooperation.[101] In the recollection of a 2021 Congressional Research

---

[100] Michael J. Waller, "Blue Team Takes on Red China," *Insight on the News*, 4 June 2001, 23–25.
[101] The most comprehensive accounts remain Goldgeier and McFaul 2003 and Stent 2014.

Service report, important less on account of its historical accuracy than as a reflection of recent sentiment, the story is one of failure. "For almost 30 years," the report reads, "the United States and Russia have struggled to develop a constructive bilateral relationship."[102] In terms similar to the failure of Engagement frame, the report goes on to describe how "in the early 1990s, a spirit of U.S.-Russia 'strategic partnership' and hopes for Russia's integration with the West were gradually overtaken by increasing tension and mutual recrimination, largely as a consequence of disagreements over Russian efforts to reestablish a sphere of influence in the post-Soviet region, U.S. promotion of NATO enlargement, and NATO's military intervention in the former Yugoslavia." The State Department's "Bilateral Relations Fact Sheet" recounts a similar story: "Following the dissolution of the Soviet Union in 1991, the United States adopted a bipartisan strategy to facilitate cooperation on global issues and promote foreign investment and trade. The United States supported Russia's integration into European and global institutions and a deepened bilateral partnership in security cooperation to reinforce the foundations of stability and predictability."[103] In short: we tried to cooperate with Russia, but "Russia ultimately rejected this approach."[104]

There is more to the story of U.S. policy toward Russia since 1989 than frustrated attempts to foster cooperation. Current recollections downplay how the end of the Cold War and the breakup of the Soviet Union posed to U.S. policymakers a host of complex problems, at a time when the urgency of the issue was waning. Should America provide aid to its former enemy and, if so, what sort? How could the United States help Moscow secure the USSR's nuclear stockpile and prevent such weapons falling into the wrong hands? More broadly, should the failing Soviet Union or its constituent parts—Russia paramount among them—be the chief focus of U.S. efforts? These questions remind us that U.S. Russia policy has always been less a Russia than a post-Soviet space policy—inseparable from the implications for Moscow's neighbors. Like China policy, moreover, U.S. policy toward Russia and the countries of the former Warsaw Pact formed part of America's overall foreign relations, and were often impacted significantly by domestic and international concerns.

During the early 1990s, America's policy of engagement with Russia crossed economics, security and diplomacy, and democracy assistance. In the economic sphere, initial postwar bilateral assistance was limited, with a skeptical Congress providing only some $480m during the George H. W. Bush administration. A multilateral conference held in Washington in January 1992 was more successful, generating some $24bn for a move away from the rigid controls of the

---

[102] *Russia: Foreign Policy and U.S. Relations*, Congressional Research Service, updated 15 April 2021, at https://crsreports.congress.gov/product/pdf/R/R46761.
[103] "Bilateral Relations Fact Sheet," https://www.state.gov/u-s-relations-with-russia/.
[104] "Bilateral Relations Fact Sheet."

Soviet economic system. U.S. policy in the initial aftermath of the Soviet Union's demise also covered U.S. Agency for International Development aid, which went from zero to $400m to a peak of $1.6bn in 1994; World Bank loans worth roughly $3bn; and the formation of the "Systemic Transformation Fund." Provision of extensive technical and scientific expertise on the part of the United States is well known due to later criticisms of the effects of "shock therapy." Despite its contribution to the downturn in U.S.-Russia relations as the 1990s progressed, U.S. economic engagement was revived as part of the 2009 reset, leading to Russian accession to the WTO in August 2012.

The demise of the Soviet Union posed equally complex challenges in the area of security, with the threat of extensive nuclear proliferation to the USSR's former constituent parts. Secretary of State James Baker engaged in shuttle diplomacy over the spring of 1992 to persuade Ukraine, Belarus, and Kazakhstan to transfer nuclear arms back to Russia. U.S. negotiators concluded an agreement with their Russian counterparts on the updated Strategic Arms Reduction Treaty soon after. Signed by Bush and Yeltsin on 3 January 1993, shortly before the former left office, START II committed both sides to reduce their strategic forces to a maximum of 3,500 and eliminate all MIRVed land-based ICBMs.[105] Although again wrinkles appeared in the relationship as Yeltsin handed power to Putin, the policy of closely managing matters of nuclear security remained, as indicated first by the formation of the NATO-Russia Council, created in 2002, and later the extension of New START signed by Biden shortly after entering office in 2021.[106]

The final pillar of America's engagement with Russia as policy covers significant investment in democracy assistance, which, limited under Bush Sr., became a marked feature under his successor, Bill Clinton. As James Goldgeier and Michael McFaul note, "Clinton was a regime transformer ... he believed that active promotion of the enlargement of the community of market democracies was a fundamental national security objective of the United States."[107] U.S. policy at the highest level sought to bolster the domestic position of Yeltsin and reformers such as Yedor Gaidar, prime minister in charge of economic reform, and Deputy Prime Minister Anatoly Chubais. In addition, the United States provided support to the activities of other nongovernmental actors working to promote a transition to democracy in Russia, such as the National Endowment for Democracy, the National Democratic Institute, the International Republican Institute, and the AFL-CIO.[108]

All three aspects of Engagement as policy were salient during the Obama administration's effort to kick-start U.S.-Russia relations following the nadir of

---

[105] Goldgeier and McFaul 2003: 58.
[106] https://www.nato.int/cps/en/natohq/topics_50091.htm.
[107] Goldgeier and McFaul 2003: 11.
[108] Goldgeier and McFaul 2003: 29.

the 2008 Russo-Georgian war. Dubbed the "reset," and complete with a large red button presented by Secretary of State Hillary Clinton to Russian foreign minister Sergei Lavrov to "push" at a meeting in Geneva in March 2009, the reset enjoyed significant early policy successes. As Undersecretary of State for Political Affairs William Burns explained one year in, the United States was "in a significantly better place with Russia.... Many challenges and difficulties remain.... But we've made a promising start."[109] As evidence, Burns pointed to the New START arms control agreement signed in April 2010 with Russian president Dmitry Medvedev. Illustrative of how U.S. foreign policy toward Russia and China takes place in a broader context than bilateral relations, the reset was designed in part to enable progress on curtailing Iran's nuclear program, including the P5 + 1 program, and UN Security Council Resolution 1929 aimed at leveraging sanctions on Iran to persuade the latter to live up to commitments, which required Moscow to renege on a delivery of S-300 missiles. Russian cooperation was also sought on matters in relation to Afghanistan—the formation of the Northern Distribution Network—and North Korea, with both Russia and the United States voting for UN Security Council Resolution 1874 in response to Pyongyang's test of a nuclear device on 25 May 2009.[110]

Once again, while engagement with Russia as policy centered on high-level diplomacy, including the formation of a Presidential Bilateral Commission, creating working groups on a host of issues, a key component remained democracy promotion. This so-called dual-track approach promoted liberal democratic legal and political modes via governmental and nongovernmental engagement with civil society groups in Russia. As a September 2021 State Department fact sheet described, "Obama Administration officials meet frequently and directly with Russian civil society leaders, be it through President Obama's attendance at parallel civil society summit in Moscow last July, President Obama's meeting with human rights activists from Russia and other countries in February 2010, Secretary Clinton's meeting with human rights activities and civil society leaders in Moscow in October 2009, or everyday encounters between U.S. government officials and Russian civil society leaders in Moscow and Washington."[111] Moreover, "In June 2009, the U.S.-Russia Foundation for Economic Advancement and the Rule of Law (USRF) registered in Russia as an affiliate of the non-profit organization USRF in the United States and has begun

---

[109] 14 April 2010, https://www.americanprogress.org/events/u-s-russia-relations-in-a-new-era-one-year-after-the-reset/.

[110] For an assessment of the state of U.S.-Russia relations soon after the reset was announced, see Colton, Frye, and Legvold 2010, especially chapter 8; Steven Pifer, "Formulating U.S. Policy Toward Russia," 2010.

[111] "Bilateral Relations Fact Sheet."

to work with Russian institutions to develop projects that encapsulate the principles of enterprise, accountability, and partnership."[112]

The failure of the reset is well known, with the Arab Spring movements and fear of its spread leading to the events in Ukraine 2014 and Russia's invasion of Crimea in February 2014. Afterward, the short-lived re-emergence of a policy of engagement morphed into what can be better described as "engagement amid containment," including the stepwise construction of the comprehensive sanctions regime in place at the time of writing. Limited engagement, such as U.S. participation in the Organization for Security and Co-operation in Europe–negotiated Minsk Agreements of 2015—a 13-point agreement on a ceasefire between Ukrainian and Russia-backed forces in eastern Ukraine, prisoner exchanges, and OSCE monitoring—demonstrate that engagement has not entirely disappeared. But even before the invasion of February 2022, concrete engagement policies were complicated by two factors: an emerging great power politics grand strategy, and the intermingling of domestic and foreign policy on account of Russian meddling in the 2016 election.

Russia policy became wrapped up with a broader grand strategy developing during the second Obama administration: great power competition. As Wess Mitchell, assistant secretary of state for European and Eurasian affairs, told the Senate Armed Services Committee in August 2018, "The starting point of the National Security Strategy is the recognition that America has entered a period of big-power competition. . . . Contrary to the hopeful assumptions of previous administrations, Russia and China are serious competitors that are building up the material and ideological wherewithal to contest U.S. primacy and leadership in the 21st Century."[113]

Russia: the Pro-engagement Community

As a community, the American Russia field has displayed a different set of dynamics and distinct connections to the U.S. government since 1989. A rapidly shrinking community after the end of the Cold War, in sharp distinction to the still-mushrooming China field, it had no comparable group of "Engager" Russia watchers nor—as we have seen—an engagement frame. Engagement policies were designed largely by policymakers balancing Russia with other regional and international priorities. Some favored engagement in the guise of "resets," until the Trump administration, which explicitly did not try to effect a reset. The Russia field thus featured no paradigmatic turnover as both policy, frame, and

---

[112] "Bilateral Relations Fact Sheet."
[113] https://www.foreign.senate.gov/imo/media/doc/082118_Mitchell_Testimony.pdf.

community, replacing a set of previously more marginal views at the center of decision-making and frame-making power.

In trying to explain the "limits of partnership," Angela Stent refers to "The Stakeholder Problem." What constituencies in the United States and Russia have a vested personal and professional interest in fostering and, more importantly, maintaining, positive bilateral relations? In Stent's view, "The first Obama administration, like its predecessors, understood that one continuing problem in US–Russian relations is the lack on both sides of stakeholders with a commitment to sustaining and nurturing the bilateral relationship."[114] Stent focuses on the business community, an important constituency among China Engagers too. "A significant group of stakeholders from the business sector in both Europe and Russia are dedicated to promoting commercial and political ties. No similarly robust broadly based groups exist either in Russia or the United States to advocate for the relationship,"[115] given largely non-complementary economies of Russia and the United States. But the point holds equally within the Russia expert community and the broader public. "In contrast," Stent goes on, "there are vocal critics of Russia and of the U.S.-Russian reset in the United States, whereas such groups are generally more muted in Europe. Anti-Americanism has also been on the rise in Russia and critics of the U.S.-Russian relationship abound."[116]

To be clear, the U.S. Russia-watching community does feature individuals calling for engagement, a reset, or some combination thereof. Thomas Graham and Matthew Rojansky's 2016 election year critique of the failure of America's Russia policy was one such example: a clear call for engagement with a small *e*. The pro-engagers are also, to be sure, aware of allies within the broader community, in particular arms controllers and many academics and former policymakers critical of America's handling of the post–Cold War transition.

But they are not "Engagers" calling for *Engagement*, either today or as a retroactive account of post–Cold War Russia strategy. The Obama reset—the closest recent years has seen to engagement as policy—was forged by engagers of a specific sort and for a specific rationale. Key architects Michael McFaul and Celeste Wallander saw the reset as a diplomatic move to achieve particular aims. As Wallander told an audience at the Council on Foreign Relations in October 2009, "The reset was a moment," less a strategy or policy, "a determination to end the atmosphere of invective and acrimony that had bedeviled U.S.-Russian relations for quite some time.... We had gotten to the point where we couldn't even talk about things that we fundamentally agree about, let alone talk about things where we might have differences of views. And that was not good for American

---

[114] Stent 2014: 17.
[115] "U.S.-Russia Relations in the Second Obama Administration," 31 December 2012, https://www.brookings.edu/articles/u-s-russia-relations-in-the-second-obama-administration/.
[116] "U.S.-Russia Relations in the Second Obama Administration."

national security interests."[117] The reset was tied to identifiable progress—New START, WTO membership—and, once again, contained within it support for Medvedev, democratization, and civil rights. The reset's authors then were pragmatic human rights and democracy engagers, not Russia "Engagers," and got off the train after Putin's return to power and the events in Ukraine and Crimea.

Why does this matter? It matters because, *in its absence*, it helps explain why U.S. China policy under Trump and his successor has been couched as a rejection of capital-E Engagement. The rejection of Engagement with China was not just a rejection of Engagement as policy, but of Engagement as a paradigm of policy, frame, and—crucially—the community involved in the formulation and justification of each. The effect is to render even the notion of a "Russian reset," much less "Engagement," unnecessary as a framing strategy in struggles within the Russia-watching community, for policy initiative, professional status, and personal reasons.

Conclusion

Juxtaposition of the rise and fall of engagement with China and Russia reveals similarities amid telling differences. Relations with both Beijing and Moscow follow a similar trajectory—optimism unrealized, and an ongoing attempt to relitigate America's part in how events turned out. Was the United States wrong to try to integrate Beijing and Moscow into the liberal international order? Should Washington have blocked rather than promoted China's entry into the WTO? Should U.S. policymakers have opposed, or at least acted to slow, NATO expansion?

While healthy as self-assessment, there is no "smoking gun" evidence that will convince all parties to the debate. Litigants disagree on the historical evidence, lacking a common referent for the simple reason that there isn't one. Participants in the debate invariably fall into the traps of assuming Engagement with China and engagement with Russia are unitary things explicable solely within the history of U.S. China and Russia policy. Slipping between describing engagement as "policy," "strategy," or "approach," the scholarly and policy debates fail to see engagement as a multifaceted phenomenon with policy, frame, and community aspects.

Disaggregating engagement in this way justifies recent proclamations of its demise—if anyone was still in doubt. More significantly, parsing Engagement with China as policy, frame, and community, and noting the *absence* of an explicit framing of engagement with Russia, points to an explanation. The end

---

[117] https://www.cfr.org/event/russia-update-reset-working.

of Engagement with China was not simply a shift in policy or strategy. Again, Engagement with China was not simply a policy, or strategy, or approach. Engagement's demise was what can best be described as a paradigmatic turnover in America's approach to China's rise, in the sense popularized by philosopher of science Thomas Kuhn.[118]

Opponents of this thesis might make two counterarguments. Realists will point to the power disparities between China and Russia to explain the lack of a frame for engagement with Moscow, as opposed to Engagement with China. In so doing, however, they would once again fall into the traps outlined previously, conflating E/engagement with policy. Disaggregating Engagement as frame, policy, and community demonstrates that while aspects of Engagement policy remain, the core faces of the Engagement frame and the community of Engagers are now unrecognizable. Not only does this justify the conclusion that Engagement is over, but it also points to a possible explanation, in the dynamics of the China and Russia sub-communities in the U.S. national security field, and their shifting relationship to the U.S. government.

The second is that U.S. Russia policy has also featured framing dynamics, but rather than the word "Engagement," the operative term is "reset." The notion is seemingly indelibly tied to Russia policy in the same way Engagement is for U.S. China policy, both as a policy proposal and as a term of opprobrium for those making the suggestion. As explored in the rest of the book, the term works to divide professionals in the Russia-watching community. Once again, the prominence of the reset, *not engagement*, in this division proves the point: the roots of U.S. policy toward Russia lie in the relationship between the national security community and the government. To that relationship we now turn, tracing first in more detail the shift from Engagement to Strategic Competition under Trump and Biden.

---

[118] Kuhn 1962.

2
From Engagement to Strategic Competition

The previous chapter interrogated the notion of engagement in relation to China and Russia. What *was* engagement? Was it a singular strategy designed to bind Beijing and Moscow to the U.S.-led international order? Engagement was a feature unique to China, absent vis-à-vis Russia. Aaron Friedberg's rendering is typical: the United States and "other liberal democracies opened their doors to China in the belief that . . . they would cause its system to converge more closely with their own. . . . But trade and societal interaction did not yield the broader benefits for which the democracies had hoped. Instead of a liberal and cooperative partner, China has become an increasingly wealthy and powerful competitor, repressive at home and aggressive abroad."[1] Friedberg captures how Engagement framed policy initiatives, designed by a distinct community of policymakers, advisors, and officials who were convinced positive relations with Beijing could offer net benefits to America. Engagement was a rhetorical device, crucially, constructed largely after Trump came into office, such that Friedberg's retelling could by 2020 appear commonsensical.

Disaggregating Engagement between frame, policy, and community is not just an academic exercise, therefore. Rather, it helps identify *precisely* what must be explained about Engagement's demise, as well as the downward trajectory of relations with Moscow. First, how after the critical turning point of Trump's election did his administration achieve a reframing of U.S. relations with China? Which community of national security experts, particularly those with a China specialty, carried out such a reframing? And what policy changes did the shift away from Engagement enable? Second, why did the Biden administration not turn back toward the Engagers and the Engagement frame, instead expanding its predecessor's post-Engagement policies?

In this chapter I adopt the frame, community, and policy disaggregation to trace the shift from Engagement to a new paradigm—one that over the course of the Trump administration crystallized as "Strategic Competition." Critical of China on the campaign trail, Trump closed the White House door on

---

[1] Friedberg 2022: 1.

The End of Engagement. David M. McCourt, Oxford University Press. Oxford University Press 2024.
DOI: 10.1093/9780197765241.003.0003

pro-Engagement constituencies and brought in a set of advisors and officials opposed to anything smacking of engagement—the Strategic Competitors. Under Biden, modifiers like "responsible" and "managed" emerged to temper the more conflictual associations of the competition frame. But in essence, as community and policy, Strategic Competition was retained as the Biden administration's approach to relations with Beijing.

We should here recall the common-sense counterargument to mine. Was the turn away from Engagement not simply a story of a failed policy, objective changes in China's domestic governance and global ambitions necessitating—forcing—a new approach on policymakers?

Any account of Engagement's demise that depicts events as either inevitable or unidirectional is misleading, however. China policy was a priority of the Trump administration's foreign policy; but it was not the only one. Withdrawing from the Iran nuclear deal and Paris climate accord and dealing with North Korea's nuclear program filled up plenty of bandwidth—including a historic summit between Trump and Kim Jong-un in June 2018. At various points events could have turned out very differently, not only the 2016 and 2020 elections. Trump reportedly respected Xi, heaping praise upon the Chinese leader for limits to his term in office.[2] Arguably the Trump administration's approach to China was heading toward settlement with the agreement of the so-called Phase 1 trade deal signed on 15 January 2020. But that was before the emergence of Covid-19, further suppression of democracy in Hong Kong, and full revelations of widespread internment of Uighurs in Xinjiang, which together strengthened the hand of the Strategic Competitors and their China-skeptical allies.

The chapter first details the reframing of America's approach to the PRC and the community of Strategic Competitors who made it possible, before exploring its policy outputs. It then moves to the Biden team's choice of competition-focused experts, who—with some wrinkles—maintained Strategic Competition as frame and policy. A final section notes the muted inclusion of Russia on the list of Washington's strategic competitors—again absent all the policymaking energy, despite Moscow's direct use of force in Ukraine throughout the period.

---

[2] See, for example, "15 Times Trump Praised China as Coronavirus Was Spreading across the Globe," *Politico*, 15 April 2020, https://www.politico.com/news/2020/04/15/trump-china-coronavirus-188736.

Strategic Competition: Reframing America's Approach to China under Trump

Donald Trump's election sounded the death knell for Engagement with China as a frame, community, and policy. Staffed with anti-Engagement China advisors, the Trump administration developed a new frame for America's approach to China labeled "Strategic Competition." Strategic Competition provided the rhetorical support for an array of initiatives across government seeking to counter, rather than accommodate, the PRC. The Trump administration's robust stance neither came out of left field nor emerged fully formed, however, evolving from the first to almost the last day of his presidency.

During campaigning, Trump adopted a tough position on China,[3] seeking distance from opponent Hillary Clinton, who was heavily associated with Engagement as secretary of state under Obama (2009–2013) and First Lady during the high point of Engagement prior to China's WTO accession. While Clinton too promised not to join the Trans-Pacific Partnership free trade deal[4]— the electoral price paid by the Democrats after the North American Free Trade Agreement no doubt in mind—Trump railed against China's "theft" of American jobs and promised to get tough with Beijing. In a sharp departure, he explicitly cast China as an enemy of the United States,[5] acknowledging in pre-election writing, "There are people who wish I wouldn't refer to China as our enemy. But that's exactly what they are."[6]

Trump was not the first presidential hopeful to promise a reassessment of U.S. policy toward China. The 1992 campaign saw Bill Clinton attack opponent George H. W. Bush for the incumbent's muted criticism of China's leaders during the Tiananmen Square massacre.[7] The George W. Bush administration made similar noises and went some way to putting them into effect. In what Nina Silove terms the "pivot before the pivot," the Bush Jr. administration began a reorganization of U.S. defense priorities toward East Asia, before the events of 11 September 2001 refocused its gaze on the Middle East and the global war on terror.[8] In the words of China hands Kenneth Lieberthal and Susan Thornton,

---

[3] For example, "Donald Trump Vows to Rip Up Trade Deals and Confront China," *New York Times*, 28 June 2016, https://www.nytimes.com/2016/06/29/us/politics/donald-trump-trade-speech.html.

[4] "Clinton Does Not Back Obama Trade Vote in Post-election Congressional Session," *Washington Post*, 5 May 2016, https://www.washingtonpost.com/politics/clinton-does-not-back-obama-trade-vote-in-post-election-congressional-session/2016/05/05/ce94f76e-12d7-11e6-8967-7ac733c56f12_story.html.

[5] See https://archive.org/details/WMUR_20151103_120000_Good_Morning_America.

[6] Trump 2015: 43.

[7] "American Presidents Have a Long History of Walking Back Tough Talk on China," *Washington Post*, 6 December 2016, https://www.washingtonpost.com/news/wonk/wp/2016/12/06/american-presidents-have-a-long-history-of-walking-back-tough-talk-on-china/.

[8] Silove 2016.

however, "All U.S. presidents who have come to office since the normalization of relations with China began their presidencies with the explicit intention of changing U.S. policy toward China. And yet, each eventually tacked back to a position that looked remarkably like his predecessor's—a mix of cooperation, cajoling, and censuring; pushing for progress in some areas, while hedging or resisting in others."[9]

All, that is, except Trump. While other administrations promised a tougher approach toward Beijing but later softened their stance in office,[10] the Trump administration was unique from the beginning. The new president offered very different high-level direction when it came to China policy. As a former State Department official commented in late 2018 on "the arguments that I'm hearing (China threat, engagement was wrong) . . . [F]or 25 years, the same people [from the same] part of the political spectrum and the same institutions held those views."[11] Yet, "For all the administrations up through the end of the Obama first term . . . at the most senior levels, there was a vision which A) supported Engagement and B) sought to pursue both managing or dealing with the frictions and differences and enhancing cooperation."[12] As this interviewee went on, "Now . . . it's, sort of, bash China all the time basically. The FBI, the DOD, DHS . . . all these people who have consistently been on a leash."[13] Trump untied the leash. The effect was a green light for key figures in the Trump administration to set about reframing China in the U.S. foreign policy imagination, laying the groundwork for a different narrative of where U.S.-China relations have been and where they need to go, enabling different policies, effected by a different set of actors.

Reframing China: From Great Power to Strategic Competition

Framing America's approach anew began on the Trump administration's first day, with National Security Council appointee Matthew Pottinger brushing off a paper he had prepared prior to the election outlining a potential new U.S. China strategy. As journalist Josh Rogin reports, "Bill's Paper"—Bill is a pseudonym, there is no "Bill"—made the case for "a broad reset of US-China relations based on recognizing the principle that the United States was not going to be able to fundamentally change the nature of the Chinese system—nor should it try."[14]

---

[9] Lieberthal and Thornton 2021: 375.
[10] "Presidents Have a Long History."
[11] China interview 056, 12 November 2018, Washington, DC.
[12] China interview 056, 12 November 2018, Washington, DC.
[13] China interview 056, 12 November 2018, Washington, DC.
[14] Rogin 2021: 37.

Developing language that would make its way into two classified strategies and the China section of the public-facing NSS of December 2017, Bill's Paper's main "idea was to deal with the reality of China, to focus on stopping the worst of its behaviors and building resilience against the rest—all while protecting American values and interests."[15] Bill's Paper reflected an understanding of China with three main aspects, which together would frame Strategic Competition: (1) American policymakers had thought they could change China, but they were wrong; (2) China represents a challenge both internationally and domestically, with economic, military, and political components, and addressing this China challenge requires a "whole of government" response; (3) the United States is in a decades-long competition with China over strategic primacy in the Indo-Pacific and globally.

Engagement Failed: Getting China Wrong

As explored in Chapter 1, at the center of the Strategic Competition frame was the claim that America tried to change China through Engagement and it had failed. The argument featured in the 2017 NSS, published in December at the end of Trump's first year in office, which recounted how for "decades, U.S. policy was rooted in the belief that support for China's rise and for its integration into the post-war international order would liberalize China." However,

> Contrary to our hopes, China expanded its power at the expense of the sovereignty of others. China gathers and exploits data on an unrivaled scale and spreads features of its authoritarian system, including corruption and the use of surveillance. It is building the most capable and well-funded military in the world, after our own. Its nuclear arsenal is growing and diversifying. Part of China's military modernization and economic expansion is due to its access to the U.S. innovation economy, including America's world-class universities.[16]

Hidden midway through the document and easy to miss, the argument that America got China wrong was repeated in all the administration's major policy statements.[17] Each time, new wrinkles crept in, as personal touches and embellishments added rhetorical flourish to new iterations.

Vice President Mike Pence amplified the point in a highly anticipated speech in October 2018, penned by Pottinger. "After the fall of the Soviet Union," Pence told his Hudson Institute audience, "we assumed that a free China was inevitable. Heady with optimism at the turn of the 21st Century, America agreed to

---

[15] Rogin 2021: 37.
[16] *National Security Strategy of the United States*, December 2017, https://trumpwhitehouse.archives.gov/wp-content/uploads/2017/12/NSS-Final-12-18-2017-0905.pdf, 25.
[17] *National Security Strategy of the United States*, December 2017, 25.

give Beijing open access to our economy... in the hope that freedom in China would expand in all of its forms... [T]hat hope has gone unfulfilled."[18] Assistant Secretary of State for East Asian and Pacific Affairs David Stilwell restated the case the following December: "U.S. policy for many years was largely premised on a version of the Golden Rule," he told the Brookings Institution. "American officials hoped that demonstrating the benefits of openness would move Beijing onto a more liberal path that led to greater economic and political openness... it has become clear that many of our hopeful assumptions were wrong."[19]

By spring and summer 2020 the claim was firmly embedded in Trump administration language, opening the May 2020 *United States Strategic Approach to the People's Republic of China*, and prominent in each of a series of four coordinated speeches given by high-level administration officials. As National Security Advisor Robert O'Brien told the Arizona Commerce Authority on 24 June, "For decades, conventional wisdom in both U.S. political parties, the business community, academia, and media, has held that it was only a matter of time before China would become more liberal, first economically and then, politically." Again, American hopes went unrealized.[20] "We imagined engagement with China would produce a future with bright promise of comity and cooperation," Secretary of State Mike Pompeo said in a July capstone to the series at the Nixon Library in Yorba Linda, California.[21] Embedding while adapting the narrative, he said, "But today... we're all still wearing masks and watching the pandemic's body count rise because the CCP failed in its promises to the world. We're reading every morning new headlines of repression in Hong Kong and in Xinjiang."[22]

Through this rhetorical effort, the Trump administration at the same time depicted and realized an "awakening" to the China challenge—an opening of the country's eyes to a new reality of the PRC. "America, under President Trump's leadership, has finally awoken to the threat the Chinese Communist Party's

---

[18] "Remarks Delivered by Vice President Mike Pence, the Hudson Institute, Washington DC, 4 October 2018." The major Trump speeches have been helpfully collected in Robert O'Brien, ed. *Trump on China: Putting America First*, available at https://trumpwhitehouse.archives.gov/wp-content/uploads/2020/11/Trump-on-China-Putting-America-First.pdf. The publication is self-described as "A collection of speeches laying out the most significant foreign policy shift in a generation." References to Trump speeches included in the volume are to pages in the O'Brien 2020 volume.
[19] "The United States, China, and Pluralism in International Affairs," remarks by David Stilwell, Assistant Secretary Bureau of East Asian and Pacific Affairs at the Brookings Institution, 2 December 2019, available at https://china.usembassy-china.org.cn/the-u-s-china-and-pluralism-in-internatio nal-affairs/.
[20] "Remarks Delivered by National Security Advisor Robert C. O'Brien," Arizona Commerce Authority, Phoenix, 24 June 2020, in O'Brien, *Trump on China*, 41.
[21] Pompeo's speech was penned by his China policy advisor, and strident critic of Beijing, Miles Yu. Yu is senior fellow and director of the China Center at the Hudson Institute.
[22] "Remarks Delivered by Secretary of State Michael R. Pompeo," Richard Nixon Library and Museum, Yorba Linda, California, 23 July 2020, in O'Brien, *Trump on China*, 91.

actions pose to our very way of life," O'Brien said in Phoenix.[23] The United States should not feel guilty about having tried, as it was for the national security advisor a reflection of America's innate optimism as a nation: "As China grew richer and stronger, we believed, the Chinese Communist Party would liberalize to meet the rising democratic aspirations of its people. This was a bold, quintessentially American idea, born of our innate optimism and by the experience of our triumph over Soviet Communism. Unfortunately, it turned out to be very naïve."[24]

The Engagement-failed line was a departure from Trump campaign rhetoric, which centered more narrowly on challenging China's predatory economic practices. The new claim was that U.S. policymakers had naively tried to change China, and it had not worked. Gesturing to a long history of American attempts to change China—rooted in the work of missionaries, traders going back to the Open Door policy, educators, scientists, and doctors[25]—the Strategic Competitors promised a sharp break with American proselytization. "Our approach is not premised on determining a particular end state for China," the May 2020 strategy claimed. In language strikingly similar to the Russia debate, Pompeo told an audience at the Hudson Institute that "it's critical that as Americans, we engage China as it is, not as we wish it were."[26] "We now see China for what it is, not what we wish it would be," Pompeo later told the Commonwealth Club of San Francisco.[27]

The "We got China wrong" line had a critical inconsistency at its heart: at the same time it acknowledged America's inability to shape Beijing's choices, it rendered any improvement in relations conditional on structural changes in China's economy and governance. In other words, dealing with China "as it is" still meant hoping for a China America "would wish it to be"—namely a country with stronger firewalls between the state and the economy, greater protections for private industry, domestic and foreign, and respect for the sort of personal liberties cherished in the West. This inconsistency aside, the notion that America got China wrong formed a central pillar of the construction of Strategic Competition as a new frame for U.S.-China relations.

---

[23] O'Brien, *Trump on China*, 41.
[24] O'Brien, *Trump on China*, 42.
[25] See, among others, Bradley 2015; Gewirtz 2017; Pomfret 2017; Tuchman 1971; Winchester 2009.
[26] "The China Challenge," speech by Michael R. Pompeo, Secretary of State, Hudson Institute, New York, 30 October 2019, https://sv.usembassy.gov/secretary-pompeo-the-china-challenge/.
[27] "Remarks by Secretary Pompeo on Technology and the China Security Challenge," Commonwealth Club, San Francisco, 14 January 2020, https://id.usembassy.gov/remarks-by-secretary-pompeo-on-technology-and-the-china-security-challenge/.

The U.S.-China Strategic Competition

The aim of the negative "Engagement failed" argument was not, of course, rhetorical consistency. Rather, it was to enable a positive case to be made for a post-Engagement approach. As codified in NSS 2017, the argument was that the United States had failed to see that it was already in a likely decades-long competition with Beijing for global power, leadership, and influence. Again, the claim would coalesce piecemeal rather than all at once as Strategic Competition.

NSS 2017 began the process, setting "a positive strategic direction for the United States that is meant to reassert America's advantages on the world stage and to build upon our country's great strengths."[28] The United States "will respond to the growing political, economic, and military competitions we face around the world."[29] Alongside Iran, North Korea, and transnational terrorist groups, the document names China and Russia as competitors that "challenge American power, influence, and interests, attempting to erode American security and prosperity. They are determined to make economies less free and less fair, to grow their militaries, and to control information and data to repress their societies and expand their influence."[30] China and Russia "aspire to project power worldwide," it went on.[31]

Where did the language of Strategic Competition come from? The concepts of strategic challenge and competition had been around thinking on China for some time. Most notably, it was standard in defense-planning discussion inside the Pentagon from the early 2010s at the latest. Using language explicitly rejected by the Obama administration when used by Secretary of Defense Ashton Carter in May 2015, for example, the Third Offset Strategy depicted China and Russia as great power competitors.[32] In an interview in October 2016, Deputy Secretary of Defense Bob Work explained the thinking behind the strategy as the challenge posed by "pacing competitors," a notion that that would become prominent under Biden.[33] In a measured tone, Work identified China and Russia as the "pacing competitors—not adversaries . . . because they're developing advanced capabilities that potentially worry us."[34] "China and Russia," Work went on, "now have theater-wide battle networks that are approaching parity with us, so

---

[28] *National Security Strategy of the United States*, December 2017, 55.
[29] *National Security Strategy of the United States*, December 2017, 45.
[30] *National Security Strategy of the United States*, December 2017, 45.
[31] *National Security Strategy of the United States*, December 2017, 45.
[32] See Gentile et al. 2020.
[33] Jim Garamone, "Defense Official Says Indo-Pacific is the Priority Theater; China Is DOD's Pacing Challenge," 9 March 2022, https://www.defense.gov/News/News-Stories/Article/Article/2961183/defense-official-says-indo-pacific-is-the-priority-theater-china-is-dods-pacing/.
[34] See "Deputy Secretary: Third Offset Strategy Bolsters America's Military Deterrence," Department of Defense, https://www.defense.gov/News/News-Stories/Article/Article/991434/deputy-secretary-third-offset-strategy-bolsters-americas-military-deterrence/.

to strengthen conventional deterrence, we have to extend our advantage in that area."[35]

Under Trump such language no longer had to be hidden, coming to the fore especially in the 2018 National Defense Strategy summary, which named China as a strategic competitor,[36] proclaiming, "Inter-state strategic competition, not terrorism, is now the primary concern in U.S. national security."[37] If there was still any doubt, the 2018 NDS laid bare the new post-global war on terror focus of U.S. military security policy. "The central challenge to U.S. prosperity and security," it stated, "is the reemergence of long-term, strategic competition by what the National Security Strategy classifies as revisionist powers. It is increasingly clear that China and Russia want to shape a world consistent with their authoritarian model—gaining veto authority over other nations' economic, diplomatic, and security decisions."[38]

Framing China and Russia as strategic competitors—with the emphasis firmly on the former—provided the rhetorical hook on which to hang a multifaceted depiction of the China challenge. At its core was the claim that America had missed the first laps of a race for global power, with China years into the pursuit of "economic and military ascendance, asserting power through an all-of-nation long-term strategy."[39] The China challenge comprised economic, military, political, and ideological elements, at once regional, global, and—crucially—*internal* to America. As the 2017 NSS laid out, "China and Russia challenge American power, influence, and interests, attempting to erode American security and prosperity. They are determined to make economies less free and less fair, to grow their militaries, and to control information and data to repress their societies and expand their influence."[40] Vice President Pence described in October 2018 how "Beijing is employing a whole-of-government approach, using political, economic, and military tools, as well as propaganda, to advance its influence."[41]

The China Challenge

In line with the Trump administration's early focus on trade, economics remained at the forefront of its depictions of the China challenge. As Pence explained in his first major China speech,

> Over the past 17 years, China's GDP has grown nine-fold; it's become the second-largest economy in the world. Much of this success was driven by

---

[35] See "Deputy Secretary: Third Offset Strategy."
[36] *2018 National Defense Strategy*, 2.
[37] *2018 National Defense Strategy*, 1.
[38] *2018 National Defense Strategy*, 2.
[39] *2018 National Defense Strategy*, 2.
[40] *National Security Strategy of the United States*, December 2017, 2.
[41] O'Brien, *Trump on China*, 6.

American investment in China. And the Chinese Communist Party has also used an arsenal of policies inconsistent with free and fair trade, including tariffs, quotas, currency manipulation, forced technology transfer, intellectual property theft, and industrial subsidies that are handed out like candy to foreign investment. These policies have built Beijing's manufacturing base, at the expense of its competitors—especially the United States of America."[42]

Such rhetoric hardened over the next two years. When Attorney General Bill Barr gave a fiery speech in July 2020—the economics pillar of the four coordinated speeches laying out the Trump strategy toward China—Barr explained how the PRC "is now engaged in an economic blitzkrieg, an aggressive, orchestrated, whole-of-government (indeed, whole-of-society) campaign to seize the commanding heights of the global economy and to surpass the United States as the world's preeminent technological superpower."[43] Barr laid out the administration's special concern with the "Made in China 2025" initiative. "Despite World Trade Organization rules prohibiting quotas for domestic output," Barr explained, "'Made in China 2025' sets targets for domestic market share ... in core components and basic materials for industries such as robotics and telecommunications... [T]he PRC seeks not merely to join the ranks of other advanced industrial economies, but to replace them."[44]

Barr's emphasis on leadership echoed a second aspect of the China challenge framing: Beijing's plan to knock America off its geopolitical perch. As Pompeo told his Nixon Library audience in June 2020, China wants to dominate the world. The Trump administration's framing of China "had a very clear purpose, a real mission ... to explain the different facets of America's relationship with China, the massive imbalances in that relationship that have built up over decades, and the Chinese Communist Party's designs for hegemony."[45] For Pompeo, China's economic designs were one manifestation of a broader plan to dominate global politics.

Making the case for a Chinese challenge to American predominance required two further rhetorical maneuvers. The first was a renewed emphasis on the "Rules-Based International Order," which responded to the question of what—precisely—Chinese hegemony threatened. Mentioned no fewer than 13 times in NSS 2017, the 2018 NDS summary noted how America faced "increased global disorder, characterized by decline in the long-standing rules-based international order—creating a security environment more complex and volatile than any we have experienced in recent memory."[46] Americans should be concerned, then,

---

[42] O'Brien, *Trump on China*, 8.
[43] O'Brien, *Trump on China*, 77.
[44] O'Brien, *Trump on China*, 77.
[45] O'Brien, *Trump on China*, 91.
[46] *2018 National Defense Strategy*, 1.

because the RBIO has proven an effective and legitimate set of norms of global governance. By the May 2020 *Strategic Approach*, the full phrase was operative, vowing the United States would not "accommodate Beijing's actions that weaken a free, open, and rules-based international order."

Foregrounding the RBIO was a holdover from the Obama administration—and would be retained under Biden. The phrase was mentioned 11 times in NSS 2015. Its introduction, with telling divergences from the Trump version, "redoubles our commitment to allies and partners and welcomes the constructive contributions of responsible rising powers. It signals our resolve and readiness to deter and, if necessary, defeat potential adversaries. It *affirms America's leadership role within a rules-based international order* that works best through empowered citizens, responsible states, and effective regional and international organizations."[47]

A second rhetorical maneuver was new: an emphasis on something called the "Free and Open Indo-Pacific." Initially floated by Japanese prime minister Shinzo Abe in 2016,[48] and subsequently making its way into the Australian foreign policy lexicon,[49] the term was absent from NSS 2015.[50] The Obama administration utilized the term "Asia-Pacific" to describe the broader context of its relationship with Beijing; the Indo-Pacific was a novel development. Under Trump, however, the 2017 document identified the Indo-Pacific as a specific region for the implementation of America's new global strategy.[51]

The genesis of the Indo-Pacific concept in the Trump administration can be gleaned from a declassified but undated document released at the very end of its tenure labeled the "U.S. Strategic Framework for the Indo-Pacific."[52] The document describes America's main challenge in this newly identified region as "How to maintain U.S. strategic primacy in the Indo-Pacific region and promote a liberal economic order while preventing China from establishing new, illiberal spheres of influence."[53] Under the section "Top U.S. Interests in the Indo-Pacific," it lists maintaining "U.S. primacy in the region while protecting American core values and liberties at home."[54]

The aim of such an initially classified document with limited distribution was to lay the groundwork for a later public statement, which appeared in the

---

[47] *National Security Strategy*, February 2015, https://obamawhitehouse.archives.gov/sites/default/files/docs/2015_national_security_strategy_2.pdf, 1.
[48] Tsuneo "Nabe" Watanabe, "Japan's Rationale for the Free and Open Indo-Pacific Strategy," https://www.spf.org/iina/en/articles/watanabe_01.html.
[49] See Medcalf 2019a; Medcalf 2022.
[50] See *National Security* Strategy, February 2015.
[51] *National Security Strategy of the United States*, December 2017, vi, 45–47.
[52] "U.S. Strategic Framework for the Indo-Pacific," https://trumpwhitehouse.archives.gov/wp-content/uploads/2021/01/IPS-Final-Declass.pdf.
[53] "U.S. Strategic Framework for the Indo-Pacific," 1.
[54] "U.S. Strategic Framework for the Indo-Pacific," 1.

November 2019 Department of State report entitled *A Free and Open Indo-Pacific: Advancing a Shared Vision*.[55] Beginning with "The United States is and always will be an Indo-Pacific nation," the report "outlines renewed U.S. engagement in the Indo-Pacific, which Trump announced in Vietnam in November 2017," including "$4.5 billion in foreign assistance since Trump came in to office."[56] Tying together the report's identification of the Indo-Pacific with the notion of defending the RBIO, the report explains, "Today, Indo-Pacific nations face unprecedented challenges to their sovereignty, prosperity, and peace. The U.S. National Security Strategy, released in December 2017, recognizes that the most consequential challenge to U.S. and partner interests is the growing competition between free and repressive visions of the future international order."[57] Cautioning that "competition . . . is not conflict,"[58] the report promises the United States "will compete vigorously against attempts to limit the autonomy and freedom of choice of Indo-Pacific nations."[59]

Tacked onto the twin notions of an RBIO that needs defending, especially in the Indo-Pacific, was a renewed interest in parts of the developing world susceptible to Chinese influence—notably Africa and Latin America. As NSS 2017 noted, "China and Russia target their investments in the developing world to expand influence and gain competitive advantages against the United States. China is investing billions of dollars in infrastructure across the globe."[60] This was a reference to Beijing's Belt and Road Initiative (BRI), formerly One Belt One Road. Announced in 2013 and modeled on the old Silk Road, BRI is an ambitious project of outbound investment, including ports and rail and road links, with its purpose being—in Xi Jinping's words—to "release the growth potential of various countries and achieve economic integration and interconnected development and deliver benefits to all."[61] For Trump administration officials, the reality of the BRI was different. As Vice President Pence told the Hudson Institute, the BRI was a form of "'debt diplomacy' to expand [China's] influence . . . offering hundreds of billions of dollars in infrastructure loans to governments from Asia to Africa to Europe and even Latin America . . . [with] the benefits invariably flow overwhelmingly to Beijing."[62]

---

[55] *A Free and Open Indo-Pacific: Advancing a Shared Vision*, Bureau of East Asian and Pacific Affairs, 2 November 2019, https://www.state.gov/a-free-and-open-indo-pacific-advancing-a-shared-vision/.
[56] *Free and Open Indo-Pacific*, 5.
[57] *Free and Open Indo-Pacific*, 5.
[58] *National Security Strategy of the United States*, December 2017, 52.
[59] *National Security Strategy of the United States*, December 2017, 5.
[60] *National Security Strategy of the United States*, December 2017, vi, 45–47.
[61] "How Is the Belt and Road Initiative Advancing China's Interests?," https://chinapower.csis.org/china-belt-and-road-initiative/.
[62] O'Brien, *Trump on China*, 11.

Behind the concern with the economic and geopolitical implications of Beijing's deepening connections with the world beyond the West was the broader context of a competition with China—and Russia—over values and ideology. As NSS 2017 made clear, "China and Russia want to shape a world antithetical to U.S. values and interests."[63] Pompeo later knit the challenge to U.S. values to the failure of Engagement: "We accommodated and encouraged China's rise for decades," he told the Hudson Institute in October 2019, "even when that rise was at the expense of American values, Western democracy, and security, and good common sense."[64] The effect was to connect the dots of the China challenge, linking a diverse web of international and domestic concerns vis-à-vis China—or developments internal to the PRC and the United States.

The central node of such a web was the CCP, its leader Xi, and the CCP's Marxist-Leninist ideology. In the words of National Security Advisor Robert O'Brien, "The competition with which we are faced is not China versus the United States. It is the Chinese Communist Party, with its Marxist-Leninist and mercantilist vision for the world, versus freedom-loving people everywhere."[65] As the May 2020 *Strategic Approach* explained,

> Beijing's efforts to compel ideological conformity at home . . . present an unsettling picture of what a CCP-led "community" looks like in practice: (1) an anticorruption campaign that has purged political opposition; (2) unjust prosecutions of bloggers, activists, and lawyers; (3) algorithmically determined arrests of ethnic and religious minorities; (4) stringent controls over and censorship of information, media, universities, businesses, and nongovernmental organizations; (5) surveillance and social credit scoring of citizens, corporations, and organizations; and (6) and arbitrary detention, torture, and abuse of people perceived to be dissidents. In a stark example of domestic conformity, local officials publicized a book burning event at a community library to demonstrate their ideological alignment to "Xi Jinping Thought."[66]

Further evidence for the domestic Chinese driver of ideological competition with the United States was deepening reports of mass internment of Uighurs in Xinjiang, "where since 2017," the *Strategic Approach* explained, "authorities

---

[63] *National Security Strategy of the United States*, December 2017, 25.
[64] "2019 Herman Kahn Award Remarks: U.S. Secretary of State Mike Pompeo on the China Challenge," Hudson Institute, Washington DC, 31 October 2019, https://www.hudson.org/national-security-defense/2019-herman-kahn-award-remarks-u-s-secretary-of-state-mike-pompeo-on-the-china-challenge.
[65] O'Brien, *Trump on China*, 3.
[66] *United States Strategic Approach to the People's Republic of China*, May 2020, https://trumpwhitehouse.archives.gov/wp-content/uploads/2020/05/U.S.-Strategic-Approach-to-The-Peoples-Republic-of-China-Report-5.24v1.pdf, 5.

have detained more than a million Uighurs and members of other ethnic and religious minority groups in indoctrination camps, where many endure forced labor, ideological indoctrination, and physical and psychological abuse."[67] The implication of such actions was increasingly clear: whether Americans realized it or not, they were in a part economic, part geopolitical, part ideological contest with a hostile competitor.

Military developments in China were therefore, perhaps paradoxically, the easiest to connect to the overall challenge posed by Beijing. Annual reports submitted to Congress on military developments involving the People's Liberation Army (PLA) had mapped the increased capacity and spending of China's forces, especially in the area of ballistic missile technology, as had yearly reports of the United States–China Economic and Security Review Commission. The raw facts of Chinese military capabilities, however, were less central to the reframing of China under Trump than the symbolism. As Pence said in October 2018, once again highlighting past failures, "While China's leader stood in the Rose Garden at the White House in 2015 and said that his country had, and I quote, 'no intention to militarize' the South China Sea, today, Beijing has deployed advanced anti-ship and anti-air missiles atop an archipelago of military bases constructed on artificial islands."[68]

For those wondering why the construction of artificial islands in the South China Sea should be of concern to the United States—reminiscent of notions of "far away countries of which we know little"—the China challenge was increasingly connected in official Trump administration statements about threats to and vulnerabilities inside the U.S. homeland stemming from China. As the 2018 NDS summary stated, "It is now undeniable that the homeland is no longer a sanctuary. America is a target, whether from terrorists seeking to attack our citizens; malicious cyber activity against personal, commercial, or government infrastructure; or political and information subversion."[69]

The defense of U.S. predominance in Asia thus had an explicit domestic rationale that was furthered, finally, in depictions of widespread foreign interference—beginning with but expanding beyond the sort of electoral interference witnessed during the 2016 election. As May 2020 *Strategic Approach* laid out, "The CCP's campaign to compel ideological conformity does not stop at China's borders . . . PRC authorities have attempted to extend CCP influence over discourse and behavior around the world, with recent examples including companies and sports teams in the United States and the United Kingdom and politicians in Australia and Europe."[70] As Pence voiced in October 2018, usefully

---

[67] *United States Strategic Approach to the People's Republic of China*, May 2020, 5.
[68] O'Brien, *Trump on China*, 9.
[69] *2018 National Defense Strategy*, 3.
[70] *United States Strategic Approach to the People's Republic of China*, May 2020, 5.

deflecting ongoing attention from Russian interference in support of Trump, "China has initiated an unprecedented effort to influence American public opinion, the 2018 elections, and the environment leading into the 2020 presidential elections. To put it bluntly, President Trump's leadership is working; and China wants a different American President."

The construction of Strategic Competition as frame did not close the door on engagement with a small *e*. In October 2019, Pence noted, "We will continue to negotiate in good faith with China to bring about long-overdue structural reforms in our economic relationship," with Trump optimistic "that an agreement can be reached."[71] What was gone, however, was what Pompeo would the following year term "engagement for engagement's sake." America has "to admit a hard truth ... that should guide us in the years and decades to come, that if we want to have a free 21st century, and not the Chinese century of which Xi Jinping dreams, the old paradigm of blind engagement with China simply won't get it done. We must not continue it and we must not return to it."[72] Though "We'll continue to forge bonds between our two peoples through education, travel, and cultural exchange [and] continue in a spirit of engagement to work together to secure the full, final, and verifiable denuclearization of North Korea," Pence noted, engagement must show results. "America is reaching out our hand to China," Pence closed, as he had in October 2018, "And we hope that, soon, Beijing will reach back, this time with deeds, not words, and with renewed respect for America."[73] As the *Strategic Approach* made clear, "We remain open to constructive, results-oriented engagement and cooperation from China where our interests align. We continue to engage with PRC leaders in a respectful yet clear-eyed manner, challenging Beijing to uphold its commitments."[74]

The Strategic Competitors: Trump's National Security Team and China

Within its first two years, the Trump administration had fundamentally reframed China as a strategic competitor of the United States. The process was far from linear, weaving together an array of economic, ideological, geopolitical, and military issues, events, and trends before the Strategic Competition frame crystallized in spring and summer 2020. As the *Strategic Approach*

---

[71] "Remarks by Vice President Pence at the Frederic V. Malek Memorial Lecture," Washington DC, 24 October 2019, https://trumpwhitehouse.archives.gov/briefings-statements/remarks-vice-president-pence-frederic-v-malek-memorial-lecture/.
[72] O'Brien, *Trump on China*, 92–93.
[73] "Remarks by Vice President Pence."
[74] *United States Strategic Approach to the People's Republic of China*, May 2020, 16.

summarized: America "recognizes the long-term strategic competition between our two systems. Through a whole-of-government approach and guided by a return to principled realism, as articulated by the NSS, the United States Government will continue to protect American interests and advance American influence."[75]

The construction of the Strategic Competition frame was an achievement of a set of advisors who came into the Trump administration from parts of the U.S. national security community distinct from their predecessors. Trump's election severed the links between established China constituencies in academia, the mainstream Washington think tanks, and business—the home of the pro-Engagement frame. While too much coherence can be read into Trump's appointments—as Rogin quips, "Trump chose his national security cabinet mostly on a series of whims"[76]— the Trump administration brought in a set of individuals and associated views from the anti-Engagement part of Washington. Although the inner workings of any administration are difficult to assess—and the Trump administration was certainly no exception—some connections can be mapped with a degree of certainty.[77]

Closing the White House Door on the "Panda Huggers"

First, Trump's election closed the White House door on individuals and institutions with long-standing connections to Engagement as frame and policy: the Engagers. As a leading think tank-based Engager expressed in an interview in March 2018, Trump's election resulted in "the takeover of the management of this [U.S.-China] relationship" by people "not anywhere near my group. And we're pretty immobilized, frankly."[78] Whoever they were, Trump's appointees were very much *not* Engagers.

Indeed, part of the rationale for constructing the Strategic Competition frame was to point the finger of blame for the failure of America's previous approach at those invested in its success: the newly identified Engagers. As Mike Pompeo told the Hudson Institute, singling out not previous administrations but their advisors, "Beijing's intransigence creates a permanent class of China lobbyists in the United States. Their primary job is to sell access to Chinese leaders and connect business partners. And frankly, whenever there was a dispute or tension in the relationship, many of our scholars blamed the United States for misrepresenting the nature of the Chinese Communist Party."[79] Just

---

[75] *United States Strategic Approach to the People's Republic of China*, May 2020, 16.
[76] Rogin 2021: 33.
[77] Also Davis and Wei 2020; Denmark 2020; Rogin 2021.
[78] China interview 035, 23 March 2018, Washington DC.
[79] "2019 Herman Kahn Award Remarks."

a week earlier, Vice President Pence had called out prior administrations as well as Washington special interests: "Past Administrations have come and gone.... None were willing to upset the established Washington interests who not only permitted these abuses, but often profited from them. The political establishment was not only silent in the face of China's economic aggression and human rights abuses, but they often enabled them."[80]

The Trump administration sidelined traditional constituencies like America's main business associations. "The U.S.-China Business Council isn't on the list [to be consulted]," a senior Washington think tanker explained in November 2018.[81] Trump had "no interest really in hearing from the business community and certainly not the major business organizations... [T]hey view[ed] them as a bunch of panda huggers."[82] A key force behind Engagement, notably during the 1990s debates over Most Favored Nation status, business interests had been a constant feature pushing Engagement as frame and policy.[83] Figures like Henry Paulson, treasury secretary under Bush Jr. (2006–2009), embodied the connections.[84] Voices supportive of business with China remained in important positions, including treasury secretary Steven Mnuchin and Gary Cohn, both formerly of investment house Goldman Sachs. As Rogin recalls, the Goldman Sachs clique gelled with elite DC Republicans, including Trump's son-in-law Jared Kushner, who gravitated to each other in the administration. "For Jared, Cohn and Mnuchin just made him more comfortable than a goofy California professor [Navarro] or a raspy voiced trade lawyer from Ashtabula, Ohio [Lighthizer]" one White House official said.[85] Nevertheless, the broader business community was viewed with skepticism. For many critics, including those close to the president, the business community "sold out... preach[ing] engagement all these years and look where it got us."[86]

In line with his pledge to "drain the Swamp"[87] of Washington interest groups, Trump also loosened ties to America's mainstream think tanks, including conservative organizations a Republican would normally plumb for expertise. Soon after entering office, a group of 150 GOP-leaning national security experts signed an open letter that labeled the president's "vision of American influence and power in the world ... wildly inconsistent and unmoored in principle."[88]

[80] "Remarks by Vice President Pence."
[81] China interview 056, 12 November 2018, Washington, DC.
[82] China interview 056, 12 November 2018, Washington, DC.
[83] Hung 2021.
[84] Paulson 2016.
[85] Rogin 2021: 19.
[86] China interview 056, 12 November 2018, Washington, DC.
[87] "Trump Wants to 'Drain the Swamp,' but Change Will Be Complex and Costly," *New York Times*, 10 November 2016, https://www.nytimes.com/2016/11/11/us/politics/trump-government.html.
[88] "Open Letter on Donald Trump from GOP National Security Leaders," *War on the Rocks*, 2 March 2016, https://warontherocks.com/2016/03/open-letter-on-donald-trump-from-gop-national-security-leaders/.

Coordinated by prominent neoconservative and former State Department counselor (2007–2009) Eliot Cohen, the signatories listed what they saw as Trump's various failings—including a loose grip on truth, an admiration for authoritarian leaders like Putin, and "his insistence that close allies such as Japan must pay vast sums for protection is the sentiment of a racketeer, not the leader of the alliances that have served us so well since World War II." Put together, the signatories concluded Trump would "make America less safe, and ... diminish our standing in the world."[89]

In the words of one conservative-leaning think tanker, the result of what became known as the "Never Trump" letter was that "a lot of the people who normally would have gone into a Republican administration from places like AEI, Heritage and Project 2049 didn't do so."[90] Signatories included the Robert Blackwill,[91] Aaron Friedberg,[92] Peter Feaver,[93] William Inboden,[94] Paul Haenle,[95] Kori Schake,[96] Michael Auslin,[97] and Rebecca Heinrichs[98]—all either important past or possible future Republic advisors. As my interviewee explained, some did choose to serve under Trump: "Randy Schriver[99] went in, [and] one person from [AEI's] Foreign and Defense Policy program ... went into State Department ... but it was sort of a weird time"[100] when many who normally would serve not only declined, but publicly vowed never to work under Trump. The result was to limit the Trump administration's connections to the mainstream Washington scene. As a consequence, Trump's distance from the Washington foreign policy establishment increased the seemingly ad hoc nature of its appointments.

In place of traditional connections to the Washington "Blob," Trump forged links with individuals unassociated personally or institutionally with Engagement. These advisors and policymakers were critical of the assumptions

---

[89] Open Letter on Donald Trump."
[90] China interview 097, 22 November 2021, via video call.
[91] Diplomat and author, senior fellow at the CFR, former ambassador to India.
[92] Princeton political scientist and former deputy assistant for national security affairs and director of policy in the office of the vice president (2003–2005).
[93] Duke political scientist and former special advisor for strategic planning and institutional reform on the National Security Council (2005–2007).
[94] Writer and academic, served on the State Department's Policy Planning Staff before taking up the role of senior director for strategic planning and institutional reform at the NSC (2005–2007).
[95] Think tanker and former NSC director for China, Taiwan, and Mongolia Affairs (2007–2009).
[96] Think tanker and experienced defense and security advisor, including as deputy director of policy planning at the Department of State (2007–2008) and director for defense strategy and requirements at the NSC (2002–2005).
[97] Historian and think tanker.
[98] Think tanker and commissioner on the Senate Armed Services Committee's Strategic Posture Commission (see https://www.armed-services.senate.gov/press-releases/armed-services-committees-leadership-announces-selections-for-commission-on-the-strategic-posture-of-the-united-states).
[99] Think tanker, chairman of the Project 2049 Institute, and former assistant secretary of defense for Indo-Pacific security affairs (2018–2019).
[100] China interview 097, 22 November 2021, via video call.

underpinning Engagement and the policies flowing from them. With some exceptions, crucially, these individuals were neither recognized China experts nor recognized members of the broader U.S. national security community in Washington, hailing instead from Trump's business and political connections and the U.S. military. Among them were his first two national security advisors, H. R. McMaster and John Bolton, NSC Asia director Matthew Pottinger (the one respected China expert at the highest level of Trump's staff), Deputy National Security Advisor K. T. McFarland, advisor Steve Bannon, trade advisor Peter Navarro, and CIA director and subsequently secretary of state Mike Pompeo. The Trump national security team brought with it three distinct but related sets of views of China, associated with unique bases outside the administration, which at times sat uneasily with one another.

"They're Screwing Us!": The Economic Perspective

The first and most immediately consequential perspective in policy terms foregrounded economic relations with Beijing, especially trade. Here Trump himself was the key figure, with his own long-standing opposition to America's dealings with China. Beyond the president, those in the Trump administration coming at China from an economics perspective were a mixed bunch.

Trump chose Robert Lighthizer as U.S. trade representative. Born in the Rust Belt in Ashtabula, Ohio, Lighthizer was set apart from his Republican colleagues and the Washington mainstream in his opposition to free trade agreements like NAFTA, and by extension, America's acquiescence on China's WTO accession.[101] According to reports, Lighthizer's appointment was looked upon with apprehension by the staff of the Office of the Trade Representative, who worried he'd follow the tone set by Trump in ridiculing those in charge of U.S. trade policy.[102] But Lighthizer was well respected as a tough but experienced trade representative. His credentials were also mainstream, having served as deputy U.S. trade representative under Ronald Reagan, following a career in law—including a stint at prominent firm Covington and Burling.

If Lighthizer was coming from a traditionally marginalized economic perspective but recognized sources of expertise, the choice of Peter Navarro as presidential advisor and subsequently director of a new Office of Trade and Manufacturing is the clearest example of the ad hoc Trump appointment process. An outsider to Beltway politics to say the least, University of California, Irvine

---

[101] Lydia DePillis, "Robert Lighthizer Blew Up 60 Years of Trade Policy. Nobody Knows What Happens Next," *ProPublica*, 13 October 2020, https://www.propublica.org/article/robert-lighthizer-blew-up-60-years-of-trade-policy-nobody-knows-what-happens-next.
[102] DePillis, "Robert Lighthizer Blew Up 60 Years."

economic historian Navarro was an unlikely choice for top office. He reportedly came to Trump's attention via an internet search for China-skeptical experts conducted by son-in-law and informal advisor Jared Kushner, which returned Navarro's 2011 book *Death by China*.[103] Whether apocryphal or not, as Rogin explains, although Navarro faced repeated attempts to sideline him, he was not inconsequential, often being the closest to the president's natural inclinations on China.[104]

The trio of Trump, Navarro, and Lighthizer forged a unique alliance combining the respect and experience of Lighthizer and the incredulity toward established modes of Trump and Navarro. This combination enabled the marked departure from the free trade norm in Washington embodied in the trade war, launched in January 2018. In doing so, it reflected the connection forged between the Trump administration and interest groups and industry associations that typically had lesser access to the White House compared their counterparts from Wall Street and America's tech and manufacturing powerhouses. One such organization is the Coalition for a Prosperous America (CPA).[105] Formed in 2007, the CPA represented the interests of farmers, ranchers, and small- to medium-sized manufacturing, each feeling the effects of offshoring to China and especially the U.S. trade deficit and its connection to the China's artificially weak currency.

Rooted in a litany of economic charges against China—from unfair trading practices and currency manipulation, to forced technology transfer and an unwillingness to commit to the rules of the WTO—the tough views shared by Trump, Navarro, and Lighthizer would not by themselves have resulted in the reframing of U.S.-China relations as a Strategic Competition. As Rogin asks, "Did Trump see China as a threat? Economically, sure. But on national security, certainly not at first."[106] Two further sets of views, first a military security view, then a values-based—even civilizational—view, underpinned the reframing of the China challenge.

The Military Security View

The construction of Strategic Competition as frame came largely from initiatives of Trump appointees holding a second, military security, perspective. The key

---

[103] See Sarah Ellison, "The Inside Story of the Kushner-Bannon Civil War," *Vanity Fair*, 14 April 2017, https://www.vanityfair.com/news/2017/04/jared-kushner-steve-bannon-white-house-civil-war.
[104] See Rogin 2021: 31–35.
[105] See Coalition for a Prosperous America, https://prosperousamerica.org/about/history/.
[106] Rogin 2021: 39.

figures here were the team assembled at the National Security Council under McMaster, including Matthew Pottinger—as described in greater detail in Chapter 5, and others such as Randy Schriver at the Pentagon. What held this perspective together was a firm rejection of the notion that China's rise was peaceful—what journalist and fierce China critic Bill Gertz called the "China Is Not A Threat Mantra."

Repeated by successive presidents and high-level officials seeking to keep a lid on Sino-U.S. tensions, a core component of Engagement as policy, the China Is Not A Threat mantra denied the central tenets of the sort contained in Strategic Competition. President George W. Bush, for example, had stated in May 2006, "I wouldn't call China an enemy," a claim repeated in December 2007 by his defense secretary, Robert Gates, who said, "I don't consider China an enemy," and later CIA director Michael Hayden, for whom it was "not inevitable that [China] will be an enemy."[107]

For the military security specialists on Trump national security team, developments inside Beijing rendered such a conclusion unsustainable, even laughable. For them, China is a bad international actor, a serial human rights abuser, and a clear military security threat to American hegemony.[108] Rogin reports that "the China hawks" who entered government believed China has a plan to emerge as a global great power by 2049, the 100-year anniversary of the CCP's victory in the Chinese civil war.[109] They were convinced in particular that the CCP views America is a threat, even if some Americans do not see—and do not want to see—China in the same way.

More important than the anti-Engagers' views, however, was the group's coherence and the coherence of their vision. The "China hawks were prepared; they had a well-developed strategy to disrupt the way Washington and Beijing did business," Rogin reports.[110] As noted, putting into effect the military security view of U.S.-China relations began with Pottinger's dusting off Bill's Paper and the drafting of the *Indo-Pacific Strategic Framework*. Effecting a military security view of China continued with patient effort to insert key ideas into the 2017 NSS, and to communicate those ideas to the American public in major speeches—beginning with Pence's speech of October 2018.

As in the economic sphere, those adopting a military security perspective were not a set of isolated policymakers in the White House, cut off from the government and broader national security community. Given the prominence of military appointments in the Trump administration, the most obvious

---

[107] Gertz 2019: 174.
[108] See Canfield 2002; Easton 2022; Fish 2022; Mosher 2017; Schweizer 2022; Spalding 2022. Ward 2019.
[109] Navarro and Autry 2011.
[110] Rogin 2021: 27.

connections were to the Pentagon and those military planners looking beyond the war on terror during the mid-2010s to the return of great power competition. From the military perspective, developments in the PLA's capabilities could only point in one direction: China was a potential threat, rendering an Engagement frame unworkable.

Concerns about the U.S. military's position vis-à-vis China—and Russia— emerged specifically from a series of working groups at Defense beginning in 2014 under the leadership of former deputy secretary Robert Work, which became known as the Third Offset Strategy. "The Third Offset emerged," a Rand account of the strategy explains, "at a time of important transition within the U.S. Department of Defense. In 2014, the U.S. wars in Afghanistan and Iraq . . . seemed to be winding down. . . . As senior U.S. defense leaders looked at the worldwide security environment, they saw an increasingly militarily capable China and Russia and a U.S. military that had consumed its energies in two-decades-long small wars and lost its conventional warfighting edge."[111] Work and his colleagues would develop an approach to countering improvements in China's and Russia's military capabilities focusing on investments in high-technology areas such as artificial intelligence, unmanned systems, and machine learning.

More important than suggestions for investment in specific areas in which the United States could maintain an edge over Beijing and Moscow, however, was Work and company's thinking on the broader questions posed by China's and Russia's military modernization. "One of these ideas was the conviction that China and Russia (especially China) were in fact strategic competitors of the United States. This ran counter to what amounted to official thinking until well into the second administration of President Barack Obama (2013–2017)."[112] A second innovation—telling in light of the achievements of Matthew Pottinger and others within the Trump administration—"was the conviction that the United States needed to develop a strategy for competing with China and Russia and make that strategy the centerpiece of its national defense strategy. This meant, among other things, refocusing the military on acquiring the kinds of capabilities required to confront strategic competitors, which was something that it had not been doing for at least a decade."[113]

The Defense planners were not concerned solely with advising the Pentagon on procurement of specific systems, therefore, but changing department thinking on China's rise to the status of peer competitor. As the Third Offset's historians note, the "Third Offset's real accomplishment [was] opening the door

---

[111] Gentile et al. 2020: ix.
[112] Gentile et al. 2020: 2.
[113] Gentile et al. 2020: 2.

to a new way of thinking about great-power competition and the relationship between DoD and industry."[114] Work and company realized that the sources of America's future edge could not be guaranteed to come from traditional relations with the major arms manufacturers. "DoD could no longer drive innovation... given that most technological innovations were now coming from the commercial sector—especially Silicon Valley, which was not particularly interested in selling to the U.S. military. The Third Offset therefore featured a drive to find new ways to cultivate technological innovations and interact with the commercial world."[115]

Work and his colleagues' thinking meshed with other inputs into the military security perspective. Yearly reports sent to Congress by the United States–China Economic and Security Review Commission, for example, detailed concerning developments in China's economic and military modernization, and raised concerns about America's lack of response. The 2016 report included a review of sweeping organizational reforms in the PLA and major acquisitions, as well Chinese naval activities in the South China Sea—and Beijing's response to a ruling against it in a case brought by the Philippines in 2013 at the Permanent Court of Arbitration at The Hague. The report's conclusions echoed those of the DoD's annual report to Congress *Military and Security Developments Involving the People's Republic of China* for 2017, which conveyed the message that "China's leaders seek ways to leverage China's growing military, diplomatic, and economic clout to advance its ambitions to establish regional preeminence and expand its international influence."[116]

Inputs extended, crucially, to other countries also "awakening" to the China challenge.[117] Former Australian journalist and government advisor John Garnaut was reportedly an influential outside voice among Trump's Strategic Competitors. In Rogin's retelling, "Garnaut was one of a small group of Australian journalists and scholars who had spent years exposing corrupt and covert efforts by Chinese agents to infiltrate Australian society."[118] Efforts included seeking influence over Australian politicians, a story given legs when evidence emerged in September 2016 that Labor senator Sam Dastyari had been less than candid over travel and legal payments made on his behalf by Chinese donors.[119] Dastyari became a poster child for Chinese influence operations and

---

[114] Gentile et al. 2020: 2.
[115] Gentile et al. 2020: 3.
[116] *Military and Security Developments Involving the People's Republic of China*, Department of Defense, 2016, i.
[117] On the Australia case, see in general Curran 2022; Medcalf 2019b. For contrasting takes, see Brophy 2021; Hartcher 2021; and Joske 2022. See also McCourt 2021.
[118] Rogin 2021: 80.
[119] "Sam Dastyari May Have Broken Federal and NSW Labor Party Rules on Donations," *Sydney Morning Herald*, 7 September 2016, https://www.smh.com.au/politics/federal/sam-dastyari-may-have-broken-federal-and-nsw-labor-party-rules-on-donations-20160907-graqsy.html.

would eventually step down the following December.[120] Garnaut's investigations into the CCP's united front work in Australia seemed to give myth to the lie that China was primarily a regional challenge, a status quo power, demonstrating clear intent to spread Beijing's influence globally—including to Europe, Canada, and the United States.[121]

A Clash of Civilizations? The Ideological Challenge

A final perspective brought into the U.S. government with Trump was an ideological, even civilizational, view of China associated with advisors Steve Bannon, Stephen Miller, and, to a degree, Navarro. The ideological view again ported connections to outside constituencies, like Newt Gingrich and a reformed Committee on the Present Danger: China (CPD-China).[122] The ideological view agreed on the economic and military security challenge posed by Beijing but added profound pessimism at the possibility of coexistence with an inherently evil CCP.

The ideological perspective was embodied in the strident form of neoconservativism of individuals like Robert Kagan and prominent ex-military and former intelligence officers, such as Brigadier General Robert Spalding.[123] As one analyst at a traditionally conservative think tank explained, "A classically neoconservative view or Bush era neoconservative view, which was far more controversial a decade ago is now mainstream. Conservative analysis is in reference not to China or to Beijing, but to the Chinese communists... [T]here's been an embrace of the idea that it's the party that's the problem."[124]

Not all neoconservatives supported the Trump administration. The "Never Trump" letter took many of them—including one of the letter's lead authors, former counselor of the Department of State Eliot Cohen (2007–2008)—off the table as inputs into the formation of Strategic Competition. Nevertheless, the ideological competition constituency focused attention on the CCP as the root cause of America's problem with China. "If it's the party that's the problem, that means the crimes against humanity in Xinjiang and repression in Tibet and offensive against human rights lawyers and its South China Sea island building and

---

[120] "China Scandal: Embattled Labor Senator Sam Dastyari Resigns from Parliament," *Sydney Morning Herald*, 13 December 2017, https://www.smh.com.au/politics/federal/china-scandal-embattled-labor-senator-sam-dastyari-resigns-from-parliament-20171211-h02ddn.html.

[121] Later detailed in Hamilton 2018 and Joske 2022.

[122] Gingrich 2019. Also Matthew Kroenig, "The Power Delusion," *Foreign Policy*, 11 November 2020, https://foreignpolicy.com/2020/11/11/china-united-states-democracy-ideology-competition-rivalry-great-powers-power-delusion/.

[123] Kagan 2019; Spalding 2019, Spalding 2022.

[124] China interview 097, 22 November 2021, via video call.

its pressure campaign against Taiwan and its united front work—these things are all interrelated."[125]

The ideological view emerged largely from the right of the Republican Party. As one analyst noted, "The Republican Party [now] has this kind of discourse of China being a civilizational threat, and strategic bogeyman, and you know it's coming from the grassroots as well, and it's affecting primary races."[126] Here Arkansas senator Tom Cotton, Florida's Marco Rubio, and Ted Cruz from Texas all staked out strong anti-China positions. Anti-China messaging even made it into leaked Republican strategy documents for coordinated campaigning during the 2020 election.[127] Dated April 2019, the document urged Republican candidates to adopt a set of clear talking points on China, describing how China "caused this pandemic by covering it up, lying, and hoarding the world's supply of medical equipment; my opponent is soft on China, fails to stand up to the Chinese Communist Party, and can't be trusted to take them on; I will stand up to China, bring our manufacturing jobs back home, and push for sanctions."[128]

The ideological view has institutional grounding, finally, in the reformed CPD-China, which collects a group of strong China critics with a civilizational view of the threat posed by Beijing—such as former Trump advisors Steve Bannon and Peter Navarro.[129] According to its mission statement, the CPD-China aims to "defend America through public education and advocacy against the full array of conventional and non-conventional dangers posed by the People's Republic of China. As with the Soviet Union in the past, Communist China represents an existential and ideological threat to the United States and to the idea of freedom—one that requires a new American consensus regarding the policies and priorities required to defeat this threat."[130] The CPD-China in turn connects organizationally current China critics with long-standing opponents of U.S. policy, self-labeled the "Blue Team"—a playful inversion of the military tactic of "Red Teaming"[131]— discussed at greater length in Chapter 5.

---

[125] China interview 097, 22 November 2021, via video call.
[126] China interview 104, 11 May 2021, via video call.
[127] "Republican Strategy Memo Advises GOP Campaigns to Blame China for Coronavirus," *Washington Post*, 25 April 2020, https://static.politico.com/80/54/2f3219384e01833b0a0ddf95181c/corona-virus-big-book-4.17.20.pdf.
[128] "Republican Strategy Memo."
[129] See https://presentdangerchina.org/.
[130] See https://presentdangerchina.org/.
[131] Michael J. Waller, "Blue Team Takes on Red China," *Insight on the News*, 4 June 2001, 23–25.

Operationalizing Strategic Competition as Policy

As Matt Turpin, a former army officer and assistant to Pottinger on Trump's NSC recalls, "As the Trump administration came in, everyone was beginning to realize that our grand forty-year experiment with Beijing was not working out as we'd planned, not because we didn't try, not because it wasn't well intentioned. It's just the CCP had a different view."[132] The CCP doesn't want "political liberalization. They are going to fight us on that as much as possible."[133] There was only one conclusion for Turpin: the era of Engagement was over, and Americans needed to realize it. Convinced of this view, the Strategic Competitors "succeeded in changing official US policy on China in the most significant way in a decade—on paper. Those inside the government who wanted to confront China now had explicit guidance how to do it. Initiatives in various departments gained steam."[134]

Ending Engagement for Engagement's Sake and the Trade War

The first policy manifestation of Strategic Competition was negative: halting Engagement done the old way—Engagement "for Engagement's sake"—and prioritizing strict reciprocity from Beijing. As one high-ranking diplomat, a holdover from the Obama administration, recalled: after Trump's election "we weren't doing diplomacy anymore. We weren't even talking to them [the Chinese]. We weren't working on any problems. We weren't . . . we were just not doing anything."[135] The Strategic Competitors were convinced that engaging counterparts in Beijing meant playing on China's terrain, and that they must halt engagement before re-engaging on their own terms.

Pompeo outlined the reasoning, post facto, in his July 2020 Nixon Library speech. "We'll keep on talking," he explained. "But the conversations are different these days. I traveled to Honolulu just a few weeks back to meet with [former PRC foreign minister] Yang Jiechi. It was the same old story—plenty of words, but literally no offer to change any of the behaviors. Yang's promises, like so many the CCP made before him, were empty. His expectations, I surmise, were that I'd cave to their demands, because frankly this is what too many prior administrations have done. I didn't, and President Trump will not either."[136] The end of Engagement meant changing the terms of conversation: from talking for talking's sake, to talking with specific goals in mind.

---

[132] Rogin 2021: xviii.
[133] Rogin 2021: xviii.
[134] Rogin 2021: 78.
[135] China interview 085, 22 October 2021, via video call.
[136] O'Brien, *Trump on China*, 95.

The shift to Strategic Competition was not, Pompeo explained, "just be about getting tough. That's unlikely to achieve the outcome that we desire."[137] Channeling an ideological-cum-neoconservative view, and mixing his messages along the way, Pompeo included a vague reference to engaging ordinary Chinese citizens, saying, "We must also engage and empower the Chinese people—a dynamic, freedom-loving people who are completely distinct from the Chinese Communist Party."[138] On the more solid ground of halting high-level dialogue with little to show for it, Pompeo "call[ed] on every leader of every nation to start by doing what America has done—to simply insist on reciprocity, to insist on transparency and accountability from the Chinese Communist Party.... For too long we let the CCP set the terms of engagement, but no longer. Free nations must set the tone."[139]

With America's diplomats at the State Department out of the business of Engagement for Engagement's sake, positive moves toward operationalizing Strategic Competition as policy came initially in the sphere of trade. At their first meeting in April 2017, Trump and Xi established a "100-day plan on trade" and a new U.S.-China Comprehensive Economic Dialogue to discuss economic and trade issues,[140] which was followed by reciprocal actions that seemed to signal the desire to build goodwill: China opening its markets to beef, biotechnology products, and some financial services; America to Chinese cooked poultry.[141]

The relationship between Trump's Comprehensive Economic Dialogue and the Obama-era Strategic and Economic Dialogue—the sort of talking shop Pompeo would later criticize—is unclear. The forum appears to have met only once, on 19 July 2017, with no concrete outcomes reported.[142] A short post-meeting statement reported only that "China acknowledged our shared objective to reduce the trade deficit which both sides will work cooperatively to achieve."[143] Reciprocity remained the name of the game, however, as "President Trump in a series of tweets appeared to indicate that he would link U.S. trade policy toward China with China's willingness to pressure North Korea to curb its nuclear and missile programs."[144] Reporting suggested that disagreements over how far China should reduce its excess steel production hamstrung the Comprehensive Economic Dialogue,[145] with cochairs treasury secretary Stephen Mnuchin and

---

[137] O'Brien, *Trump on China*, 99.
[138] O'Brien, *Trump on China*, 100.
[139] O'Brien, *Trump on China*, 100.
[140] "U.S.-China Trade Issues," Congressional Research Service, 30 July 2018, https://sgp.fas.org/crs/row/RL33536.pdf, 56.
[141] "U.S.-China Trade Issues," 56.
[142] U.S. Department of the Treasury, n.d, https://home.treasury.gov/policy-issues/international/us-china-comprehensive-economic-dialogue. Accessed 27 February 2024.
[143] "U.S.-China Trade Issues," 57.
[144] "U.S.-China Trade Issues," 56.
[145] Megan Cassela, "Steel Topples U.S.-China Talks," *Politico*, 20 July 2017, https://www.politico.com/tipsheets/morning-trade/2017/07/20/steel-topples-us-china-talks-221440.

commerce secretary Wilbur Ross noting, "The principles of balance, fairness, and reciprocity on matters of trade will continue to guide the American position so we can give American workers and businesses an opportunity to compete on a level playing field."[146]

Lack of progress at the Comprehensive Economic Dialogue appears to have convinced Trump to switch to a more combative approach. On 14 August, Trump sent a memo to Trade Representative Lighthizer and senior economic advisors instructing them to launch a Section 301 investigation into Chinese activities, to determine whether "to investigate China's laws, policies, practices, or actions that may be unreasonable or discriminatory and that may be harming American intellectual property rights, innovation, or technology development."[147] Lighthizer's report, submitted on 22 March 2018, found widespread evidence of forced technology transfer and theft of intellectual property, multiple intrusions into and theft from U.S. computer networks, and numerous agreements reneged upon by China.[148] Lighthizer was instructed to consider whether the United States should adopt tariffs in response, and on what goods, and to pursue WTO dispute resolution, while Mnuchin was instructed to "propose executive branch action . . . to address concerns about investment in the United States directed or facilitated by China in industries or technologies deemed important to the United States."[149]

In the meantime, Trump had launched the first salvo in a trade conflict that initially inflicted collateral damage on European nations and others, imposing tariffs in January 2018 from all sources of washing machine parts and solar panels, and in March imposing tariffs of 25% on steel and 15% on aluminum, again from all sources.[150] The real U.S.-China trade war began, however, after China responded with tariffs on 128 products, including soybeans and aircraft, followed in July by 25% levies on $34bn of Chinese goods. Further tariffs kicked in in August and from China in September, before a 90-day truce called in December 2018 led to a postponement of a $200bn set of U.S. tariffs, and the start of talks toward a full agreement. A draft trade agreement on 1 May 2019 suggested

---

[146] See "Statement from Secretary Mnuchin and Secretary Ross Following the U.S.-China Comprehensive Economic Dialogue," Department of the Treasury, 19 July 2017, https://home.treasury.gov/news/press-releases/sm0128.

[147] See "Actions by the United States Related to the Section 301 Investigation of China's Laws, Policies, Practices, or Actions Related to Technology Transfer, Intellectual Property, and Innovation," 27 March 2018, *Federal Register*, https://www.federalregister.gov/documents/2018/03/27/2018-06304/actions-by-the-united-states-related-to-the-section-301-investigation-of-chinas-laws-policies.

[148] See "Actions by the United States."

[149] See "Actions by the United States."

[150] "Timeline: Key Dates in the U.S.-China Trade War," 15 January 2020, https://www.reuters.com/article/us-usa-trade-china-timeline/timeline-key-dates-in-the-u-s-china-trade-war-idUSKBN1ZE1AA.

a breakthrough, but two days later Beijing sent a late-night cable to Washington backtracking on almost all of its provisions. Threats of further U.S. tariffs and vague promises of "substantial" Chinese purchases continued throughout until 11 October 2019, when an agreement was struck on a "Phase 1" deal, which included a suspension of planned tariffs and yet more—unspecified—promises of Chinese purchases of U.S. goods.[151]

The Gloves Come Off: Strategic Competition as Policy and the Phase 1 Deal

Signed on 15 January 2020, the Phase 1 trade deal would turn out to be one of two major turning points in the operationalization of Strategic Competition as policy under Trump in early 2020, the other being the onset of the Covid-19 pandemic. One former diplomat stationed in Beijing perceived "a serious break . . . after the Phase 1 trade agreement . . . [T]he high point of the guardrails that existed beforehand were completely lifted . . . I think Trump himself wanted to preserve some relationship with Xi."[152] But as 2020 wore on, the Trump administration "took the gloves off": "There was a lot more strong sanctions, a lot more Hong Kong sanctions, no interest in real diplomacy . . . I see that break as [after] a high point of January 20 and then all the Covid stuff."[153]

In reality, the administration's gloves had not been fully "on" for much of the previous 18 months, as the trade war had become inseparable from initiatives across government to counter Chinese influence. Shortly after the submission of Lighthizer's Section 301 report, Navarro's Office of Trade and Manufacturing released another report on trade with China. The June 2018 report, titled "How China's Economic Aggression Threatens the Technologies and Intellectual Property of the United States and the World,"[154] detailed a litany of mechanisms economic coercion and aggression, from physical and cyber-enabled theft of U.S. tech and IP theft to harvesting of data on American consumers to state-sponsored technology-seeking investment. Together, the report painted a picture of an economic competitor seeking to "acquire key technologies and intellectual property from other countries, including the United States," and "capture

---

[151] "Timeline: Key Dates."
[152] China interview 088, 28 October 2021, via telephone.
[153] China interview 088, 28 October 2021, via telephone.
[154] Office of Trade and Manufacturing, *How China's Economic Aggression Threatens the Technologies and Intellectual Property of the United States and the World*, 19 June 2018, https://trumpwhitehouse.archives.gov/briefings-statements/office-trade-manufacturing-policy-report-chinas-economic-aggression-threatens-technologies-intellectual-property-united-states-world/.

the emerging high-technology industries that will drive future economic growth and many advancements in the defense industry."[155]

On 16 May 2019, the United States banned Chinese telecommunications giant Huawei from buying parts and components from U.S. companies. In October, Huawei was added to the Commerce Department's "Entities List" of firms subject to export licenses, which promised to limit Huawei's ability to use Android software on its smartphones.[156] Huawei's addition to the list had the further effect of persuading other countries—notably the United Kingdom—to follow the United States in banning Huawei from their telecommunications networks, given the difficulties of maintaining connections through American export barriers.

The administration's actions against Huawei were indicative of the breadth of initiatives either underway or in planning across the U.S. government, aimed at resisting Chinese influence in America and abroad. At the Justice Department, a "China Initiative" complemented the 301 investigation and Office of Trade and Manufacturing's efforts by "identifying and prosecuting those engaged in trade secret theft, hacking, and economic espionage ... [and] protecting our critical infrastructure against external threats through foreign direct investment and supply chain compromises, as well as combatting covert efforts to influence the American public and policymakers without proper transparency."[157] High-profile cases brought under the initiative included that of Oklahoma-based engineer Hongjin Tan, sentenced to two years in federal prison for stealing next-generation battery storage technology,[158] and Shan Shi, from Houston, Texas, convicted of conspiracy to steal trade secrets by enticing employers of a syntactic foam technology firm to leave for a Chinese company, taking their knowledge with them.[159] The initiative would later uncover Harvard University professor of chemistry Charles Lieber's lying to government investigators about an affiliation with Wuhan University of Technology (WUT) and China's Thousand Talents Program, and for failing to disclose income he received from WUT.[160]

---

[155] Office of Trade and Manufacturing, *China's Economic Aggression*.
[156] https://www.bis.doc.gov/index.php/federal-register-notices/17-regulations/1541-federal-register-notices-2019#fr54002.
[157] See https://www.justice.gov/archives/nsd/information-about-department-justice-s-china-initiative-and-compilation-china-related, last updated 19 November 2021.
[158] "Chinese National Sentenced to Prison in $1bn Trade Secret Theft Case," *Wall Street Journal*, https://www.wsj.com/articles/chinese-national-sentenced-to-prison-in-1-billion-trade-secret-theft-case-11582839551.
[159] "Houston Businessman Convicted of Conspiring to Steal Trade Secrets, Acquitted of Economic Espionage for China," *Washington Post*, 29 July 2019, https://www.washingtonpost.com/local/legal-issues/houston-businessman-convicted-of-conspiring-to-steal-trade-secrets-acquitted-of-economic-espionage-for-china/2019/07/29/92418df2-b245-11e9-8f6c-7828e68cb15f_story.html.
[160] "Ex-Harvard Professor Sentenced in China Ties Case," *New York Times*, 26 April 2023, https://www.nytimes.com/2023/04/26/science/charles-lieber-sentence-china.html.

As O'Brien explained in the first of four coordinated speeches in summer 2020, "Under President Trump's leadership, we know what the Chinese Communist Party is doing, we are calling it out, and we are taking decisive action to counter it across the board."[161] As O'Brien told his Arizona Commerce Authority audience, these initiatives included stopping the flow of U.S. information and data to China, with Huawei the headline case; designating operations of nine pro-China outlets in America as "foreign missions"; placing export restrictions on 21 Chinese government entities over their treatment of ethnic Uyghurs in Xinjiang; leaving a United Nations Human Rights council "coopted by China"; preventing members of the PLA from accessing the U.S. visa program; moving to prevent U.S. retirement savings being invested in China-related securities; and sending a list of PLA-linked U.S. defense firms to Congress for further scrutiny.[162] "The days of American passivity and naivety regarding the People's Republic of China and its communist rulers are over," O'Brien warned.[163] The FBI, it is estimated, had some 5,000 active cases against China by the time of Director Christopher Wray's July 2020 speech to the Hudson Institute, and was opening one case every 12 hours to counter China's "whole-of-state effort to become the world's only superpower by any means necessary."[164]

As Rogin chronicles, "Throughout the summer of 2020, as the virus ... and Trump's election prospects looked increasingly dim, the president gave the green light for his national security team to take whatever policies to push back on China's malign behavior they had sitting on the shelf and let them fly."[165] The last weeks of the administration saw a series of initiatives bolstering U.S. support for Taiwan and opposition to developments inside China, as well as drawing attention to the PRC's growing global power—the culmination of the Trump administration's lifting the lid on China. "As Trump's national security officials, led by Pottinger, contemplated ... the end of their time in government, they worked to cement as many wins as possible in the US-China competition before a new administration might come in and change the rules of engagement."[166]

Joe Biden's victory in the 2020 election ended the Trump administration's control over U.S. China policy and raised the question of whether a return to Engagement might be around the corner. In so doing, it foregrounds the question of how different Trump's tenure had been from a hypothetical Hillary Clinton administration. As Rogin claims, "Toward the end of the Obama administration, there was mounting evidence not only that the CCP under Xi Jinping was headed

---

[161] O'Brien, *Trump on China*, 53.
[162] O'Brien, *Trump on China*, 53.
[163] O'Brien, *Trump on China*, 56.
[164] O'Brien, *Trump on China*, 61.
[165] Rogin 2021: 281.
[166] Rogin 2021: 299.

in the opposite direction of what their leaders were professing but also that Xi was determined to shape the international environment in his favor."[167] In other words, even had Clinton won, Engagement was over: a Clinton "administration undoubtedly would have used different language, focused more on multilateral cooperation and alliances, [and] perhaps figured out a way to have the United States join the Trans-Pacific Partnership. But it's unlikely she would have been able to continue the Obama approach to China."[168] For Rogin, Clinton "would not have been able to avoid the conclusion that Washington had lost the bet it made twenty years ago, when it had granted China permanent normal trade relations in the hope that helping China expand economically would cause it to liberalize politically and that would lead to peaceful coexistence."[169]

Doing things differently, and ending Engagement, however, are two different things—as the immense effort needed to effect a change in China policy described here demonstrates. The Strategic Competitors brought in with the Trump administration worked from the first day until almost the last—little was likely done after the insurrection of 6 January 2021—on laying the reframing groundwork for a change in concrete policies toward China. Biden's victory offers another window into how a Clinton administration might have gone about dealing with Beijing.

Strategic Competition and the Biden Administration

A corollary of the common feeling that, whoever who won the 2016 election, a new China strategy would have been the result is the argument that "no matter who won the 2020 election, the US-China relationship would be forever changed and the new normal was no longer based on engagement and 'win-win cooperation.'"[170] Put differently, common sense holds that Biden was *bound* to continue Strategic Competition. As Rogin contends, "There was no going back to the stance that the Obama administration had taken toward China in 2016, when Susan Rice[171] and John Kerry[172] had attempted to shape the U.S.-China relationship into one where any opportunity for cooperation took priority, and where most uncomfortable issues were swept under the rug."[173]

Such common sense is illustrative less for being uncontestable truth than for what it conveys of how important actors recall events. The Biden administration

---

[167] Rogin 2021: 11.
[168] Rogin 2021: xxiii.
[169] Rogin 2021: xxiii.
[170] Rogin 2021: 287.
[171] National security advisor (2013–2017).
[172] Secretary of state (2013–2017).
[173] Rogin 2021: 288.

was likely to continue Strategic Competition, but it was not set in stone. Biden would bring in his own policy team and feel the imperative to distance his framing and policies toward China as he sought to "build back better" from the tumultuous years of Donald Trump. The Biden administration did so against the backdrop of the ongoing Covid-19 pandemic, ratcheting threats from Beijing against Taiwan including two war scares, further limits placed on democracy in Hong Kong, and concern over the extent of Russia-China links since the invasion of February 2022.

Biden's Strategic Competitors

The Biden administration appointed a set of advisors and officials in agreement with the basic contours of the Strategic Competition frame and policy. Biden's Strategic Competitors began with his NSC appointments, most notably new "China czar" Kurt Campbell, alongside key China advisors at State—including Secretary Antony "Tony" Blinken—and Defense, like Ely Ratner. The temptation to recount Biden's appointments solely through a China-focused lens is strong but should be resisted. A minority were China specialists. But with China a top-tier issue during confirmation hearings, few could avoid taking a stance. The style and rhetoric of these Democratic Strategic Competitors was distinct from their Trump Republican counterparts. But on China, similarities outweighed the differences.

At the National Security Council, Biden named Kurt Campbell coordinator for the Indo-Pacific—maintaining the Trump team's language for the region.[174] Campbell was a key architect of the "pivot to Asia" under the first Obama administration, the stalled plan to reposition the United States to "intensify its bilateral relationships with nearly every Asian state from India to Vietnam and from Malaysia to Mongolia, and to embed itself in Asia's growing web of regional institutions."[175] As Campbell detailed in a 2016 monograph—part pivot memoir, part advertisement for a job in government should a Democrat win the White House—the United States needed a new strategy for "dealing with discord" and "managing competition" with China.[176] Campbell's 10-point strategy included mobilizing the U.S. public with "clear and authoritative declarations of U.S. Asia strategy" while doing more to "consequentially shape the contours of China's rise." In a phrasing both prescient and telling for how a Clinton administration

---

[174] For Campbell's reflections on the mandate he and his team received from Biden, see Bob Davis, "Q&A: Kurt Campbell on Talking to China Again," *Wire China*, 16 July 2023, https://www.thewirechina.com/2023/07/16/kurt-campbell-on-talking-to-china-again/.
[175] Campbell 2016: 15.
[176] Campbell 2016: 237.

would have prioritized Asia, Campbell asserted the United States could achieve this by "embedding China policy fully within a larger Asia policy framework, as well as by refraining from adopting a 'China first' strategy that focuses inordinately on communiqués and grand bargains and regards China as the key to all U.S. efforts in Asia."[177] Campbell was also coauthor of the March 2018 "China Reckoning" article in *Foreign Affairs* excoriating Engagement. With Strategic Competitor Laura Rosenberger as Campbell's deputy,[178] Campbell was well placed to advocate for a deepening of Strategic Competition with China, rather than a return to Engagement.

Also appointed to the Biden NSC was academic and think tanker Rush Doshi,[179] whose credentials included having worked as a research assistant on Campbell's *The Pivot* and Aaron Friedberg's *Getting China Wrong*. Doshi's own book *The Long Game* traces China's decades-long plan to return to a point of global power and influence. For Beijing, Doshi argues, events like Brexit and Trump's election signaled that "the world's most powerful democracies were withdrawing from the international order they had helped erect abroad and were struggling to govern themselves at home."[180] Covid added to the feeling that the West was in terminal decline, "a sense that "time and momentum are on our side," as Xi put it. Relying on primary source material rather than anecdote, Doshi's book intellectualized the tenor of Pillsbury's *Hundred Year Marathon*. Rather than contain China, however, Doshi supported Campbell's suggestions of managing competition, following Beijing's strategy of shaping the strategic context—deepening relationships with allies in Asia, while blunting China's influence by seeking to join and dilute Chinese-led governance institutions.[181]

As national security advisor Biden appointed Jake Sullivan,[182] who in August 2019 had made the case in *Foreign Affairs* for "competition with China without catastrophe."[183] The article, coauthored with Campbell, agreed with the Trump administration's choice of competition to describe U.S.-China relations but disagreed with the label "strategic." "Foreign policy frameworks beginning with the word 'strategic' often raise more questions than they answer," they argued in

---

[177] Campbell 2016: 198.

[178] See Alex Thomson, Phelim Kine, and Max Tani, "Jake's Nest of China Hawks," *Politico*, 13 April 2022, https://www.politico.com/newsletters/west-wing-playbook/2022/04/13/jakes-nest-of-china-hawks-00024976.

[179] Prior to entering government Roshi was the director of the Brookings Institution China Strategy Initiative, where he was a fellow of foreign policy.

[180] Doshi 2021: 2.

[181] "Biden's China Team: Who Is Rush Doshi?," *U.S. China Perception Monitor*, 3 April 2023, https://uscnpm.org/2023/04/03/bidens-china-team-who-is-rush-doshi/.

[182] Sullivan was director of policy planning in Hillary Clinton's State Department (2011–2013), and prior to entering government was a fellow at the Carnegie Endowment for International Peace.

[183] Kurt M. Campbell and Jake Sullivan, "Competition without Catastrophe: How America Can Both Challenge and Coexist with China," *Foreign Affairs*, September–October 2019, https://www.foreignaffairs.com/articles/china/competition-with-china-without-catastrophe.

a clear attack on Trump China policy. "'Strategic patience' reflects uncertainty about what to do and when. 'Strategic ambiguity' reflects uncertainty about what to signal. And in this case, 'strategic competition' reflects uncertainty about what that competition is over and what it means to win."[184]

Reporting on Biden's appointments thus termed the NSC Sullivan's "nest of China hawks."[185] This characterization is arguably an exaggeration, but it reflects the widespread view in Washington that the Biden NSC was set up from the beginning to continue course, rather than fundamentally challenge Strategic Competition as the frame for U.S.-China relations. The task was to prudently oversee, rather than resist, competition with Beijing.

With Antony Blinken as secretary of state, the State Department was similarly staffed to continue to build out a competitive approach with China, rather than attempt to reframe China in ways akin to Engagement.[186] Blinken spent his teenage years in Paris with his mother and stepfather and was respected for his experience and knowledge of world affairs—not to mention a diplomatic poise that marked him out from his tough-talking Trump-era predecessors—rather than any specific views on China.[187] Blinken was thus trusted by the president and attractive to Democrats. He was also reassuring to allies, having authored a scholarly work critical of the Reagan administration's policy of seeking to prevent Western European nations cooperating with Moscow over the building of the trans-Siberian gas pipeline. Blinken priced the costs to alliance unity higher than the geoeconomic effects of the Reagan administration's attempts to halt the project. Blinken was also likely able to survive confirmation.[188] Blinken was sure to raise Republican suspicions, having worked with Obama and supported the Iran nuclear deal, but supporters on the Hill could also point to Blinken's support for the Iraq War and interventions in Syria after Assad used chemical weapons as evidence for his robust foreign policy views.

At Defense, Campbell's "China Reckoning" coauthor Ely Ratner assumed the role of assistant secretary of defense for Indo-Pacific security affairs, and was in

---

[184] Campbell and Sullivan, "Competition without Catastrophe."
[185] See Alex Thomson, Phelim Kine, and Max Tani, "Jake's Nest of China Hawks," *Politico*, 13 April 2022, https://www.politico.com/newsletters/west-wing-playbook/2022/04/13/jakes-nest-of-china-hawks-00024976.
[186] For example, Melanie Hart of the Center for American Progress was made China policy coordinator for undersecretary for economic growth, energy, and the environment, and tasked with reviewing the Trump administration's economic initiatives, including policies toward Huawei, about which her previous research had raised serious concerns. https://www.bloomberg.com/news/articles/2021-02-16/biden-builds-out-china-team-with-staff-who-reflect-tougher-tone.
[187] Nicholas Romanow and William Inboden, "The Lessons of Reagan's Pipeline Crisis for Competing with China," *War on the Rocks*, 5 April 2022, https://warontherocks.com/2022/04/the-lessons-of-reagans-pipeline-crisis-for-competing-with-china/.
[188] Conor Finnegan, "Who Is Tony Blinken? Biden Taps Close Confidante, Longtime Aide for Secretary of State," ABC News 24 November 2020, https://abcnews.go.com/Politics/tony-blinken-biden-taps-close-confidante-longtime-aide/story?id = 74363232.

February 2021 named head of a Department China task force with a "specific two-fold mission: to conduct a baseline assessment of China-related programs, policies, and processes at the Department of Defense; and to provide the Secretary with a set of top priorities and recommended courses of action for the Department."[189] While the results, released on 9 June 2021, were classified, the headline goal of the 2022 NDS to place "a primary focus on the need to sustain and strengthen U.S. deterrence against China" provides evidence of its contents. As Ratner told the House Armed Services Committee on 9 March 2022, China is America's "pacing challenge," the Indo-Pacific its principal strategic theater.[190]

New director of intelligence Avril Haines brought another tough set of views of the China challenge. As she told her confirmation hearing on 19 January 2021 when pointedly asked whether she supported an aggressive stance, "Our approach to China has to evolve and essentially meet the reality of the particularly assertive and aggressive China that we see today," she said. "I do support an aggressive stance, in a sense, to deal with the challenge that we are facing."[191] Like Biden's other appointments, Haines promised a measured but forthright approach, noting that "China is adversarial and an adversary on some issues and on other issues, we try to cooperate with them," citing climate change as "one area where the United States has sought Beijing's cooperation."[192]

The business and economic wings of the Biden administration were, as might be expected, less clearly disposed toward dispensing with small-*e* engagement in the form of oversight and management of U.S. business interests in China. Treasury secretary Janet Yellen and Gina Raimondo at Commerce sought to retain department links to Chinese counterparts.[193] There too, however, appointees brought with them an acceptance of Strategic Competition as the frame and operative mode for policymaking toward China. At Commerce, tellingly, longtime CFR fellow Elizabeth Economy was appointed senior advisor, bringing with her a conviction that Engagement was over. As she reflected on Engagement,

---

[189] See "Secretary of Defense Directive on China Task Force Recommendations," 9 June 2021, https://www.defense.gov/News/Releases/Release/Article/2651534/secretary-of-defense-directive-on-china-task-force-recommendations/.

[190] See https://www.defense.gov/News/News-Stories/Article/Article/2961183/defense-official-says-indo-pacific-is-the-priority-theater-china-is-dods-pacing/.

[191] "Biden Intelligence Pick Favors 'Aggressive' Stance on China Threat," *Reuters*, 19 January 2021, https://www.reuters.com/article/us-usa-biden-intelligence/biden-intelligence-pick-favors-aggressive-stance-on-china-threat-idUSKBN29O18J.

[192] https://www.washingtonpost.com/national-security/biden-haines-director-national-intelligence/2021/01/19/8ed875a2-5a7f-11eb-a976-bad6431e03e2_story.html.

[193] Katrina Northrop, "Commerce at the Center: How the Commerce Department Became Central to the U.S.'s China Policy," *Wire China*, 28 May 2023, https://www.thewirechina.com/2023/05/28/department-of-commerce-at-the-center/.

At the heart of engagement is a simple belief: integrate China into the system of international organizations and agreement that underpin the liberal international order, and China will become a pillar of that order and embrace its values such as freedom of navigation, human rights, and free trade. This belief in the power of the US model and the liberal international order underpinned U.S. policy toward China for almost forty years. But in the end China lost interest, and the United States lost faith. Engagement is no longer a credible, much less the best, U.S. policy for China.[194]

At Treasury, Elizabeth Rosenberg assumed the role of assistant secretary for terrorist financing and financial crimes. Another affiliate of the Center for a New American Security (CNAS), while there Rosenberg had coauthored a report with CNAS colleagues Ratner, Doshi, and others detailing the "China challenge" and what concrete steps the United States should take to "renew American competitiveness in the Indo-Pacific."[195]

The coherence of Biden's Strategic Competitor community should not be overstated. Divisions reportedly emerged within the administration between convinced Strategic Competitors like Ratner and Campbell, and those hoping for limited re-engagement. New labels such as "managed coexistence" and "responsible competition" waxed and waned—to the alarm of anti-Engagers on the outside.[196] A May 2022 speech by Blinken outlining the administration's approach was notable mostly for its change of emphasis vis-à-vis the Trump administration, focusing more on diplomacy and good relations with allies, democracy, and "defend[ing] and reform[ing] the rules-based international order—the system of laws, agreements, principles, and institutions that the world came together to build after two world wars to manage relations between states, to prevent conflict, to uphold the rights of all people."[197] Blinken's comments—a "nothingburger"[198] to his critics—accurately reflected the diverse imperatives of the Biden foreign policy team within the post-Trump context. The priorities of strong Democratic liberal internationalists and human rights proponents, like Samantha Power as ambassador to the United Nations, inevitably clashed with those of former secretary of state and climate envoy John Kerry—an object of suspicion due to his insistence on working with Beijing.

---

[194] Economy 2022a: 31.

[195] Ely Ratner, et al. *Rising to the China Challenge: Renewing American Competitiveness in the Indo-Pacific* Center for a New American Security, 28 January 2020, https://www.cnas.org/publications/reports/rising-to-the-china-challenge.

[196] As Kurt Campbell and Sullivan laid out in "Competition Without Catastrophe: How America Can Both Challenge and Coexist with China," *Foreign Affairs* September/October 2019, https://www.foreignaffairs.com/articles/china/competition-with-china-without-catastrophe.

[197] https://www.state.gov/the-administrations-approach-to-the-peoples-republic-of-china/.

[198] https://thechinaproject.com/2022/05/26/editors-note-for-thursday-may-26-2022/.

Beyond the administration, finally, Strategic Competitors continued to prepare the U.S. government for competition with China, most notably via the formation in January 2023 of the bipartisan House Select Committee on Strategic Competition Between the United States and the Chinese Communist Party. "Committed to working on a bipartisan basis to build consensus on the threat posed by the Chinese Communist Party and develop a plan of action to defend the American people, our economy, and our values," during the committee's first hearing in February it heard from Pottinger and McMaster, in addition to human rights activist Tony Yi and Scott Paul from the Alliance for American Manufacturing.[199]

Framing Competition with China under Biden: Managed, Responsible, and Otherwise

Composed of Strategic Competitors rather than Engagers, the Biden administration did not attempt a reframing of China back to something like Engagement. Early speeches and the key strategy documents retained the competition and Indo-Pacific regional framings. As the NDS opened, "The PRC remains our most consequential strategic competitor for the coming decades."[200] Blinken made clear the reasons in his speech at George Washington University on 26 May, saying, "[We see the challenge posed by China] in how Beijing has perfected mass surveillance . . . and exported that technology to more than 80 countries; how it's advancing unlawful maritime claims in the South China Sea . . . ; how it's circumventing or breaking trade rules . . . ; and how it purports to champion sovereignty and territorial integrity while standing with governments that brazenly violate them."[201]

Also prominent was the notion of defending the RBIO. Pointing to the "UN Charter and the Universal Declaration of Human Rights, which enshrined concepts like self-determination, sovereignty, the peaceful settlement of disputes," Blinken denied these are "Western constructs. They are reflections of the world's shared aspirations."[202] America, however, faces a China "with both

---

[199] https://selectcommitteeontheccp.house.gov/committee-activity/hearings/chinese-communist-partys-threat-america.

[200] *2022 National Defense Strategy of the United States of America, Including the 2022 Nuclear Posture Review and 2022 Missile Defense Review*, Washington DC, 27 October 2022, https://media.defense.gov/2022/Oct/27/2003103845/-1/-1/1/2022-NATIONAL-DEFENSE-STRATEGY-NPR-MDR.PDF, iii.

[201] "The Administration's Approach to the People's Republic of China," Speech, Secretary of State Anthony J. Blinken, George Washington University, Washington DC, 26 May 2022. Available at https://www.state.gov/the-administrations-approach-to-the-peoples-republic-of-china/.

[202] "The Administration's Approach to the People's Republic of China," Speech, Secretary of State Anthony J. Blinken, George Washington University, Washington DC, 26 May 2022. Available at https://www.state.gov/the-administrations-approach-to-the-peoples-republic-of-china/.

the intent to reshape the international order and, increasingly, the economic, diplomatic, military, and technological power to do it."[203] America's strategy should be to secure "a free, open, prosperous, and secure international order."[204]

The Biden team's rhetoric on China differed from its predecessors in telling ways, however. In each, innovations were reportedly tied to the president's own foreign policy perspective. Rather than individual advisors or departments pushing for rhetorical novelty, it was Biden himself shaping America's framing of the China challenge.[205]

A first innovation was the notion of the 2020s as the "decisive decade" in the competition with Beijing. Blinken teased the concept in his May speech at George Washington University, telling his listeners, "President Biden believes this decade will be decisive,"[206] before it was laid down in in the Biden-Harris NSS: "We are now in the early years of a decisive decade for America and the world. The terms of geopolitical competition between the major powers will be set."[207] Echoing Blinken's language, "The People's Republic of China harbors the intention and, increasingly, the capacity to reshape the international order in favor of one that tilts the global playing field to its benefit," and "In the contest for the future of our world, my Administration is clear-eyed about the scope and seriousness of this challenge."[208]

The idea of a decisive decade was tied to a second framing innovation connecting the struggle with China to a broader defense of democracy against an autocracy seen as resurgent globally. "There's another core source of national strength that we'll be relying on in this decisive decade," Blinken said, "our democracy."[209] "Beijing believes that its model is the better one; that a party-led centralized system is more efficient, less messy, ultimately superior to democracy. . . . Our task is to prove once again that democracy can meet urgent challenges, create opportunity, [and] advance human dignity."[210] As NSS 2022 explained,

---

[203] "The Administration's Approach to the People's Republic of China," Speech, Secretary of State Anthony J. Blinken, George Washington University, Washington DC, 26 May 2022. Available at https://www.state.gov/the-administrations-approach-to-the-peoples-republic-of-china/.

[204] *National Security Strategy*, October 2022, https://www.whitehouse.gov/wp-content/uploads/2022/10/Biden-Harris-Administrations-National-Security-Strategy-10.2022.pdf, 10–11.

[205] Steve Clemons, "Is there a Biden Doctrine?" *The Atlantic* 22 August 2016, https://www.theatlantic.com/international/archive/2016/08/biden-doctrine/496841/.

[206] "The Administration's Approach to the People's Republic of China," Speech, Secretary of State Anthony J. Blinken, George Washington University, Washington, DC, 26 May 2022. Available at https://www.state.gov/the-administrations-approach-to-the-peoples-republic-of-china/.

[207] *National Security Strategy*, October 2022, 8.

[208] *National Security Strategy*, October 2022, foreword.

[209] "The Administration's Approach to the People's Republic of China," Speech, Secretary of State Anthony J. Blinken, George Washington University, Washington DC, 26 May 2022. Available at https://www.state.gov/the-administrations-approach-to-the-peoples-republic-of-china/.

[210] "The Administration's Approach to the People's Republic of China," Speech, Secretary of State Anthony J. Blinken, George Washington University, Washington DC, 26 May 2022. Available at https://www.state.gov/the-administrations-approach-to-the-peoples-republic-of-china/.

America's "most pressing strategic challenge... is from powers that layer authoritarian governance with a revisionist foreign policy. It is their behavior that poses a challenge to international peace and stability—especially waging or preparing for wars of aggression, actively undermining the democratic political processes of other countries, leveraging technology and supply chains for coercion and repression, and exporting an illiberal model of international order."[211] The message was directed not only at China but also Russia, and—crucially—Trumpism in America as well: "Autocrats are working overtime to undermine democracy and export a model of governance marked by repression at home and coercion abroad."[212]

Threading the needle of maintaining a competitive framing for China while pushing back against Trumpism led to attempts to find alternatives to "strategic" to define the nature of U.S.-China competition. "Managed" and "responsible" competition, and "coexistence" in place of competition, were the most frequent. In his meeting with Chinese foreign minister Jang Jiechi in Zurich in October 2021, National Security Advisor Jake Sullivan "discussed the importance of maintaining open lines of communication to responsibly manage the competition between the United States and the People's Republic of China."[213] "We are not looking for conflict or a new Cold War. To the contrary, we're determined to avoid both," Blinken proclaimed in May 2022. "We'll engage constructively with China wherever we can, not as a favor to us or anyone else, and never in exchange for walking away from our principles, but because working together to solve great challenges is what the world expects from great powers, and because it's directly in our interest."[214] At the time of writing, in summer 2023, however, no label had replaced Strategic Competition to frame the Biden administration's approach to China.

Competing with China as Policy under Biden

The ongoing Ukraine conflict may have knocked China off the headlines for much of 2022, but operationalizing competition with Beijing remained the Biden's administration foreign policy focus. As Blinken told his George Washington audience, the United States was developing a strategy "summed up

---

[211] *National Security Strategy*, October 2022, 8.
[212] *National Security Strategy*, October 2022, foreword.
[213] https://www.whitehouse.gov/briefing-room/statements-releases/2021/10/06/readout-of-national-security-advisor-jake-sullivans-meeting-with-politburo-member-yang-jiechi/.
[214] "The Administration's Approach to the People's Republic of China," Speech, Secretary of State Anthony J. Blinken, George Washington University, Washington DC, 26 May 2022. Available at https://www.state.gov/the-administrations-approach-to-the-peoples-republic-of-china/.

in three words—"invest, align, compete.""[215] Channeling language popular in Washington, notably by CFR president Richard Haass, that foreign policy starts at home,[216] the "Biden administration is making far-reaching investments in our core sources of national strength—starting with a modern industrial strategy to sustain and expand our economic and technological influence, make our economy and supply chains more resilient, sharpen our competitive edge."[217] Aligning with "allies and partners" was the strategy's second pillar, from a renewed commitment to the Association of Southeast Asian Nations (ASEAN) to convening global summits aimed at defeating Covid.[218] Indicatively, competing with China was the strategy's final pillar: "Thanks to increased investments at home and greater alignment with allies and partners, we are well-positioned to outcompete China in key areas," Blinken made clear.[219]

The passage of three large-scale spending bills formed the core of the invest pillar, marking a departure from the Trump administration's use of tariffs to achieve policy ends on China. The first was the Bipartisan Infrastructure Investment and Jobs Act, signed by Biden on 15 November 2021.[220] Much of the bill's content—like clean water and reliable high-speed internet for all Americans—is unrelated to China. Upgrades to rail networks, roads, and ports to ensure "resilience" against threats—including cyberattack—however, had a clearer geostrategic rationale. Touted as "a once-in-a-generation investment in our nation's infrastructure and competitiveness,"[221] the bill was explicitly sold by the Biden administration to better position the United States in its competition with China.[222]

---

[215] "The Administration's Approach to the People's Republic of China," Speech, Secretary of State Anthony J. Blinken, George Washington University, Washington DC, 26 May 2022. Available at https://www.state.gov/the-administrations-approach-to-the-peoples-republic-of-china/.

[216] For example, "we have broken down the dividing line between foreign policy and domestic policy. We understand that if the United States is to succeed abroad, we must invest in our innovation and industrial strength, and build our resilience, at home," *National Security Strategy*, October 2022, 11. See also Hass 2021.

[217] "The Administration's Approach to the People's Republic of China," Speech, Secretary of State Anthony J. Blinken, George Washington University, Washington DC, 26 May 2022. Available at https://www.state.gov/the-administrations-approach-to-the-peoples-republic-of-china/.

[218] "The Administration's Approach to the People's Republic of China," Speech, Secretary of State Anthony J. Blinken, George Washington University, Washington DC, 26 May 2022. Available at https://www.state.gov/the-administrations-approach-to-the-peoples-republic-of-china/.

[219] "The Administration's Approach to the People's Republic of China," Speech, Secretary of State Anthony J. Blinken, George Washington University, Washington DC, 26 May 2022. Available at https://www.state.gov/the-administrations-approach-to-the-peoples-republic-of-china/.

[220] "Biden Signs Infrastructure Bill, Promoting Benefits for Americans," *The New York Times* 15 November 2021, https://www.nytimes.com/2021/11/15/us/politics/biden-signs-infrastructure-bill.html.

[221] https://www.whitehouse.gov/briefing-room/statements-releases/2021/11/06/fact-sheet-the-bipartisan-infrastructure-deal/.

[222] "Biden Sells Infrastructure Improvements as a Way to Counter China," *The New York Times* 16 November 2021, https://www.nytimes.com/2021/11/16/us/politics/biden-infrastructure-china.html.

August 2022's CHIPS and Science Act—or the "Creating Helpful Incentives to Produce Semiconductors" and Science Act—was more squarely aimed at competition with the PRC.[223] Combining bipartisan bills introduced in the Senate and by Republicans in the House, the bill made "historic investments that will poise U.S. workers, communities, and businesses to win the race for the 21st century."[224] Investments took the form of seed funding, roughly $280bn of it, to induce private U.S. industry to "strengthen American manufacturing, supply chains, and national security, and invest in research and development, science and technology, and the workforce of the future to keep the United States the leader in the industries of tomorrow, including nanotechnology, clean energy, quantum computing, and artificial intelligence."[225] Early successes included a $40bn commitment from chip maker Micron to build a factory in New York State, and a new partnership between semiconductor producers Qualcomm and Global Foundries.[226]

A final large spending bill, the Inflation Reduction Act—signed 16 August 2022—also had a strong, if more hidden, China focus.[227] The bill provided tax incentives of up to $30bn to promote U.S. wind and solar manufacturing, as well as batteries for electric vehicles and power storage. A further $20bn was made available to promote America's electric car industry, with another $10bn in the form of an investment tax credit.[228] Although a "real win for U.S. climate advocates," for CSIS analyst Ilaria Mazzocco, much of the bill was "also squarely aimed at enhancing competition with China," with the latter "perceived as the largest commercial beneficiary of the clean energy transition thanks to its centrality in clean energy technology supply chains."[229]

In addition to investments in U.S. manufacturing, the Biden administration pushed forward Trump-era efforts to regulate Chinese technology in the United States deemed a national security risk, including apps such as TikTok and WeChat. But in an initial rebuke to his predecessor, Biden began by revoking Trump's executive order of 6 August 2020 targeting TikTok's parent company

---

[223] https://www.congress.gov/bill/117th-congress/house-bill/4346.
[224] https://www.whitehouse.gov/briefing-room/statements-releases/2022/08/09/fact-sheet-chips-and-science-act-will-lower-costs-create-jobs-strengthen-supply-chains-and-counter-china/.
[225] https://www.whitehouse.gov/briefing-room/statements-releases/2022/08/09/fact-sheet-chips-and-science-act-will-lower-costs-create-jobs-strengthen-supply-chains-and-counter-china/.
[226] https://www.whitehouse.gov/briefing-room/statements-releases/2022/08/09/fact-sheet-chips-and-science-act-will-lower-costs-create-jobs-strengthen-supply-chains-and-counter-china/.
[227] https://www.whitehouse.gov/briefing-room/speeches-remarks/2022/08/16/remarks-by-president-biden-at-signing-of-h-r-5376-the-inflation-reduction-act-of-2022/.
[228] "Building a Clean Energy Economy: A Guidebook to the Inflation Reduction Act's Investments in Clean Energy and Climate Action," January 2022. Available at https://www.whitehouse.gov/wp-content/uploads/2022/12/Inflation-Reduction-Act-Guidebook.pdf.
[229] Ilaria Mazzocco, "Why the New Is Also About Competition with China," Center for Strategic and International Studies, 25 August 2022, https://www.csis.org/analysis/why-new-climate-bill-also-about-competition-china.

ByteDance.[230] Trump's order had not been carried out "in the soundest fashion," Biden administration officials told reporters.[231] To inevitable charges that the United States seeks to "contain" China's economic development,[232] Biden signed a new order requiring security reviews of these and other apps in the jurisdiction of foreign adversaries.[233]

The "align" pillar centered a reinvigorated diplomatic and economic effort to court countries in East Asia and beyond to Washington's side in its rivalry with Beijing. In May 2022, the United States launched the Indo-Pacific Economic Framework for Prosperity—a partnership with 13 other countries in the region, from Australia, India, and Japan to Indonesia, Vietnam, and the Philippines.[234] Proclaiming a commitment "to a free, open, fair, inclusive, interconnected, resilient, secure, and prosperous Indo-Pacific region that has the potential to achieve sustainable and inclusive economic growth," the framework's signatories promised cooperation on supply chains, trade, clean energy, and anticorruption efforts.[235] The framework responded to the criticism of the Trump administration as having ignored America's allies in the region. Where China sent leaders and high-ranking officials to regional forums like ASEAN, the United States sent lower-status officials, seemingly signaling a low priority of East and Southeast Asia in Washington. Biden's decision in May 2023 to skip a regional visit to remain at home amid dispute with congressional Republicans over raising the debt ceiling was indicative, being quickly labeled a "win" for Beijing.[236]

Alignment in the military intelligence sphere was more sustained and high profile under Biden than the attempt to increase America's diplomatic projection in the region. As the 2022 NDS explains, "Close collaboration with allies and partners is foundational for U.S. national security interests and for our collective ability to address the challenges that the PRC and Russia present, while responsibly managing the array of other threats we face."[237] The so-called Five Eyes intelligence pact—connecting America's intelligence services to those of

---

[230] "Executive Order on Addressing the Threat Posed by TikTok," 6 August 2020, https://trumpwhitehouse.archives.gov/presidential-actions/executive-order-addressing-threat-posed-tiktok/.
[231] "Biden Revokes and Replaces Trump Order That Banned Tik Tok," *The New York Times* 9 June 2021, https://www.nytimes.com/2021/06/09/us/politics/biden-tiktok-ban-trump.html.
[232] Edward Luce, "China is Right About US Containment," *The Financial Times* 8 March 2023, https://www.ft.com/content/bc6685c1-6f17-4e9e-aaaa-922083c06e70.
[233] "Biden Revokes and Replaces Trump Order That Banned Tik Tok," *New York Times* 9 June 2021, https://www.nytimes.com/2021/06/09/us/politics/biden-tiktok-ban-trump.html.
[234] https://www.whitehouse.gov/briefing-room/statements-releases/2022/05/23/statement-on-indo-pacific-economic-framework-for-prosperity/.
[235] https://www.whitehouse.gov/briefing-room/statements-releases/2022/05/23/statement-on-indo-pacific-economic-framework-for-prosperity/.
[236] "Biden Abruptly Cuts Short an Asia-Pacific Visit, to China's Benefit," *The New York Times* 17 May 2023, https://www.nytimes.com/2023/05/17/world/australia/biden-pacific-papua-new-guinea.html.
[237] *National Security Strategy*, October 2022, 14.

Canada, New Zealand, Australia, and Britain—took on a higher profile.[238] A virtual summit of the Quadrilateral Security Dialogue with India, Australia, and Japan—the "Quad" for short—held in March 2021 followed a joint naval exercise in November of the previous year, and demonstrated the Biden administration's focus on incorporating India in particular into a regional security architecture aimed at balancing China's influence.[239]

A new trilateral security pact with Australia and the UK—dubbed AUKUS—was the most ambitious addition to the military security alignment in the Indo-Pacific. Announced on 15 September 2021, Australia's participation immediately triggered a diplomatic crisis with France, since it involved Canberra pulling out of an agreement to purchase submarines from Paris, now to be provided by the United States and Britain.[240] Initially a vague set of promises, based on an Australian plan, the three countries' leaders announced more concrete proposals at a glitzy press conference in San Diego, California, on 13 March 2023. Cooperation between the Australian, British, and U.S. navies would begin immediately, including the embedding of military personnel and increased port visits by U.S. and UK navies. With the provision of SSN-AUKUS class submarines not expected until the late 2030s or early 2040s, congressional approval will be sought for the sale of three to five Virginia-class SSNs (i.e., nuclear-powered submarines) directly from the United States starting early in the 2030s.[241] Labeled by some as an investment deal with a security component—the tab to Australia will run to $368bn[242]—a joint leaders' statement emphasized how AUKUS "elevates all three nations' industrial capacity to produce and sustain interoperable nuclear-powered submarines for decades to come, expands our individual and collective undersea presence in the Indo-Pacific, and contributes to global security and stability. In these outcomes, AUKUS reflects the principle that shared action, taken in partnership, can benefit all."[243]

AUKUS, together with a reinvigorated Quad and Five Eyes, also formed part of the "compete" pillar of the Biden administration's China policy, as Strategic Competitors pushed forward a set of organizational changes aimed at bolstering the capacity for coordinated action aimed at China. Ratner's temporary China

---

[238] "What Is the Five Eyes Intelligence Pact?," *CNN*, 26 May 2017, https://www.cnn.com/2017/05/25/world/uk-us-five-eyes-explainer/index.html.
[239] Sheila Smith, "The Quad in the Indo-Pacific: What to Know," *Council on Foreign Relations* 27 May 2021, https://www.cfr.org/in-brief/quad-indo-pacific-what-know.
[240] "Aukus: France Recalls Envoy after Security Pact Row," *BBC News Online* 17 September 2021, https://www.bbc.com/news/world-europe-58604677.
[241] "Joint Leaders Statement on AUKUS," *White House* 13 March 2023, https://www.whitehouse.gov/briefi ng-room/statements-releases/2023/03/13/joint-leaders-statement-on-aukus-2/.
[242] See Sam Roggeveen, "Australia is Making a Risky Bet on the U.S.," *New York Times*, 20 September 2021, https://www.nytimes.com/2021/09/20/opinion/AUKUS-australia-us-china.html.
[243] "Joint Leaders Statement on AUKUS," White House, 13 March 2023, https://www.whitehouse.gov/briefing-room/statements-releases/2023/03/13/joint-leaders-statement-on-aukus-2/.

Task Force at Defense was "a 'sprint effort' ... [to] examine high-priority topics including strategy, operational concepts, technology and force structure, force posture and force management and intelligence."[244] Delivered on 9 June, the task force's recommendations remained mostly classified, feeding directly into national security and defense strategies, but evidently framed China as America's number one "pacing threat."[245] Permanent organizational changes at the Central Intelligence Agency and State, however, solidified Strategic Competition as the operative policy mode. A new "Mission Center" at Langley offered the CIA, in the words of Director William Burns, the ability to "further strengthen our collective work on the most important geopolitical threat we face in the 21st century, an increasingly adversarial Chinese government."[246]

At State, meanwhile, Blinken formed a new Office of China Coordination—unofficially known as a "China House"—touting the new body's ability to "ensure the U.S. government is able to responsibly manage our competition with the People's Republic of China ... and advance our vision for an open, inclusive international system."[247] Recognizing how competition connects and cuts across the department's work—indeed that the entire government's—Blinken went on, "China House brings together a group of China experts from throughout the Department and beyond it to work shoulder to shoulder with colleagues from every regional bureau and experts in international security, economics, technology, multilateral diplomacy, and strategic communications."[248]

The Biden administration's invest, align, compete policy framework sought to balance operationalizing Strategic Competition with Beijing and the danger of slipping into hostility, even conflict. Like its predecessor, no new high-level dialogues as had underpinned Engagement were initiated, but regular top-level communication was continued. A first meeting between officials in Anchorage in March 2021 highlighted the difficulty of the task of signaling something new while accepting core aspects of the previous administration's framing of the China challenge. After trading barbs and accusations, mostly for show, Blinken and his team "made clear that Beijing's perception of America in inexorable decline is misguided and that the United States sees itself locked in intense competition with China—particularly in the realms of cyber conflict and technological

---

[244] https://www.defense.gov/News/News-Stories/Article/Article/2500271/biden-announces-dod-china-task-force/.
[245] "Secretary of Defense Directive."
[246] "CIA Creates New Mission Center to Counter China," *Washington Post*, 7 October 2021, https://www.washingtonpost.com/national-security/cia-china-mission-center/2021/10/06/fd477 142-26d4-11ec-8d53-67cfb452aa60_story.html#:~:text = The%20CIA%20is%20creating%20 a,years%2Dlong%20struggle%20with%20Beijing.
[247] "Secretary Blinken Launches the Office of China Coordination," U.S. Department of State, 16 December 2022, https://www.state.gov/secretary-blinken-launches-the-office-of-china-coord ination/.
[248] "Secretary Blinken Launches the Office."

innovation—for years to come."[249] On 9 September 2021, a phone call between Biden and Xi discussed areas of overlap in interests, values, and perspectives, and was presented to the press as "part of the United States' ongoing efforts to responsibly manage the competition between the United States and the PRC."[250] A virtual summit two months later included a three-and-a-half hour chat between the two leaders, who agreed "to ensure that the competition between our countries does not veer into conflict, whether intended or unintended. Just simple, straightforward competition. It seems to me we need to establish a common-sense guardrail, to be clear and honest where we disagree and work together where our interests intersect, especially on vital issues like climate change."[251]

The language of "guardrails" became prominent in late 2021, as bilateral relations soured from their already-low point at the end of the Trump administration. Taiwan was a flashpoint, but not the only one. Biden twice openly claimed the United States would intervene to support Taipei in the event of a Chinese invasion.[252] Repeated attempts by administration staff to walk back the comments could not mask the impression that U.S. policy had changed, especially when set against congressional discussion of the Taiwan issue that suggested a decision to defend Taiwan had been made.[253] The issuance of new guidelines allowing U.S. officials to meet more freely with officials from Taiwan,[254] freedom of navigation operations in the Taiwan Strait,[255] numerous high-level meetings between Taiwanese and U.S. officials—most notably House Speaker Nancy Pelosi's trip in August 2022—and moves toward sustained economic investment in the island furthered the impression.[256]

---

[249] "Where the US and China Go from Here," *Washington Post*, 22 March 2022, https://www.washingtonpost.com/world/2021/03/22/united-states-china-relations-anchorage-analysis/.
[250] "Readout of President Joseph R. Biden Jr. Call with President Xi Jinping of the People's Republic of China," 9 September 2021, https://www.whitehouse.gov/briefing-room/statements-releases/2021/09/09/readout-of-president-joseph-r-biden-jr-call-with-president-xi-jinping-of-the-peoples-republic-of-china/.
[251] "Readout of President Biden's Virtual Meeting with President Xi Jinping of the People's Republic of China," 16 November 2021, https://www.whitehouse.gov/briefing-room/statements-releases/2021/11/16/readout-of-president-bidens-virtual-meeting-with-president-xi-jinping-of-the-peoples-republic-of-china/.
[252] "Biden Says U.S. Troops Would Defend Taiwan in Event of Attack by China," *Washington Post*, 19 September 2022, https://www.washingtonpost.com/politics/2022/09/18/biden-taiwan-military-china-attack/.
[253] Michael D. Swaine, "U.S. Official Signals Stunning Shift in the Way We Interpret 'One China' Policy," *Responsible Statecraft*, 10 December 2021, https://responsiblestatecraft.org/2021/12/10/us-official-signals-stunning-shift-in-the-way-we-interpret-one-china-policy/.
[254] "New Guidelines for U.S. Government Interactions with Taiwan Counterparts," U.S. Department of State, 9 April 2021, https://www.state.gov/new-guidelines-for-u-s-government-interactions-with-taiwan-counterparts/.
[255] See "Taiwan: Two US Warships Sail through Strait," *BBC Online*, 26 August 2022, https://www.bbc.com/news/world-asia-62704449; "U.S. Military Releases Video of Near-Collision with Chinese Destroyer," *Washington Post*, 5 June 2023, https://www.washingtonpost.com/national-security/2023/06/05/china-ship-us-destroyer-taiwan-strait/.
[256] See, for example, "President Tsai Meets Atlantic Council Delegation," 19 July 2022, https://www.atlanticcouncil.org/insight-impact/in-the-news/president-tsai-meets-atlantic-council-del

To label the Biden administration indistinct from its predecessor would be inaccurate. The post-Trump context, and especially the progressive elements in the Democratic coalition, came strongly to the fore in the manner—if not the frame—of dealings with Beijing. Fear of backlash against ordinary Asian Americans was an important factor in the decision to suspend the Trump-era "China Initiative" at the Justice Department.[257] As concern at the prospect of military conflict with China spiked periodically in 2021 and 2023, the Biden team also pushed for increased crisis management measures, from floating the idea of a defense hotline between the Pentagon and Beijing[258] to sending CIA director William Burns on a secret trip in May 2023.[259] The Chinese leadership, however, was reportedly uninterested in either picking up the phone or meeting with American counterparts below the level of strategic dialogue,[260] leaving Blinken and Sullivan to engage in rhetorical gymnastics—"de-coupling" and "de-risking"—to describe a frozen bilateral relationship.[261]

Whither Russia? Containing and Engaging with Moscow under Trump and Biden

The sort of paradigmatic turnover in the U.S. approach toward China, effected under the Trump administration and continued under his successor, was absent in the Russia case. There was no reframing of Russia, carried out by policymakers

egation/; "Biden Sending Delegation to Taiwan to Reaffirm Commitment amid Russia's Invasion of Ukraine," *Washington Post*, 28 February 2022, https://www.washingtonpost.com/politics/2022/02/28/biden-delegation-taiwan-commitment-russia-invasion-ukraine/; "Nancy Pelosi Visits Taiwan Despite Warnings from China," *Washington Post*, 3 August 2022, https://www.washingtonpost.com/world/2022/08/02/nancy-pelosi-taiwan-visit/; "Media Note: 2021 U.S.-Taiwan Economic Prosperity Dialogue, 19 November 2021, https://www.state.gov/2021-u-s-taiwan-economic-prosperity-partnership-dialogue/; "Biden Administration Begins Trade Dialogue with Taiwan," *New York Times*, 1 June 2022, https://www.nytimes.com/2022/06/01/business/economy/biden-taiwan-trade.html; "New Trade Deal Signed as China Tensions Rise," *BBC*, 1 June 2023, https://www.bbc.com/news/business-65773797.

[257] "Justice Department Shutters China Initiative, Launches Broader Strategy to Counter Nation-State Threats," *Washington Post*, 23 February 2022, https://www.washingtonpost.com/national-security/2022/02/23/china-initivative-redo/.
[258] Jack Destch, "Biden Looks for Defense Hotline with China," *Foreign Policy*, 10 May 2021, https://foreignpolicy.com/2021/05/10/biden-china-xi-jinping-defense-hotline-pentagon/.
[259] "CIA Chief Made Secret Visit to China in Bid to Thaw Relations," *Financial Times*, 2 June 2023, https://www.ft.com/content/5fdfed4f-7270-455f-ac33-fedbef887423.
[260] "China Rebuffs Pentagon Chief, Blunting Push for Rapprochement," *Wall Street Journal*, 30 May 2023, https://www.wsj.com/articles/china-rebuffs-pentagon-chief-blunting-push-for-rapprochement-dd78d9bf?mod=hp_lead_pos2.
[261] "Remarks by National Security Advisor Jake Sullivan on Renewing American Economic Leadership at the Brookings Institution," 27 April 2023, https://www.whitehouse.gov/briefing-room/speeches-remarks/2023/04/27/remarks-by-national-security-advisor-jake-sullivan-on-renewing-american-economic-leadership-at-the-brookings-institution/

with different convictions and producing a distinct set of policy manifestations. Trump entered office with Russian forces active in eastern Ukraine, against a backdrop of allegations of election meddling in Trump's favor. With U.S.-Russia relations already seemingly at a nadir, there was neither under Trump nor or Biden a more hawkish position or the inverse—despite the existence in each case of calls for a new approach. With China the overwhelming focus, Russia remained an afterthought, tacked onto descriptions of Beijing as America's major geopolitical challenge, with little conviction or direction.

Trump and Russia

Unlike with China, Trump was on record as desiring better relations with Moscow. In his pre-election writings, he connected Russia and China as America's "biggest challenge long term."[262] But in a major foreign policy speech early in campaigning, he noted Russia's knowledge of the "horror of Islamic terrorism" and expressed optimism that this "horrible cycle of hostility must end and ideally will end soon." As he told an audience at the Center for the National Interest in Washington in April 2016, "An easing of tensions, and improved relations with Russia from a position of strength only, is possible, absolutely possible."[263]

For Trump, Pompeo told the Senate Foreign Relations Committee soon after entering office, competing with Russia—at least—did not necessitate conflictual relations: "President Trump believes that two great nuclear powers should not have such a contentious relationship," Pompeo stated. "This is not just in our interest, but in the interest of the whole world."[264] Proposing direct engagement in ways similar to the engaging China debate, Pompeo argued, "We can't make progress on issues of mutual concern unless we are talking to them. I am referring to key issues like stopping terrorism, obtaining peace in Ukraine, stopping the civil war in Syria ... and shutting down all of Iran's malign activity."

But already by the time he entered the White House, Trump was under a cloud of suspicion that his victory was owed to disinformation spread among the U.S. public by state-directed Russian influence agents, possibly in collusion with Trump allies. Allegations of criminal conspiracy by members of the Trump campaign team led Acting Attorney General Rod Rosenstein in May 2017 to nominate a special counsel to investigate. Robert Mueller's investigation would find evidence of links between the Trump team and Russian interlocutors, but

---

[262] Trump 2015: 42.
[263] "Transcript: Donald Trump's Foreign Policy Speech," *New York Times*, 27 April 2016, https://www.nytimes.com/2016/04/28/us/politics/transcript-trump-foreign-policy.html.
[264] https://www.foreign.senate.gov/imo/media/doc/072518_Pompeo_Testimony.pdf.

insufficient evidence for either criminal conspiracy to direct Russian interference or obstruction of justice on the part of Trump himself.[265] With the Mueller report not published until April 2019, the ongoing investigation helped stymy policymaking toward Russia for much of the Trump administration's first two years.

Early turmoil among Trump's foreign policy team, including rapid turnover of senior officials like National Security Advisor Michael Flynn, also acted against significant policy change toward Russia. Some commentators suggest Flynn was tapped by Trump for the role in part to facilitate a "reverse Nixon"—an overture to Moscow with the aim of preventing a deepening China-Russia axis.[266] But Flynn had no chance to settle into the role nor effect any such overture, leaving the White House in February 2017 after it became known he had discussed sanctions against Russia—and presumably their possible removal—with Russia's ambassador to Washington, Sergey Kislyak. The Flynn affair quashed any attempt to act on hopes to—as he later told reporters for an investigation into his ouster—"figure out how to work with Russia instead of making it an enemy. We have so many problems that we were handed on a plate from [Obama]."[267]

Trump's Russia-focused appointments were less optimistic about a thaw in relations. At the National Security Council, Fiona Hill was brought in from the Brookings Institution as senior director for European and Russian affairs. Author of the most authoritative biography of the Russian leader,[268] Hill had a reputation "as a blunt speaker and independent thinker and analyst"—and no friend of Putin.[269] Hoping to be an "adult in the room" in relation to a crucial set of bilateral and multilateral relationships, Hill instead gained almost no access to the president before leaving in summer 2019, later caught up in the impeachment proceedings against the president.[270] Hill's lack of success offers a point of illustrative comparison with Trump's chief China hand, Matthew Pottinger, a comparison I explore in detail in Chapter 5.

Despite Flynn's rapid exit, the specter of investigation by a special counsel, and limited interest in a rethinking of U.S. policy toward Russia among key members

---

[265] Robert S. Mueller, *Report on the Investigation into Russian Interference in the 2016 Presidential Election*, March 2019, https://www.justice.gov/archives/sco/file/1373816/download.

[266] Also "Flynn's Contradictory Line on Russia," *NPR*, 19 May 2017, https://www.npr.org/sections/parallels/2017/05/19/529148729/michael-flynns-contradictory-line-on-russia.

[267] Nicholas Schmidle, "Michael Flynn, General Chaos," *New Yorker*, 18 February 2017, https://www.newyorker.com/magazine/2017/02/27/michael-flynn-general-chaos.

[268] Hill and Gaddy 2015.

[269] Adam Entous, "What Fiona Hill Learned in the White House," *New Yorker*, 29 June 2020, https://www.newyorker.com/magazine/2020/06/29/what-fiona-hill-learned-in-the-white-house#:~:text = McMaster%20rushed%20in%20behind%20her,her%20work%20speak%20for%20 itself.

[270] As recounted in Hill 2021. See also "Top Russia Expert Leaving Trump's National Security Council," *CNN*, 18 June 2019.

of Trump's national security team, Trump himself remained open to the possibility. His warm views toward Moscow were most evident during an infamous summit with Putin in Helsinki in July 2018, when the U.S. leader stated plainly he believed Putin's denials that operatives for his government interfered in the 2016 election—over the convictions of members of his own party and conclusions of his own intelligence services.[271] "They think it's Russia," he told the final press conference, referring to U.S. intelligence assessments. "I have President Putin ... he just said it's not Russia. I don't see any reason why it would be."[272]

The effect of cross-cutting dynamics and tensions in the Trump administration on relations with Moscow was to prevent any positive framing or reframing of Russia as an object in U.S. national security policy. NSS 2017 depicted Russia as, alongside China, "challeng[ing] American power, influence, and interests, attempting to erode American security and prosperity ... China and Russia want to shape a world antithetical to U.S. values and interests."[273] Singling out Moscow was "using information tools in an attempt to undermine the legitimacy of democracies,"[274] and seeking to divide the United States from its allies. The 2018 NDS still saw Russia as an addendum to China, stating, "Long-term strategic competitions with China and Russia are the principal priorities for the Department."[275]

The most comprehensive Trump administration document on Russia, the Russia Integrated Strategy of 2019, thus lays out what might be termed "limited engagement amid containment": "In light of the current context and lack of mutual trust, engaging constructively with the Russian Federation is a challenge. As we continue to impose escalating costs for Russian malign behavior, we leave the door open for dialogue, giving Russia the opportunity to demonstrate its willingness to be a constructive interlocutor." The document laid out four key mission goals: (1) to persuade Russia to respect territorial sovereignty of states, especially in relation to Ukraine; (2) to engage constructively with Russia on resolution of international conflicts and global challenges; (3) to see that Russian society becomes more resilient and democratic; and (4) to keep trade open and spread American business values.[276] The emphasis here on spreading U.S. values demonstrates the decided weighting of the 2019 Russia Integrated Strategy toward containment.

---

[271] "Trump-Putin Summit Is Over: The Head Scratching? Not So Much," *New York Times*, 16 July 2018, https://www.nytimes.com/2018/07/16/world/europe/trump-putin-summit-helsinki.html.
[272] "Trump-Putin Summit Is Over."
[273] *National Security Strategy of the United States*, December 2017, 2.
[274] *2018 National Defense Strategy*, 14.
[275] *2018 National Defense Strategy*, 4.
[276] https://www.state.gov/wp-content/uploads/2019/06/ICS-Russia_UNCLASS_508.pdf. The document was subsequently removed from the State Department's website.

The handover from Trump to Biden brought with it little expectation of a change in policy toward Russia. Staffed with advisors strongly critical of Putin—including Toria Nuland[277] as assistant secretary of state for political affairs—any unilateral attempt by the United States to improve bilateral relations was unlikely. Expiration of the New Start arms control treaty in February 2021 offered one possible basis for dialogue, as the authors of the open letter of June 2020 seeking improved U.S.-Russia relations realized, and the Biden team agreed to a five-year extension. With the exception of a June 2021 meeting in Geneva—notable largely for agreeing little, except for the need to maintain such routine diplomacy[278]—by late 2021 mounting evidence of Russian preparation for a full-scale invasion of Ukraine shifted U.S. Russia policy from competition to all-out containment. As NSS 2022 denounced "Russia's brutal and unprovoked war on its neighbor Ukraine . . . shatter[ing] peace in Europe. . . . We are constraining Russia's strategic economic sectors, including defense and aerospace, and we will continue to counter Russia's attempts to weaken and destabilize sovereign nations and undermine multilateral institutions."[279]

Conclusion

In his introduction to a collection of Trump administration speeches on China, former national security advisor Robert O'Brien described its policy toward the PRC as the "most significant United States foreign policy shift in a generation."[280] O'Brien was not exaggerating. Trump's election in 2016 was a critical juncture in America's relations with Beijing. Unlike previous administrations, which entered office promising a tougher approach, but which eventually dialed back criticism in search of common ground, Trump offered different high-level direction. Drawing on inputs from China-skeptic advisors with overlapping concerns about Beijing—economic, military security, and ideological—Trump "unleashed" lower-level officials and bureaucrats across the government to develop policy initiatives likely to anger China's leaders. The result was to lay the groundwork for a reframing of China that crystallized in official statements and strategy documents as "Strategic Competition." Policy manifestations of the new

---

[277] Nuland previously served as principal foreign policy advisor to Vice President Dick Cheney (2003–2005) and as assistant secretary of state for European and Eurasian affairs (2013–2017). Prior to entering the Biden administration, Nuland was senior counselor at the Albright-Stonebridge consulting firm, and a fellow at the Brookings Institution.

[278] See Michael Kimmage's reflections, https://www.wilsoncenter.org/article/biden-putin-summit-expert-analysis.

[279] *National Security Strategy*, October 2022, 26.

[280] O'Brien, *Trump on China*.

approach remained limited to a provisional Phase 1 trade deal until 2020, when anger at the effects of Covid-19 led Trump to "take the gloves off."

When the Biden administration entered office, it had the opportunity to return to Engagement as frame, policy, and community. Staffed with experts convinced of the benefits of the new competitive framing, the Biden administration did the opposite, continuing to "build out" Strategic Competition as a frame and policy direction. The two administration's approaches were not, of course, identical—the Biden team seeking a modifier to "strategic" in "Strategic Competition" that signaled prudence in the management of the relationship. Nonetheless, the shift from Trump to Biden was one of continuity, not change.

Why? To that question, the book now turns, first to the polarized, professionalized, and personalized struggles that forged the Engagers and anti-Engagers, before Part III traces the formation of the Russia-we-havers and Russia-we-wanters among America's Russia expert community.

PART II
THE END OF ENGAGEMENT WITH CHINA

3
Beyond Hawks and Doves
Polarization in the U.S. China Field

"There is a history in the China field of people wanting to talk about China watchers as either apologists or hawks," one interviewee told me with evident concern, before asking, "You're not doing that, are you?"[1] The language of hawks and doves is ubiquitous in U.S. foreign policy, seeming to grasp an essential truth about how Washington works. For one think tanker, in "almost every area for policy [there are] the people who want [America] slightly more engaged, with military restraint, and the people that want to take a tougher line."[2] Being honest with my interviewee, I said I had been tempted early in the project to talk about the China field as irrevocably split between hawks and doves. Struck by talk of "dragon slayers" or "panda sluggers" lined up against "panda huggers" or "panda greasers"—common terms for pro- and anti-China experts—a hawks-and-doves story of Engagement's demise seemed to fit, on its face.

A simplistic account of the transformation in U.S. China policy since 2016 is that with Trump's victory, control passed into the hands of the China hawks, who set about reframing the PRC in the public mind and designing policies aimed at countering China's misdeeds. With Biden's election, control then passed to Democratic China hawks like Kurt Campbell and Ely Ratner, who sought to carry on the Trump China hawks' work. Depending on one's views, the hawks are either right or wrong that engagement is impossible. Either way, a plausible hawk/dove story can be told about Engagement's end.

I quickly discarded the idea of telling the story of Engagement's demise via hawk-and-dove imagery, however. With some exceptions, such as the influence of the neoconservatives under George W. Bush,[3] the hawk and dove labels obscure more than they illuminate. Neither hawks nor doves are of the same stripe. Those hawkish toward one country might be dovish toward another. Some China skeptics, such as former defense planner Elbridge Colby,[4] for example, have counseled engagement with Russia to enable a shift in military capabilities

---

[1] China interview 066, 6 December 2018, Cambridge, MA.
[2] Russia interview 004, 24 November 2020, via video call.
[3] See Smith 2007; Mann 2004.
[4] Cofounder and principal of the Marathon Initiative. Former deputy assistant secretary of defense for strategy and force development, 2017–2018.

The End of Engagement. David M. McCourt, Oxford University Press. Oxford University Press 2024.
DOI: 10.1093/9780197765241.003.0004

to East Asia.[5] Moreover, doves may be doves and hawks may be hawks for different reasons, as when human rights advocates and military-security specialists find common interventionist ground. The hawk/dove labels thus mask more consequential if cross-cutting political, ethical, and professional divisions.

This chapter is *not*, therefore, about the Engagers and the Strategic Competitors as reflections of a fundamental hawk-dove binary in U.S. foreign relations. The story is more complicated. The chapter is also not one about partisan polarization. Division into more pro- and anti-engagement groups does not track with party affiliation. Again, if only the story were so straightforward. Party politics certainly matters. As the previous chapter detailed, no account of the end of Engagement with China can ignore the pivotal impact of the 2016 election. But identification as Republican or Democratic runs orthogonally to national security professionals' policy views.

Instead, the chapter tracks the emergence and consolidation of opposed camps in the China sub-field of the American national security community, not limited to partisan affiliation. I term these camps the China "Engagers" and "anti-Engagers." Put plainly, *without the emergence and consolidation of these camps prior to and during the Trump administration, the shift from Engagement to Strategic Competition with China would have been impossible.*

No assumptions are made for the moment about what structures the Engager and anti-Engager camps and defines their prevailing viewpoints—be it hawkish or dovish disposition or party affiliation, for example. The task for this chapter is descriptive: to trace polarization among America's China experts, the bases for which I explore in the following chapters. As emphasized in the previous chapter, it is imperative to be clear about what, precisely, is being polarized. In a point of marked division between the two cases, the Engager/anti-Engager camps are split not only over policy, but also over the *framing* of China, whereas Russia experts remain divided principally over policy.

The chapter opens with a review of the Engager/anti-Engager distinction. I then explore the longer-term origins of these divisions. The anti-Engagers have their roots in the Clinton administration, with the so-called Blue Team questioning the president's relationship with Beijing. I then trace the polarization of Engagement under Trump, as the Engager's split over how to deal with a more authoritarian and bellicose Beijing, leading to the emergence of the Strategic Competitors. I detail the strange bedfellows thereby created, as disillusioned left-wing academics made common cause with military hawks and

---

[5] For example, Elbridge Colby and Alex Velez-Green, "To Avert War with China, the U.S. Must Prioritize Taiwan over Ukraine," *Washington Post*, 18 May 2023, https://www.washingtonpost.com/opinions/2023/05/18/taiwan-ukraine-support-russia-china/.

human rights defenders, while libertarian think tankers came to agree with former diplomats who defend the record of Engagement.

The Engagers and their Critics: Taking Sides over China

The previous two chapters introduced the major groups within the U.S. China-watching community: the Engagers and the Strategic Competitors, without which there would have been no shift from a more engaged to a more competitive approach toward Beijing since 2016. Here I dive more deeply into the major divisions within the American China field. Readers by now comfortable with the major dynamics among America's China watchers can move forward to the next section. Readers who want to know, stick with me.

Before revisiting the engagers and their critics, we might fruitfully recall that in his *Perception and Misperception in International Politics*, political scientist Robert Jervis demonstrated how different perceptions of a rival's intentions underlie foreign policy polarization.[6] Taking U.S.-Soviet relations as his example, Jervis showed that those pushing hardline policies assumed Moscow to be an implacable aggressor bent on expansion. Those holding what Jervis termed "the deterrence model"—where appeasement breeds conflict—held that only strength begets security. Those pushing more conciliatory policies, by contrast, tended to see the Soviet Union as oriented toward defense and the status quo, leading them to advocate the "spiral model"—whereby overly hostile previous policies lead to a spiraling downward into mutual suspicion and tit-for-tat policymaking. The debate continues to echo vis-à-vis China.[7]

My approach differs from Jervis's in adopting a sociological view attuned to group dynamics rather than a psychological one attuned to perception and misperception. Yet the two are not mutually exclusive. Interpretations of Beijing's drives and intentions are important, which a refresher on Jervis's insights helps sharpen. The Engagers and anti-Engagers are split on China's intentions. Is China a normal great power, anxious to exert greater influence in its region? Or is it an expansionist power seeking global domination?

---

[6] Jervis 1976: 58-113.
[7] See especially Lyle Goldstein's call for Washington and Beijing to initiate "cooperation spirals" as a means to improve relations. See Goldstein 2015.

America's China Experts: Engagers, Anti-Engagers, and More

America's China watchers are split into two broad camps: the Engagers and the anti-Engagers. Neither group is institutionalized. One's position within these groups is always a matter of degree, recognition, and negotiation. Following the logic of fractionation,[8] where any two China experts can be divided into more competitive and the more cooperative, moreover, the Engagers and anti-Engagers have themselves separated between those willing to adopt the post-Trump competitive framing of U.S.-China relations, a group I term "Competitive Coexisters," and an even more hardline group, the "New Cold Warriors."

The Engagers

The Engagers can be defined as China experts who seek to defend Engagement, remaining optimistic about what cooperation with Beijing can achieve, at least in the (very) long term. At the heart of the Engager group is a set of former policymakers and diplomats—notable among them Charles "Chas" Freeman,[9] Kenneth Lieberthal, Michel Oksenberg, Susan Shirk, J. Stapleton Roy, and Jeffrey Bader—who worked to maintain a degree of cooperation between the United States and China despite the shifting pendulum of Sino-U.S. relations and occasional crisis. Others include former U.S. trade representative Michal Froman and former national security advisors Stephen Hadley (2005–2009),[10] Susan Rice (2013–2017), and Tom Donilon (2010–2013). Beyond them, the Engager group includes individual like Jan Berris and Steve Orlins, experienced China watchers associated with the cultural exchange organization the National Committee on U.S.-China Relations. It also includes others coming to the same place on China but from distinct professional viewpoints. One thinks here of think tankers like Carla Freeman at the United States Institute of Peace and Cheng Li at the Brookings Institution, or individuals like Craig Allen from the U.S.-China Business Council. Finally, a core constituency of the Engager group is academics: including political scientists Taylor Fravel (MIT), Mary Gallagher (Michigan), Avery Goldstein (Pennsylvania), Thomas Christensen (Columbia); legal scholars Neysun Mahboubi (Pennsylvania), Benjamin Liebman (Columbia), and Nico Howson (Michigan). Another key constituency is think tankers, like Scott Kennedy from the Center for Strategic and International

---

[8] See Abbott 2001, especially chapter 3, "The Fraction of Construction."
[9] Longtime diplomat, including as ambassador to Saudi Arabia (1990–1992), and assistant secretary of defense (1993–1994).
[10] See Bob Davis, "Q&A: Stephen J. Hadley on Keeping China Relations on Track," *Wire China*, 2 April 2023, https://www.thewirechina.com/2023/04/02/stephen-j-hadley-on-keeping-china-relations-on-track/.

Studies (CSIS), and "restraint"-focused security specialists like Lyle Goldstein[11] and Michael Swaine.

As detailed in Chapter 1, for the Engagers, Engagement *as policy* was not a failure. It was justified from the 1970s onward, first as a means to counter the Soviet Union and later to raise living standards both in America and in China, while promoting international peace and security, as—for them—it remains.[12] For one think tanker, critics of engagement

> speak as though the advent of Xi Jinping was always written, that it could have been foreseen in Deng Xiaoping and Hu Jintao. And it's not true. In fact, China was getting more open and more integrated during that time. Not entirely. I don't mean to be naive about that, but . . . at the level of personal freedom to shape [their] everyday lives, . . . at the level of their personal health, their global integration, [China was opening up].[13]

In the Engager's view, at no point was a policy aimed at arresting China's development morally or politically defensible. What the Strategic Competitors get wrong, in the Engagers' view, is to confuse outcomes in China—which Engagers agree have not been what Americans would hope—with the intentions of American diplomacy, given that such intentions are not promises. Precisely what, Engagers ask, should American have done differently? WTO membership stands here as a signal event the United States might not have pushed so heavily. Engagers counter, however, by asking whether successive governments themselves have been sufficiently committed to such global institutions, and might have done more to hold Beijing's feet to the WTO fire.

For the Engagers, moreover, the terms of the debate are not only stacked against the policies many had a hand in effecting, but also intellectually incoherent. As one senior ex- diplomat to me, "The current rhetoric . . . about the 'failure' of 'the engagement policy' is a gross misreading of the intentions and substance of U.S. policy."[14] For Stape Roy, for example, Engagement was not really "a thing." What is now known as Engagement was simply the prudent conduct of U.S.-China relations. "Since there was never an 'engagement' strategy with uniform contents and goals, it is equally absurd to maintain that 'it' was a 'failure,'" Roy argues.[15]

---

[11] Director of Asia engagement at the think tank Defense Priorities. Formerly research professor in the China Maritime Studies Institute at the U.S. Naval War College.
[12] For an insightful set of reflections on Engagement, including contributions by many Old Engagers, see Thurston 2021.
[13] China interview 083, 12 October 2021, Washington, DC.
[14] China interview 057, 13 November 2018, Washington, DC.
[15] Roy 2018.

For a former senior intelligence official, not squarely an Engager but critical of the claims of the anti-Engagers,

> Engagement has worked.... It's still a work in progress, and there have been some setbacks, but my view is that it hasn't failed. It just hasn't fully succeeded yet. It's going to take more time than we thought 30 years ago, right? ... I just think that this idea that engagement is dead is ridiculous because even when you listen to the Biden administration, they will acknowledge what we need to have some kind of a dialog process for interaction with the Chinese. Well, that's engagement.... We can't address all of the challenges of our relationship with China if we're unwilling to engage in diplomacy with them.[16]

In their pro-Engagement open letter,[17] the signatories argued that Trump's militarized anti-China rhetoric, together with the trade war, risked creating the type of zero-sum security dilemma diplomacy the United States should be trying to avoid. Many question what America a risen China threatens. For one think tanker, today's "China is a threat to the George H.W. Bush new security concept that we mustn't allow the emergence of any regional hegemon."[18] Referring to post–Cold War optimism in U.S. foreign policy circles and the expansive view of American capabilities that came with it, this interviewee went on: "We all understand what that concept comes from ... it's born of a certain era and a certain sense of what we're capable of. And at the time, it was a radical departure from our traditional concepts of security. And I think we've forgotten that. Because we've gotten accustomed to that concept and it is now baked in."[19]

Against the Trump administration's rhetoric that previous U.S. policies had sought to "change China," the Engagers charge that in reality it was the Trump administration that was failing to accept China as it is. For the Engagers, while the Chinese government is engaging in policies and actions we find abhorrent, Engagement as policy—engagement with a small *e* we might call it—remains the best way to keep America safe while advancing its interests.

The Competitive Coexisters

The development of Strategic Competition as frame and policy under the Trump administration stimulated the consolidation of a new group of broadly pro-Engagement China experts I term the "Competitive Coexisters." Unlike

---

[16] China interview 078, 27 September 2021, via video call.

[17] See M. Taylor Fravel, J. Stapleton Roy, Michael Swaine, Susan Thornton, and Ezra Vogel, "China Is Not An Enemy," *Washington Post*, July 19, 2019, https://www.washingtonpost.com/opinions/making-china-a-us-enemy-is-counterproductive/2019/07/02/647d49d0-9bfa-11e9-b27f-ed2942f73d70_story.html.

[18] China interview 083, 12 October 2021, Washington, DC.

[19] China interview 083, 12 October 2021, Washington, DC.

the Engagers, the Competitive Coexisters are less motivated to defend the old Engagement as frame and policy and more energized by the question of how to promote cooperation within a new competitive climate inherited. Critical of the rhetorical and conceptual basis of Strategic Competition, yet recognizing that 2022 is not 2002, the group seeks a broader understanding of the U.S. national interest than zero-sum competition with Beijing. In the think tank space, the Competitive Coexister group includes Brookings's Ryan Hass, New America's Samm Sacks, and Damien Ma from the Paulson Institute. The Competitive Coexisters also have a strong base in new media outlets, such as Kaiser Kuo's *Sinica* podcast, Jeremy Goldkorn's *SupChina*, and roving China watchers Graham Webster and Matt Sheehan.[20]

For the Competitive Coexisters, the rejection of Engagement was a political or tactical move by the Strategic Competitors rather than a rational policy response to changing conditions in China. Like the Engagers, Competitive Coexisters worry about threat escalation, the securitization of China in the American political mind, and the creation of faits accompli, in which future leaders are locked into conflict even where they might hope to escape.

For the Competitive Coexisters, like the Engagers, China is more than the Chinese Communist Party and its military-security apparatus. Competitive Coexisters deeply care for Chinese people too, often having strong connections to real Chinese people. As one told me, "I have friends there, friends I would give a kidney to."[21] For another senior legal academic, "There's people who have become very close friends who we have no contact with. . . . I think a lot of us feel starved for that type of contact right now."[22] Like the Engagers, the Competitive Coexisters do not deny China is going through a period of increased authoritarianism. But unlike the Strategic Competitors, the Competitive Coexisters do not see the change as having been inevitable, nor a return to openness impossible.

While the Competitive Coexister group varies internally about how necessary the change in China policy developed by the Trump administration was, they see the "competition" frame as vague and problematic—smuggling in imagery of great power struggle ill-suited to the reality of a multipolar, globalized world. Moreover, the imagery of competition with Beijing ignores important domestic challenges America faces. This willingness to cast a critical gaze at America when considering China marks the Competitive Coexisters off from the anti-Engagers and, to an extent, the Engagers themselves. Here the generational difference between the Competitive Coexisters and the Engagers becomes salient. Where many of the Engagers came of educational and professional age during

---

[20] See https://supchina.com; https://gwbstr.com/. See Eliot Chen, "Matt Sheehan on How China Is Shaping Its AI World," *Wire China*, 20 August 2023.
[21] China interview 083, 12 October 2021, Washington, DC.
[22] China interview 093, 10 November 2021, via video call.

the heady years of opening to a still exotic China—roughly the 1970s through the early 1990s—the Competitive Coexisters did the same in a very different domestic and international context. The Competitive Coexisters thus view current debates against a backdrop of post-9/11 cultural malaise, including a marked concern about the future of democracy and the socio-psychological effects of technological change.

Originally, I thought to label this group the "New Engagers," in part to capture the generational dynamic. But as one Competitive Coexister requested, "Rather than calling it the new engagers, please call it something... between competitive coexistence or managed coexistence. I don't know. Ryan [Hass] has something like 'competitive interdependence.' Just don't saddle this group with the word 'engagement.'... You can tell I care about this group."[23] Engagement is politically toxic, this Coexister explained: "I don't know anybody who would say that they are not on board with the strategic competition frame. Right?"[24] As a consequence, "I wouldn't wear a name tag that said that I was a competitor. I don't love that. [I prefer] something... like 'responsible' or 'managed coexistence' or something [like] 'prudent coexistence.' I mean, honestly, even coexistence is sometimes fraught, but it's way, way better than engagement."[25]

The Competitive Coexisters accept that Engagement is over. As one senior think tanker explained, now "the real policy division is between those who seek to manage [competition] or win [it]...... For me, the issue is okay: this is a competition long term, high stakes, high costs in all likelihood, given the complexity of the world.... The goal should be to manage competition as well as possible in support of clearly defined American interests over the long term, knowing we're going to win some and we're going to lose some."[26] For them, the competition is not zero sum, and so winning makes no sense. Hence,

> I'm a manager. I don't think there's any other way to come at it. It's too complex. We're also constrained, domestically and internationally. So we need to name our interests. We need to prioritize. We need to be very honest about costs.... Doesn't mean we sing the Internationale, but we don't prevail in this competition. No one's honest about costs. [The anti-Engagers] are very clear about what we object to about China, and they like to stick a finger in the eye and, you know, usually for good reason. But what does this cost?[27]

---

[23] China interview 103, 25 March 2022, via telephone.
[24] China interview 103, 25 March 2022, via telephone.
[25] China interview 103, 25 March 2022, via telephone.
[26] China interview 083, 12 October 2021, Washington, DC.
[27] China interview 083, 12 October 2021, Washington, DC.

For the Competitive Coexisters, "Foreign policy begins at home."[28] Against arguments that the United States should invest domestically to compete with China—from childcare to infrastructure to vital manufacturing materials and components—for many Competitive Coexisters, the United States should do those things *because they are good regardless*. Competitive Coexisters are also marked by concerns over possible implications of a new cold war with China, particularly anti-Asian sentiment in the United States and possible violence.[29] Others marry concerns over prudent policymaking toward Beijing with a wish to promote female voices in the traditionally male-dominated national security space.[30]

The Anti-Engagers

As I explored in Chapter 2, the anti-Engagers see Washington as locked with Beijing in a long-term competition across geopolitics, economics, and technology. As one former Defense Department planner turned think tanker reflected, "How do I look back at [Engagement] historically? As an epic failure. I don't claim to have had sort of perfect clairvoyance or anything like it on the China challenge. But, I think, looked at empirically, I agree with Mearsheimer: we basically enabled the rise of our superpower rival without holding them to the commitments that they made, say in the WTO."[31]

At the core of the anti-Engager group are the Strategic Competitors—those who theorized and then effected the shift away from Engagement, first from within the Trump administration, later continuing under Joe Biden. The group also includes those within the broader China-watching community supportive of the new frame of strategic or major power competition. The group is, broadly speaking, bipartisan, despite the clear importance of the Trump presidency for the change in rhetoric and approach.

Although Pottinger and his team were at the heart of shift from Engagement to Strategic Competition, the anti-Engagers as a group is wider. Their military-security view of the China challenge resonated with others inside and outside government. For example, organizations like the U.S.-China Economic and Security Review Commission and the Center for Strategic and Budgetary Assessments and Project 2049, along with its director, Randall Schriver—are in a similar place and have been for some time. So too, crucially, are a group of

[28] As outlined by Council on Foreign Relations president Richard Haass (2014).
[29] Russell Jeung and Jessica Lee, "Rivalry without Racism: Can America Compete with China and Avoid Fueling Anti-Asian Hate?," *Foreign Affairs*, 28 July 2021, https://www.foreignaffairs.com/articles/united-states/2021-07-28/rivalry-without-racism.
[30] Anne-Marie Slaughter and Samm Sacks, "Changing the Face of Sino-American Relations," *Project Syndicate*, April 2, 2021, https://www.project-syndicate.org/commentary/us-china-alaska-summit-diplomacy-women-by-anne-marie-slaughter-and-samm-sacks-2021-04.
[31] China interview 094, 16 November 2021, via video call.

Democratic-affiliated experts and organizations—many with connections to the Center for a New American Security (CNAS)—including current NSC Asia director Kurt Campbell, and other members of Biden's team, such as Ely Ratner and Rush Doshi. Despite the turnover of administration from Trump to Biden, therefore, the operating mode within the U.S. government remained hostile to Engagement as policy and frame.

The Strategic Competitors' dominance challenged America's China watchers to adapt to the new reality: either rethink their own views, defend the old approach, or advocate a perspective yet more critical of China and the CCP. In this sense, the Strategic Competitors group includes—and has drawn inspiration from—long-standing experts who have changed their interpretations of the wisdom of Engagement, including Jerome Cohen, Winston Lord, Orville Schell, and David Shambaugh. Previously associated with America's embrace of China in different ways—as academics, journalists, diplomats, and activists—they have all become China skeptical. For one, we might call these "lapsed" or "disillusioned Engagers."[32] As Shambaugh notes in a review of recent trends in U.S.-China relations, for example, while some argue for a "'balance' between cooperation and competition," others, including Shambaugh, "find the scope for concerted and coordinated cooperation to be very limited" and see "full-spectrum competition" as reality, desirable, and necessary.[33]

Like Engagement before it, Strategic Competition occupies the mainstream view—the intellectual center of gravity—within the Washington think tank space—as evidenced by its position at core think tanks such as CSIS's China Power Project, CNAS, and even Brookings and the Council on Foreign Relations. The group also includes mid- and early-career military-security specialists, like Elsa Kania,[34] Oriana Mastro,[35] Elbridge Colby, and Hal Brands.[36] Several China-skeptic journalists also fall into this category, such as Andrew Browne,[37] James Mann,[38] John Pomfret, Bill Bishop,[39] and, before joining the marines, Matthew Pottinger.

---

[32] Personal communication with the author.

[33] Shambaugh 2023: 376. For Shambaugh's account of the demise of Engagement, see "Q&A: David Shambaugh on Why U.S. Engagement with China Is Already Dead in Spirit," *Wire China*, 7 November 2021, https://www.thewirechina.com/2021/11/07/david-shambaugh-on-why-u-s-engagement-with-china-is-already-dead-in-spirit/.

[34] PhD student at MIT and adjunct senior fellow with the Technology and National Security Program at the Center for a New American Security.

[35] Center fellow at the Freeman Spogli Institute for International Studies and courtesy assistant professor in political science, Stanford University.

[36] Henry A. Kissinger Distinguished Professor of Global Affairs at the Johns Hopkins University School of Advanced International Studies.

[37] Editorial director of the Bloomberg New Economy Forum. Previously of the *Wall Street Journal*.

[38] Longtime journalist, including as chief of the Beijing bureau of the *Los Angeles Times*, 1984–87.

[39] Bishop is the editor of the *Sinocism* newsletter, which he founded after a career as an entrepreneur and media executive in China. *Sinocism* currently has over 170,000 subscribers.

The boundaries of the anti-Engager camp are nevertheless fuzzy; the aforementioned might well disagree with their inclusion. Take, for example, a China expert such as Elizabeth Economy. Is Economy a Strategic Competitor or a Competitive Coexister? Forthright scholarship focused particularly on Chinese leader Xi Jinping's role in the PRC's global ambitions would suggest a closer affinity to the Strategic Competition position than that of the Engagers or the Competitive Coexisters.[40] Yet Economy has not been as critical of long-standing policy as others, highlighting what ties the center of the Strategic Competitor group together.

Beyond the question of inclusion, then, the degree of "groupness" of the anti-Engagers is also debatable. No suggestion of homogeneity is implied here. What is implied is a shared location or positioning within the China field. The expression of that location is the belief that Engagement did not work—that U.S. policy was predicated on an economic and political opening in China that has not taken place, and a mistaken belief that America could "change China," rendering Engagement in need of replacement. Some focus more on the rise to power of Xi Jinping, some on the fundamental nature of the Chinese Communist Party, some say another successor might have gone the same way. For all of them, however, the United States is locked in a long-term competition with China, of China's, not America's, choosing. The United States, they believe, must recognize this and mobilize all its economic, military, and diplomatic resources for the challenge.

The New Cold Warriors

The anti-Engagement camp includes an important subgroup of China critics, many of whom take a line more strident than the Strategic Competitors—the New Cold Warriors. Convinced that China is not just a competitor but already an enemy, all support Strategic Competition as a frame for U.S.-China relations because it is explicitly couched as a rejection of Engagement, the long persistence of which many consider a dangerous failing on the part of America's foreign policy elite. For the New Cold Warriors, the first Cold War is not just a metaphor for contemporary U.S.-China relations,[41] moreover, but a very real description of what they see as a new period of global existential struggle for the hearts and minds of people around the world in which the United States and China are now embroiled, necessitating the expenditure of all military and economic resources on the part of Washington.[42]

As noted in Chapter 2, these strident China critics include military-security hawks and some neoconservatives. Former secretary of state Mike Pompeo is an

---

[40] See Economy 2022c.
[41] Brands and Gaddis 2021.
[42] See, for example, Spalding 2022.

important node in the group.[43] Pompeo was a key figure as the Trump administration shifted America's approach to China, channeling the economic, military, and economic critiques of China running through the Trump team's approach. As he reports in his recent autobiography, *Never Give an Inch,* he told business leaders they should prioritize U.S. national security interests vis-à-vis China over profits, telling one health sector CEO: "Why do you think the Chinese like you so much?" He didn't appreciate the question.... But he knew as well as I did that his access to senior Chinese leaders was not secured by his good looks or brains but from the fact that he was simply their next target."[44] For Pompeo, "No segment of American society is safe from the CCP's United Front operations, which are run out of the Chinese embassy in DC."[45] Advised by historian and New Cold Warrior, Miles Yu,[46] Pompeo highlights a concern with China that encompasses the ideological critique of some neoconservatives and right-wing Republicans. Recalling a proposed speech at MIT—"Assuming MIT to be an open, tolerant, pro-America Campus"—canceled due to concern for the safety of students of Asian heritage, Pompeo notes that MIT is "awash in Chinese money."[47] Pompeo wears his CCP sanctions, announced shortly after leaving office, as a badge of honor: "It means we did our job to hold China accountable."[48]

The New Cold Warrior group includes those with a professional interest in Taiwan and the military-security threat from China—such as Ian Easton and Mark Stokes from the Taiwan-funded Project 2049. Easton is the author of a 2019 report on the military balance around the island titled *The Chinese Invasion Threat*.[49] A declassified version of a report for the Department of Defense, the report ran through various invasion scenarios, concluding, at the time, that "Taiwan has little to fear of invasion for right now."[50] Given the serious logistical difficulties the PLA and People's Liberation Army Navy (PLAN) will face to take and hold Taiwan, Easton considered mobilization would provide further warning time to Taipei and outside forces. Easton's report was objective, therefore, but anti-Engagement in tone—by openly assuming China's desire to retake Taiwan by force—and in the assumption that the United States would respond to prevent such an outcome. In a subsequent work—a "must-read for anyone who

---

[43] See Bob Davis, "Q&A: Mike Pompeo on Sounding the Alarm about China," *Wire China,* 19 March 2023, https://www.thewirechina.com/2023/03/19/mike-pompeo-on-sounding-the-alarm-about-china/.
[44] Pompeo 2023: 298–99/498. Kindle edition consulted.
[45] Pompeo 2023: 300/498. Kindle edition consulted.
[46] See https://www.hudson.org/foreign-policy/are-us-china-new-cold-war-miles-yu.
[47] Pompeo 2023: 304/498. Kindle edition consulted.
[48] Pompeo 2023: 308/498. Kindle edition consulted.
[49] Easton 2019.
[50] Easton 2019: 272.

cares about freedom's future"—according to Pompeo's blurb, Easton provides another take on Xi Jinping's "final struggle" to shape a world safe for autocracy.[51]

The New Cold Warrior sub-camp also includes long-standing public critics of the CCP—such as Gordon G. Chang,[52] Newt Gingrich,[53] Bill Gertz,[54] and journalists critical of U.S. China policy, such as the *Washington Post*'s Josh Rogin.[55] Unlike those who point to the CCP's strength and longevity, Chang has remained consistent since his 2001 book *The Coming Collapse of China*, where he describes an internally weak regime on the brink of failure and prone to outward aggression to maintain domestic control.[56] Chang has become a trusted commentator on mostly right-wing outlets, such as Fox News. From within the media mainstream, meanwhile, Rogin has used his perch at the *Post* to maintain public awareness about Beijing's misdeeds, such as large-scale military incursions into Taiwanese airspace, while cautioning about efforts to restart Engagement as policy, especially in the economic sphere.[57]

Advocates of a human rights-focused foreign policy, such as Peter Mattis of the Jamestown Foundation,[58] the American Enterprise Institute's Michael Mazza,[59] Axios's Bethany Allen,[60] and strategist Isaac Stone Fish,[61] are on similar ground, as are several younger congressional staffers and politicos. As detailed further in the following chapter, although coming from a human rights perspective, these mostly younger China watchers thus share a broad position on the nature of the new cold war with China with a set of most more senior military and national security China hawks. Defense consultant Jonathan Ward, for example, has issued another call for a coordinated response to China's "vision of victory," while *The Hill* opinion contributor Joseph Bosco has—like Rogin—sought to keep Washington's watchful eye on Beijing.[62]

---

[51] Easton 2022.
[52] Chang 2001.
[53] Gingrich 2019.
[54] Gertz 2000.
[55] Rogin 2021.
[56] Chang 2001.
[57] See, among others, "China Is Testing the West. We Shouldn't Back Down," *Washington Post*, 23 December 2021, https://www.washingtonpost.com/opinions/2021/12/23/china-is-testing-west-we-shouldnt-back-down/; "Americans Shouldn't Be Forced to Invest in China's Military," *Washington Post*, 27 August 2020, https://www.washingtonpost.com/opinions/global-opinions/americans-shouldnt-be-forced-to-invest-in-chinas-military/2020/08/27/e027b6f4-e89f-11ea-97e0-94d2e46e759b_story.html; "The State Department Is Wrong to Play Down China's Bad Actions," *Washington Post*, 16 March 2023, https://www.washingtonpost.com/opinions/2023/03/16/state-department-softening-china/.
[58] Mattis 2018).
[59] https://globaltaiwan.org/2021/12/vol-6-issue-24/#MichaelMazza12152021.
[60] Allen 2023.
[61] Stone Fish 2022.
[62] See, among others, Joseph Bosco, "Biden Needs to Upgrade Weapons to Ukraine, Defense Commitment to Taiwan," *The Hill*, 4 April 2023, https://thehill.com/opinion/international/3931586-biden-needs-to-upgrade-weapons-to-ukraine-defense-commitment-to-taiwan/.

A further, important, anchor is Committee on the Present Danger–China, which collects a group of strong China critics with a civilizational view of the threat posed by Beijing—such as former Trump advisors Steve Bannon and Peter Navarro.[63] In so doing, the CPD-China amplifies criticisms of author and journalist Peter Schweizer that the Biden administration is soft on Beijing due to Joe Biden's son, Hunter's, business dealings.[64] The CPD-China in turn connects current China critics with long-standing opponents of U.S. policy, self-labeled the "Blue Team"—a playful inversion of the military tactic of "Red Teaming"[65]— discussed further in Chapter 5.

For the New Cold Warriors, the approach brought in by Trump usefully focused U.S. attention on developing a robust China policy, while offering the rhetorical space for calling what—for them—China is: a threat. In short, the New Cold Warriors believe much of what the Strategic Competitors believe, but cast in darker and more urgent terms. For them, China is a bad international actor, a serial human rights abuser, and a clear military-security threat to American hegemony—particularly evident in the naval sphere.[66] Before Strategic Competitor Rush Doshi's work on China's "long game" to challenge U.S. power, and Michael Pillsbury's own *Hundred Year Marathon*, New Cold Warriors like Navarro had come to the conclusion that China has a real plan to emerge as a global great power by 2049, the 100-year anniversary of the CCP's victory in the Chinese civil war.[67] Former naval intelligence officer James Fanell, for instance, warned with growing urgency of the PLAN's growing strength, rendering the next 10 years a "decade of concern" in U.S.-China relations.[68]

This depiction of the predominant groups within the China expert community is not intended to capture each group's views in their entirety. Given both the nuances of people's opinions and the presence of in-betweeners—those who do not fit neatly in any box—the task is impossible. Nonetheless, these sketches capture the contours of broad camps holding opposed views as articles of faith. The Engagers, the Competitive Coexisters, the Strategic Competitors, and the New Cold Warriors believe what they believe.

---

[63] https://presentdangerchina.org/.
[64] Schweizer 2022. See "Release: The Chi-Den Administration: Is It Possible to Defeat the CCP If Our Leaders Work for It?," 30 March 2023, https://presentdangerchina.org/release-the-chi-den-adm inistration-is-it-possible-to-defeat-the-ccp-if-our-leaders-work-for-it/.
[65] Michael J. Waller, "Blue Team Takes on Red China," *Insight on the News*, 4 June 2001, 23–25.
[66] See Canfield 2002; Easton 2022; Mosher 2017; Schweizer 2022; Spalding 2022; Stone Fish 2022; Ward 2019.
[67] Navarro and Autry 2011.
[68] "China's Global Naval Strategy and Expanding Force Structure: Pathway to Hegemon." Fanell's testimony in a hearing before the U.S. House of Representatives Permanent Select Committee on Intelligence, May 17, 2018, https://docs.house.gov/meetings/IG/IG00/20180517/108298/HHRG-115-IG00-Wstate-FanellJ-20180517.pdf.

The question is, *why*? The following two chapters explore the professional and personal commitments leading people to "just believe what they believe." Before turning to them, the remainder of this chapter explores the historical development of the pro- and anti-engagement camps in the American China-watching community.

Knowing Your Enemy... and Your Friends

What explains the views of the Engagers and the anti-Engagers? Again, in some ways, they represent common divisions in any country's foreign policy thinking, typically labeled hawkish and more dovish dispositions. According to others, they are baked specifically into the DNA of America's international relations. However, the Engager/anti-Engager groups are not inevitable divisions, nor did they emerge overnight in recent years. The Engager/anti-Engagers have more proximate origins, with antecedents in the Cold War and immediate post–Cold War years. The aim here is not to adjudicate between competing understandings of the past, to access the past *as it really was*. Rather, the task is to explore America's China experts' beliefs of about the longer-term origins of the views to which they subscribe. However sparse on details, vague on specifics, and contested, if experts believe a given depiction of history, it forms part of the reality they act upon.

The Origins of Engagement and Anti-Engagement

Engagement, as community, frame, and set of policy manifestations, is inextricably tied to the origins and development of the field of China scholarship and expertise in the United States. Many interviewees traced the interconnections to divisions sown during the McCarthyite Red Scare of the late 1940s and 1950s, and the fate of China sympathizers and alleged communists like Owen Lattimore and John Paton Davies.[69] The opening of the early 1970s, on this account, was in part the making up for lost time, as U.S. knowledge and understanding of China was sharply curtailed following what would become three decades of separation with Beijing.

A second occasional referent is the Committee of Concerned Asian Scholars (CCAS) and splits in the nascent China community over the Vietnam War.[70] As a recently retired think tanker, longtime China hand, and well-known Engager

---

[69] Newman 1992; Davies 2012.
[70] See Lanza 2017; Committee of Concerned Asian Scholars 1972.

explained, "There were two fundamentally different kinds of people in CCAS."[71] The first group "believed that the U.S. was, essentially, an imperialist power and was behaving as an imperialist power and, therefore, you could never have a sensible foreign policy unless you had ... revolutionary change in the governance of America, so that the Vietnam War was a reflection of the rotten core of the United States. That's, sort of, one group of people."[72] This first group included historians "Perry Link,[73] Paul Pickowicz[74] to a lesser extent ... [the] group that was opposed to the Vietnam War."[75] One historian recalls it like this:

> We all start going to China. I can remember very vividly in the spring of 1980, I was with the first group of scholars that went to China on the U.S.-China exchanges, and those things were announced when diplomatic relations were established in January of seventy-nine. It came in a great hurry, and, quite frankly, my interpretation is that the more senior or the more conservative scholars decided, "I don't want to do this now. Let's see how it goes." And so the people that went were all us panda huggers or whatever you want to call us—I mean the people who were sympathetic to the revolution.[76]

A second group within the CCAS, this interviewee described

> were people like me that had been in the army, and there were lots of people that saw the war as a tragic mistake. We didn't know what the hell we were doing and we stumbled into this, and, once you stumble in, you dump more in. But it wasn't because of the nature of America. It was a mistake, so get the war over and learn the lessons and move on. America's not rotten. So one [group] was, essentially, sort of, conservative people that thought this was a terrible mistake, and others were revolutionary [and] thought America was the mistake.[77]

For this interviewee, then, a division within the CCAS during the 1970s lies at the heart of the contemporary split within America's China experts. The division centers on moral outrage at developments in China, rather than America. On the one hand are those who opposed the Vietnam War as a mistake, rather

---

[71] China interview 035, 23 March 2018, Washington, DC.
[72] China interview 035, 23 March 2018, Washington, DC.
[73] Distinguished professor of comparative literature/Chinese at the University of California, Riverside, and emeritus professor of East Asian studies, Princeton University, where he taught from 1973 to 1977 and 1989 to 2008. Between 1977 and 1988 Link taught at the University of California, Los Angeles.
[74] Distinguished professor emeritus of history and Chinese studies at the University of California, San Diego.
[75] China interview 035, 23 March 2018, Washington, DC.
[76] China interview 075, 7 March 2019, Berkeley, CA.
[77] China interview 075, 7 March 2019, Berkeley, CA.

than a sign of America' moral corruption, leading to an opposition to the Trump administration's development of a strategy of Strategic Competition coupled with tough, anti-China rhetoric. On the other hand, and "I hesitate to put Perry [Link] in one group and me in the other, but that's the way I look at it," one Engager noted, are those who "are morally outraged at what China is doing. Before, they were equally morally outraged at what the U.S. was doing. So they seem to me to be people that are always morally outraged, right?"[78] What was "one unified group when it came to the Vietnam War, after the war—the Vietnam War ended in seventy-five—this group flew apart."[79]

Yet what some term the paradigm of "Engagement 1.0"—Engagement as frame, community, and policy that held from the opening and normalization in the 1970s through the 1990s—contained both factions within the CCAS and beyond. Driven by "the desire for an entente against the Soviet Union,"[80] deepening interconnections between China and the United States—beginning, admittedly, from a very low base—made Engagement and the development of China studies in the United States one and the same, practically as much as intellectually. As the above think tanker notes, splits within the CCAS were papered over by a shared, pragmatic concern with gaining and widening interconnections with China. Although "every bit as opposed to the Vietnam War as Perry Link was, [together] we organized to try as young Asian scholars to do research and write and speak in public and have teachings about the history of Vietnam, the history of China, how it bore on America's involvement in Asia in a war that we all disagreed with."[81]

As community, not just frame and policy, however, Engagement 1.0 was based on an ever-expanding set of practical relations, a shaking free of the strictures of the 1950s and 1960s and the last vestiges of McCarthyism. For one longtime China watcher and business leader, during the 1980s, "It became possible to be a China expert, or somebody focused on China, not in academia or journalism, for example, and government, where the engagement with China, particularly after normalization, it expanded so enormously and so rapidly. There so many agencies at the U.S. government, and not just the security ones."[82]

The events of 4 June 1989 in Tiananmen Square rocked the Engager community, effectively destroying Engagement 1.0 as frame, community, and policy. The leadership in Beijing's response proved that, beneath surface rhetoric of opening in China, coupled with good diplomatic relations and military cooperation with

---

[78] China interview 035, 23 March 2018, Washington, DC.
[79] China interview 035, 23 March 2018, Washington, DC.
[80] China interview 061, 20 November 2019, via telephone.
[81] China interview 035, 23 March 2018, Washington, DC.
[82] China interview 068, 29 January 2019, via telephone.

the United States, at its core the CCP remained a repressive force. Tiananmen thus opened up fissures within the Engager community.

On one side were those concerned with human rights in China, many the same "morally outraged" members of the CCAS. Without the Cold War anti-Soviet logic, some China watchers, including human rights critics and some anti-communist holdovers from before the opening, no longer advocated sweeping China's human rights record under the rug in search of encouraging ever-closer engagement with the West. This sentiment had public expression in Congress, as prominent Republicans and Democrats, notably Nancy Pelosi, sought action against China.[83] On the other side were those hopeful of putting Tiananmen behind them as soon as possible, including some academics, think tankers, and, notably, members of the business community.[84]

Beyond the Engagers, the fallout from Tiananmen consolidated a group of anti-Engagers with a notable partisan bent, namely in the form of the stridently China-skeptical Blue Team during the late 1990s. Blue Teamers accused the Clinton administration of being enmeshed in webs of corruption with the PRC that included hundreds of thousands of dollars in Chinese contributions to the national committee of the Democratic Party, the theft of American military technology, and Chinese espionage activities in the United States.[85] Such accusations entered the political mainstream via a June 1998 report of a House Select Committee on U.S. National Security and Military/Commercial Concerns and with the People's Republic of China, released after redaction by Republican chair Christopher Cox.[86] While a group of leading security scholars rebutted the report's conclusions as "inflammatory" and based on serious mischaracterizations and oversimplifications,[87] the broad sense that U.S. intelligence agencies had missed important warning signs in relation to the PRC gained traction in Washington. At the Pentagon, the Office of Net Assessment issued a December 2020 report critical of U.S. intelligence on the issue of Taiwan's defense.[88] Blue Team members also took part in a commission tasked with overseeing CIA analysis on China, which found no evidence of explicit bias,

---

[83] Mike Ives, "Nancy Pelosi Has a Long History of Criticizing China's Human Rights Record," *New York Times*, 2 August 2022, https://www.nytimes.com/2022/08/02/world/asia/nancy-pelosi-china-history.html.

[84] Hung 2021.

[85] China interview 072, 19 February 2019, via video call. For example, "Ex-DIA Analyst Admits Passing Secrets to China," *Washington Times*, 23 June 2006.

[86] *U.S. National Security and Military/Commercial Concerns with the People's Republic of China*, available at https://www.govinfo.gov/content/pkg/GPO-CRPT-105hrpt851/pdf/GPO-CRPT-105hrpt851.pdf.

[87] Alistair Iain Johnston et\ al., "The Cox Committee Report: An Assessment," December 1999, at https://carnegieendowment.org/pdf/npp/coxfinal3.pdf.

[88] See Bill Gertz, "Panel Finds CIA Soft on China," 6 July 2001, *Washington Times*, https://www.washingtontimes.com/news/2001/jul/6/20010706-024147-1037r/.

but an "institutional predisposition" to minimize issues of concern in relation to China.[89] The Blue Team is analyzed in greater depth in Chapter 5.

Divisions within today's China field have their roots in long-standing disputes over the nature of the Chinese regime and the proper basis for U.S.-China relations, disputes going back several decades. This is not to suggest stasis. Contemporary splits are not replicas of previous fissures. How could they be, given turnover in personnel and changes in international context, most notably the shifting balance between Washington and Beijing? Rather, the question is when, how, and why these latent divisions in the China field developed into the clear distinctions between Engagers and anti-Engagers under Trump and Biden.

To the Open Letters: The Consolidation of the Engagers and Anti-Engagers

Today's splits within the China expert community in the United States have their roots in Cold War schisms among policymakers, academics, and think tankers, which impacted both how those in the fields perceived political developments in the late 1980s and 1990s and—for those in positions of authority—how they went about designing policy. Even younger scholars entering the respective fields years, if not decades, after the Cold War's end see the years before and after 1989 as formative for their profession and the broader context of policy. The question remains how expert and policy struggles after the Cold War were transformed between the 1990s and recent years. While China policy was always polarized to a greater and lesser extent, what processes led to the specific polarization witnessed since the mid-2010s?

The previous two chapters explored China policy in some detail. The next section picks up the story on the China side with the effects of the Trump election, the hypothetical of a Clinton victory in 2016, and the second of the book's puzzles: why the Biden administration continued with the operationalization of Strategic Competition as frame and policy, rather than returning to Engagement.

The Engagement Community Fractures

Would Engagement have been replaced had the 2016 election turned out differently? The answer revolves around the individuals a Clinton administration would have imported. A Clinton administration would likely have also adopted a stiffer stance toward Beijing, as—in addition to Defense Department

---

[89] Gertz, "Panel Finds CIA Soft."

planning—stronger notes of skepticism were gaining volume in the broader China field prior to 2016.[90] Events like Beijing's declaration of an Exclusive Economic Zone in the South China Sea were increasingly difficult to square with the Engagement frame. Even pro-Engagement experts adopted a cautious tone.[91] Engagement would therefore likely have come under strain whoever had won in 2016. Trump's tough rhetoric and economic policy measures nonetheless accelerated the polarization of Engagement as policy and community, visible outside the Beltway as 2018 proceeded.[92] Trump's approach forced China professionals to take sides, not only on the substantive issue of the trade war, but on the history of U.S. strategy toward Beijing. A notable consequence was the emergence of strange political bedfellows and an increasingly restricted space for those in favor of something like Engagement.

Engagement's demise ran orthogonally to common divisions in U.S. politics—left/right, liberal/conservative, hawk/dove. Human rights advocates found common cause with military hawks and opponents of Chinese economic practices. Libertarian groups pushing restraint found allies in leftist critics of the military industrial complex.

One human rights advocate, for example, not a natural Trump supporter, was "thrilled" with the shift in China policy: "I don't care who is in the White House . . . , not because it's poking a stick in the eye of an extremely repressive and dangerous China . . . but . . . on its own terms."[93] As a journalist, based in Beijing in the Trump years, confessed, "I'm . . . an outlier on this among journalists because most people are so knee-jerk. . . . They hate [Trump] so much that they can't even contemplate the idea that . . . he could ever possibly in any way ever have been right about anything under the face of the sun. And I think that a lot of times Trump probably actually got, like, a corner of the stick that was the right stick."[94] A former diplomat, stationed in Beijing in the mid-2010s with a remit covering business and trade, "congratulate[d] him [Trump] for doing something [about China]. I don't think his strategy was very good. . . . But something had to be done."[95]

A senior humanities professor described how "the [conservative] American Enterprise Institute invites me and they pretty much love what I say. On the other hand . . . I'm writing for the *New York Review of Books* . . . so there's a left/

---

[90] Blackwill and Tellis 2015.
[91] David Lampton, "The Tipping Point," speech co-organized by The Carter Center and the Shanghai Academy of Social Sciences," May 2015, available at https://www.cirsd.org/en/horizons/horizons-summer-2015--issue-no4/the-tipping-point---can-we-amplify-what-we-have-in-common-. On China's actions in the South China Sea, see Hayton 2015; Kaplan 2014; Poling 2022.
[92] Evan Osnos, "Making China Great Again," *New Yorker*, January 2018, https://www.newyorker.com/magazine/2018/01/08/making-china-great-again.
[93] China interview 041, 24 March 2018, Washington, DC.
[94] China interview 107, 13 July 2022, via video call.
[95] China interview 109, 7 September 2022, via video call.

right split there."[96] As this professor, with a long track record of China human rights issues activism explained, "In the middle . . . , people don't warm to my critical point of view as much. In the business world a few years ago, this sort of 'Rumble through and everything will be OK' . . . those people just don't want to hear about human rights or topics like that."[97]

Campbell and Ratner's critique of Engagement in early 2018 encapsulated the emerging dynamic.[98] As a former State Department official stated plainly, Campbell and Ratner's was "a political argument."[99] Far from hawkish critics, Campbell and Ratner were *internal* critics of a policy with which both were previously involved. "They're Engagers . . . [Their argument is] an exaggeration based on the need to position themselves politically." One think tanker and Competitive Coexister explained their motivations.

> In part . . . this reflects their views. They have been skeptical for some time of the benefits of deep engagement with China and have wanted to push American policy toward a more competitive approach. . . . They saw a window of opportunity when the ground was shifting and realized that they could really have an impact at a moment when things were sort of all up in the air, because for 40 years previously in Democratic and Republican administrations we'd transferred from center-right to center-left to center-right and center-left administrations. [You could] sort of close your eyes and listen to the words [of] Steve Hadley and Susan Rice and say they're not that distinguishable, right? They sort of all blend together with little bit of variance on the margins, right? And this was a moment where the whole playbook was being thrown under the bonfire and something was being written afresh and they had a chance to impact it.[100]

Specifically, Campbell and Ratner sought a distinctly Democratic viewpoint, with future political appointments in mind. "They're positioning a Democratic Party position. . . . They're the Democratic Party foreign policy realists . . . defining that position as it relates to China and East Asia."[101] As one think tanker and Competitive Coexister complained, Kurt and Ely

> worried that the Republicans would take control of China as a political issue and own it for the next generation unless the issue could be neutralized.

---

[96] China interview 027, 2 February 2018, via telephone.
[97] China interview 027, 2 February 2018, via telephone.
[98] Campbell and Ratner 2018.
[99] China interview 055, 12 November 2018, Washington, DC.
[100] China interview 091, 9 November 2021, via telephone.
[101] China interview 055, 12 November 2018, Washington, DC.

And the way to neutralize the issue and to prevent sort of being significantly outflanked on it was to agree that engagement had failed and a new approach was needed, right, to be defined later. And from that bipartisan consensus, it's sort of generated a momentum of its own.[102]

(In my interviewee's opinion, "It's not necessarily the responsibility of the Democratic Party to provide a veneer of legitimacy to making a radical departure" in U.S. China policy. "Adjustments were more appropriate than radical shifts" like the ones they called for.)[103]

The fracturing of the center of the Engagement community prompted a defense of Engagement mounted by a group of mostly former diplomats and policymakers,[104] who argued that, while things had not turned out as planned, Engagement was sound at the time. As one former diplomat explained, "the current rhetoric . . . about the 'failure' of 'the engagement policy' is a gross misreading of the intentions and substance of U.S. policy."[105] For J. Stapleton Roy, as a political argument, the notion that Engagement failed "is the contention that Presidents Nixon, Ford, Carter, Reagan, Bush #41, Clinton and then Bush #43 and Obama *all* misconceived 'the national interest' and proceeded willy-nilly into something called an 'engagement' strategy toward China."[106] Other leading Engagers echoed Roy's warnings.[107] Discarding Engagement, they argued, risked "demonizing" China precisely when pressing global problems required cooperation.

Intellectually, such arguments had weight. Yet within a polarized context, they were suspect. Indicatively, few interviewees proactively defended Engagement, only a small number of typically senior Engagers expressing the optimism to which Engagement's critics point. Although China was not without problems, one such senior Engager commented, "We've got a huge trade deficit, and the Chinese are trading unfairly. . . . Xi Jinping is not the continuation of Jiang Zemin and Hu Jintao . . . [but] most foreign policies don't last 40 years. . . . And on balance, it's been positive . . . so let's not blow up the world."[108] But by 2018, such previously mainstream views were increasingly marginal. In the words of one long-standing and prominent Engager: "What's in the middle of the [political] road? Roadkill."[109]

---

[102] China interview 055, 12 November 2018, Washington, DC.
[103] China interview 091, 9 November 2021, via telephone.
[104] For example, Roy 2018; Chas Freeman, "On Hostile Coexistence with China," remarks at Stanford University, 3 May 2019, https://chasfreeman.net/on-hostile-coexistence-with-china/.
[105] China interview 069, 7 February 2019, via email correspondence.
[106] Roy 2018.
[107] Fravel et al., "China Is Not An Enemy."
[108] China interview 035, 23 March 2018, Washington, DC.
[109] China interview 035, 23 March 2018, Washington, DC.

"Not blowing up the world" and presenting new policy solutions in the face of accepted shifts in predominant views of China are two different propositions, which over time led the pro-Engagement group to struggle to maintain coherence. As one interviewee described, the Engagers as a group are "splitting apart."[110] The reports of two U.S.-China expert task forces highlight the processes by which the group's unity frayed. The issue is who participates, who signs, and who dissents—choices part intellectual, part political, and part personal, as explored further below.

A first task force presented its "recommendations for a new administration" in February 2017.[111] Describing a "China now more assertive in Asia, more mercantilist in its economic policies, and more authoritarian in its domestic politics,"[112] the report urged the Trump administration to adopt a policy characterized by "greater firmness, more effective policy tools, and a greater insistence on reciprocity."[113] However, while reflective of the overall shift in thinking in Washington, DC, the report affirmed that "a rising power need not become an adversary of the established power" and, reprising the basic principles of Engagement, concluded that the Trump administration "should recognize that U.S. engagement with China from a principled position of strength in Asia has generally served these interests well."[114] It is telling, then, that the report split individuals broadly on the same page on China. Of the participants, 12 chose to sign—including former US ambassador to China Winston Lord and Kurt Campbell—while six other participants, including Jeffrey Bader, Mike Lampton, Douglas Paal,[115] Stape Roy, Michael Swaine, and declined.

When a second report appeared in February 2019, tellingly titled *Course Correction: Toward an Effective and Sustainable China Policy*,[116] some original participants declined to take part at all. As one explained, "At some point, you just become too far away from the group. Why would I sign that . . . ? And so you can see this thing [the Engager group] . . . pulling apart."[117]

Donald Trump's election in 2016 was a crucial turning point in U.S.-China relations, fostering a polarized China field, splintering and weakening a hitherto

---

[110] China interview 035, 23 March 2018, Washington, DC.
[111] See *US Policy toward China: Recommendations for a New Administration*, https://china.ucsd.edu/_files/02072017_US_China_task-force_report.pdf.
[112] *US Policy toward China: Recommendations for a New Administration*, 65.
[113] *US Policy toward China: Recommendations for a New Administration*.
[114] *US Policy toward China: Recommendations for a New Administration*.
[115] Distinguished fellow in the Asia Program at the Carnegie Endowment for International Peace. Formerly vice chairman of JP Morgan Chase International and director of the American Institute in Taiwan (2002–2006). Paal served on the National Security Council staffs of Presidents Reagan and George H. W. Bush, as director of Asian Affairs and senior director and special assistant to the President (1986–1993).
[116] http://china.ucsd.edu/_files/2019-CourseCorrection.pdf.
[117] China interview 035, 23 March 2018, Washington, DC.

largely united group of pro-Engagement China experts. This is not to say that China policy would have stayed unchanged had Clinton, not Trump, triumphed in 2016. Objective changes in China—from Beijing's militarization of the South China Seas to everyday difficulties faced by U.S. companies in doing business in China—would have Clinton too to adopt a tougher line with Beijing, as evidenced by the continuation of Trump's China policy under his successor. It was clear by 2016 that, as almost all interviewees told me, China had changed. However, it is unlikely the Clinton team would have fashioned such a signal move away from the status quo. But Trump's election brought in a set of experts from the China-watching community and the broader national security community. Some were outsiders and wildcards, like Navarro. Some, like Matthew Pottinger, were not exactly outsiders but brought a different set of foci and shaper criticisms of China. In "calling China bad," launching the trade war, and moving away from Engagement policies of economic and strategic dialogue toward a new security-framing of the China challenge, the Trump administration was supported by some, like the old Blue Teamers, who were out of the mainstream of the China field—of which more in Chapter 5. The result was a thoroughly polarized Engagement frame, policy, and community.

Conclusion

In the rare cases when accounts of U.S. foreign policymaking explore the policy preferences of individuals, especially beyond the top decision-making positions, they typically stop at hawkish or dovish disposition, or a description of policy preference and general worldviews. By exploring the formation and crystallization of the more complex social universe of America's China experts, the present chapter highlights the inadequacies of such an approach. Questions remain. *Why* do America's China watchers believe what they believe? In the following two chapters, I explore the professional and personal origins of the major distinctions traced here. America's China experts, I show, believe different things due to the types of experts and, indeed, types of people they are.

4
Professional Status Oppositions and the Wisdom of Engagement

The previous chapters have told a familiar story, if with a widened aperture: foreign policy knowledge communities divided over how forcefully to respond to national security challenges. Should the United States engage with China? Or is engagement impossible given the bellicose authoritarian regimes currently in power in Beijing? Under Trump, a paradigmatic turnover saw the Engagers replaced by the Strategic Competitors, with Biden bringing in his own set of Strategic Competitors to continue the tough policy toward Beijing. Is there anything more to the story?

We should expect so, because policy struggles are never *just* struggles over policy and the ideas and beliefs underpinning them. They are *always* also contests over prestige, influence, and legitimacy within a professional space—here the American national security community, and its sub-communities of China and Russia experts. The China and Russia expert fields are what can be termed "interstitial" arenas, where individuals with different affiliations—think tanks, universities, media, and business organizations—struggle over recognition as experts.[1] The larger goal, at least for some, is policy influence, as professionals seek access to the "revolving door." To access the revolving door, one does not need to be correct all of the time, but one has to be *legitimate*.

When did Engagement stop being a legitimate policy position? How did Strategic Competition become legitimate? The common-sense answer is that changes in China since the 2000s weakened the claims of the Engagers, thereby weakening the Engager group itself. Put differently, the Strategic Competitors won the battle for policy control because their description of the world is superior to that of the Engagers, who are naive, rosy-eyed, either too gullible or too weak in believing the United States must accommodate China's views as the price for good relations.

In this chapter, I show there is more to the story of the end of Engagement with China than the victory of the Strategic Competitors at the level of policy ideas. What appears at first blush as purely a debate over ideas—was Engagement with

---

[1] Medvetz 2013.

China a failure? What forms of engagement remain possible, or how should the United States operationalize strategic competition?—is always connected with struggles over prestige, status, reputation, and legitimacy. As important as who argues what is *where* they argue it from, be it a social position of greater or lesser prestige, influence, reputation, and power. What matters is not only what experts argue but also who gets to argue as an expert at all. This chapter shines a light on this often-ignored aspect of contestation over national security policy and the struggle over the meaning of China expertise.

The chapter first traces a fault line separating the China Engagers and anti-Engagers—the former holding traditional markers of intellectual prestige and policymaking experience that distinguish them from those either lacking such status or holders of narrower, national security expertise, often not limited to China. Here calls for "nuanced" knowledge of China betray different worldviews and investments. Essential for those with Engagers with professional interests in cooperation, nuanced knowledge of China is not seen as a necessary good by those for whom the nature of China—as a pressing military-security threat—is clear, rendering arguments for a partial return to Engagement weaker than those seeking firmer policies. The shift from the Engagement frame and community to Strategic Competition was thus also effected by different *kinds* of China expertise entering office under Trump, particularly those with a military-security orientation.

Engagement in the U.S. China Field's Professional Status Competition

Professional competition over Engagement with China presents an axis of opposition distinct from that between the Engagers and anti-Engagers described in the previous chapter. In the place of a "with us or against us" political logic, professional competitions are over knowledge, prestige, and status: in short, recognition as an expert. Both before and during the Trump administration, Engagement as frame supported and was supported by claims to "nuanced" understanding of China. In that context, key organizations in Washington—notably two congressional commissions on China—provided much-needed legitimacy to skepticism about Engagement and its bearers, and it was some of the very same Engagement-skeptics who effected the shift to Strategic Competition.

The Professional Bases of Engagement and Anti-Engagement

The Engagers not only believe different things about U.S.-China relations than do their anti-Engagement colleagues; they also see themselves, and are seen by their anti-Engagement counterparts, as different *types* of experts. The Engagers' belief in engaging with China as the best approach for dealing with Beijing is not merely a policy preference but a reflection of their understanding of what it means to be a China expert, to *know* China—as explored over the next sections. The anti-Engagers reject the implication that only the Engagers can know China, asserting that their own understandings of the intentions of the CCP are not only equally legitimate, but more correct, and were for too long ignored.

The open letters of 2019 represent an—admittedly partial—snapshot of the professional bases of the Engager and anti-Engager communities. To recap, the first letter was an attempt by a set of China watchers critical of the shift to Strategic Competition under the Trump administration urging U.S. elites to reject a framing of China as an enemy. Tough U.S. policy, they asserted, risked making China an enemy. In so doing, the authors[2] and the signatories nailed their Engager credentials to the mast.

Before exploring the Engagers' professional credentials more closely, it is important to stress that too much can be read into the open letters. Penning and signing such letters reflects a certain kind of investment in policy and desire for policy relevance, often from people less relevant to policy discussions than they would like to be. Often more indicative than who signs is who does not, which may suggest a desire to keep one's head below the parapet in case an opportunity to serve in government comes along. Among other absentees, Thomas Christensen, Elizabeth Economy, Michael O'Hanlon,[3] Harry Harding,[4] Melanie Hart,[5] Winston Lord, Evan Madeiros,[6] Andrew Nathan,[7] Daniel Rosen,[8] David Shambaugh, Orville Schell, and Susan Shirk are notable in not signing the

---

[2] Academics and former policymakers Taylor Fravel, J. Stapleton Roy, Michael Swaine, Susan Thornton, and Ezra Vogel. Vogel (1930–2020) was then Henry Ford II Professor of the Social Sciences, Emeritus, at Harvard University.

[3] Director of research and senior fellow of the Foreign Policy Program at the Brookings Institution.

[4] University professor emeritus and professor emeritus of public policy at the University of Virginia.

[5] Center for American Progress. At the time of writing, Hart was China policy coordinator for undersecretary of state for economic growth, energy, and the environment.

[6] Penner Family Chair in Asian Studies and the Cling Family Senior Fellow in Asian Studies Relations at Georgetown University. Madeiros previously served as advisor to treasury secretary Hank Paulson working on the U.S.-China Strategic Economic Dialogue (2007–2008), later spending six years on Obama's National Security Council, first as director for China, Taiwan, and Mongolian affairs and later special assistant to the president and senior director for Asian affairs.

[7] Class of 1919 professor of political science at Columbia University.

[8] Cofounder of the Rhodium Group independent research firm. Former senior advisor for international economic policy at the National Economic Council and National Security Council (2000–2001).

"China Is Not an Enemy" letter. Signatories often cross between professional location, having positions—either synchronously or over the course of a career—in academia, business, think tanks, and government. In short, the letters do not exhaust the Engager community, nor are all signers "Engagers" in the same way. Those hoping for a more systematic delineation of the professional bases of the Engager and anti-Engager crowds will be dissatisfied. Surely a more determinative connection between professional position and policy disposition is possible, they believe. Unfortunately, the world doesn't work that way—the same policy views can emerge from different professional investments, just as different policy convictions can come from the same professional investments.

Nevertheless, the letter suggests a more expanded typology of Engagers. The 94 signatories are split between think tankers (20), academics (40), and a third group made up of former policymakers, government officials, and leaders of business and cultural organizations like the National Committee of U.S.-China Relations (27).[9] Many, if not most, have affiliations that cross these categories and thus could be placed in more than one. Nonetheless, each is invested in practical ways with deepening America's engagement with China.

A first group is professionally located in major East Coast think tanks and professional schools, with the Brookings Institution, Johns Hopkins School of Advanced International Studies (SAIS), and Peterson Institute for International Economics (PIIE), all heavily represented. Eleven members of this group were China-focused experts, including well-known Engagers, including Richard Bush (Brookings), Robert Daly (Wilson Center), Jamie P. Horsley (Paul Tsai Center at Yale), David Lampton (SAIS), Cheng Li (Brookings), Yawei Liu (Carter Center), Douglas Paal (Carnegie Endowment for International Peace), Jonathan Pollack (Brookings), and Anne Thurston (SAIS). Seven think tankers had an economics focus, including Fred Bergsten (PIIE), David Dollar (Brookings), Yukon Huang (Carnegie), and Nicholas Lardy (PIIE). Their role in think tanks is predicated on the ability to maintain and deepen links with Chinese individuals and organizations.

The same push to forge and maintain links to individuals and organizations in China applies, if at a further degree of remove from Washington policymaking, for another third, approximately, of the signatories who were academics, mostly from elite northeastern universities, plus top China centers at Stanford, Berkeley, and Michigan. A heavy concentration of the group (some 19) were political scientists, including Kevin O'Brien (Berkeley), Bruce Dickson (George Washington), Mary Gallagher (Michigan), Avery Goldstein (Pennsylvania), Robert Jervis (Columbia), Robert Keohane (Princeton), Jean Oi (Stanford),

---

[9] The remainder (7) are interested outsiders to the China field, not easily slotted into these categories.

Elizabeth Perry (Harvard), Barry Posen (MIT), Shelley Rigger (Davidson), Robert Ross (Boston), and Scott Sagan (Stanford). Other disciplines like history (five, including Alice Miller of Stanford and Michael Szonyi of Harvard), business studies (two, William Kirby and William Overholt of Harvard Business School), law (one, Jerry Cohen of NYU), and sociology (two, Amitai Etzioni of George Washington and Andrew Walder of Stanford), were less well represented, which is probably explained by those discipline's greater distance from national security policy.

A final sub-group of former policymakers (13) is made up of those diplomats, advisors, and officials involved in the Engagement as the major operating mode of the U.S. government: Jeffery Bader;[10] David Gordon;[11] Philip Gordon;[12] Morton Halperin;[13] Clifford A. Hart Jr.;[14] Ambassador Carla Hills;[15] Mickey Kantor;[16] Herbert Levin;[17] Kenneth Lieberthal; Daniel W. Piccuta;[18] David Shear;[19] Anne-Marie Slaughter;[20] James Steinberg;[21] and Daniel B. Wright.[22] Other officials from the military and intelligence services (nine in number) include Dennis Blasko;[23] Bernard Cole;[24] Peter Dutton;[25] Thomas Fingar;[26] Paul Heer;[27] John Mclaughlin;[28] Michael Nacht;[29] and Paul Pillar.[30] A small but important final group are located outside government, in business organizations

---

[10] Special assistant to President Obama for National Security Affairs at the NSC (2009–2011).
[11] Head of research at Eurasia Group and former director of policy planning at the State Department (2007–2009).
[12] Assistant secretary of state for European and Eurasian affairs (2009–2013), subsequently deputy national security advisor (2021–2022) and national security advisor to Vice President Kamala Harris (2022–).
[13] Director of policy planning at the State Department (1998–2001).
[14] Former U.S. consul general to Hong Kong and Macau (2013–2016).
[15] United States trade representative (1989–1993).
[16] United States trade representative (1993–1996) and secretary of commerce (1996–1997).
[17] Staff Office for Japan and Korea on Henry Kissinger's National Security Council (1970), assistant in the National Intelligence Office for East Asia and South Asia (1981–1983), staff member on the Policy Planning Staff (1983–1985).
[18] Deputy chief of mission in Beijing (2007–2009), chargé d'affaires in Beijing (2009).
[19] Assistant secretary of defense for Asian and Pacific security affairs (2014–2016).
[20] Director of policy planning at the U.S. Department of State (2009–2011).
[21] Deputy national security advisor (1996–2000) and deputy secretary of state (2009–2011).
[22] Managing director for China and the Strategic Economic Dialogue US at the U.S. Treasury Department, under Hank Paulson.
[23] Former U.S. Army attaché in Beijing and Hong Kong (1992–1996) and senior military fellow at the National Defense University.
[24] Professor emeritus at the National War College.
[25] Former director of the China Maritime Institute at the Naval War College.
[26] Assistant secretary of state for intelligence and research (2004–2005) and chair of the National Intelligence Council (2005–2008).
[27] National intelligence officer for East Asia (2007–2015).
[28] Deputy director of central intelligence (2000–2004).
[29] Assistant secretary of defense for global security affairs (2009–2010) and assistant director of the U.S. Arms Control and Disarmament Agency (1994–1997).
[30] National intelligence officer for the Near East and South Asia (2000–2005).

and lobbies, including Craig Allen,[31] Robert Kapp,[32] James McGregor,[33] Jan Berris[34] and Stephen Orlins from the National Committee on U.S.-China Relations (NCUSCR), and Helena Kolenda[35] from the Luce Foundation.

Again, generalizing about the professional investments of the Engagers should be done with caution. The "China Is Not an Enemy" letter of July 2019 represents only a snapshot, specifically over developments under the early Trump administration. Nonetheless, the three major overlapping groups of establishment think tankers, elite academics, and former Engager-associated officials tell us something about the professional bases of Engagement.

A similar exercise can be done with the social bases of anti-Engagement, if with more caution. Unlike the "Kramer letter," which pushed back against a call for engagement with Moscow, the "Stay the Course" letter—organized by retired naval intelligence officer James Fanell[36]—did not appear in an establishment outlet, say the *Washington Post* or a more policy-focused online magazine like *Politico* or *Foreign Policy*. Appearing instead in the *Journal of Political Risk*, edited by risk analyst and strong China critic Anders Corr,[37] the letter reflected associations among an informal group of self-identified anti-Engagers.

Some 57 of the 133 U.S.-based signatories (as of 18 July 2019) were retired armed forces. Others included long-standing and well-known China critics, including commentator Gordon Chang, journalist Bill Gertz,[38] and sociologist Stephen Mosher.[39] Mark Stokes[40] and Ian Easton[41] from Project 2049 signed on, as did Frank Gaffney,[42] chair of the re-formed Committee on the Present Danger China and member of the Blue Team—on which more later. As with the letter of Swaine et al., some signatories represented exceptions that proved the rule.

---

[31] President, U.S.-China Business Council (2018–).

[32] President, U.S.-China Business Council (1994–2004).

[33] James (Jim) McGregor is chairman of public relations firm APCO Worldwide's greater China region.

[34] NCUSCR vice president.

[35] NCUSCR president (2005–).

[36] Fanell's near 30-year career in naval intelligence concluded with the role of director of intelligence and information operations for the U.S. Pacific Fleet, ending in 2015.

[37] Strategic analyst. Founder of Corr Analytics.

[38] Editor and reporter for the *Washington Times*. Gertz is discussed further in the following chapter.

[39] President of the Population Research Institute and author of *Hegemon: China's Plan to Dominate Asia and the World* (New York: Encounter, 2023). Mosher was barred from China after reporting on alleged forced abortion practices while conducting fieldwork in his rural site and was later dismissed from his Stanford PhD program. See Wallace Turner, "Stanford Ousts Ph.D. Candidate over His Use of Data on China," *New York Times*, 26 February 1983, https://www.nytimes.com/1983/02/26/us/stanford-ousts-phd-candidate-over-his-use-of-data-on-china.html.

[40] Executive director.

[41] Senior director.

[42] Founder and president of the Center for Security Policy and former assistant secretary of state for international security affairs (1987).

With some exceptions, such as University of Miami political scientist June Teufel Dreyer, signatories held professional investments distinct from the Engagers.

To Know China: Or, Who Get to Call Themselves China Experts?

As suggested by the new sociology of expertise, China expertise is less natural than grounded in a specific-type of performance of unique insight into China. In addition to general attributes of professional esteem—affiliations with prestigious universities and think tanks, public notoriety, prizes won—the performance of China expertise is underpinned by special markers like language ability, time spent "in country," and demonstrated commitment to understanding China.

China experts attach special significance to language skills, frequently distinguishing between those with real linguistic ability from those merely "throwing around buzzwords" in Chinese. As one senior legal academic, a strong proponent of Engagement with China, explained, "My worry is that there are people in the field now ... who are ambitious to become China watchers, [but are] people who speak on China without much language ability ... without in many cases much real experience living a day-to-day life in China and understanding what the political and governance culture is.... That makes me really sad."[43] For most Engagers, China is too complex to be able to speak authoritatively about without deep immersion in the country.

Generalists such as Elbridge Colby and Ely Ratner are thus viewed skeptically by some self-professed China specialists. Colby is "not a China scholar. He doesn't really know China," one senior think tanker told me. "Everything contributes [and so] I don't slam the door on any of this stuff, but it's the absolutist case [Colby makes] that worries me, especially when it always involves the omission of diplomacy."[44] For his part, "Ely was one of these Ash Carter fellow travelers back in 2014, 2015, 2016. He was always super hawkish on China, very outraged about the South China Sea stuff. He's a kind of a Southeast Asia person. ... I don't consider him to be a China person, to be honest. He doesn't have any real China experience."[45] As this interviewee went on,

> Everyone now is talking about China constantly, even if they've never met a Chinese person.... It's very easy for me to spot, but impossible for normal people to spot, the difference between someone who's actually lived in China or speaks Chinese or knows something about China and people who are

[43] China interview 084, 12 October 2021, via video call.
[44] China interview 083, 12 October 2021, Washington, DC.
[45] China interview 085, 22 October 2021, via video call.

transferring over from the Middle East or transferring over from Russia or transferring from the IR [international relations] theory group [who have] never thought about China before, but because now it's all of a sudden the flavor of the month, I have to focus on this. So that's a huge part of the story, I would say. All these former Soviet Cold War people now do China—Mike McFaul, Hal Brands,[46] Tom Wright,[47] all these people who never met a Chinese person in their life."[48]

For one Engager, these individuals have important *viewpoints*, not *expertise*. "There's a difference. . . . Viewpoint tends to be mostly military folks, intel[igence] kind of people . . . some generalists, IR theorists . . . people who are just more on the popular end of things."[49] Some slip into the territory of having less a viewpoint than a "shtick," "because there's a difference between having an argument and having a shtick."[50] Gordon Chang, this interviewee suggested, has a shtick: for Chang, China is weak and on the point of collapse,[51] a view—in my interviewee's opinion at least—unsupported by on-the-ground observation. For a prominent mid-career think tanker, John Mearsheimer fits the bill too: even if

> he's right in pure realist logic, it's ethically monstrous to me [to argue as Mearsheimer does that the United States should have sought to prevent China's rise]. . . . I lived in China for 10 years [and] we're going to deny 1.4 billion people an opportunity at the good life? Mearsheimer has never really been to China or hasn't spent a long time [there]. He's thinking purely about nation-state on nation-state.[52]

Time spent in country was another frequently noted marker of true China expertise. As a diplomat turned academic noted, "I'm deeply skeptical of people who spend six months or a year, maybe even a year and a half doing some dissertation research and otherwise are always based overseas. . . . I don't think they really can catch all the nuance."[53] Beyond time spent in country, time out of country was also noted as a factor in the degree of insight one can profess. "China changes so fast that if you haven't been there in the last year, you're really a bit out of touch," this interviewee continued.[54]

---

[46] Senior fellow at the American Enterprise Institute. See Brands 2022; Brands and Beckley 2022.
[47] Senior director for strategic planning at the National Security Council and former director and senior fellow of the Center on the United States and Europe at the Brookings Institution.
[48] China interview 085, 22 October 2021, via video call.
[49] China interview 083, 12 October 2021, Washington, DC.
[50] China interview 083, 12 October 2021, Washington, DC.
[51] See Chang 2001.
[52] China interview 095, 19 November 2021, via video call.
[53] China interview 081, 4 October 2021, via video call.
[54] China interview 081, 4 October 2021, via video call.

Critics respond that language ability plus time spent in country does not automatically confer insight. One well-connected, longtime China watcher and fierce opponent of the CCP noted how "a lot of the people who speak very good Chinese are not very good analysts. The difficulty of Chinese becomes a kind of code. So you have to break it first. But once you've broken it, it still does not necessarily mean that that you are capable of good and analysis.... Language skill and analytical skill are not the same."[55] For such critics, former National Security Council China director Matt Pottinger is a rare example of someone combining both. "Matt Pottinger has both analytical skill and policy skill. Usually people have one or the other. Very seldom do they go together."[56] But in general, in this interviewee's opinion, "Frankly, the knowledge of the CCP is very low among the so-called experts on China. And you can quote me on that, in fact. [I've been] saying that for decades."[57]

Others question the incentive structure produced by the need to go to China. "I have to be able to go to China," one legal academic stated plainly.[58] "I have to be able to speak to my interlocutors. I have to be able to travel around the country without concern, right? If the relationship gets to a point where I can't do those things, then that directly impacts my ability to do my research."[59] For anti-Engagers, this admission raises the suspicion that analysts who need to go to China are thereby beholden to the Chinese in some way, potentially biased in their conclusions.

Given that Engagers and anti-Engagers disagree about whether they agree that the need to engage China brings with it pro-China sympathies, a safer space for the type of knowledge sought is "analysis." As a think tanker explained,

> My tribe, if I were to articulate one, is really not one about what position you hold. It's about the quality of your thought process.... I find myself aligning with people... who show their math.... I don't so much care where you come down. I don't hold the preexisting ideological view about what China policy should be. My... strongly held ideological conviction is diagnosis needs to be separated from prognosis.... I'm genuinely fascinated about what the hell's going on in China.[60]

---

[55] China interview 090, 8 November 2021, via telephone.
[56] China interview 090, 8 November 2021, via telephone.
[57] China interview 090, 8 November 2021, via telephone.
[58] China interview 080, 30 September 2021, via video call.
[59] China interview 080, 30 September 2021, via video call.
[60] China interview 095, 19 November 2021, via video call.

Similarly, for a well-known new Cold Warrior, "I'm a minority of one... I'm not doing this to build a consensus.... I'm not a political activist. I am an analyst."[61]

As a central figure in the China business field told me, "The loudest people in China today in Washington are the least informed. As you can tell, I'm no panda hugger. I'm very clear eyed. I've got great affection for the Chinese people. I spent 30 years there. I'm not anti-China, but I'm very clear on what China is up to. Let's say this: I'm anti-Xi Jinping and where he's brought China. It's really devastating what it's doing to China and Chinese people's opportunities globally. But who do you hear from in Washington on China? You hear Tom Cotton [and] Marco Rubio."[62] Cotton and Rubio are not, in this interviewee's estimation, knowledgeable interlocutors on China—they don't count as experts.

Engagement Expertise under Trump

As a community, therefore, many Engagers viewed themselves as differentiated from the sort of defense and security generalists on Trump's national security team by their attachment to China-specific expertise. Prior to Trump, Engagers used these credentials to form tight connections to the main foreign policymaking positions of the U.S. government, from where they promoted cooperation with China—differences of opinion with Beijing notwithstanding. The paradigm shift away from Engagement was therefore also a turnover in the type of China expertise held by key policymakers. For the first time in decades, a varied group of critics found themselves in the position of sharing a vision of U.S.-China relations with the occupant of the White House. For these self-professed China hawks, the demise of Engagement meant the welcome end to the influence and epistemic hegemony of the elite China hands whose connections to China had rendered it—in their view—blind to Beijing's increasing bellicosity. These critics were located institutionally outside the main international affairs think tanks, research centers, and academic departments, frequently retired from the military and intelligence services, or employed in for-profit companies, like risk consulting.[63]

Anti-Engagers viewed—and continue to view—the Engagers as disconnected from what they see as the new reality in China and Sino-U.S. relations. In the anti-Engager's view, the Engagers rely on academic credentials and long-standing ties to China to prove their status, both of which they see as politically

---

[61] China interview 089, 2 November 2021, via video call.
[62] China interview 108, 20 August 2022, via video call.
[63] For example, the signatories to "Stay the Course," 18 July 2019, https://www.jpolrisk.com/stay-the-course-on-china-an-open-letter-to-president-trump/.

compromised—a view difficult to dismiss given the Trump administration's politicization of Engagement, described above. While "all very respected and all very erudite," one interviewee noted, this erudition enabled the Engagers to evade the criticism of other China watchers, particularly on the issue of China's increasingly militaristic behavior on the global stage.[64] The problem, my interviewee went on, is that the Engagers had been "indoctrinated" in the "Kissinger School," meaning a "corpus of thought on China, which was to say . . . China's not really an aggressive nation. They've always been an inward nation."[65] This interviewee's career in intelligence, spent reading Chinese propaganda and classified material, leads to a thorough repudiation of the view that China is not a threat to the United States. Nothing could be further from the truth, for this anti-Engager.

Engagers, by contrast, question the anti-Engagers' knowledge of China, noting a relative discrepancy in terms of academic qualifications and credentials, and criticizing the anti-Engagers for their lack of contacts inside China. Engagers think that the anti-Engagers' forthright views on China policy are a reflection of their focus on defense and security matters. This leads the anti-Engagers, in the Engagers' view, to miss the broader cultural, historical, and political factors in China's behavior. Crucially, the Engagers also consider the anti-Engagers' perspective to reflect their lack of the same credentials the anti-Engagers' believe compromise the Engagers' arguments. Engagers expressed deep concern about the lack of influence of established China hands in the Trump administration—with Matthew Pottinger at the NSC again an important exception. As one senior China scholar argued, the problem with the Trump administration was that it failed to recruit or retain any "good China watchers."[66]

The expertise of the anti-Engagers therefore differs markedly from that of the Engagers. Each side was aware the debate was in part over their respective status as China experts, which amplifies ill will—as detailed in the next chapter. An important background context frequently noted by Engagers in particular was the sense that Trump's China policy reflected a broader crisis of expertise. As one China expert in the legal field suggested, the most troubling thing about Trump's China policy was "the more general rejection of expertise" it reflected.[67] Acknowledging bias—"I, of course, speak from a point of extreme bias because I consider myself an expert on foreign relations in the China sphere, so I think we are valuable people," said one business school academic—this interviewee affirmed that Engagement's chief critics are not China experts at all.[68]

---

[64] China interview 072, 19 February 2019, via video call.
[65] China interview 072, 19 February 2019, via video call.
[66] China interview 067, 9 January 2019, via video call.
[67] China interview 029, 26 February 2018, via telephone.
[68] China interview 029, 26 February 2018, via telephone.

Together, these impressions highlight the interconnections between the professional investments of different China experts and their views of Engagement and U.S. China policy under Trump. Navarro et al., the previous interviewee went on, "just believe things that I simply don't believe, which is that we are on our way to having some sort of conflict with this country, and the less economic engagement we have, the better decision-making we can have. We don't want our decision-making clouded by the facts of [America's deep interconnection with China.]" From the opposite perspective, that of the anti-Engagers, it is the Engagers' very credentials that have clouded them to the facts of Chinese aggression.

Nuance and the End of Engagement

Central to the Engagers' performance of expertise is the claim to "nuanced" understanding of China. Nuance fits with Engagement as frame—a master narrative of relations between Washington and Beijing that rejects black-and-white conclusions about China in the vaguely defined hope of improved relations going forward. For anti-Engagers, "nuance" is a term Engagers invoke to avoid accepting the undeniable facts of the China threat. With the fracturing of the Engagement community and the paradigmatic shift to Strategic Competition, members of the China field faced the challenge of adjusting their claims to nuance to new conditions. Why is a nuanced view of China needed in the face of a documented arms buildup, human rights violations in Xinjiang, and Beijing's impeding of international investigations into the origins of Covid-19? Engagers were faced with the choice to either reject Strategic Competition, and thereby risk forfeiting relevance, or to reassert the need for a nuanced approach in operationalizing Strategic Competition.

The means by which China professionals critical of anti-Engagement have sought to nuance the debate depends largely on their field position. One group, former diplomats in particular, continued to defend Engagement as a natural part of international relations. Thus, "The argument that engagement is the wrong approach is absurd. Engagement is always the right approach.... But engagement may not necessarily be done properly."[69] Noteworthy among such voices are former ambassadors Staple Roy and Chas Freeman,[70] who each argue that while things have not turned out as planned, Engagement as both policy and frame was sound *at the time*: "The current rhetoric, or narrative, about the 'failure' of 'the engagement policy' is a gross misreading of the intentions and

---

[69] China interview 027, 2 February 2018, via telephone.
[70] For example, Roy 2018.

substance of U.S. policy. It is born of ignorance—some of it willful—about the nature of foreign policy.... But even more it is an expression of a political view."[71] Baked into this perspective is a claim to a certain kind of nuanced expertise, derived from experience and exposure to China and its people, and a rejection of politicized policymaking.

Others seek nuance by focusing on historical counterfactuals. "What," one interviewee asked, "was the alternative [to Engagement]?"[72] At what point in the last four decades should Engagement have been abandoned? After Tiananmen? At the time of the Taiwan Straits Crisis of 1996? "If you're saying that engagement was such a terrible idea, you know, what should the U.S. have done differently?"[73] Another China watcher, professionally located at a top business school, who agreed that Engagement had a utopian tinge, said, "I don't think there was anything else we could have done.... If we had tried to contain China in that late 1990s, where would we be?"[74] Still others questioned why the role of America—especially U.S. businesses—in facilitating China's rise was absent from the failures of Engagement debate. For another popular China watcher, "I mean it's not like China came here in the middle of the night, broke into our house, and stole our factories, and brought them over to Shenzhen..... It was American actors with perfect agency who did this. This is on us."[75]

Both members of the old Engager and Competitive Coexisters camps stress the importance of nuance to the formulation of good policy: "Policies need to be a lot more nuanced," one explained.[76] Another think tanker and Competitive Coexister who worked in the Obama administration harked back to its approach: "President Obama's view was ... you make good policy. Good policy will produce good results. [The anti-Engagers'] argument sort of flips it on its head, which is politics should drive policy, right? And I'm not comfortable with that... . Good politics isn't always good policy."[77]

As a performance, however, China expertise is based on recognized understanding of China, not knowledge of the United States or American politics and society. Consequently, few interviewees questioned America's motives and the nature of American national interest in China's rise. One retired political scientist asked why "anybody [should] want to be subordinated to the United States ... as if they don't think their own nation is great to be independent is really a radical American parochial discourse that's no good for anybody."[78] For another

---

[71] China interview 069, 7 February 2019, via email.
[72] China interview 030, 28 February 2018, via telephone.
[73] China interview 066, 6 December 2018, Cambridge, MA.
[74] China interview 029, 26 February 2019, via telephone.
[75] China interview 050, 2 May 2018, via telephone.
[76] China interview 103, 25 March 2022, via telephone.
[77] China interview 091, 9 November 2021, via telephone.
[78] China interview 028, 21 February 2018, via telephone.

former ambassador, "We need to be clear about what's at stake [in the China challenge]. It is—not yet anyway—the defense of the United States. It's the defense of American primacy in the Pacific.... [But] American primacy like any primacy is not eternal and cannot be preserved forever."[79] For them, "The thesis is that China must not be allowed exercise influence, governance, or, you know, achieve a military capability in its own neighborhood.... That's pretty absurd."[80] Such reflections, however, were rare.

Alastair Iain Johnston's attempts to nuance the end-of-Engagement debate through empirical assessments of such notions as China as a "revisionist" or "status quo" power typifies the dynamic.[81] Johnston demonstrates that China cannot be understood as seeking to overturn the "international order" since there is no single international order. In some regional and issue-specific areas China strongly upholds the global order, such as over arms control agreements, open trade, and the norm of sovereign independence.[82]

Anti-Engagers reject such arguments and the attempt to nuance the debate over U.S. China policy they typify. Especially for many in the military and intelligence, the aim of the China's military buildup is clear: "To kill Americans. You can't be rosy about things when you have that fundamental reality."[83] As one China scholar with military experience explained, you could ask theoretical questions such as, "Is China really challenging the international order?" But for people in the Defense Department, "We don't care.... The weapons systems the Chinese are developing can only be understood as targeting the United States."[84]

For one Engager in the legal field, consequently, "It's frustrating and discouraging to me because when I began my career, there was an idea that our job was to study and interact with another nation, but from a fairly objective viewpoint. So you could celebrate successes, criticize difficulties. But it wasn't such a one-note wonder as it is now, right?"[85] A strong position pro- or anti-China might be expected from "people at the Council on Foreign Relations in New York or Washington, or people in government or, you know, the people that populate think tanks."[86] Inside the Beltway, for this interviewee, "If you're young and ambitious and you stand up and say, 'Well, things are very complex in China, and here's the good, the bad, [and] the ugly,' you may not progress in accordance with your ambitions."[87] What is more discouraging, the interviewee went on, is "that

---

[79] China interview 061, 20 November 2019, via telephone.
[80] China interview 061, 20 November 2019, via telephone.
[81] Johnston 2003.
[82] Johnston 2019.
[83] China interview 045, 5 April 2018, San Francisco.
[84] China interview 043, 4 April 2018, San Francisco.
[85] China interview 084, 12 October 2021, via video call.
[86] China interview 084, 12 October 2021, via video call.
[87] China interview 084, 12 October 2021, via video call.

it's sort of infected the views of people who present themselves to the world as objective scholars.... They're doing it from, you know, the purchase of political science departments, law schools, sociology departments."[88]

Opponents of Engagement see in the views of its senior defenders the doubling down on four decades of head-in-the-sand thinking on China. For Michael Pillsbury, former consultant to the Defense Department and advisor to President Trump, China's leaders are committed to a long-term plan to replace America as the leading superpower, beginning with removing the U.S. Navy from the western Pacific.[89] One leading critic of Engagement explained the issue as follows: "For 40 years we engaged. We engaged on [the Engagers'] advice, on their expert testimony.... They were all the intellectual foundation for advising every administration, Republican and Democrat to engage, to engage, to engage. ... You can't say that China's got nice intentions when they build seven islands in the South China Sea. And that's really what busted open the floodgate, in my opinion, was the actual undeniable physical evidence."[90] For the anti-Engagers, the facts are clear: the Chinese "are out to clean our clocks."[91]

Enter the Generalist: The Expanding China Field and the Demise of Engagement

From a small and relatively collegial group—as compared with the old Sovietologists—the American China community compartmentalized and fragmented over time.[92] As one journalist reminisced, an annual dinner of China hands—journalists, diplomats, and think tankers—that congregated in the 1980s would be impossible today because the American China community has ballooned to multiple thousands.[93] As late as the late 1980s and into the 1990s, Asia was still a backdrop to U.S. foreign policy. In the early 1980s, only the Brookings Institution, SAIS, and George Washington University's Institute for Sino-Soviet Studies had serious capacity in Washington for studying the PRC. Subsequent years saw a proliferation of China-related positions at the major think tanks and research organizations, as well as an increase in the number of think tanks themselves, including the Center for a New American Security, founded 2007), the Center for American Progress (started in 2003), the Global Taiwan Institute (initiated in 2016) and, beyond the Beltway, the School of

---

[88] China interview 084, 12 October 2021, via video call.
[89] Pillsbury 2015.
[90] China interview 072, 19 February 2019, via video call.
[91] China interview 072, 19 February 2019, via video call.
[92] On the latter, see Engerman 2009.
[93] China interview 051, 31 July 2018, Washington, DC.

Global Policy and Strategy at the University of California at San Diego (beginning in 1986).

The number of specialists on the PRC in the U.S. government has mirrored this expansion. At the State Department, "Now there is virtually no desk... that doesn't need a China expert," a senior academic explained.[94] As one former diplomat noted, "One of the things that's changed clearly is who's considered [a] China expert has broadened a fair amount... almost every issue from technology to trade has the China component."[95] From cyber to climate to global fisheries, the PRC impacts U.S. interest formation requiring specialist understanding. "When I was in Beijing [during the late 1970s]," one ex-diplomat recalled, "the entire staff of the U.S. Liaison Office numbered 25." A few years later, the American mission had grown to approximately 100. When this interviewee returned in the late 1980s as head of section in the U.S. Embassy in Beijing, he supervised 13 officers with a staff of some 250. Later, when he was a political appointee under President George W. Bush, "The embassy in Beijing had metastasized to a behemoth of well over 1,000 staff while my old political section had grown to 30-plus officers."[96] The sheer size of the community, here solely within one section of the U.S. Embassy in the PRC, militated against, for this interviewee, close personal contacts compared to subsequent generations.

The China field's expansion is far from a negative phenomenon, bringing more specialized knowledge and openings for a wider range of individuals than traditionally. As one mid-career think tanker explained, "We have a far wider variety now of younger people with really strong China backgrounds.... It used to be [a]... cohort of top China scholars, and everybody would just sort of listen to them. Now it's a lot more dynamic."[97] As one think tanker stated, China watchers are everywhere in Washington, DC, providing knowledge on a plethora of issues. Take pandas, for example. "If you talk about zoologists and the community in the United States that wants to protect pandas in China, ... those are China [watchers.] If you want to know about pandas, go over to the Resources for the Future," a Washington nonprofit.[98] An important recent pattern, then, in the American China community is its spectacular growth, in terms not just of numbers, but of the diversity of its expertise.

Nonetheless, many interviewees lamented the loss of collegiality and the consequent decline of the "Engager" as a particular social type, coming from a specific location within the American China community, with an associated set of pro-cooperation dispositions. In the recollection of one journalist, "There was

---

[94] China interview 039, 24 March 2018. Washington DC.
[95] China interview 088, 28 October 2021, via telephone.
[96] China interview 069, 7 February 2019, via email.
[97] China interview 049, 19 April 2018, via telephone.
[98] China interview 035, 23 March 2018, Washington, DC.

tremendous togetherness from how small the community was in the seventies." A bond formed in part because "You couldn't get to China" as a result of the "whole legacy of McCarthyism," and Engagers shared educational trajectories at the small number of top departments—like Columbia, Harvard, Michigan, Stanford, and the University of Washington—where many China experts trained. With the opening came "a tremendous sense of change, and of relief"— and opportunity.[99]

As one senior Engager explained, with the opening to China, "Our careers very much began. We saw ourselves ... picking up where the people who taught us began. And that is engage, engaging China. [China's subsequent growth] created so many opportunities, in business, in NGOs, in government for engagement in China, and the field grew substantially." The field's expansion, however, renders its boundaries less well defined. "If you're interested in economic questions, then the boundary includes the Federal Reserve System, Wall Street, corporations, with vice presidents for international relations [having] big departments that deal with China.... The bigger a community gets and the more specialized, the less of a sense of community," the senior Engager elaborated. The natural result was "more pluralism, more impersonal relationships, propping up more factionalism."[100]

Alongside expansive growth, the American China community has diversified and specialized. Although it's "very cliché, China's so big," one junior think tanker noted. "There's so much going on that you really have to specialize ... to have a competitive advantage."[101] The trend is not limited to the Beltway but extends across academia. Nor is it new. Already in 2011, political scientist Kevin O'Brien chronicled the trade-offs between the field's deepening through specialization and a "hollowing out" of the core.[102] The process underpins what many consider a growing gap between the academy and the policy community, bringing with it the weakening of the scholarly community and the disappearance of a particular type of China scholar-cum-policymaker—the *Engager*.

O'Brien's target, political science, offers a good example. There disciplinary incentive structures—particularly the rise of quantitative methods and hypothesis-testing methodology, including most recently, experiments—have pushed against the formation of generalist China expertise. "Political science [has] a real hierarchy of methods ... [and] it makes sense that somebody who wants to be successful ... would seek to do the things that are most applauded and rewarded," one interviewee observed.[103] More clearly scientific approaches

---

[99] China interview 051, 31 July 2018, Washington, DC.
[100] China interview 035, 23 March 2018, Washington, DC.
[101] China interview 052, 1 August 2018, Washington, DC.
[102] O'Brien 2011.
[103] China interview 025, 24 March 2018, Washington, DC.

occupy top status, tied also to the academic job market. "If the job market is producing, if the high-tech people are to invest," another interviewee noted, "they tend to distort it [as students] flock in that direction."[104] "If you have to choose between Chinese [language] and computer modeling," one retired political scientist argued, "you should do computer modeling."[105] Yet the trend is especially problematic in research areas like IR. "I tell students who are interested in . . . Chinese foreign policy . . . they should definitely not go into political science," he explained. "They should go do diplomatic history . . . [because] when you have a magic method which solves all problems for all places and people, why would you do something as parochial as caring about China?"[106]

Other disciplines repeat this trend, with different wrinkles, but the same implications for the formation of broadly trained China experts. For many interviewees, the core issue is the trade-off between detail and the ability to see the "big picture." Many argued that analysis of the PRC is improving—"Granular is better."[107] But for a former diplomat, too much knowledge of the trees and not enough of the forest takes "us away from the ability to synthesize from disparate elements of the relationship and away from interdisciplinary examination of China."[108] One senior political scientist recounts urging one PhD student to "expand a little." While the student did good work, "it is very narrow and . . . their demands of being convinced of something are really high. [They've] written a very, very tight dissertation. It's a typical kind of research now that has five different kinds of evidence that all point at one thing. . . . I said, 'You don't just need to repeat what you've said, we believe you now. . . . Now use up a little bit [of] what you've earned to explain to us what's—expand beyond it . . . speculate.'"[109]

Numerous interviewees thus suggested that the U.S. academy is not training "broad-gauge" China experts, as specialization in graduate school instruction hammered home early a narrow understanding of empirics.[110] The overall effect of these trends is impossible for an observer to gauge. In part, the assessment of decreased influence may be more perception than reality, with reminiscences of the influence of prominent China field figures such as Ken Lieberthal and Susan Shirk in government poorly reflecting the persistent gap between the ivory tower and government. For one prominent China historian, however, the impact seems clear: "The scholarly China-watching community is frankly less important" than it used to be.[111] Attempts to bridge the gap between the scholarly

---

[104] China interview 040, 16 March 2018, Berkeley, CA.
[105] China interview 032, 16 March 2018, Berkeley, CA.
[106] China interview 028, 21 February 2018, via telephone.
[107] China interview 014, 17 October 2017, Washington, DC.
[108] China interview 061, 20 November 2019, via telephone.
[109] China interview 031, 16 March 2018, Berkeley, CA.
[110] See also Shambaugh 2023. Examples of what might be considered broad-gauge scholarship include Brown 2020; Economy 2022b; Shambaugh 2014, 2020; Shirk 2022.
[111] China interview 039, 24 March 2018, Washington, DC.

field and the world of policy—such as the National Committee on U.S.-China Relations' Public Intellectuals Program—reflect the growing divide they seek to overcome.[112]

Whatever the truth of perceptions of a growing separation between the China field and the policy community in Washington, several interviewees pointed to related decline of the China generalist, and consequent rise in the public debate on the PRC of the foreign policy / national security generalist. As one Beltway think tanker noted, in the policy analysis community, "If you're too general, you're vulnerable," leading to the specialization pressures described above, making "the *China* generalist a dying species [emphasis added]." At the same time, however, greater media appetite for commentary on all things China offers rewards to those willing to talk on a range of topics, whether in one's wheelhouse or not, the same interviewee noted, with audiences "assuming you should know everything about everybody in the Chinese government and poverty eradication and economic growth . . . , futurology, technical advance[s] and U.S.-China relations and China-everything-else relations." Thus, at the same time as the China generalist is declining, he lamented, the putative China expert—a label mostly self-applied inside the Beltway—"basically has to be able to comment on everything."[113]

Enter the U.S. foreign policy / national security generalist. Early in the shift from Engagement to Strategic Competition in 2018, one senior political scientist sensed a rising prominence in the public debate of the non-China expert. "China . . . will be taken over by the generalists, rather than by the area studies people," he remarked, "people who know about the world market and economics or people who know about military strategy or stuff like this rather than China people." With increased salience of the PRC across the U.S. government, "It's going to go less and less to so-called China specialists . . . [because] to know about China you don't have to know about China."[114]

The centrality of military-security strategists, such as Elbridge Colby and Hal Brands, and a militarized frame on the PRC question are a case in point.[115] In his *Strategy of Denial*, Colby, a former deputy assistant secretary of defense for strategy and force development, lays out a comprehensive military approach to counter the PRC's growing international influence. Historian Brands—who shares with Colby government experience in strategy and planning as special assistant to the secretary of defense for strategic planning (2015–2016)—explores

---

[112] Public Intellectuals Program, National Committee on U.S.-China Relations, https://www.ncuscr.org/program/public-intellectuals-program; see also the Bridging the Gap project at American University in Washington, DC, https://bridgingthegapproject.org/.
[113] China interview 038, 24 March 2018, Washington, DC.
[114] China interview 028, 21 February 2018, via telephone.
[115] See Colby 2021; Brands 2022.

the lessons of the Cold War for the U.S. response to the PRC challenge. To label Colby and Brands as "not knowing about China" is unfair—both are well read and deeply engaged on the topic. The point, rather, is that they bring a specific type of knowledge to the conversation—military-security expertise—framing China in a specific, militarized, fashion.

Other examples of the trend toward increased prominence of generalists include Harvard University political scientist Graham Allison, whose *Destined for War* brought the notion of the "Thucydides Trap"—familiar in IR scholarship—to the PRC debate. The Thucydides Trap refers to the Greek historian's location of the origins of the Peloponnesian War (431–404 BCE) in the fear the rise of another state (Athens, here the PRC) aroused in an established one (Sparta, read the United States). Allison's generalist status was unquestioned, and his position in favor of engagement with Beijing acknowledged, but more than one interviewee suggested that one was not to take *Destined for War* as a serious piece of scholarship on the question of contemporary U.S.-PRC relations.[116] Niall Ferguson of Harvard University and later Stanford was another common reference, whose concept of "Chimerica" conferred on him prominence in the debate far outstripping Ferguson's regional knowledge.[117]

Beyond the rise of the military-security strategist and IR generalist, an increased prominence of China in the writings of national security commentators in the mainstream media furthers the trend toward generalists predominating in the policy debate on the PRC.[118] The *Washington Post*'s Josh Rogin has been a strident critic of the CCP, translating the Trump administration's strategy to the broader public.[119] Midway through the Trump administration, *New York Times* columnist David Brooks identified a tougher view of the PRC as a bipartisan issue in Washington, DC.[120] More recently, Nicholas Kristof and Thomas Friedman have each questioned the Biden administration's understanding of the PRC threat.[121] But the trend is not unidirectional. Not all national security generalists are PRC skeptics. Former political scientist and CNN talking head Fareed Zakaria, for one, has spoken out strongly against demonizing the PRC

---

[116] China interview 010, 25 October 2017, Washington, DC.
[117] Ferguson and Schularick 2007.
[118] See Feldman 2015; Nye 2015.
[119] See, for example, Josh Rogin, "If China Wants a Better Relationship with the U.S., It Must Behave Better," *Washington Post*, 18 June 2020, https://www.washingtonpost.com/opinions/global-opinions/if-china-wants-a-better-relationship-with-the-us-it-must-behave-better/2020/06/18/fd9e50b0-b18d-11ea-8758-bfd1d045525a_story.html. See Rogin 2021.
[120] David Brooks, 'How China Brings Us Together: An Existential Threat for the 21st Century," *New York Times*, 14 January 2019, https://www.nytimes.com/2019/02/14/opinion/china-economy.html.
[121] Nicholas Kristof, "Biden's Nightmare May Be China," *New York Times*, 30 January 2021, https://www.nytimes.com/2021/01/30/opinion/sunday/foreign-policy-china.html; Thomas L. Friedman, "Is There a War Coming between China and the U.S.?," *New York Times*, 27 April 2021, https://www.nytimes.com/2021/04/27/opinion/china-us-2034.html.

and the risks of economic decoupling.¹²² In so doing, Zakaria has echoed the views of prominent Engagers, like the Quincy Institute's Michael Swaine. IR scholar Stephen Walt, meanwhile, has questioned the commonplace that few countries prefer the Chinese to the U.S. vision of international order.¹²³ Each redirects the focus of attention regarding the PRC to U.S. domestic politics. As the Council on Foreign Relations' Richard Haass puts it, good foreign policy "begins at home."[124]

What is significant, therefore, is not the rise of the generalist per se, but rather the marginalization of a particular type of pro-engagement U.S. China expert who—in previous years—might have made arguments similar to those of Swaine, Walt, Ryan Hass, and others, *without* the association of being pro-Beijing. The issue is less the substance of the debate, therefore—over the nature and extent of China's global ambitions—than who gets to participate, with what degree of legitimacy. Over time, generalists and military-security specialists more inclined toward anti-Engagement gained a solid foothold in the China conversation and, subsequently, policymaking.

Institutionalized Engagement Skepticism

The ability of anti-Engagers to perform a legitimate kind of China expertise was facilitated in large measure by an institutionalized form of Engagement skepticism prior to Trump's election, located within particular institutions such as human rights organizations like the National Endowment for Democracy and military-security organizations like the Center for Strategic and Budgetary Assessments. Even more important, arguably, were two China congressional commissions set up after China's accession to the WTO in 2001, from which Engagement skeptics kept a close eye on developments in Beijing. In so doing, these institutions afforded Engagement skepticism and its bearers the necessary legitimacy within the China field to perform a different type of China expertise than the Engagers—a posture more forthright in its assessments of China, especially the CCP, yet still grounded in recognized Chinese expertise.

During the debate over Chinese WTO accession, many opponents feared accession would weaken U.S. leverage over Beijing—notably in the human rights sphere. As a quid pro quo, two congressionally funded commissions were created

---

[122] See, for example, Fareed Zakaria, "The New China Scare: Why America Shouldn't Panic about Its Latest Challenger," *Foreign Affairs*, January–February 2020, https://www.foreignaffairs.com/articles/china/2019-12-06/new-china-scare.

[123] Stephen M. Walt, "The World Might Want China's Rules," *Foreign Policy*, 4 May 2021, https://foreignpolicy.com/2021/05/04/the-world-might-want-chinas-rules/.

[124] Haass 2014.

to oversee China's behavior on an ongoing basis. The first was included as a provision within the legislation that gave China permanent Most Favored Nation status (H.R. 4444, 10 October 2000). The task of the Congressional-Executive Commission on China (CECC) is to "monitor the acts of the People's Republic of China which reflect compliance with or violation of human rights, in particular, those contained in the International Covenant on Civil and Political Rights and in the Universal Declaration of Human Rights."[125] A second commission—the U.S.-China Economic and Security Review Commission, or USCC—was created three weeks later on 30 October and tasked to "monitor, investigate, and report to Congress on the national security implications of the bilateral trade and economic relationship" between the United States and China.

The scope of research and testimony sought by the CECC and USCC is objective, spanning the China field. Accordingly, the twin commissions have provided an outlet for both pro- and anti-Engagement views. A February 2007 USCC hearing is indicative. The commission heard from Deputy Assistant Secretary of State for East Asian and Pacific Affairs Thomas Christensen, who articulated the George W. Bush's administration's vision of a China "that is more open, transparent, and democratic," contributing to "a global system that has provided peace, security, and prosperity to America, China, and the rest of the world."[126] Noting, tellingly, that China was not yet the "responsible stakeholder" so envisioned, Christensen said that "encouraging China to move in that direction continues to be the foundation of our policy; the question, as this Commission has correctly pointed out, is how we can most effectively do that."[127]

The commission also heard, however, from China skeptics whose ideas have formed a key part of the shift from Engagement to Strategic Competition. Journalist James Mann argued, in terms strikingly similar to those used after 2017, that U.S. policymakers were operating with a mistaken paradigm, with "Americans, particularly in our political and business elites, regularly talk[ing] as though China is inevitably destined for political change as well [as economic]."[128] For Mann, the Engagers were wrong: "While China will certainly be a richer and more powerful country 25 years from now, it could still be an autocracy of one form or another. Its leadership ... may not be willing to tolerate organized political opposition any more than it does today."[129]

---

[125] https://www.cecc.gov/about/legislative-mandate.
[126] Thomas J. Christensen, "The State of U.S.-China Diplomacy," https://www.uscc.gov/sites/default/files/2.1.2007christensen_thomas_statement.pdf.
[127] Christensen, "State of U.S.-China Diplomacy."
[128] James Mann, statement before the U.S.-China Economic and Security Review Commission hearing on "U.S.-China Relationship: Economics and Security in Perspective," 1 February 2007, https://www.uscc.gov/sites/default/files/2.1.2007mann_james_statement.pdf.
[129] Mann, statement before the U.S.-China Economic and Security Review Commission.

The next day the commission heard from Peter Navarro. Then a professor of economics and public policy at the University of California, Irvine, Navarro was not a central figure in China circles. Nonetheless, he told commissioners, "While American politicians, policymakers, and journalists remain dangerously preoccupied with events in the Middle East, China has emerged, largely unchallenged, as an economic superpower with an ever-growing ability to exert significant influence over U.S. economic, financial and political institutions."[130]

Engagement skepticism also had an institutional home in a set of organizations funded by the Department of Defense's Office of Net Assessments (ONA), under the directorship of legendary strategist and futurologist Andrew Marshall,[131] himself convinced of the long-term threat posed by China and the need for concrete planning.[132] So-called ONA shops, like the Center for Strategic and Budgetary Assessments and later Project 2049, have focused on the balance of forces in the Pacific theater.[133] The Center for Strategic and Budgetary Assessments (CSBA), under the leadership of Andrew Krepenevich, took the lead in envisioning and conceptualizing possible conflict with China, putting out in 2010 the influential concept paper coining the term "Air Sea Battle."[134] Michael O'Hanlon and James Steinberg, both associated more with Engagement than its critics,[135] later warned of the concept becoming a self-fulfilling prophesy.[136] Nonetheless, as one interviewee told me in late 2017, the CSBA's strong position on the long-term threat from China was now firmly in the center of U.S. strategic discussions on China: "We [at the CSBA] have stayed where we [were]" on China; "the rest of the community [came] to us."[137]

While Engagement was predominant at the top levels of the government until the second Obama administration, therefore, the professional community of China watchers featured a lively discussion about developments in Chinese politics, economy, and society, far more variegated than critics of a pro-Engagement groupthink. Together, the USCC, CECC, and ONA shops preserved a space within the China community for forthright and increasingly skeptical voices. In so doing, they institutionalized legitimate Engagement skepticism.

---

[130] https://www.uscc.gov/sites/default/files/2.1.2007navarro_peter_statement.pdf. The USCC heard testimony from Navarro's future colleague Robert Lighthizer concerning China's predatory trade practices in 2009.

[131] Marshall (1921–2019) was ONA director from 1973 to 2015.

[132] See https://www.nytimes.com/2019/03/26/us/politics/andrew-marshall-dead.html.

[133] For example, https://project2049.net/wp-content/uploads/2019/01/Chinas-Top-Five-War-Plans_Ian_Easton_Project2049.pdf.

[134] https://www.washingtonpost.com/world/national-security/us-model-for-a-future-war-fans-tensions-with-china-and-inside-pentagon/2012/08/01/gJQAC6F8PX_story.html.

[135] See their 2014 call for a policy of "strategic reassurance and resolve" vis-à-vis Beijing. Steinberg and O'Hanlon 2014.

[136] https://www.washingtonpost.com/opinions/beyond-air-sea-battle-a-military-concept-that-challenges-policymakers/2012/08/23/8fd4f8fa-ed31-11e1-9ddc-340d5efb1e9c_story.htm.

[137] China interview 004, 1 September 2017, San Francisco.

Conclusion

Accounts of U.S. foreign policy typically depict struggle over policy as *only* struggle over policy. The tendency to do so ignores, however, how contestation over policy is also always a struggle among different types of experts, who bring with them perspectives rooted in distinct professional statuses and trajectories. Which ideas win out is not, therefore, a matter of which ones accord most with "reality"; the ideas that win out are also the most legitimate.

Here too questions remain. Ideas, political scientist Thomas Risse-Kappen reminds us, do not float freely.[138] Ideas do not exist in the ether. They are tied instead to particular individuals and groups who believe what they believe, often with almost religious fervor. If ideas are to be legitimate, therefore, so too must be their bearers, who must also have the skill or good fortune to see their policy projects to fruition. The following chapter thus turns to the deeply personal struggles over policy and expertise that saw Engagement overturned in favor of Strategic Competition.

[138] Risse-Kappen 1994.

5
Engagement Is Personal

This chapter explores an aspect of Engagement's demise frequently left out of scholarly and popular analysis of U.S. foreign policymaking: the intense personal struggles that underpin the contestations over policy ideas and professional status described in the previous two chapters. Despite decades of expansion, the U.S. national security community is still small at its upper levels. The intimate dinners of the 1980s where the then-dozens of America's China hands would congregate are today longer be possible—a conference center would be needed, at the least. But America's China people typically know many of their colleagues. Key ideas and decisions are tied to specific individuals. The quintessential example is Henry Kissinger, synonymous with Engagement.[1] Other examples include Kurt Campbell and the pivot to Asia, and of course George Kennan and "containment." The rise and fall of Engagement with China, then, was more than an outcome of polarized professional contestation. Running orthogonally to struggles over policy ideas and expert status was a personal story of hopes realized or frustrated, agendas fulfilled or denied, as America's China experts waged intellectual and bureaucratic battles.[2]

Telling the personal story of Engagement's end feels taboo, however. Most writing on U.S. foreign policy resists personalizing policy, remaining in the register of what "America" or "Washington" has done and should do. Individuals further away from policy feature even more rarely—think, on the China side, of former U.S. trade representative and keen Engager Charlene Barshefsky,[3] Chinese law expert Jerome Cohen,[4] or podcaster Kaiser Kuo.[5] When specific

---

[1] A view Kissinger has continued to defend. Tom Porter, "Henry Kissinger Has Warned of the Doomsday Potential of the Weapons US-China Possess as Relations between the 2 Superpowers Worsen," *Business Insider*, 2 May 2021, https://www.businessinsider.com/henry-kissinger-in-doomsday-warning-over-us-china-conflict-2021-5. Kissinger visited China, at the age of 100, in July 2023. "Frustrated by Biden, China Courts 'Old Friends' Like Kissinger," *New York Times*, 20 July 2023, https://www.nytimes.com/2023/07/20/world/asia/china-kissinger-visit-us.html.

[2] Mann 1998: 11.

[3] United States trade representative (1997–2001). See Bob Davis, "Q&A: Charlene Barshefsky on Why Engagement with China Is More Important Than Ever," *Wire China*, 8 May 2022, https://www.thewirechina.com/2022/05/08/charlene-barshefsky-on-why-engagement-with-china-is-more-important-than-ever/.

[4] Professor of law, emeritus, New York University School of Law.

[5] Freelance writer, journalist, and podcaster. Cofounder of the *Sinica* podcast and editor-at-large of the China Project. Former member of Chinese rock band Tang Dynasty.

people do appear, they are typically presidents and their advisors. Even then, top leaders are often also pictured as throughputs of structural forces, like the balance of power, Thucydides's Trap,[6] or a general realization that the world changed. In short, people matter, but *not too much*.

The reasons for the mismatch between the importance of individuals in foreign policymaking and how they are mostly downplayed in scholarly work are twofold. First, individual policymakers—much less academics or journalists—do not determine policy. Nixon and Kissinger could not have engineered the opening to China without the exigencies of the Vietnam War and the Sino-Soviet split. If presidents are not determinative, why expand the scope of analysis to more seemingly marginal figures? Second, authors are often removed from the world they write about only by the thinnest of scholarly veils. Unlike the food critic, who is more than willing to trash a head chef knowing they are never going to be reviewed, foreign policy commentators are connected to the policy enterprise. They may know the policymakers involved. Or they may hope for positions of authority in future administrations themselves. Better not to name names.

We should, consequently, resist the taboo against personalizing U.S. foreign policy. Engagement and the story of its end is personal. The Engager and anti-Engagers on China are constituted not only by policy preference and professional investment but also by personal dispositions and connections. Moreover, Engagement with China and frame was the professional achievement of a relatively small number of individuals, leading Engagement to become a focal point for individualized disagreement in the broader China field, a lightning rod for emotive attacks and defenses of career legacies, personal investments, and connections—disagreements often long-standing for more senior members of the China community. Similarly, Strategic Competition was the achievement of the individuals described in Chapter 2.

Engagement's demise saw the vindication of China skeptics over those Engagers whose connections to China often go back to their first encounter with the country. Some of the vindicated were associated with the so-called Blue Team critics of Engagement, whose role in Engagement's demise is examined further. Noting the ubiquity of George Kennan in China commentary, I show how the Strategic Competitors have sought to relive the 1940s, "waking America up" to the threat from Beijing as Kennan and others did vis-à-vis the Soviet Union. A deeper analysis of the part played by Deputy National Security Advisor Matthew Pottinger in the making of Strategic Competition demonstrates how Engagement's end rested in large measure on Pottinger's unique personal capacities. Consideration of the cases of Susan Thornton under the Trump

---

[6] The fear generated in an established power by the rise of a peer competitor, derived from the lessons of Athens and Sparta. See Allison 2017.

administration and Jessica Chen Weiss under Biden demonstrate the stakes for the Engagers.

Engagement's End: Vindication and Commiseration among America's China Watchers

The end of Engagement, one interviewee explained, generated a lot of "personal antipathy in the community.... A lot of these people are ones whose career didn't go so well because they were effectively sidelined because they were not on the [right side]."[7] The election of Donald Trump and authoritarian turn in China emboldened such individuals. "For them what I'm seeing is a lot of real personal vindication in what's going on."[8] Many China skeptics were, this interviewee goes on, "marginalized... [as] kind of the China hawks, the scaremongers in the eighties and nineties who are coming back and saying, 'Look, we were right.'"[9]

For supporters of good relations with China in the policy and professional communities, the dynamic is reversed. Widespread criticism of Engagement, amplified after Trump's election, placed many individuals in the position of having to either justify or reverse track on often-long careers contributing to or operating under Engagement as policy and frame. One interviewee, an emeritus professor of political science, pointed to former business leader—a central figure in the opening up of China to American investment during the 1990s and well known in the China community—as someone who's entire professional life was placed at stake in the debate over Engagement. This individual "clearly experiences the turn [away from Engagement] as saying he wasted his life and so he almost doesn't want to hear the conversations.... You can see him tuning out.... I think he's feeling... that no one wants to listen to him anymore."[10]

When Did You First Go to China? Generational Experience and Engagement Sentiment

For many China professionals, inside and outside government, their careers were shaped by Engagement. This is especially the case for the small group of China watchers whose careers happened to coincide with the opening to China during the 1970s and early 1980s, such that they were able to visit a country few westerners had seen since the communist revolution in 1949. As one

---

[7] China interview 070, 8 February 2019, via telephone.
[8] China interview 070, 8 February 2019, via telephone.
[9] China interview 070, 8 February 2019, via telephone.
[10] China interview 028, 21 February 2018, via telephone.

interviewee—a prominent think tanker and Engager—described, "We were not expecting to ever get to China and know people. In other words, we expected to go through a career and never really talk to a resident Chinese person in the leadership or in society.... Our careers did not follow the pattern we thought. It was almost the exact opposite of what we thought it would be."[11] From this interviewee's perspective, their career had tracked closely the enormous change in China from when they first visited. "Not all," "but almost all," had been "positive change."[12]

The effect is a deep attachment to China—not always to Engagement as policy or frame, but as an intertwined personal and professional investment. For my political scientist interviewee, "Petit bourgeois neurotics tend to have their own identity at risk, whether it's their farm, their small business, or their intellectual positions. Petit bourgeois neurotics are petty bourgeois neurotics.... I'm including me in this. We are sick people. We really, really care and identify ourselves with these things we thought [about the possibilities of engagement]."[13] The idea that years of labor—reading, writing, traveling, institution and friendship building—have been wasted is a difficult notion to accept.

Another senior Engager, a professor of law, lamented his colleagues' turn against Engagement:

> I want to leave you with this. It's difficult because the fault is in us as observers. It's not just a question of integrity, it's a question of backbone. It's really, really hard to approach any complicated question and resist what is the groupthink or what is the desired conclusion [the new consensus on Strategic Competition]. And for me, it's disillusioning because I have a different view of my fellow humans, whether they're professionals or intellectuals. I don't think we should be moved in that way.... The easy response is, "Oh, you're pro-China or you're anti-China."... That's not the problem. The problem is that we're human beings. And we are moved in ways that we can't resist. I find that so sad.... I love some of these characters. So you put that down in the interview. But there are some people that I'm sure we did not name who—I just I feel sad, sad because I love them and I don't want them to be that way.[14]

The personalized struggle over China in U.S. foreign policy is not simple careerism, nor only a manifestation of general U.S. foreign policy personalization. The rise and fall of Engagement with Beijing were tied to the attachment to China of pro-Engagement experts—an attachment often more accurately described

---

[11] China interview 035, 23 March 2018, Washington, DC.
[12] China interview 035, 23 March 2018, Washington, DC.
[13] China interview 028, 21 February 2018, via telephone.
[14] China interview 084, 12 October 2021, via video call.

as love. Many China watchers have strong friendships in the country—for one leading think tanker, "I have friends there I'd give a kidney to, no hesitations."[15] From houses adorned with Chinese art and imagery, they eagerly await their next trip, a wait prolonged during the interviewing period by Covid and uncertain entrance policies emanating from Beijing. Not all experts share the sentiment, with skeptics either barred from or reluctant to travel to China, creating a dividing line in the field based on *which* China people experienced, with *when* people first went to China crucial. The Engager group is demarcated, then, not just by views of American policy, nor types of expertise, but by personal investments in positive U.S.-China relations.

The date or period of one's first encounter with China is a crucial formative factor in one's views. Up through the 1990s, going to China was unusual—for most foreigners, but especially Americans, with contacts only re-established at the end of the 1970s. Going to China at all has rarely been easy apart from a brief period in the first decade of this century, a window that closed during the second. For those who visited China when relatively few did or could, there remains a degree of romanticism. "It's sort of like if you met Nelson Mandela at 20 years old, it would probably affect everything you would do vis-à-vis South Africa for the rest of your life," one academic Engager confessed.[16] For some, the romanticism remains; for others, the downturn in U.S.-China relations led to a sense of betrayal, as if lives and careers have been wasted, hopes left unfulfilled.

"I do think it matters a lot [when you first went to China]. I think generation, age, it matters. I think it affects a lot when, when you first went," one Los Angeles–based China academic explained. It mattered "whether you first got interested in Chinese studies when China was this place that you weren't sure you could visit, or whether, like me, your first experience with doing research in Asia was to go to the PRC. You didn't have to go to Taiwan first."[17] For many Americans, lack of official contact meant the British-controlled Hong Kong or Taiwan was the only option. "I think it makes a difference if you became interested in China after Tiananmen rather than before, and so it all makes a difference. If it was after the Olympics [of 2008] rather than before, I just think . . . there are different sort of questions in your mind one way or another."[18]

---

[15] China interview 083, 12 October 2021, Washington, DC.
[16] China interview 080, 30 September 2021, via video call. As this interviewee continued, "I think there's a lot of Americans who work on Chinese law who have a similar kind experience. And those are the kinds of people who built up something called the Committee on Legal Education Exchange with China, which is a Ford Foundation–funded project that ran from the mid-eighties or the mid-nineties and trained something like 200 Chinese legal specialists in the U.S., meaning Chinese law professors, recent law graduates who came to the U.S."
[17] China interview 026, 31 January 2018, via telephone.
[18] China interview 026, 31 January 2018, via telephone.

As an early career think tanker explained, "There's been different phases of when you go to China and how you deal with it from the people who ... went on totally guided tours in the seventies to the people that went in the eighties when everything was totally opening and great."[19] Even into the 1990s, "People ... still thought of it as the Wild West, and they were doing great, cool stuff, but thought of them[selves] as sort of more adventurous."[20] While "Life was tougher, when I was there, it was sort of another golden age in the early 2000s when China was entering the WTO. China was booming. Anyone could get a job, whether you were Chinese or American, right? ... and, in some ways, live a better lifestyle than they would have in the U.S. and in certain ways on the pay they were getting.... So I think it was another golden age where a lot of people of my generation maybe had a much better experience, of course, than people now."[21] Other China specialists who went at the same time include Michigan political scientist Mary Gallagher, former *Time* magazine reporter Susan Jakes, and MIT political scientist Taylor Fravel.

The most senior group are now in their eighties and beyond, the last remnants of the children of missionaries—who were some of the only Americans in China prior to the civil war. As one former ambassador explained, the effect was not to romanticize China, but the opposite, to see the Chinese as normal in every respect. "The advantage of growing up in China is I grew up with the Chinese being ordinary people, no special glamour attached to them."[22] The Chinese are, in this view, neither fundamentally good or bad: "I mean, I don't find that Chinese human nature is any different from human nature elsewhere."[23]

The next generation of U.S. visitors was also small in number, having gone to China before normalization in 1979, comprising the officials who traveled with Nixon, the student members of the Committee of Concerned Asia Scholars, and the limited educational exchanges of the late 1970s.[24] At a time of rapidly warming diplomatic relations, they became witnesses to history, returning with positive views of the country. Joe Esherick,[25] Perry Link, and Paul Pickowicz are some of those in this group.

A second generation had it easier. Born in the late 1960s, these visitors could see Deng Xiaoping's China in great numbers. As one think tanker explained, "People of my generation ... started our interest in China at a time when China was backward and undeveloped, a bit of a mystery.... We were really among the first to go to China in large numbers and live and work there."[26] With few

---

[19] China interview 077, 24 May 2022, via video call.
[20] China interview 077, 24 May 2022, via video call.
[21] China interview 077, 24 May 2022, via video call.
[22] China interview 057, 13 November 2018, Washington, DC.
[23] China interview 057, 13 November 2018, Washington, DC.
[24] See Platt 2010.
[25] Emeritus professor of modern Chinese history, University of California, San Diego.
[26] China interview 031, 3 May 2018, via video call.

traveling to China, a degree of "generational fortuitousness" allowed these intrepid westerners "to get into China relatively early and set ourselves apart."[27] As one journalist recalled, the 1980s was a heady time of opening and discovery: "China itself was exciting."[28]

The affective component here should not be played down. As someone involved in the WTO accession confessed, the mid- to late 1990s was "the most energized and the most electrifying few months of my whole time in Washington, DC."[29] Developments in U.S.-China policymaking were exciting, intoxicating. For one academic Engager, "We should acknowledge that being an American in China in the 1980s was pretty damn awesome.... China was completely safe. You could travel for almost nothing.... Like, literally people would bicycle up to you on the street in Tiananmen Square and invite you home for dinner. And you go because it was fine in the glory days. So that definitely affects us. And then we watched our friends get rich,"[30] from their engagements with China.

Mid-career and junior cohorts of China experts experienced different Chinas. As one business academic explained, "I started [my doctoral research] in 2004 and finished in 2011. And when I was there as a PhD student, it was an interesting time. Obviously it was the Hu Jintao era, and it was kind of—at least before 2008—a really open time in China."[31] Many report a change with the Olympics, and especially after Xi Jinping's rise to power in 2012, leading to a closing down, as greater strictures were placed on what visitors could see, where they could go. Such developments did not lead automatically to anti-Engagement positions on U.S.-China relations, but absent is the romance associated with a China both accepted as a major power already and a difficult one to deal with, to boot.

The Blue Team and the Origins of Anti-Engagement

Where the Engagers feel an attachment to China forged in personal connections and by extension the notion of engagement, many anti-Engagers share an equal and opposite commitment to China skepticism, often—although not always—because they lack the same sort of personal connections to the country of their Engagement colleagues. Anti-Engagers have long harbored concerns about the Engagers' interests in the cooperative policies toward Beijing they prescribed. In conversation, anti-Engagers express the suspicion that pro-Engagers echo the propaganda of the CCP, rendering them captured by the government in

---

[27] China interview 031, 3 May 2018, via video call.
[28] China interview 051, 31 July 2018, Washington, DC.
[29] China interview 068, 29 January 2019, via telephone.
[30] China interview 093, 10 November 2021, via video call.
[31] China interview 066, 6 December 2018, Cambridge, MA.

Beijing.[32] For one anti-Engager, for example, the Engagers "were captured by the CCP, many of them, like Susan Shirk. I first met her when she just came out of China after this momentous trip. She and her cohort [were captured]." The Wilson Center's Robert Daly is another pro-Engagement expert accused of being "captured by the CCP elite. His Chinese is very good, but he got captured," one strong critic suggested.[33]

Such accusations are not made in public, for the most part. But the history of anti-Engagement has periodic bouts of more vitriolic personalized struggle. The lineage of today's anti-Engagers can be traced to the late 1990s and early 2000s activities of the so-called Blue Team.

The Blue Team, according to a *Washington Post* report from 2000, was "a loose alliance of members of Congress, congressional staff, think tank fellows, Republican political operatives, conservative journalists, lobbyists for Taiwan, former intelligence officers and a handful of academics, all united in the view that a rising China poses great risks to America's vital interests."[34] Blue Teamers and fellow travelers, like William Triplett,[35] Bill Gertz, and Michael Pillsbury, offered fervent criticism of Engagement-associated individuals, including Eric McVadon, former naval attaché in Beijing;[36] Dennis Wilder, former national security director for China (2004–2006); and Paul Heer, national intelligence officer for East Asia (2007–2015). In the words of journalist Bill Gertz, the Blue Team's task was to expose how "a community of current and former officials, known derisively as 'Panda huggers' for their pro-China views, has gained enormous influence over U.S. policies and programs related to China."[37] The Blue Teamers especially resented those they termed "the Relationship Police," "those who seek a close and cooperative U.S. relationship with Beijing" and argued against any congressional or executive-level action likely to anger the Chinese.[38]

Much of the animus motivating personal struggles among the U.S. China community has its roots in the charges leveled by the Blue Team and the perception that differential fortunes over two decades had been reversed under Trump. As one long-standing Blue Team target recalled, there were

> the Blue Teamers and then there were the panda huggers like me and Dennis Wilder and others.... At the time, China policy was highly politicized and very

---

[32] China interview 072, 19 February 2019, via video call.
[33] China interview 090, 8 November 2021, via telephone.
[34] "'Blue Team' Draws a Hard Line on Beijing," *Washington Post*, 22 February 2000, https://www.washingtonpost.com/wp-srv/WPcap/2000-02/22/004r-02220.
[35] Deputy special assistant to President Ronald Reagan (1981–1983) and contributing writer at the *Washington Times*.
[36] McVadon retired from the U.S. Navy in 1992 at the rank of rear admiral.
[37] Gertz 2008: 169–70.
[38] "Blue Team Draws a Hard Line."

contentious. To this day, before and after that, there have always been a constituency in the policy community and in the commentariat for a very hard line, ideologically driven almost.... Anybody who didn't agree with that was seen as soft on China.[39]

As reporting at the time noted, "Scholars who have been targets of Blue Team scorn say there is an increasingly politicized atmosphere among Sinologists. 'It's not as much fun as it used to be,' said Ronald N. Montaperto, then-professor at the National Defense University considered soft on China by the Blue Team. 'Debate has become very personal and very political, and frequently generates more heat than light.'"[40] A former Defense Intelligence Agency analyst, Montaperto later pleaded guilty to passing classified material to the PRC, serving time in a federal prison.[41]

In the charged political environment of the second Clinton administration, complete with impeachment proceedings against the president, the Blue Team accused the Democrats of not only being soft on China, but enmeshed in webs of corruption with the PRC that included hundreds of thousands of dollars in Chinese contributions to the Democratic National Committee, the theft of American military technology, and Chinese espionage activities in the United States.[42] In addition, the Blue Team saw Chinese influence extending well beyond the military and Washington, to the China expert community at large.

Coming from the right wing of the Republican Party, the Blue Team's accusations entered the political mainstream via a June 1998 report of a House Select Committee on National Security and Military/Commercial Concerns with the People's Republic of China, released after redaction by Republican representative and committee chair Christopher Cox.[43] The Cox Committee report detailed accusations that the PRC had stolen classified design information on the United States' most advanced thermonuclear weapons. It charged that extensive espionage had resulted in the transfer of sensitive design information from the Loral and Howard Hughes corporations, concluding, "These thefts of nuclear secrets from our national weapons laboratories enabled the PRC to design, develop, and successfully test modern nuclear weapons sooner than would otherwise have been possible."[44] Chinese activities were not new, the report went

---

[39] China interview 036, 27 September 2022, via video call.
[40] "Blue Team Draws a Hard Line."
[41] "Ex-DIA Analysts Admits Passing Secrets to China," *Washington Times*, 23 June 2006, https://www.washingtontimes.com/news/2006/jun/23/20060623-120347-7268r/.
[42] See, for example, "Ex-DIA Analyst Admits Passing Secrets to China."
[43] *U.S. National Security and Military/Commercial Concerns with the People's Republic of China*, available at https://www.govinfo.gov/content/pkg/GPO-CRPT-105hrpt851/pdf/GPO-CRPT-105hrpt851.pdf.
[44] *U.S. National Security and Military/Commercial Concerns with the People's Republic of China*, i.

on: "PRC penetration of our national weapons laboratories spans at least the past several decades and almost certainly continues today."[45]

The Cox report's conclusions were subject to a rebuttal by a group of scholars who considered the report's language "inflammatory" and based on mischaracterizations and oversimplifications in its views of Chinese governance structures, Beijing's view of the United States, and technical matters like Beijing's theft of sensitive nuclear weapons information.[46] Led by Harvard political scientist Alistair Iain Johnston, the assessment concluded that "an appropriate relationship between the United States and China is essential to progress and peace in the coming century," that "such a relationship must be based on a realistic, informed view on each side of the capabilities, history, motivation, and likely evolution of the other," and that the Cox report was seriously flawed.[47] Nonetheless, the sense that U.S. intelligence agencies had missed important warning signs in relation to the PRC gained traction in Washington, as did the suspicion that the broader national security community was playing down the long-term threat from Beijing.

Soon after the Cox report, Blue Team members took part in a commission tasked with overseeing CIA analysis on China, which found no evidence of explicit bias, but an "institutional predisposition" to minimize issues of concern in relation to China.[48] The commission, headed by retired army general John Tilelli, included anti-Engagers and Blue Teamers, among them Aaron Friedberg, University of Pennsylvania historian Arthur Waldron, and Larry Wortzel—a former attaché in China then with the Heritage Foundation, who would serve nine terms as a commissioner on the U.S.-China Economic and Security Review Commission (2001–2020). Per reporting at the time by sources close to the Blue Team, "One U.S. intelligence official close to the CIA said the problem is that senior analysts have not done enough to foster a diversity of views on Chinese security issues. 'Their basic working assumption is that China must become a strategic partner,' this official said of the senior analysts. 'Analysts are promoted who hold those views.'"[49]

Related Blue Team initiatives included a report produced by the Office of Net Assessment—headed by the China skeptic Andrew Marshall, and an important node in the anti-Engager community—critical of U.S. intelligence on the issue of Taiwan's defense.[50] Produced pursuant to the annual defense Appropriations

---

[45] *U.S. National Security and Military/Commercial Concerns with the People's Republic of China*, i.
[46] Alistair Iain Johnston et al., "The Cox Committee Report: An Assessment," December 1999, at https://carnegieendowment.org/pdf/npp/coxfinal3.pdf.
[47] Johnston et al., "The Cox Committee Report," 10.
[48] Bill Gertz, "Panel Finds CIA Soft on China," *Washington Times*, 6 July 2001, https://www.washingtontimes.com/news/2001/jul/6/20010706-024147-1037r/.
[49] Gertz, "Panel Finds CIA Soft on China."
[50] See Gertz, "Panel Finds CIA Soft on China."

Bill for 1999, the report concluded that "despite anticipated improvements to Taiwan's missile and air defense systems, by 2005, the PLA will possess the capability to attack Taiwan with air and missile strikes which would degrade key military facilities and damage the island's economic infrastructure ... [Taipei's] success in deterring potential Chinese aggression will be dependent on its continued acquisition of modern arms, technology and equipment," presumably from the United States.[51]

The report's concern for Taiwan's readiness in the face of possible attack from Beijing spread in Washington, including via a report for the Senate Foreign Relations Committee—which included one Joseph Biden Jr.—that urged an "overhaul" of U.S. defense policy toward the island. Committee chair Jesse Helms reported back from a staff trip to Taiwan, finding "Taiwan's civilian and military officials ... prepared vigorously to defend Taiwan's democracy if the need arises." Nonetheless, "Taiwan's military possesses a number of shortcomings," with American assistance needed. "Unfortunately, current U.S. policy is totally inadequate to the task. Without radical surgery, U.S. policy toward Taiwan threatens to leave that young democracy dangerously exposed to Communist Chinese attack."[52] The USCC's annual report for 2002 concluded, similarly, that "the U.S.-PRC bilateral relationship is at best, deficient for conflict resolution, uncoordinated within the U.S. bureaucracy and, at worst, has the effect of supporting Chinese efforts to enhance their science and technology base without adequate oversight within the U.S. Government."[53]

The intense personal disputes and disagreements underpinning the shift from Engagement to Strategic Competition derive, in part, from the activities of the Blue Team and fellow travelers. Largely hidden during the Bush Jr. and Obama administrations—when the U.S. national security community's eyes were firmly fixed on the Middle East and the war on terror—the views of the staunch anti-Engagers and Blue Teamers found strong support among the proponents of ideological competition with Beijing in and around the Trump administration.

One constituency was the Cold War group the Committee on the Present Danger (CPD-C), re-formed with an explicit China focus. Under the leadership of Blue Teamer Frank Gaffney, the CPD-C seeks to "educate and inform American citizens and policymakers about the existential threats presented from the People's Republic of China under the misrule of the Chinese Communist Party," threats emerging from the "PRC's accelerating military buildup; its active

---

[51] Available at https://csis-website-prod.s3.amazonaws.com/s3fs-public/legacy_files/files/media/csis/pubs/asia_neac_dod_taiwan_1999%5B1%5D.pdf.
[52] Available at https://www.govinfo.gov/content/pkg/CPRT-107SPRT71658/html/CPRT-107SPRT71658.htm.
[53] *The National Security Implications of the Economic Relationship between the United States and China*, July 2002, https://www.uscc.gov/sites/default/files/annual_reports/2002%20Annual%20Report%20to%20Congress.pdf, 28.

information and political warfare that targets the American people and our business, political and media elites; cyber warfare; and economic warfare."[54] Members include Trump advisor Steve Bannon, Peter Navarro coauthor Greg Autry, Stephen Mosher, and active Blue Teamers Arthur Waldron[55] and author Ed Timperlake.[56] The CPD-C overlaps with the signatories of the 2020 "Stay the Course" letter, with 17 of the 132 authors members.[57]

The critique of Engagement as an overall approach at once included a criticism of the entire China community, with charges running the gamut from naiveté to bias to capture by the CCP. Support for the shift to the Strategic Competition among many China experts is tied directly to a highly emotive sense of having been long ignored, their viewpoint and expertise disparaged. As one critic of Engagement, a now-retired intelligence officer, explained, while the Engagers were talking to Chinese scholars, liberal elites, and friendly policymakers, people like my interviewee were reading classified military intelligence presenting a different aspect to China's rise. "Before 2012," the former intelligence explained, pro-Engagement China experts "ridiculed people like me. . . . They mocked us. They said we were uneducated. . . . Yet guys like me were reading what the Chinese were saying."[58] As a consequence, this interviewee considered the end of Engagement a vindication of multiple decades of effort and frustration as an intelligence officer who tried unsuccessfully to raise the alarm in Washington about the China threat.

Present at the Re-creation: A Long Telegram for China and a New Georgetown Set

One name above others bucks the tendency against personalizing U.S. foreign policymaking. Former diplomat George Kennan remains a ubiquitous reference, revered as an oracle who singlehandedly readied a war-weary Washington for the Cold War.[59] While Kennan's target was the USSR, many commentators have

---

[54] See https://presentdangerchina.org/about-us/.
[55] Lauder Professor of History, University of Pennsylvania.
[56] Assistant secretary in the Department of Veteran's Affairs (1989–1993) and principal director of mobilization planning and requirements in the Department of Defense (1983–1984).
[57] Frank Gaffney, Henry Cooper, Kenneth DeGraffenreid, Chadwick Gore, Lianchan Han, Bradley Johnson, Clare Lopez, Thomas McInerny, John Mills, Stephen Mosher, Suzanne Scholte, Mark Stokes, Bradley Thayer, Arthur Waldron, James Woolsey, Jiali Yang, James Zumwalt.
[58] China interview 072, 19 February 2019, via video call.
[59] A 2019 publication from the Wilson Center's Kennan Institute reflected on the diplomat's genius, with contributions from across the national security community, including former National Intelligence Council director Paul Heer, former Policy Planning Staff director Anne-Marie Slaughter, and Biden's national security advisor, Jake Sullivan. See Kimmage and Rojansky 2019, https://www.wilsoncenter.org/book/kennan-for-our-times-revisiting-americas-greatest-20th-century-diplomat-the-21st-century.

extolled the need for a new Kennan for an era of competition with China. For one, it is "time for some unknown diplomat in Beijing or obscure policymaker in the State Department or National Security Council to replicate George Kennan's Long Telegram to provide insight and long-term guidance to American leaders."[60] Robert Wilkie, Trump's secretary of veterans affairs, who recalled romantically how "on February 22, 1946, George Kennan, then a young American diplomat in the Soviet Union, penned a secret cable to the State Department... Kennan would have opined, China [is] undoubtedly the greatest task our diplomacy has ever faced and probably the greatest it will ever have to face."[61]

Plentiful telegrams have duly appeared. In January 2021, the Atlantic Council published an anonymous "Longer Telegram"—its writer identified only as "a former senior government official with deep expertise and experience dealing with China"—that explicitly sought to achieve the Kennan effect.[62] For the author, "The defining challenge facing the United States in the 21st century is the rise of China. This is an uncomfortable truth for the Washington foreign policy establishment to admit. Since the turn of the millennium, while the American eagle should have been soaring over the cerulean waters of the Indo-Pacific, its head instead has been buried, ostrich-like, in the Middle East's sterile sands. But while Washington has been dozing, Beijing has been dreaming—and China's dreams are the stuff of American nightmares." Next to call for a new Long Telegram was C. Lea Shea: "We need a strategy—and we need one now," Shea exhorted.[63]

Not everyone is convinced of Kennan's relevance for the contemporary era. "When George Kennan wrote his famous 'Long Telegram,'" Tanner Greer notes, "he did not appreciate the true threat the U.S. foreign-policy community would face: a future where every few years a scholar, pundit, or government official decides that they too must write a long missive that will redefine American grand strategy for the decades to come."[64] Brad Glosserman is concerned less with cliché than the differences between containment and competition, concluding that "the biggest difference would be [the competition] strategy's efforts to undermine stability within China.... This would be the most aggressive expression of containment and... hard to mistake... for anything other than... an attempt

---

[60] Francis Sempa, "Needed: a Long Telegram from Beijing," *The Diplomat*, 28 January 2016, https://thediplomat.com/2016/01/needed-a-long-telegram-from-beijing/.
[61] https://www.heritage.org/asia/commentary/who-will-write-the-next-long-telegram.
[62] Anonymous, *The Longer Telegram: Toward a New American China Strategy*, Atlantic Council, 2021, https://www.atlanticcouncil.org/content-series/atlantic-council-strategy-paper-series/the-longer-telegram/.
[63] C. Lee Shea, "The Longest Telegram: A Visionary Blueprint for the Comprehensive Grand Strategy against China We Need," *War on the Rocks*, 1 April 2021, https://warontherocks.com/2021/04/the-longest-telegram-a-visionary-blueprint-for-the-comprehensive-grand-strategy-against-china-we-need/.
[64] https://foreignpolicy.com/2021/03/04/china-us-relations-longer-telegram-response/.

to destabilize the Chinese Communist Party and promote regime change."[65] Finally, for Josh Rogin the "fact that Kennan opposed much of the Cold War policy he is often credited with inspiring is lost on most Americans... his name is casually invoked several times a month at various think tank panel events as the man who devised the Cold War plan that defeated the Soviet Union. And while it's true... that the United States won the Cold War, there's actually no agreement on why the Soviet Union collapsed."[66]

But deployment of Kennan is not just a quirk of U.S. strategic culture. Harking back to Kennan's role in the first Cold War reflects a core personalized aspect of the shift from Engagement to Strategic Competition: the Strategic Competitors' collective efforts to achieve the sort of national awakening with which Kennan is often—however misleadingly—credited.[67] To paraphrase former secretary of state Dean Acheson's autobiography:[68] the Strategic Competitors saw themselves as "present at the (re)creation" of a new Cold War with China.

Rediscovering Kennan was only one aspect of the personal efforts as Strategic Competitors inside and outside the Trump administration sought to relive the late 1940s. Inside, as Rogin goes on, Secretary of State Mike Pompeo was a convinced anti-Engager keen to "leave his mark as a China hardliner" and saw the publication of a Kennan-style document by the State Department Policy Planning Staff—the organization Kennan himself had been tapped by George Marshall to create in 1947—as the ideal vehicle.[69] As one White House official told Rogin, "Pompeo... made a political calculation almost before anyone else that taking a tougher stance on China was going to be the smart political move."[70] Pompeo, alongside the "proud hardliner" in David Stilwell appointed to the post of assistant secretary for East Asian and Pacific affairs, charged Carnegie Mellon University political scientist Kiron Skinner with the task of writing a new Kennan memo. "On paper, Skinner was perfectly qualified. Like Kennan, she had a PhD from Harvard in political science." But when she told an event at a New America Foundation event of April 2019 that "this is a fight with really a

---

[65] Brad Glosserman, "What's in a Word? Calling it "Containment" Makes a Huge Difference," *Pacific Forum* 30 November 2021, https://pacforum.org/wp-content/uploads/2024/01/PacNet55.2021.11.30.pdf.

[66] Rogin 2021: 181–82.

[67] The importance of the Long Telegram has long been overstated, its real impact lying less in what it said—again, its conclusions were precisely *not* what ended up as being codified in NSC-68 and containment—than how well it articulated the starkness of the Soviet threat for those around Truman *already* convinced of the need for a new U.S. policy. Averell Harriman, ambassador to Moscow, had raced to Washington in April 1945 following FDR's death to advocate a "get tough" policy, and was supported by diplomat Chip Bohlen. Navy secretary James Forrestal was already there and had copies of the Long Telegram widely circulated in Washington, even before its publication in *Foreign Affairs*. See McCourt and Mudge 2022.

[68] Acheson 1969.

[69] Rogin 2021: 182–85.

[70] Rogin 2021: 193.

different civilization.... It's the first time we will have a great power competitor who is not Caucasian," Skinner was widely rebuked as having seemingly proven Trump's foreign policy was fundamentally racist.[71] Skinner left the government soon after.[72]

Pompeo's hoped-for Kennan-style document appeared in November 2020. While *The Elements of the China Challenge* does not explicitly mention Kennan, it notes that "the failure to understand China's interests and objectives derives in no small measure from neglect of the CCP's governing ideas," and cites Kennan's Long Telegram—in the very first footnote nonetheless—as "another turn to authoritative assumptions and governing ideas to explain the conduct of a great-power rival."[73] As the document's executive summary states, echoing Kennan,

> China is a challenge because of its conduct. [The CCP is m]odeled on 20th-century Marxist-Leninist dictatorship.... The party today wields its economic power to co-opt and coerce countries around the world.... At the same time, the CCP is developing a world-class military to rival and eventually surpass the U.S. military. These actions enable the CCP to credibly pursue the quest—proceeding outward through the Indo-Pacific region and encompassing the globe—to achieve "national rejuvenation" culminating in the transformation of the international order.[74]

As Rogin acknowledges, "In today's chaotic information environment, no one document or one proposal could have the impact or unique insight that Kennan had in the early days of the Cold War."[75] But more important here is what Pompeo and other Strategic Competitors *believed* they were doing during the Trump administration: reliving the early Cold War, this time with China as the target. Matthew Pottinger saw "Bill's Paper," the declassified planning document that formed the foundation of the 2017 NSS and May 2020 *United States Strategic Approach to the People's Republic of China*, as the Strategic Competitors' NSC-68—the National Security Council document that turned Kennan's notion of containment of the Soviet Union into policy, much to the latter's regret.[76]

Reliving the 1940s also took place outside the government, among informal groups of anti-Engagers and Strategic Competitors who met to network and

---

[71] Rogin 2021: 185.
[72] Rogin 2021: 185.
[73] *The Elements of the China Challenge*, November 2020, https://www.state.gov/wp-content/uploads/2020/11/20-02832-Elements-of-China-Challenge-508.pdf, 51.
[74] *The Elements of the China Challenge*, 1.
[75] Rogin 2021: 196.
[76] See Rogin 2021: 197: "Pottinger, the document's lead author, told me this was the closest thing the Trump administration would be able to issue to NSC 68, the Truman-era document that sought to provide the actual programmatic plan to respond to Kennan's Long Telegram and his Letter X."

strategize a new, more robust strategy toward Beijing. "Pompeo held what he called 'Saturday Sessions' on China outside the Statement Department and invited outside experts like Michael Pillsbury to come and talk through various China-related issues," Rogin reports.[77] Another self-styled salon met at the home close to Capitol Hill of fierce CCP critic Dimon Liu. Nicknamed the "Bingo club," the group was started because Liu had given up on the older generation of China hands, who were too set in their ways. She set upon convincing the younger generation that the United States needed to change its China policy, "before it's too late."[78] Liu's "first convert" was Peter Mattis, a young anti-Engager convinced of the need for a combative approach to dealing with the CCP.[79] Another recruit was Rogin himself, who "over the next months and years ... witnessed this group of young, patriotic Americans work together to combat CCP influence operations."[80]

Noting the activities of the salons that served to connect China skeptics should not be confused with conspiracy theorizing. Such groups are a constant feature of Washington life—other China groups were "popping up everywhere" after 2017, from Washington, DC, to Stanford University on the West Coast.[81] They were also common during the late 1940s, as historian Greg Herken has explored.[82] One such informal network was the "Georgetown Set" that centered on the house of prominent journalist Joe Alsop and wife Mary, whose Sunday suppers collected the great and the good to discuss—among other topics—the emerging Cold War. Another group met on Monday nights at the home of Democratic National Committee chair Oscar Ewing, and included Truman advisor and anti-communist Democrat Clark Clifford.[83] As Liu realized, "I used my kitchen to slowly build a community by feeding them. Good food and good conversation was an old-fashioned approach, popular in the eighteenth century, and it is still going."[84]

It would be naive to ignore the anti-Engagers who gathered at Pompeo's Saturday Sessions and around Dimon Liu's table as mere throughputs of broader structural forces, like the changing balance of global power and an objective threat from a changed China. These were current, former, and possible future policymakers, journalists, think tankers, military officers, congresspeople, and their staff—those whom policymakers have in mind when making and framing policy. The anti-Engagers' activities demonstrate the inadequacy of seeing the

---

[77] Rogin 2021: 183.
[78] Rogin 2021: 113.
[79] Rogin 2021: 113.
[80] Rogin 2021: 113.
[81] Rogin 2021: 114.
[82] Herken 2015.
[83] See McCourt and Mudge 2022: 20.
[84] Rogin 2021: 114.

Engagers and anti-Engager groups as constituted solely by different policy views and professional status. Engagement was a personal struggle, one lived in the minds of its architects as the beginnings of a second Cold War.

Matthew Pottinger and Strategic Competition Paradigm

Nowhere is the importance of individual people and personalities and the paradox of how to capture such influence without losing sight of broader factors more clear than in the central role played in Engagement's demise by Matthew Pottinger. Asia director on Trump's NSC and from September 2019 deputy national security advisor, it was Pottinger who set about from the administration's first day to fundamentally change America's approach to the PRC. As Pottinger later explained, "In 2017, [we crafted] our national security strategy, national defense strategy and our Indo-Pacific strategic framework—which was really a China strategy—as well as a still-classified strategy called 'Countering Chinese Economic Aggression.' Those four strategies laid out the policy case for the end of what is broadly termed engagement... [and] were very sharp departures from their predecessor documents."[85] Pottinger was a, if not *the*, main architect of the Strategic Competition frame.

How far can the emergence of Strategic Competition really be placed at Pottinger's feet? Pottinger's impact on U.S. China policy as a member of Trump's National Security Council appears both profound and predictable. As one journalist has recalled, Pottinger's story also "highlights the reality that today's U.S. elites who are familiar with China are not like the Americans before reform. ... Nor are they like the academics and reporters who were passionate, admiring, and hopeful about the transformation of this ancient civilization. ... U.S. elites are mostly suspicious about China's rise, or individuals who had their China dream dashed. Pottinger is but one of them."[86] Pottinger was not alone in his frustration with Engagement as frame, community, and set of policies by the end of Obama's second term.

If Pottinger's role seems unsurprising, we should remember salient features of the Trump administration that rendered the task of shifting U.S. China policy far from an automatic outcome. First, all previous administrations had come in tougher on China only to backtrack. Second, as president, Trump strongly

---

[85] Bob Davis, "Matthew Pottinger on Flipping the U.S.-China Paradigm on Its Head," *Wire China*, 26 June 2022, https://www.thewirechina.com/2022/06/26/matthew-pottinger-on-flipping-the-u-s-china-paradigm-on-its-head/.

[86] See Han Yong Hong, "Friends to Foes: Matthew Pottinger's Mandarin Speech to China and US-China Relations," *Think China*, 8 May 2020, https://www.thinkchina.sg/friends-foes-matthew-pottingers-mandarin-speech-china-and-us-china-relations.

desired a deal on trade with Xi Jinping and met and communicated with Xi numerous times over the course of 2017–2019 to that end. Third, the Trump administration was split between the national security-focused China skeptics—Navarro, Pottinger, McMaster—and those like treasury secretary Stephen Mnuchin, economic advisor Gary Cohn, and commerce secretary Wilbur Ross—who also sought a deal with China. It was far from guaranteed that the more hawkish line would win out within the Trump administration. And finally, Trump was notoriously difficult to work for and his administration suffered from higher turnover and greater attrition than most. Pottinger himself would eventually resign on 6 January 2021, following the storming of the U.S. Capitol by supporters of Trump.

Pottinger's ability not only to survive until the last days of the administration itself is surprising, therefore—to say nothing of his hand in effecting the shift from Engagement to Strategic Competition. Pottinger's skill as an entrepreneur of a new frame for U.S.-China relations was part professional—a matter of his credentials and legitimacy as a China expert; partly a matter of his policy views as a strong China skeptic; and partly a matter of his own personal abilities, as he navigated the tumultuous waters of the Trump administration and national security bureaucracy.

Senior Engagers decried the lack of what they perceived as "real" China expertise, as detailed in the previous chapter. But Pottinger was for many an exception. A journalist by vocation, he was therefore recognized as knowledgeable without sitting at the center of the China expert community. For fellow journalist David Ignatius of *The New York Times*, for example, Pottinger was "one of our country's leading, most knowledgeable China experts."[87] Pottinger checked the boxes for language ability—being fluent in Mandarin—and time spent in country—having been the *Wall Street Journal*'s on-the-ground reporter, prior to joining the marines in 2005, which gave Pottinger yet another form of legitimacy. A 2011 introduction by Peter Osnos in *The Atlantic* ended with a "salute to Capt. Matt Pottinger and [the] hope our leaders and the public can take advantage of his insights. He has earned the right to those views at great risk to himself and out of devotion to American ideals."[88] Pottinger also had China business acumen, having set up his own consulting firm—ChinaSix—before working for the hedge fund DavidsonKempner. Finally, Pottinger had personal connections to the Trump team, having been brought in by short-lived national security advisor

---

[87] David Ignatius, "Transcript: World Stage: China with Matthew Pottinger," 6 March 2023, https://www.washingtonpost.com/washington-post-live/2023/03/06/former-deputy-national-security-adviser-matthew-pottinger-us-china-tensions/.

[88] Peter Osnos, "Meet Captain Matt Pottinger, United States Marine Corps," *The Atlantic*, 5 April 2011, https://www.theatlantic.com/national/archive/2011/04/meet-captain-matt-pottinger-united-states-marine-corps/236825/.

Michael Flynn, for whom he worked when in the marines, and having K. T. McFarland as "a friend from New York."[89]

Pottinger married recognized China expertise, however, with a form of insight into China more aligned to the anti-Engager camp—a black-and-white perspective on the ill intent of the CCP, rather than nuanced knowledge of China writ large, which the anti-Engagers consider nuance for nuance's sake. Like some anti-Engagers, Pottinger drew on a close reading of the speeches of key Chinese leaders, including Xi himself. As he later explained to journalist Bob Davis, "We know a lot more about Xi now—those of us who pay attention to what he's been saying in speeches that are addressed to his internal audience, the Central Committee of the Communist Party."[90]

Outlining for Davis the policy conclusions he drew, Pottinger tellingly quoted Biden appointee Rush Doshi to describe China's 30-year "Long Game" strategy[91] to replace American power in East Asia in testimony to the Senate Armed Services Committee in June 2019:[92] "The grand strategy set in motion by China's rulers aimed first to *dilute* American influence in Asia, then to *displace* American power more overtly from the region and, ultimately, to *dominate* a global order in ways that suit and promote Beijing's authoritarian model." Trump policy, he went on, was "best thought of as a *counterstrategy* to the thirty-year-old grand strategy that Beijing set in motion," and had three key components: to defend "free and open societies" by making it "easier for Chinese people to access information from outside China's 'Great Firewall' "; by blocking U.S. money from "being directed toward Beijing's military modernization and toward Chinese entities complicit in genocide and other crimes against humanity"; and by "beat[ing] Beijing in the race for high-tech supremacy."[93]

Here was a strategy Pottinger would later describe as "constrainment"—a newly minted portmanteau that "unlike containment... accounts for the current realities of economic interdependence and seeks to tilt them to Washington's advantage. Constrainment should seek to puncture Beijing's confidence that it can achieve its aims through war."[94] Constrainment was sure to appeal to the trade hawks in the Trump administration, especially Navarro. As Pottinger noted in a *Wall Street Journal* op-ed in March 2021, "It's not enough to run faster at home and in the free world, although that's one of the things we need to do. We need to

---

[89] Davis, "Matthew Pottinger on Flipping the U.S.-China Paradigm."
[90] Davis, "Matthew Pottinger on Flipping the U.S.-China Paradigm."
[91] Doshi 2021.
[92] Matthew Pottinger, Testimony to US Senate Armed Services Committee, 8 June 2019. Available at https://www.hoover.org/sites/default/files/written_testimony_to_sasc1.pdf.
[93] https://www.hoover.org/sites/default/files/written_testimony_to_sasc1.pdf.
[94] See Pottinger's testimony to the Select Committee on the CCP, 28 February 2023, https://selectcommitteeontheccp.house.gov/media/press-releases/pottinger-mcmaster-yi-paul-witness-testimony.

ensure that there are viable alternatives to Huawei and that there are incentives for those companies to innovate and grow and compete. But at the same time, we have to *constrain* Huawei."[95] Addressing the role of U.S. multinationals, a favored target of Navarro's, Pottinger did not separate economic from ideological competition with Beijing: "American businessmen, wishing for simple, lucrative commercial deals, have long resisted viewing U.S.-China relations as an ideological struggle. But strategic guidance issued by the leaders of both countries make[s] clear the matter is settled: The ideological dimension of the competition is inescapable, even central."[96]

The combination of traditional Engagement-inflected credentials with anti-Engagement-inflected views thus strengthened Pottinger's position as he navigated the factional divides within the Trump administration. For Josh Rogin, Pottinger felt comfortable with the so-called super hawks in the administration—Steve Bannon, Stephen Miller, and Navarro. "Matt Pottinger was this group's platoon commander and Marco Rubio was their spirit animal."[97] He had the metaphorical scars to prove it, having endured as a reporter in China "numerous instances of harassment, including being videotaped by security agents, being forced to flush his notes down a toilet to keep the police from getting them, and being punched in a Beijing Starbucks by "a government goon.""[98] When talking tough, therefore, Pottinger had the necessary legitimacy. As he explained to Davis about the Chinese playbook and the Engagement response, "The evidence, though, really mounted over the course of those 25 years that China would, in fact, work very hard to subvert U.S. power and influence—first within China, then regionally, and then globally. I thought that we were behaving as though we were blind and deaf to the reality of the Chinese Communist Party's ambitions, its hostility to the end-state that we were trying to achieve, and its resourcefulness in working to achieve its ambitions globally."[99]

Pottinger's views were both credible *and* legitimate, never too far from those Engagers concerned about developments under Xi Jinping, and especially the tough line taken by the emerging Democratic Strategic Competitors aligned with Campbell and Ratner. As he later told Mike Gallagher's special committee on the CCP, it was important that while the United States waged competition with Beijing, the government "protect the rights of Chinese Americans. Protect, also, Chinese nationals studying and working in the United States so

---

[95] Davis, "Matthew Pottinger on Flipping the U.S.-China Paradigm."
[96] Matthew Pottinger, "Beijing Targets American Business," *Wall Street Journal*, 26 March 2021, https://www.wsj.com/articles/beijing-targets-american-business-11616783268.
[97] Rogin 2021, xxv.
[98] Hong, "Friends to Foes." See also "A Veteran China Hand Advises Trump for Xi's Visit," *New York Times*, 4 April 2017, https://www.nytimes.com/2017/04/04/world/asia/matthew-pottinger-trump-china.html.
[99] Davis, "Matthew Pottinger on Flipping the U.S.-China Paradigm."

they can enjoy the freedoms that so starkly distinguish the American way of life from the increasingly oppressive atmosphere in China today. This means standing up against bigotry and discrimination here at home." Also important was preventing competition from spilling into open conflict, necessitating "high-level channels open with Beijing. This is to help prevent Xi from making grave miscalculations—an occupational hazard for long-serving dictators, as his friend Putin reminds us."[100]

Pottinger thus skillfully utilized his unique blend of mainstream-yet-hawkish credentials. As one of his predecessors, Michael Green, explained in early 2017, "He's a very effective bureaucratic player, which is saying something because he's never had a policy job before."[101] The example used to back up the assertion was in the sphere of trade issues, "the subject of fierce, unsettled debate between mainstream advisers like Gary D. Cohn, the former Goldman Sachs banker who now runs the National Economic Council, and hard-liners like Stephen K. Bannon, the president's chief strategist, and Peter Navarro, a strident anti-China scholar who is the director of the National Trade Council," the article went on. "In a recent session in the Oval Office, a frustrated Mr. Pottinger watched as Mr. Bannon and Mr. Kushner complained to Mr. Trump that China was deliberately depressing its currency, which undercuts American goods (in fact, China has recently been trying to do the opposite). Mr. Pottinger, according to a person briefed on the exchange, drew Mr. Cohn, who was standing nearby, into the conversation, and Mr. Cohn contradicted the other two men."[102] While speaking Navarro's language, Pottinger was sure not to alienate the few Engagers in the administration.

Pottinger's skill extended to both the reframing of China as a case of policy failure and the foregrounding of his position as a former optimist about what Engagement might achieve. Again, Pottinger was far from alone in his dissatisfaction with China policy under Trump's predecessors. But telling a new story about the past and future of U.S.-China relations was a deliberate rhetorical tactic, one that worked. As he explained to Ignatius, "The United States made a big gamble in the 1990s . . . that we would bring China into the world, really enrich China, train its experts, its new business leaders and technocrats, even military officers, scientists and open our markets. It was an explicit hope of successive administrations in the United States—that over time, China would evolve into something friendlier and more liberal."[103] Expressing a degree of empathy with the Engagers, however, Pottinger went on, "I don't think it was a crazy idea.

---

[100] Pottinger's testimony to the Select Committee on the CCP, 28 February 2023, https://selectcommitteeontheccp.house.gov/media/press-releases/pottinger-mcmaster-yi-paul-witness-testimony.
[101] "Veteran China Hand."
[102] "Veteran China Hand."
[103] Ignatius, "Transcript: World Stage."

If you think back to our victory in the Cold War where we were able to peacefully bring the Cold War to a soft landing, we saw . . . all the Eastern Europeans become] market democracies. I think that it was a reasonable strategy to try."[104] As he told Davis, "Early in my career as a journalist in China, when I was writing for *Reuters*, I covered the negotiations to bring China into the WTO. I was among those who were optimistic that this would unleash not just economic growth, but reforms that would further liberalize the Chinese economy."[105]

Empathy did not mean sympathy, however. The Engagement "strategy has failed categorically," Pottinger explained, and therefore "we should not be clinging to an engagement strategy, even though there should always be elements of engagement in our current strategy. I'm not saying we don't engage. I'm saying that the emphasis now needs to be on protecting the national security interests and prosperity of free countries, the United States and our allies and other partners around the world."[106] In its place, Pottinger was outspoken in his willingness to label Beijing a "revisionist power," with which the United States is in a "strategic competition."[107] Like the anti-Engagers, moreover, Pottinger pointed the finger of agency squarely at Beijing and Xi himself, with the United States reacting—*waking up*—to reality, rather than making it. In reference to Taiwan, for example, Pottinger told Ignatius that "Xi Jinping is the protagonist in this story. He's trying to actively change the status quo from one of a stable modus vivendi where Taiwan does not have de jure independence and where countries around the world recognize their other own one-China policies. Xi wants to move towards an active annexation of Taiwan."[108] China, under Xi, had changed.

The outbreak of Covid-19 in early 2020 further strengthened Pottinger himself as a voice in the White House beyond matters of geopolitics, as well as the anti-Engagers in the administration like Navarro, and the case for Strategic Competition with Beijing. Initially unsure how to respond, Pottinger and Navarro reportedly took Covid more seriously than others inside the White House, due surely to a lack of faith in China's likely response—duly given credence as Xi played down the scale of the outbreak, hampering the actions of the World Health Organization, while initiating a steep lockdown on Hubei Province in mid-January 2020. Pottinger had covered SARS in 2003 while at the *Wall Street Journal*, "So he dusted off his contacts in China and spoke with doctors on the ground," finding unsurprisingly, "the narrative they were telling (bad, asymptomatic spread, etc.) was not what the Chinese government were saying."[109]

---

[104] Ignatius, "Transcript: World Stage."
[105] Davis, "Matthew Pottinger on Flipping the U.S.-China Paradigm."
[106] Ignatius, "Transcript: World Stage."
[107] Ignatius, "Transcript: World Stage."
[108] Ignatius, "Transcript: World Stage."
[109] "Transcript: Matthew Pottinger on Face the Nation," *CBS News*, 21 February 2021, https://www.cbsnews.com/news/transcript-matt-pottinger-on-face-the-nation-february-21-2021/.

Pottinger was early and clear in communicating to Trump his conviction that the virus represented a major national security threat. It was also Pottinger's idea for Trump to refer to the "Wuhan virus," not shying away from assigning blame for the outbreak. Trump went further, calling Covid the "Chinese virus."[110] As he later told Davis, the outbreak of Covid was crucial for converting Strategic Competition as frame, into policy: "When it comes to seeing that paradigm shift—the move from theory to practical application—2020 and the Covid crisis were the catalyst for those policies being put into action in a significant way."[111]

Pottinger remained a policy and rhetorical entrepreneur after leaving office. In a May 2023 interview, he tried a new image for the failure of Engagement: "We saw a baby shark and thought that we could transform it into a dolphin," he explained. "We kept feeding the shark and the shark got bigger and bigger. And now we're dealing with a formidable, great white."[112] Time will tell whether the shark imagery will have the same traction as the failure of Engagement. But Pottinger's personal influence on Engagement's demise is undeniable. Pottinger was not simply Trump's China hawk—he was, and remains, a legitimate China expert who is also a strong critic of the CCP and its modes of interacting with the United States and—crucially—a dogged and skilled bureaucratic operator within the contemporary Republican Party.

The Shaky Ground of Competitive Coexistence: The Case of Jessica Chen Weiss

Engagement's demise was personal: a matter of individual beliefs, dispositions, and convictions. It was also personal*ized*: a matter of the views, credentials, and initiatives of specific people and the groups that coalesce around them. The case of political scientist Jessica Chen Weiss's time in the Biden administration shines further light on the personal dynamics of pro- and anti-Engagement. As a Council on Foreign Relations fellow in the State Department's Policy Planning unit (August 2021–July 2022)—Weiss lacked the policymaking initiative of Pottinger or his successor Kurt Campbell, and is not therefore a direct comparison. But her case illustrates the shaky personal and professional ground of what can be called competitive coexistence—the space between Engagement and Strategic Competition. In short, how could individuals like Weiss at once make the case for careful management of the now-competitive U.S.-China relations,

---

[110] Hong, "Friends to Foes."
[111] Davis, "Matthew Pottinger on Flipping the U.S.-China Paradigm."
[112] "China Is a 'Great White Shark' Fed by the West, Ex-Trump Adviser Pottinger," *Nikkei Asia*, 24 May 2023, https://asia.nikkei.com/Editor-s-Picks/Interview/China-is-great-white-shark-fed-by-West-ex-Trump-adviser-Pottinger.

smoothing the sharper rhetorical and framing edges of U.S. China policy, while remaining credible by downplaying their own affiliations with the Engagers and their specific form of China expertise?

For Weiss, the problem with strategic competition as frame and policy under Trump and Biden is that it creates rather than alleviates tensions. As she explained in a *Foreign Policy* interview after leaving government, "Policymakers are locked in an escalatory spiral."[113] Strategic competition, she elaborated in *Foreign Affairs*, "has begun to consume U.S. foreign policy. Seized with the challenge of a near-peer rival whose interests and values diverge sharply from those of the United States, U.S. politicians and policymakers are becoming so focused on countering China that they risk losing sight of the affirmative interests and values that should underpin U.S. strategy."[114] Like other critics of the competition frame, Weiss noted that American policymakers have failed to define success. What does "winning Strategic Competition" mean? Competition tends, for Weiss, to become an end in itself, as leaders are overwhelmed by "the instinct to counter every Chinese initiative, project, and provocation remains predominant, crowding out efforts to revitalize an inclusive international system that would protect U.S. interests and values even as global power shifts and evolves."[115] Even the war in Ukraine is seen primarily through a U.S.-China competition lens.[116]

The effect, in Weiss's view, is to measure success in the competition with Beijing by China's loss, not what the United States hopes to achieve: "So long as outcompeting China defines the United States' sense of purpose, Washington will continue to measure success on terms other than on its own.... If the pursuit of human progress, peace, and prosperity is the ultimate objective ... then the United States does not need to beat China in order to win."[117] A better guide, she continues, would "be the world that the United States seeks: what it wants, rather than what it fears ... policies should be judged on the basis of whether they further progress toward that world rather than whether they undermine some Chinese interest or provide some advantage over Beijing."[118] Put differently, Strategic Competition with Beijing risks collateral damage in America and can be done better. "The current course will not just bring indefinite deterioration of the U.S.-Chinese relationship and a growing danger of catastrophic conflict;

---

[113] "Is America's China Policy Too Hawkish?," *Foreign Policy* 8 March 2023, https://foreignpolicy.com/2023/03/08/us-china-economic-competition-policy/?utm_source = PostUp&utm_medium = email&utm_campaign = FP.

[114] Jessica Chen Weiss, "The China Trap: U.S. Foreign Policy and the Perilous Logic of Zero-Sum Competition," *Foreign Affairs*, September/October 2022, https://www.foreignaffairs.com/print/node/1129143.

[115] Weiss, "The China Trap."
[116] Weiss, "The China Trap."
[117] Weiss, "The China Trap."
[118] Weiss, "The China Trap."

it also threatens to undermine the sustainability of American leadership in the world and the vitality of American society and democracy at home."[119]

Weiss therefore questioned common sense on the decline of U.S.-China relations and put some of the blame at America's door: "In Washington, the standard account for why the relationship has gotten so bad," she explained, "is that China changed: in the past decade or two, Beijing has stopped 'biding its time,' becoming more repressive at home and assertive abroad even while continuing to take advantage of the relationships and institutions that have enabled China's economic growth. . . . But a complete account must also acknowledge corresponding changes in U.S. politics and policy as the United States has reacted to developments in China."[120] The United States has brought in "an array of punitive actions and protective policies," while "waver[ing] in its support for the international institutions and agreements that have long structured global interdependence."[121]

In so doing, however, Weiss risked straying onto the terrain of Engagement as a set of policy views, making apparent her personal and professional pro-Engagement affiliations, and thereby limiting her credibility. Pointing the finger back at the United States *in itself* risks committing the cardinal sin, for Engagement's critics, of moral equivalence. Statements like "The United States seeks to perpetuate its preeminence and an international system that privileges its interests and values; China sees U.S. leadership as weakened by hypocrisy and neglect, providing an opening to force others to accept its influence and legitimacy" suggest that Washington and Beijing are in some sense the same, morally and politically.[122] Moral equivalence is anathema to military hawks, those holding the ideological view of competition with China, and especially human rights people.

The problem, as Weiss seems to recognize, is that the ideational, social, and personal space between Engagement and committed Strategic Competition is narrow and shifting. Weiss has standard China expertise credentials as a prized student of the University of California, San Diego. When she says that "anyone who seeks to diverge from the consensus is accused of having sympathy for the other side,"[123] anti-Engagers likely think just that. The barriers between the groups are hard to avoid. "For those who broadly share her views," journalist Ian Johnson expressed in a *New Yorker* profile,

---

[119] Weiss, "The China Trap."
[120] Weiss, "The China Trap."
[121] Weiss, "The China Trap."
[122] Weiss, "The China Trap."
[123] "Is America's China Policy Too Hawkish?"

Weiss is a welcome change from those who don't dare say what they think for fear of being seen as weak or soft on China. "She's extremely brave," said Susan Thornton, a retired senior U.S. diplomat and now a visiting lecturer at the Yale Law School. "It's really hard to criticize Biden knowing what else is out there, but the problem is you can't do nuanced policymaking because anything you do will be ammunition for the other side."[124]

Guilt by association for the anti-Engagers.

The personalization of Engagement with China escapes neat categorization as either uniformly hostile or collegial. One long-accused "panda hugger" said of his relations with strong critic James Fanell, "I've always gotten along very well with Jim ... even to this day, we cordially correspond occasionally."[125] Others lean into the DC food fight: "It's no secret that Kurt Campbell has a very strong and assertive personality. So some people are uncomfortable with that.... I think Bridge Colby might, you know, fall in a similar category. He's got a very strong, assertive personality, very strongly held views, and he likes to debate and argue."[126] Ultimately, my interviewee went on, it "depends on personalities ... where there is strong arguments, there's going to be strong personalities.... There's a lot more hostility and resentment among a lot of people than I found it worth my time to exhibit.... I get along fine with Kurt even when I've disagreed with him. And I've debated and argue with [Colby and] we're perfectly cordial."[127] What can be said with certainty is that any account of U.S. China policy that ignores its personalized nature is missing one of its most salient features.

Conclusion

Accounts of post-1989 U.S. foreign policy typically fail to capture the deeply personal nature of the rise and fall of Engagement with China, remaining in the space of political struggle over policy ideas—to integrate China into the international order after Tiananmen. Few people are named in those accounts, beyond presidents and their top advisors. Yet, while American national security policy and diplomatic history are intensely personal, the U.S. national security community is a human space. Thirty years is, after all, about the span of an individual

---

[124] Ian Johnson, "A Professor Who Challenges the Washington Consensus on China," *New Yorker*, 13 December 2022, https://www.newyorker.com/news/persons-of-interest/a-professor-who-challenges-the-washington-consensus-on-china.
[125] China interview 078, 27 September 2021, via video call.
[126] China interview 078, 27 September 2021, via video call.
[127] China interview 078, 27 September 2021, via video call.

career. The Engagers and their anti-Engagers, then, are more than policy groups and particular kinds of experts. They are collections of people with shared hopes, convictions, and commitments, and they will stay that way, however today's policies and events turn out.

So too are America's Russia experts, to which the next part of the book turns.

PART III
ENDING ENGAGEMENT WITH RUSSIA

6

The Russia-We-Have, or the Russia-We-Want? Polarization in the Russia Field

Recall the temptation to talk of polarization among America' foreign policy experts in the language of hawks and doves. Like the end of Engagement with China, such a straightforward account of relations with Moscow since 1989 seems to fit, a story based on the dominance of Russia hawks over doves after a brief period optimism in the early 1990s. The temptation was rejected because hawk-and-dove imagery masks more complex groupings. As one senior Russia think tanker and former official stressed, "I don't think in partisan terms. . . . I worked with everybody. It doesn't make any difference. . . . In this town . . . that's what I like. [Democrat] Laura Rosenberger[1] . . . and Republicans . . . like David Kramer.[2] I see no difference between them at all."[3] Even the language used to describe hawks and doves is country specific. Animal imagery is largely absent from the Russia-watching community, for example. The term "bear hug" was taken.

Like Chapter 3, therefore, this chapter is not about a Russia expert community in the United States rent between hawks and doves. The story, once again, is more complicated. Nor, again, is the chapter about party-political polarization, despite the salience of Russia given meddling by Moscow in U.S. politics in both the 2016 and 2020 elections.

In this chapter, rather, I track the formation of the "Russia-we-havers" and the "Russia-we-wanters." For several years after the fall of the Berlin Wall, U.S. Russia strategy was largely consensual and bipartisan; both countries were viewed through a lens of opportunity and optimism. For one distinguished former ambassador to both Beijing and Moscow, "I think it's safe to say that in both the China field and the Russia field, there was by and large a bipartisan consensus until there wasn't."[4] More recently and on distinct timelines, however, America's approach polarized. In the case of Russia, the community split between two

---

[1] Senior director for China on Biden's National Security Council.
[2] Managing director for global policy at the George W. Bush Institute and former assistant secretary of state for democracy, human rights, and labor.
[3] Russia interview 035, 18 November 2020, via video call.
[4] Russia interview 043, 4 December 2020, via video call.

The End of Engagement. David M. McCourt, Oxford University Press. Oxford University Press 2024.
DOI: 10.1093/9780197765241.003.0007

broad groups that respectively want the United States to deal with Russia "as it is" and "as it could be."

I do not assume uniformity in the degree of polarization in the two fields. Interviews convey that the smaller Russia field is less contentious and divided than the U.S. China field, with experts closer in their descriptions of Russia and policy proscriptions. Finally, as emphasized earlier, it is imperative to be clear about what, precisely, is being polarized. In a point of marked division between the two cases, the Engager/anti-Engager camps are split not only over policy, but the *framing* of China, whereas Russia experts remain divided principally over policy.

The chapter again opens with a deeper description of the Russia-we-havers and the Russia-we-wanters, before exploring the longer-term origins of both groups, which I trace to Cold War American divisions over how to portray and interact with the Soviet Union. The chapter then examines the combined effects of the rise of Putin and a U.S. administration distracted after 9/11 for the consolidation of each camp, notably after Putin's return to power in 2012.

The Russia-We-Have? Or the Russia-We-Want?

At first blush the Russia watchers are a mirror image of the China watchers: split between those more and less in favor of engagement with Moscow, a division again reminiscent of hawks versus doves. However, polarization over Russia in the U.S. foreign policy conversation displays unique characteristics. Rather than Engagers pitted against anti-Engagers, as with China, what rends America's Russia watchers is whether to deal with "the Russia we have," or the Russia "we—and the Russians themselves—want."[5]

The Russia-We-Havers

As one senior think tanker and former official described it, for the authors of the "first letter"—shorthand for both the letter penned by Thomas Graham, Rose Gottemoeller, Fiona Hill, and Thomas Pickering published in *Politico*, and the general position within the debate occupied by its signatories—"The idea is that you have to accept Russia as it is . . . , and that means, you know, an authoritarian country, . . . one which is pretty antagonistic towards the West, not

---

[5] To recall, interviews were conducted in fall 2020, before Russia's military buildup and subsequent invasion of Ukraine. No interviewees—from any group described here—predicted or foresaw the invasion.

just the United States."⁶ Putin, however unsavory to Western eyes, is "in power. He's president. He's been reelected several times. And we just have to deal with him," as one member of the opposite camp explained the Russia-we-have position.⁷ Accepting Russia as it is means accepting, for those of this view, a country that does not respect "human rights . . . [that] discriminates against LGBT [communities], imprisons political dissidents, things like that. You accept that's the way Russia is, and you say, 'But we still have to deal with it on certain issues.'"⁸

Like the China Engagers, the Russia-we-havers are far from a unified bunch. Composed of former diplomats, arms control experts, academics, and think tankers, the Russia-we-havers do not form an institutionalized group. There is no single think tank one can point to. Rather, the position is a node within the Russia-watching community and the debate over how the United States should behave in its dealings with Moscow. Thomas Graham sits at the node's center, with others, like the Atlantic Council's Emma Ashford and the Wilson Center's Matthew Rojansky, seen as sympathetic.

However unpalatable, accepting Russia as it is necessary, in the opinion of the first letter's signatories and those of like mind, given the need to cooperate with Moscow on issues of shared concern. As one of writer of the Graham letter explained, "We start from the assumption that the relationship between the United States and Russia . . . is competitive and that we're deeply divided on our views on what is appropriate or proper [conduct in world politics]."⁹ The aim is less to forge a shared worldview than "to manage the competitive relationship responsibly so that you reduce the risk of nuclear conflict . . . keep[ing] competition within necessary parameters so that it doesn't escalate."¹⁰ While the relationship will remain antagonistic, it is thereby possible to "[leave] open the window for cooperation or collaboration on narrowing the issues of transnational [concern] that require the United States and Russia to work together, along with other major powers, [like] climate change, nonproliferation, international terrorism and so forth."¹¹ For one think tanker, "You have to deal with the Russia you've got, not the Russia you wish you had, right? You do have to deal with them [because] war is a terrible idea. . . . Within that universe, my position is that Russia and the United States have different interests for a variety of reasons and in a variety of places. They have similar interests in a few places, but . . . it's not a values thing."¹² Accepting Russia as it is also means, finally, accepting the need to see world politics from a Russian perspective: "I think that it's important

⁶ Russia interview 015, 19 October 2020, via video call.
⁷ Russia interview 037, 20 November 2020, via video call.
⁸ Russia interview 015, 19 October 2020, via video call.
⁹ Russia interview 030, 13 November 2020, via video call.
¹⁰ Russia interview 030, 13 November 2020, via video call.
¹¹ Russia interview 030, 13 November 2020, via video call.
¹² Russia interview 017, 20 October 2020, via video call.

to put yourself in Russia and Putin's shoes, not, you know, because you're sympathetic to him ... but just to understand where he is coming from."

Russia skeptics dispute Washington's ability to cooperate with Moscow and Putin in this way, and the wisdom of even trying given the sort of "realities" about Russia American leaders must swallow from the Russia-we-have perspective, of which more later. For the signatories of the first letter, however, the hope is based on past experience. As a junior think tanker, a non-signatory to the letter but considered a fellow traveler, commented, "The Russia-we-have folks believe the U.S. and Russia together could solve some significant problems in the world. And the reason they think that is because they did."[13] Talking about the Cold War and its immediate aftermath, this interviewee pointed out that "there was a period of time when U.S. and Russia cooperation did solve some important big things."[14] As a former arms controller explained, to name one example, our "principal concern was avoiding accidents and miscalculations.... We got down to 7,000 nuclear weapons—the two of us.... We took ourselves down now from about 12,000. About 5,000 on each side were dismantled, weapons and reserve weapons."[15]

As with the China field, the Russia-we-havers are far from united on every issue, having arrived at their views from different angles via distinct professional trajectories. The Graham crowd holds multiple types of Russia expertise, each inclined toward cooperation—among their domains are nuclear arms control, diplomacy, policymaking, and academia, as detailed in the next chapter. All share some version of a "realist" worldview—a theoretical perspective on IR stressing timeless verities of power politics, might makes right, and the conflict-prone nature of international affairs. Far from anomalous, from a realist perspective Russia's actions in its foreign relations—from the Georgia and Ukraine to American elections—are to be expected. Great powers act to further their interests, and Russia is no exception. As a senior ex-diplomat explained, among those who argue that "we can have a much better relationship with Russia if Russia will only submit potentially all of our demands... there's no recognition that Russia has vital interests. There's no willingness to declare which of those vital interests the United States considered legitimate and should respect and vice versa. By the way, it's a two-way street."[16]

For one Russia-we-haver, consequently, Putin represents

> the return of a traditional Russia ... after an abnormal period in the late nineties or in the late 1980s and 1990s. That's the Russia we have to deal with.... You

---

[13] Russia interview 039, 30 November 2020, via video call.
[14] Russia interview 039, 30 November 2020, via video call.
[15] Russia interview 042, 3 December 2020, via video call.
[16] Russia interview 009, 12 October 2020, via telephone.

have to manage relations in some fashion because it isn't going to go away. It's a player in European security, European economics. And we're not really used to dealing with Russia [the historical nation and not the] very specific Russia during the Cold War and then what we thought was going to be the total opposite in the late 1980s and early 1990s. Now we've got a historical Russia. We don't quite know what to do.[17]

The notion of "traditional Russia" goes beyond a realist theoretical disposition, hinting at an understanding of Russian history and political psychology to which not all Russia-we-havers would ascribe. The notion of traditional Russia has its lineage in American diplomat George F. Kennan's so-called Long Telegram of February 1946, published in *Foreign Affairs* the following year under the pseudonym "X."[18] There Kennan traced Russia's postwar behavior to the Russian psyche, rather than the more recent phenomenon of Soviet communism. As explored later, the Kennan telegram's impact on those around President Truman and the possibility of postwar cooperation with the USSR took on mythical status. Few interviewees, Russia-we-haver or Russia-we-wanter, expressed this understanding of the origins of Moscow's worldview. Nonetheless, whether tied to a view of Russia's natural statecraft or the dicta of great power politics, Russia-we-havers are resigned to dealing with Moscow as it is. Regular contacts must be kept, however unpleasant a taste in the mouth they leave.

In terms similar to Engagement in the China debate, Russia-we-havers advocate "continu[ing] talking," in the hope that, with "regular meetings or regular channels... the probability that you'll find some way to muddle through, which is often the best you can hope for, ... it's just much higher."[19] For think tanker Matt Rojansky and historian Michael Kimmage,[20] the aim should be to "enmesh the relationship in process."[21] U.S. leaders should resist a "friend or foe" frame, and instead view Russia as a "third neighbor," alongside Mexico and Canada.[22] To be sure, Russia is—in this image—the annoying neighbor with which one has disputes over noise and property boundaries. But while one may wish to avoid this neighbor, one also has a shared interest in the neighborhood, rendering regular, well-functioning contacts indispensable.

If Russia is the annoying neighbor, Putin is its head of the household, and the Russia-we-havers are forced to contend with him, which is duly a wedge issue in

---

[17] Russia interview 030, 13 November 2020, via video call.
[18] X [Kennan] 1947.
[19] Russia interview 005, 30 September 2020, via video call.
[20] Professor of history, Catholic University of America, Washington, DC.
[21] Matthew Rojansky and Michael Kimmage, "The Third Neighbor: Can America Live with Putin's Russia?," *National Interest*, 3 July 2020, https://nationalinterest.org/feature/third-neighbor-can-america-live-putins-russia-163806.
[22] Rojansky and Kimmage, "The Third Neighbor."

the camp. For some, like Fiona Hill, Putin's personality, and in particular his understanding of his role as a world-historical actor reshaping Russia' international relations, is central to an adequate American understanding of Moscow.[23] U.S.-Russia relations may then significantly improve post-Putin, with implications for present policy that dampen calls for enmeshed engagement.

Others resist such a personalized view. As one think tanker explained, "I'm definitely not in the camp of people who think that you can understand Russian foreign policy by just psychoanalyzing Putin."[24] Instead, "Putin is sometimes a helpful shorthand for ... the Russian elite, the political class around Putin."[25]

Another Washington-based Russia think tanker added to this line of reasoning the view that because "we tried really hard [to reset relations] and it didn't take" we should not conclude that we should "double down and cast our bets on the next guy [after Putin] or the opposition without really ... understanding that ... he's popular with Russians."[26] In particular, an opposition figure more palatable to the American taste like Alexei Navalny is "problematic for a host of other reasons.... He's just simply not as popular [as Putin]."[27]

Russia-we-havers are critical of America's own role in the decline in U.S.-Russia relations since the high point of the 1990s. For a minority of Russia watchers, mostly academics distant from policy, the issue is Russophobia.[28] A member of this group said, "[I'm] increasingly concerned at the Russophobia and the demonization of Russia [and] the team demonization of Russia's leader, which gets in the way of understanding both what's bad, but also what's—I won't say bad and good—but what's unacceptable and what we can work with, what we need. We need to understand our adversaries, as well as our friends.... We understand neither very well these days." For this interviewee, "Russophobia has gotten to the point where everything is just automatically in a box and you can't even argue for a more subtle [approach] even in the U.S. national interest. Even if you put it in terms of... 'This is good for us,' you still can't suggest that there's anything wrong with the conventional wisdom or orthodoxy without being branded a Putin lover or soft on Russia."[29]

IR scholar John Mearsheimer's interventions after the invasion of Ukraine represent a more widespread view in the policy space, one that gained rare mainstream media attention. For Mearsheimer, the West brought the invasion on itself, ignoring Russia's clear revisionist designs, and its desire to be treated as a great power with regional security interests of its own. A chief interlocutor of

---

[23] Hill and Gaddy 2015.
[24] Russia interview 034, 17 November 2020, via video call.
[25] Russia interview 034, 17 November 2020, via video call.
[26] Russia interview 046, 12 June 2021, via video call.
[27] Russia interview 046, 12 June 2021, via video call.
[28] Tsygankov 2009.
[29] Russia interview 014, 16 October 2020, via video call.

the Russia-we-havers, notably directing his comment at the views of Graham in particular, explained it this way: those who take Russia as it is "tend to think the United States was much too hard on Russia after the fall of the Soviet Union. They tend to think NATO enlargement was a mistake. Some of them think we were pressing Russia too hard on democracy. There are various views, but Tom Graham's views, and I know them well, are based on a presumption that this Western notion that Russia can be a democracy in a normal European country is fanciful, that we have to understand Russia as it really is."[30]

In sum, what holds the "diverse group that Tom Graham has gathered" together is not a coherent "assessment of Russia. There's just too many different people with very different perspectives," one academic commented. Rather, what holds the Russia-we-havers together is a shared view that "they don't want a policy to be made based on the automatic assumption that everything Russia does is hostile. That is ... dangerous for the execution of policy."[31]

The Russia-We-Wanters

The letter penned by David Kramer and company in *Politico* in response to the Graham letter crystallizes the views and dispositions of a second broad camp within the U.S. Russia-watching community. Like the Graham camp, this second group is often personalized as the "Fried camp" after longtime Russia hand Daniel Fried.[32] The Fried group is not content to deal with Russia as it is, but seeks to promote relations while leaving open the door for Russian development along more liberal, democratic lines: a Russia we, in America and by extension the rest of the world, want.

As one Russia expert and podcaster explained, the Russia-we-wanters believe we are doing "ourselves and the Russians a disservice to think that they don't want something more than what we have right now."[33] A former ambassador to Moscow and strong Russia-we-wanter expressed the view that the United States should not seek the sort of improvement in relations via loosening of the sanctions regime advocated by Graham et al., because it is not what the Russian people want: "I don't accept Russia as it is," he explained. "I think we have to continue because, if nothing else, the people of Russia, a lot of the young people who I knew ... they want to see their country ... become a democracy."[34] The task is,

---

[30] Russia interview 035, 18 November 2020, via video call.
[31] Russia interview 022, 27 October 2020, via video call.
[32] Weiser Family Distinguished Fellow at the Atlantic Council. Formerly special assistant and National Security Council senior director for Presidents Clinton (1993–1997) and Bush (2001–2005). Ambassador to Poland (1997–2000) and assistant secretary of state for Europe (2005–2009).
[33] Russia interview 017, 19 November 2020, via video call.
[34] Russia interview 018, 3 December 2020, via video call.

therefore, "to try to fashion a policy that enhances our interests and that of our allies and to do the kinds of things in the future without necessarily accepting, you know, Putin's imperialistic policies in the near abroad, undermining democracy or basically giving up on the chances for a better European security system."[35]

For Russia-we-havers and the signatories of the Kramer letter, the Graham position is "basically a call for ignoring human rights problems.... That's how I would interpret it, perhaps a little unfairly," one key signatory noted.[36] The Russia-we-have view is duly categorized by opponents as a moral position—a crusading view to its critics, justified for its proponents. One supporter of the Russia-we-want position comments, "My view is when something unacceptable happens, like ... the poisoning of [Alexander Litvinenko in London] or the murder of Nemtsov or the murder of Magnitsky, if we say those things are unacceptable, then we actually have to do something so that we don't appear as if we say it's unacceptable and then accept it. And so that's why I've supported sanctions on the regime ... whereas Tom [Graham] wants to focus on where we can find common interests. And he thinks that values are not interests. And I—that's where we really strongly disagree."[37]

For one former State Department Russia hand, a critic of the Russia-we-want view, by contrast, the 1990s saw a "kind of crusading mentality or theology," an "attempt by liberal internationalists to change the fundamental character of Russia and to export America's concept of human rights and democracy to Russia, [which led] to a lot of mistakes."[38] "How can you explain this turn away from the truth and towards a more authoritarian and unified Western position other than the fact that someone is morally deficient in way?" a leading Russia-we-haver noted.[39] For one think tanker, "[The Kramer types believe] 'We are right. They are wrong.'"[40] But "I don't think the Russians think they're evil. I think the Russians sometimes do things that are evil. I think the Americans sometimes do things that are evil, and the Europeans accidentally sometimes do things that are evil."[41]

For Russia-we-havers, while concern with such overt moralism might be justified, the nature of the Russian regime renders the meaningful cooperation engagers hope for unlikely in any case. "If you accept Russia as it is, then you focus on other issues that are important in the relationship ... [You] just have to realize that ... our ability to influence or change it ... is virtually zero."[42]

---

[35] Russia interview 018, 3 December 2020, via video call.
[36] Russia interview 006, 20 November 2020, via video call.
[37] Russia interview 006, 20 November 2020, via video call.
[38] Russia interview 011, 12 October 2020, via video call.
[39] Russia interview 007, 13 November 2020, via video call.
[40] Russia interview 008, 20 October 2020, via video call.
[41] Russia interview 008, 20 October 2020, via video call.
[42] Russia interview 006, 20 November 2020, via video call.

Moreover, as a former Obama official noted, "My problem with [the Graham] letter is that in order to cooperate, you have to have overlapping interests. There has to be something . . . you're working toward that you can agree would be useful. . . . There ain't much."[43] Calls for enmeshing the relationship in process ignore what, for this Russia hand, was years of hard work. "We tried really hard. I mean the reset. I mean, we really tried hard" to improve U.S.-Russia relations.[44] For this interviewee, we failed.

Yet, in contrast to the China debate, the notion of engagement with Russia is no longer off the rhetorical table. But what follows as policy is less the sort of "enmeshed engagement" with Russian elites advocated by Rojansky and others, and more deep engagement with ordinary Russians, especially younger, liberal-leaning citizens. As one longtime Russia-hand explained, America should return to the first principles it developed under Ronald Reagan, "which is to talk to the Russian people . . . being more coherent and comprehensive in the way [we] approach Russia. That was the main thrust."[45] The United States should not, on this view, aid the Putin regime in stealing from the Russian people their chance of a better life. In candid terms, for this Russia-we-wanter, "Putin is a motherfucker who is stealing Russia's potential . . . if Russia were left to be Russia. I mean, basically . . . the way to sum it up is, if Russia were left to be Russia and the Russian people could have the future they wanted, it would look much more European and much less adversarial."[46]

The Russia-we-wanter label is thus misleading, it should be noted. At the heart of the worldview is that it is not just that *we* in America want a more liberal, open, and democratic Russia. *The Russians want it too.* The Russia-we-havers do not agree. As the above interviewee, in government under Clinton and later Biden, said, "I'm sure the Tom Graham line would say that [encouraging ordinary Russians to think about Russia's future differently] can be dangerous, as in the CIA infiltrating the ivory tower and trying to send people back as revolutionaries. But on the other hand, there is a way to do that. Presumably that's just about creating deep links with other potential elites in other countries."[47]

The notion that the last two decades has witnessed the return of a "traditional Russia" is thus given short shrift by most Russia-we-wanters. As one explained, the "conclusion that Russia is, by virtue of this history, always going to be some variant of what it is today" is nonsense. Not only does it ignore the will of many younger, pro-Western Russians, it shifts the burden of improving relations onto America, not the autocratic regime in Moscow. "The trouble is, when you try

---

[43] Russia interview 019, 13 November 2020, via telephone.
[44] Russia interview 019, 13 November 2020, via telephone.
[45] Russia interview 020, 16 November 2020, via video call.
[46] Russia interview 020, 16 November 2020, via video call.
[47] Russia interview 020, 16 November 2020, via video call.

to put that [taking Russia as it is] into practice, it means another reset, another reset. The burden becomes on us to make things nice with Russia."[48] Why should the burden fall on the United States, Russia-we-havers ask? The United States is not denying the sovereignty of countries in Eastern Europe or interfering in democratic processes around the world.

The Russia-we-wanters by necessity play down or refute the argument, made by the Russia-we-havers, that the breakdown in U.S.-Russia relations risks nuclear proliferation or even Russian use of nuclear weapons—a risk that rose sharply with the onset of full-scale war in Ukraine in early 2022. As a former ambassador explained "[to] the hysterics who say we can't support Ukraine because Russia might nuke us . . . it's not going to happen. The Soviet Union was more powerful militarily than Russia is today and we were able to contain the Soviet Union. We could contain Russia."[49] While Moscow's nuclear capabilities should not be ignored, it follows, nor should they dictate U.S. policy.

The Russia-we-want view, then, is in some ways a *more* positive view of Russia and a more optimistic position on what the future might hold than that predominates among the Graham camp. As one academic and former official explained, "It's quite a sympathetic view, actually . . . I think Sandy Vershbow[50] [a prominent Russia-we-wanter] is not less sympathetic toward Russian culture . . . and the possibilities of Russia's future than Tom Graham." In fact, "[He is] probably more hopeful. . . . The problem is to get the Russians to do the right thing."[51] For the Graham crowd, by contrast, "There's actually a greater fatalism. . . . They say we have to accept Russia as it is . . . [and] there's a growing divide among people as to whether one should be hopeful about Russia's long-term prospects."[52] Such a split characterizes the Russia-we-wanters too. As one explained, "I found [the Kramer] letter a little strident in tone, but also kind of dismissive of negotiation and dialogue, sort of basically saying that the regime is so odious and zero sum in its thinking, it's really not worth it. That's the point. I mean, [the letter] did say that . . . certain arms control agreements were worth pursuing if we could do it. But we're a little too fatalistic in the other direction."[53]

The Russia-we-want position is also more optimistic on the United States' ability to change Russian behavior. As one critic noted, the Kramer letter "basically said just push hard and [the Russians] will drop out of the tree like a rope,

---

[48] Russia interview 035, 18 November 2020, via video call.
[49] Russia interview 040, 1 December 2020, via video call.
[50] Alexander "Sandy" Vershbow is a Distinguished Fellow with the Atlantic Council's Scowcroft Center for Strategy and Security and Eurasia Center. A career Foreign Service officer (1977–2008), Vershbow served as ambassador to the Russian Federation (2001–2005) and special assistant to the president and National Security Council senior director for Russian affairs (1994–1997).
[51] Russia interview 044, 4 December 2020, via video call.
[52] Russia interview 044, 4 December 2020, via video call.
[53] Russia interview 038, 30 November 2020, via video call.

climb into our laps, and agree to do everything we ask because, in fact, they can't take the heat any longer."[54] The Russia-we-wanters are thus "not really willing to put much on the table" in diplomacy with Moscow since,

> in their own view, some of them are a very hard-line people.... It is something of a traitorous posture on your part to try to put yourself in the other guy's shoes to understand how he or she is thinking, to listen to what they say and to see whether, in fact, that brings you a conclusion as to where are openings and how you can exploit them.... So they are basically of the unilateralist diktat school.... We morally were much better than they are. Well, you know, they're terrible people and they make awful mistakes and they're cruel and inhumane. ... Not that I would argue with them on those questions, but I would argue with them on the fact that there's a way out. They believe in pressure producing miracles. And I believe pressure produces more backbreaking work.[55]

Finally, like each of the camps described above, the Russia-we-wanters are far from unified. As one longtime Russia hand noted, while aligned with political scientist and former ambassador to Moscow Michael McFaul for the most part, "I'm not sure Mike wants to spend the kind of money to look as strong on the defense side as I [do]."[56] The Russia-we-havers have also been split on how strongly to respond to Putin's intervention in Ukraine since 2014. As one senior official noted, "I lost in the interagency [struggle] when I wanted in 2016 to expose [Putin's] money and his lovers and his children and whatever, [to] make it tough for him. So there's even a split within [the more hawkish crowd on Russia]."[57]

The Eastern Europeans

Alongside the Russia-we-have and the Russia-we-want camps sits a third group, with strong points of overlap with the latter. This group comprises individuals with personal and institutional ties to Eastern Europe countries not allied with Russia. These individuals and groups are not Russia experts precisely, located as they are where the business community and lobbyists meet the Russia field. Nevertheless, they are a crucial constituency shaping U.S. thought and policy toward Eastern Europe. At the organizational level, the Atlantic Council and the Center for European Policy Analysis are key hubs.

---

[54] Russia interview 042, 3 December 2020, via video call.
[55] Russia interview 042, 3 December 2020, via video call.
[56] Russia interview 033, 16 November 2020, via video call.
[57] Russia interview 033, 16 November 2020, via video call.

The "third letter" in *Politico*, one Russia-we-haver explained, exemplified "the more institutional elements . . . pushing this kind of stuff [i.e., a tough line on Russia] . . . based on their own organizations like, say, the Atlantic Council, people on the Russia side, like Russia Today, journalists or things like this."[58] Such influence is not new. In the 1990s, "The Brzezinski family and Zbigniew Brzezinski personally was very influential, [alongside] Central and Eastern European constituencies in battleground states, where there was support for pro-Eastern European policies."[59] Deputy Secretary of State Strobe Talbott (1994–2001) changed his view on NATO enlargement, from opposition to support, in one think tanker's view, "as a political necessity because the political winds were in favor. And the argument was, look, if Russia turns out to be good, then we'll enlarge and will be fine. And if Russia is bad, then it's fine too [because now we'll know for sure]."[60]

As a Russia-we-haver explained, "So for example, you look at the Atlantic Council and you just look at their funders, it's principally defense contractors and foundations from Eastern Europe. It's like the Baltic Freedom Forum and the Hungarian National Memory Foundation, and so on."[61] Ukrainian groups are particularly important, "like the famous Burisma [Holdings Limited], who fund [former Ukrainian president] Petro Poroshenko himself [the richest oligarch in Ukraine]. They have a hand-in-glove relationship with lobbying firms, like Blue Star Strategies, which is a democratic firm."[62]

We should avoid conspiracy theories here. First, such connections are not secret, far from it. As one deep engager with Russia explained, "I'm forgetting the names now, but . . . this is easy research to do because it's all . . . on their website."[63] According to the Atlantic Council's "Honor roll," Burisma Holdings gave between $100,000 and $250,000, while the Kiev-based Victor Pinchuk Foundation gave $250,000–$499,000, among other donors from Europe and further afield. Russians are notably absent.

More importantly, however, conspiracy theories should be avoided because, as one mid-career think tanker of Russian origin explained, individuals with Eastern European connections and organizations with Eastern European funding are not hawkish on Russia because they hate Russia. "They do not suffer from any kind of Russophobia. That's not the issue . . . "[64] The thing is that they "really like Central Europe and Eastern Europe even more. Right? They're interested in that policy. And so for the causes they are interested in and the agenda

---

[58] Russia interview 036, 19 November 2020, via video call.
[59] Russia interview 007, 2 October 2020, via video call.
[60] Russia interview 007, 2 October 2020, via video call.
[61] Russia interview 005, 30 September 2020, via video call.
[62] Russia interview 005, 30 September 2020, via video call.
[63] Russia interview 005, 30 September 2020, via video call.
[64] Russia interview 039, 30 November 2020, via video call.

they are interested in, Russia typically ends up being problematic and Russia typically ends up being a policy opportunity cost that gets raised like, Whoa, if we do this, we'll not hurt. You know, our relationship with Russia will not lead to a security dilemma in Russia. And they say fucking Russia, always Russia."[65]

At least before the invasion of February 2022, the issue was less a dislike of Russia than an exclusion of Russians and Russian perspectives in a group of individuals from "the Baltics, Ukraine, Poland and to some extent, you know, Georgia.... I think this plays a really big role as well," one Russia policy commentator explained.

> If you look at the guest list of events of... the Atlantic Council, right, to some extent, the Kennan [Institute at the Wilson] Center or something like this, you see certain people recycle the circle in and circle out. And they all come from certain camps. And the Russian liberal opposition, I think, has an outsized influence on how Americans and think tanks and academia like see the Russia problem, and then on the other hand, Central Europeans or Eastern Europeans who come through these think tanks, too.[66]

The effect is to create a third camp in the broader national security conversation undergirding the Russia-we-want position.

To Know Your Enemy

For one of the leading voices seeking to deal with Russia as it is, the Russia-we-have and Russia-we-want groups reflect enduring groupings in U.S. foreign policy. "This is traditional American foreign policy. From the moment the United States got engaged in the world today as a big power... one of the driving forces behind American foreign policy has been to transform the world."[67] Voices of restraint and a desire to avoid imperial entanglements, from Hamilton to Eisenhower, have lost out, in the words of one former ambassador in Central Asia, to "a mindset... peculiar to Americans,... who have grown up believing... that we are such an example for the world and that... everything we do is right and that although we may make mistakes, our intentions are good, you know?"[68]

However, like the Engager/anti-Engager groups on China, those seeking to deal with Russia as it is and as it could be are not inevitable groups, nor did they emerge overnight in recent years. Once again, the Russia-we-have/

---

[65] Russia interview 039, 30 November 2020, via video call.
[66] Russia interview 036, 19 November 2020, via video call.
[67] Russia interview 030, 13 November 2020, via video call.
[68] Russia interview 023, 29 October 2020, via telephone.

Russia-we-want camps have more proximate origins, with antecedents in the Cold War and immediate post–Cold War years.

The Origins of Russia as It Is and as We'd Like It

Like the China field, America's Russia watchers trace the origins of contemporary divisions in their community back decades. The post-1945 era is common referent for the long-term origins of principal divisions in the Russia community too, especially for those involved for multiple decades. For one senior academic and former policymaker, for example, beyond the relitigation of the 1990s and the expansion of NATO, present divisions can be traced further back, to lingering debates about the wisdom of promises made by President Roosevelt at the Yalta conference in February 1945.

"The Russia field has been divided ... at least since 1940 into two schools of thought, which you saw reflected in those open letters," one business academic told me.[69] On the one hand, you have "the Roosevelt view [of] Russia [as] a country that we can do business with, even though it has a different system.... And then [there is] the other view, associated with people like George Kennan and other people like that, [that] Russia has a different system domestically [so] you can't deal with it as you can deal with other countries in the international system."[70] For them, the open letters are merely an updated version of the U.S. debate over Russia at the end of World War II, "letter one saying we have to normalize relations with Russia ... and then two ... saying, no, Russia is a malign power."[71]

A senior former ambassador agreed. There "have been perhaps two broad camps in the Russian community for some time.... I can remember in my first year in graduate school, which would have been in 1954, attending a conference at West Point ... and the whole second piece of the discussion was the Soviet threat and how much communism and the Soviet Union with nuclear weapons presented an almost impossible challenge to the United States."[72]

The history of America's Sovietologists to the end of the Cold War has already been told expertly by David Engerman.[73] Suffice it here to emphasize how these divisions form a background common sense among Russia watchers who care to consider the longer-term origins of their field, whether historically accurate or not. For one senior historian and political scientist, "A group of [which Harvard

---

[69] Russia interview 015, 19 October 2020, via video call.
[70] Russia interview 015, 19 October 2020, via video call.
[71] Russia interview 015, 19 October 2020, via video call.
[72] Russia interview 042, 3 December 2020, via video call.
[73] Engerman 2009.

historian] Richard Pipes was the most prominent . . . took the view that Russia was an unchanging beast and it had to be totally destroyed rather than reformed. Could you reform it, or did the whole thing just have to collapse and then you could build something new?" The counterpoint to Pipes was "Seweryn Bialer, who was a communist who had defected in the mid-fifties and was a professor at Columbia and writing about reform in the Soviet Union and the possibility of real change. So there were different currents."[74]

The terms used to describe the schools vary. For one former ambassador to Moscow and leading political scientist, to "oversimplify . . . it was the totalitarian school versus that the interest group/pluralist politics [school], right? Zbigniew Brzezinski versus [Jerry] Hough[75] and Steve Cohen."[76] The former group held that economic and political modernization was unlikely in the Soviet Union viewed as a deeply and intrinsically authoritarian system. In part, the view was shaped by the experiences of émigrés from the region. "You had this initial moment during the Cold War, [with] the totalitarian school of Zbigniew Brzezinski and others, that said the system can never reform its totalitarian nature and eventual collapse. And remember, there was a big influx of East European exiles that came to American academia during that time. And they brought that perspective with them."[77]

In reaction, "In the late sixties and early seventies, there was a pluralism school that developed [that] said actually it's not as totalitarian as these old school people think. There's interest group politics here within the Soviet system."[78] Proponents of the pluralist view were more optimistic, rejecting the idea—clearly mirrored today—that the Soviet Union could be equated with the Russian leadership, from Khrushchev to Gorbachev. "That was basically the dominant paradigm. Gorbachev came along, and the reformers like Jerry Hough and Steve Cohen, they felt very vindicated from their theories that Gorbachev has come along and it was possible to reform communism."[79]

Like divisions with the CCAS, viewpoints on the Soviet Union during the Cold War were not easily separable from disagreements about U.S. domestic politics. "I always wondered how much of [the different viewpoints on Russia] was driven by American domestic politics," the above interviewee noted, "because this was a generation that [was] in college and getting their PhDs during the Vietnam War. . . . And they had this kind of anti-imperialist outlook towards America."[80] Not all were necessarily sympathetic to the Soviet Union, "although

---

[74] Russia interview 029, 12 November 2020, via video call.
[75] Professor of political science at Duke University (1973–2016).
[76] Russia interview 028 (second interview), 3 February 2021, via video call.
[77] Russia interview 028 (second interview), 3 February 2021, via video call.
[78] Russia interview 028 (second interview), 3 February 2021, via video call.
[79] Russia interview 028 (second interview), 3 February 2021, via video call.
[80] Russia interview 028 (second interview), 3 February 2021, via video call.

a couple of them were, guys like Steve Cohen and Jerry Hough down at Duke. I mean, Hough in particular really leaned into this. At one point he wrote this article saying [the] Soviet Union is more democratic than the United States because it has these interest groups. The workers are represented in a way that they're really not represented in American democracy. [This was] in the early seventies during a real crisis in American democracy." Nonetheless, the pluralism school "was a new school of thought."[81]

For others, the issue broke down simply as the "optimists versus the pessimists." For one political scientist, "The period up through the collapse of the Soviet Union and probably a little bit into the collapse of Soviet Union . . . [people] basically fell into the pessimists and the optimists."[82] The latter "wrote about [how there was] no change in the Soviet Union and that really it wasn't any different over the sixties, seventies and eighties."[83] Until Gorbachev came along, the "optimist[s] couldn't find a way to express how . . . their optimism would be realized. There was a kind of sense of, well, things have to change because this is such an inhuman or bizarre or totalitarian or something system that it, it will, it will change."[84]

Such long-term origins of the Russia-as-it-is and as-we'd-like-it-to-be positions became consequential during the early 1990s and have continued to shape views into the new millennium. Russia watchers do not agree, however, on precisely how, only that the way in which people interpreted the end of the Cold War mattered for how they assessed U.S. options in the 1990s.

As one former ambassador and Russia-we-wanter explained, "You can make the same argument today about splits in the Moscow-watching community as you made 50 years ago."[85] There were those, on the one hand, "who saw the two countries, the United States and Russia today, the United States and the Soviet Union then, as you might say, morally equivalent."[86] And on the other, there were those who saw the Soviet Union, and now Russia, "as a very large problem. . . . Most people have been consistent. Those of us old enough to have been engaged in the Soviet conversation, now in the Russian conversation, have been consistently on one side."[87] On the other there are people who "cheat," the interviewee went on. "If we had this conversation in the nineties, it would be a very different conversation, because while I was skeptical about Moscow's intentions in the nineties, I considered it impossible that there was going to be a real change in

---

[81] Russia interview 028 (second interview), 3 February 2021, via video call.
[82] Russia interview 022, 27 October 2020, via video call.
[83] Russia interview 022, 27 October 2020, via video call.
[84] Russia interview 022, 27 October 2020, via video call.
[85] Russia interview 040, 1 December 2020, via video call.
[86] Russia interview 040, 1 December 2020, via video call.
[87] Russia interview 040, 1 December 2020, via video call.

policy that would lead to a true period of cooperation between Washington and Moscow."[88]

Some thus made little distinction between America's new Russian interlocutors after 1991 and their old Soviet enemies. This insistence on continuity was prominent especially in the military, according to one former ambassador to the region. Those in the U.S. Navy especially retained a "kind of knee-jerk [view] of Russia is the enemy, you know, the bogeyman."[89] Beyond the military, at State and the NSC, some still held an automatic "sort of Russophobia. And I'd say that was pretty pervasive still on Capitol Hill and in many respects has remained so. I've been struck by the degree to which there is a default Russophobia that has carried over to this day, obviously strengthened since 2014."[90] Many such Russia skeptics held their views "because of personal experience and anger, not so much because they were neoconservative," one political scientist and former policymaker explained.[91]

Others read the events 1989 in the Soviet Union through their own political and academic lenses. For revisionist historians like Stephen Cohen, long skeptical of characterizations of the USSR as incapable of change, "Gorbachev [was] Russia's savior."[92] If Gorbachev was the savior, of both the USSR and their theories, we might add, some like Cohen were led to view "Yeltsin as the destroyer."[93] For them, "There was always the possibility that the Soviet system could reform. . . . And the most extreme elements of that was [the view that] they're going to become more like us, we're going to become more like them, and we're going to meet in Hungary and have the same kind of political and economic systems. . . . There is even a school of thought called that. I'm forgetting the label of it [the "convergence thesis"]."[94] For them Mikhail Gorbachev was "the guy that was proving the theory. . . . Hough and Cohen in particular were saying, 'We told you so.' There were interest group politics there. And now we have a reformer within the system who's going to democratize the Soviet system."[95]

From this perspective, the United States embraced Russian leader Yeltsin too quickly, turning its back on former Soviet leader Gorbachev, with whom they had negotiated the end of the Cold War. This latter point is important, although often lost to history. The collapse of the Soviet Union in 1991 was not the cause of the end of the Cold War for revisionists like Cohen. The Cold War had ended two years earlier via high-level negotiation, caused by changes of minds in

---

[88] Russia interview 040, 1 December 2020, via video call.
[89] Russia interview 023, 29 October 2020, via telephone.
[90] Russia interview 024, 31 October 2020, via video call.
[91] Russia interview 024, 31 October 2020, via video call.
[92] Russia interview 034, 17 November 2020, via video call.
[93] Russia interview 034, 17 November 2020, via video call.
[94] Russia interview 028 (second interview), 3 February 2021, via video call.
[95] Russia interview 028 (second interview), 3 February 2021, via video call.

Moscow and on the backs of extensive transnational efforts, not U.S. economic coercion. That the putatively democratic Yeltsin was America's choice said more about U.S. desires for Russia than the reality, which would shape U.S. policy in the 1990s, especially the decision to expand NATO.

Here the revisionist and realist perspectives converged on the concern that the United States might unwittingly usher in the return of a traditional Russian foreign policy in Eastern Europe. As one political scientist, involved at the NSC during the first Clinton administration, explained in realist terms, "There were people like myself who were opposed [to NATO expansion] largely because of the concern that when you expanded NATO to the east, you increase the likelihood that Russia would respond to build a countervailing coalition and that might scuttle the opportunity to anchor Russia in Europe. And I think that that's the view that predominated among analysts in the academic community, but not the view that ended up dominating on the inside."[96]

Other opponents of the totalitarian school came to different conclusions, however, notably the nascent "transitologists," those who would make their names (and careers) charting and theorizing the transition away from communism in the countries of the former Soviet Union. The academic work of a transitologist like Michael McFaul thus aligned with the pluralism school by rejecting the view of the USSR as a monolith and accepting a greater role for domestic interest groups and local politics than the totalitarian school allowed for. As a position within the policy debate, however, the pluralist-aligned perspective supported the views of what one interviewee called the "liberal expansionists" who argued "that NATO needed to expand as a strategy of democratic enlargement."[97] The pluralist/transitologist perspective "wasn't against Russia" but for the view that "geopolitics should not play a role. This was really about values and in some ways righting the wrong of Yalta ... and letting countries into the democratic space when and if they are ready."[98]

In the policy fight, the liberal expansionists were supported by those "of Central European extraction ... Polish Americans, Czech Americans, Estonian Americans."[99] "Americans from Central Europe lobbied hard," one former official noted, "and it's no accident that when Clinton or other top officials gave a speech about NATO enlargement, they tended to give it in Michigan or Illinois or Ohio, where there were a lot of voters from those countries."[100]

Tracing the disputed origins of the contemporary Russia-we-have versus the Russia-we-want camps prior to and after the end of the Cold War is not merely

---

[96] Russia interview 024, 31 October 2020, via video call.
[97] Russia interview 024, 31 October 2020, via video call.
[98] Russia interview 024, 31 October 2020, via video call.
[99] Russia interview 024, 31 October 2020, via video call.
[100] Russia interview 024, 31 October 2020, via video call.

an academic exercise. These origins matter. How a Russia analyst or scholar views the past and how it unfolded continues to shape perceptions about the present. As one mid-career Russia analyst observed, "There's parts of the [Russia-watching] community that are firmly stuck in the 1980s, and there are parts of the communities that are firmly stuck in the early 1970s."[101] For those "stuck in the 1970s," the era of détente and a mild improvement in U.S.-Russia relations, the aim is to "have a better relationship for the sake of having a better relationship." But "that's not politically sustainable in the United States.... But they think, hey, at any point in time it can be like [the] 1970s.... Who cares what the regime is like? . . . Let's just do another détente."[102] For those stuck in the 1980s, like "Sandy Vershbow [and] this whole group . . . for them, the Berlin Wall is always on the verge of collapse. And so they think whatever's happening in Russia, it's . . . going to lead to collapse [like in] the 1980s."[103] But central to this view is an understanding of what ended the Cold War, what the Cold War *was*: "The reason why I tend to think they're wrong is because they're wrong about what happened. So they're wrong about the causes of the dissolution of the Soviet Union and the end of the Cold War. And because they get that history wrong, from my perspective, they also get the present wrong."[104]

Yet, however much we might wish to get the history, and hence the present, right, no such certainty is forthcoming. Past, present, and future remain in dispute. The following task, therefore, is to trace how these longer-term origins of the China and Russia communities' divisions and distinctions crystallized into the Engagers versus the anti-Engagers and the Russia-we-havers versus the Russia-we-wanters.

The Polarization of U.S.-Russia Relations

U.S. Russia policy since the end of the Cold War is neither identical to nor a mirror image of China policy. At no point, either under Trump, his predecessors, or successor, did relations between the U.S. government and the Russia segment of the national security community shift to enable a rapid policy turnover. The "Russian reset" of 2009–2010, the closest Russia policy comes to large shift away from the status quo, was the initiative of Russia specialists very much within the mainstream view in the field. Russia policy became polarized under Trump in a partisan sense, with Republicans divided between wings more and less credulous of Russian interference in the 2016 election. But contra China policy, the

---

[101] Russia interview 039, 30 November 2020, via video call.
[102] Russia interview 039, 30 November 2020, via video call.
[103] Russia interview 039, 30 November 2020, via video call.
[104] Russia interview 039, 30 November 2020, via video call.

Russia-we-haver and the Russia-we-wanter camps crystallized over policy, not partisan politics or a broad framing of Russia. I pick up the story with the genesis of the reset and its failure after 2012, when Vladimir Putin returned to the Russian presidency in an ominous sign for political developments in the country, subsequently confirmed by the events in Ukraine in 2014 and the takeover of Crimea. The effect of these events was to convert liberal interventionists—who were pivotal to the reset—to the side of the Russia-we-wanters, while the United States set about building a comprehensive sanctions regime, constricting relations, and (in the view of the Russia-we-havers) ignoring arms control.

An Uneasy Peace: Russia Watching after Yeltsin

If the last years of the millennium were the high point of Engagement with China as policy and frame, yet were also when the seeds of Engagement's demise were sown, the period saw a similar apogee of U.S.-Russia policy built on foundations of sand. Russia policy was imbricated in congressional attacks on Clinton toward the end of his tenure. As one journalist recalls, "It's ninety-nine or 2000 [and Congress is] talk[ing] about the mistakes of the Clinton administration. . . . And these Republicans in Congress are like, 'Tell us more, tell us more.' . . . There's always this pressure from Congress, and it tends to be toward a more confrontational stance."[105] At the level of high politics, however, the "Bill and Boris" show of genuinely warm relations papered over tensions, centered on the 1999 bombing of Kosovo amid NATO enlargement.

Tensions would deepen when Yeltsin stepped aside in May 2000 in favor of his prime minister, Vladimir Putin, appointed the previous year. The rise of former KGB agent Putin punctured the "triumphalism in that period" among America's Russia experts, as one interviewee expressed, which stemmed from a widespread view that "we beat them, we won."[106] It cast doubt on the hope shared among America's Russia watchers that, as one 1990 official described it, "Russia would emerge as a normal democratic state that would be more focused on what a democracy [should be] focused on, which was how you ensure a good economy, meet the needs of the people, become, you know, less Soviet-like or less Russian-like."[107]

But optimism about U.S.-Russia relations did not disappear overnight. As in the case of China, 9/11 significantly affected Russia policy and expert views of Moscow. Putin's offer in the wake of the attacks to allow U.S. armed forces

---

[105] Russia interview 002, 21 September 2020, via video call.
[106] Russia interview 027, 6 November 2020, via video call.
[107] Russia interview 031, 11 November 2020, via video call.

access to its operations in Afghanistan via the northern route enamored him to George W. Bush. The effect was to push Russia further down the list of administration priorities, dominated by the soon-to-be-expanded global war on terror. The war on terror offered Putin a rhetorical frame to cover a crackdown against dissidents, especially after an attack on a school in Beslan in 2004, which left some 300 children dead.

Beyond the official views of a distracted U.S. government, however, Russia elicited greater concern among America's national security community. A 2006 Council on Foreign Relations task force, staffed by Russia watchers across what would later crystallize as the Russia-we-have and Russia-we-want camps, is indicative. Collecting Russia watchers such as Michael McFaul, Fiona Hill, Mark Brzezinski (son of Zbigniew), Stephen Sestanovich,[108] Robert Blackwill, and others, the task force concluded that Russia was "headed in the wrong direction." The "United States has generally enjoyed good relations with Russia since the dissolution of the Soviet Union fifteen years ago," but "in recent years ... Russian society and foreign policy have continued to change in ways that raise questions and cause problems for the United States."[109] Reinforcing the desire for cooperation "on a number of issues—Iran, energy, HIV/AIDS, and preventing terrorists from acquiring weapons of mass destruction— ... central to promoting American interests," the task force nevertheless recommended "the United States pursue 'selective cooperation' with Russia rather than seek a broad 'partnership' that is not now feasible."[110] It was not feasible because "domestic developments in Russia are of consequence to the United States for strategic as well as moral reasons, and ... U.S. policymakers should address themselves both to what happens inside Russia as well as to more traditional U.S. foreign policy concerns."[111] Again, Russia was headed in the wrong direction.

As in the case of the more recent China task forces, as interesting as what the report itself concludes is what the report does not say, and who dissented from its conclusions. Richard Burt[112] dissented from the report's emphasis on democratization, for example: "At this stage in the relationship, making democratization a central component of its policy toward Russia—as this report

---

[108] George F. Kennan Senior Fellow in Russian and Eurasian Studies at the Council on Foreign Relations, and Kathryn and Shelby Cullom Davis Professor of International Diplomacy at Columbia University's School of International and Public Affairs. A former policy planner at the State Department, between 1997 and 2001 Sestanovich served as special adviser to Secretary of State Madeleine Albright on the former Soviet Union.

[109] *Russia's Wrong Direction: What the United States Can and Should Do*, Council on Foreign Relations, March 2006, https://www.cfr.org/report/russias-wrong-direction, xi.

[110] *Russia's Wrong Direction*, xi.

[111] *Russia's Wrong Direction*, xii.

[112] Former assistant secretary of state for European and Canadian affairs (1983–1985), and ambassador to Germany (1985–1989). Burt was also chief American negotiator for the Strategic Arms Limitation Treaty (START 1), which was signed in 1991.

recommends—runs the risk of undermining our other critical objectives in working with Moscow."[113] Walter Slocombe,[114] Robert Blackwill, and Dov Zakheim[115] mirrored these concerns:

> The United States should accept that its main interests are not Russia's internal arrangements (though a more democratic and less corrupt Russia would probably serve U.S. interests, as it would certainly serve U.S. values). American foreign policy should cold-bloodedly realize that the United States and Russia have real differences and conflicts, but that they can cooperate when they have de facto shared goals. The United States did that with the Soviet Union; it can as well with Putin's Russia. But it should do so without either illusions or paranoia.[116]

Divisions among America's Russia watchers remained as U.S.-Russia diplomatic relations continued to decline over the decade. In a now infamous speech at the Munich Security Conference in 2007, Putin lambasted the notion of "unipolarity," which, "however one might embellish this term ... refers to one type of situation, namely one center of authority, one center of force, one center of decision-making. It is a world in which there is one master, one sovereign. ... [T]his is pernicious not only for all those within this system, but also for the sovereign itself because it destroys itself from within."[117] The short but intense Russo-Georgian War followed in August 2008, up to that point the nadir of post–Cold War relations between Washington and Moscow.

The Unrealized Reset

If 2008 represented the low point in U.S.-Russia relations after 1989 up to then, two events of that year also signaled a window of opportunity, should any American policymakers wish to chance a new approach to Russia. The first was Putin's decision to step down from the residency in May 2008 in favor of Dmitry Medvedev, with Putin retaking the role of prime minister he had vacated eight years earlier. Medvedev had a reputation as a potential reformer, at least in comparison to Putin, and might therefore be someone with whom the United States could do business. As the divisions opened up in the CFR task force report made clear, diplomatic progress with the United States would be that much easier with

---

[113] *Russia's Wrong Direction*, 73.
[114] Former undersecretary of defense for policy (1994–2001).
[115] Former deputy undersecretary of defense for planning and resources (1985–1987).
[116] *Russia's Wrong Direction*, 73.
[117] http://en.kremlin.ru/events/president/transcripts/copy/24034

an interlocutor who could at least be presented as sharing American interests in democracy, human rights, and the rule of law. The second event was the election of Barack Obama, an outsider to Washington compared to his predecessors, and a critic of foreign policy Establishment[118]—who thereby had the mandate and opportunity to attempt to reverse the slide in U.S.-Russia relations.

The Russian reset, launched by new secretary of state, Hilary Clinton, with her opposite number, Sergei Lavrov in March 2009, attempted to capitalize on Medvedev's tenure to restart U.S.-Russia relations. At the initiative's launch in Prague, the two top diplomats laughed off a mistranslation of "reset" into Russian—which instead became "overload"—as apt for the amount of work each side hoped to put in on issues of shared concern, beginning with Iran's nuclear program.[119] As a later recapitulation described, the reset

> sought to engage the Russian government to pursue foreign policy goals of common interest—win-win outcomes—for the American and Russian people. In parallel to this engagement with the Russian government, President Obama and his administration also have engaged directly with Russian society—as well as facilitated greater contacts between American and Russian business leaders, civil society organizations, and students—as a way to promote our economic interests, enhance mutual understanding between our two nations, and advance universal values.[120]

Designed to reverse the "dangerous drift" in bilateral relations, the reset's emphasis on civil society engagement and universal values reflects the input of Russia experts Michael McFaul—the Stanford political scientist who had advised Obama on the campaign trail—and think tanker and former professor of government Celeste Wallander.[121] McFaul became special assistant to the president and senior NSC director for Russian and Eurasian affairs, with Wallander undersecretary of defense for policy at the Pentagon. Both were strongly committed to human rights and democracy in Russia and convinced of the basic premises of the democratic peace thesis that democracies are less bellicose than their autocratic counterparts. As one official involved with the reset noted, "It's not just about power, it's about liberalism. It is about integration. It is about an international system that includes rule of law, protection for trade.... The Kremlin sees that as a core threat and therefore frames its interests in zero-sum terms relative

---

[118] Gideon Rachman, "Trump, Obama, and Their Battle with the 'Blob,'" *Financial Times*, 2 December 2019, https://www.ft.com/content/ab46ddd8-14e3-11ea-8d73-6303645ac406

[119] https://www.nytimes.com/2009/03/07/world/europe/07diplo.html

[120] "U.S.-Russia Relations: 'Reset' Fact Sheet," 24 June 2010, https://obamawhitehouse.archives.gov/the-press-office/us-russia-relations-reset-fact-sheet

[121] "U.S.-Russia Relations: 'Reset' Fact Sheet."

to the United States."[122] "The underlying assumption" of the reset, then, "was that the United States' national security interests are served by the existence of a community of countries that are committed to liberalism, both politically and economically, and . . . are increasingly integrated in that international system, not just economically, politically, socially, culturally, and that that's the basis for cooperation. . . . That is the premise of European security. . . . It's not rocket science."[123] While under no illusions about whether Putin would approve, the reasoning behind the reset "was the clear evidence [that] that's what Russian citizens wanted."[124]

The reset thus emerged from a particular location in the Russia field: neither hawks nor doves, but from those experts optimistic about the possibility of engagement as a means of stimulating change in Russia's external behavior and domestic governance. The view thus found support from individuals later associated with the both the Russia-as-it-is and Russia-as-we'd-like-it-to-be camps. The reset was not the brainchild of the realists, like Tom Graham, nor the arms controllers, nor the Daniel Fried camp. Yet it could garner support from each. As one official at the time, associated with the latter, confessed, "I didn't think the reset would work, and I told [McFaul so], but I thought it was worth a shot."[125] With Medvedev in the Kremlin, a reset was worth a try.

As one of its architects recalled,

> We were not naive. We knew that when Putin chose Medvedev, Medvedev was not exactly a . . . fairly elected president, and that Putin was standing behind him. But there were many other individuals that Putin could have chosen. And the debate basically came down to between Dmitry Medvedev and Sergei Ivanov, who was at that time, I think still, the defense minister. . . . But generally it was OK, they're still on the integration path . . . and so the premise of the reset was exactly that. . . . Basically it was saying, let's try again. . . . It wasn't just let's be nice again. It was, let's try again, let's push integration.[126]

Putin did not approve. While the reset was far from the uniform failure it now appears—the signing of New START treaty in April 2010 among its achievements—his return drove a wedge into the heart of America's Russia expert community. Putin's response to the events in Ukraine in 2014, including the invasion of the Crimea and the Donbas, solidified the two camps, with the liberal internationalists riven from those in favor of continued engagement. As

---

[122] Russia interview 032, 13 November 2020, via telephone.
[123] Russia interview 032, 13 November 2020, via telephone.
[124] Russia interview 032, 13 November 2020, via telephone.
[125] Russia interview 035, 18 November 2020, via video call.
[126] Russia interview 032, 13 November 2020, via telephone.

one former ambassador recalled, "I was in the thick of this and I was considered a hawk in the summer of 2014, but I was considered mainstream by the summer of 2015."[127]

Russia's invasion of the Crimea was met with a first round of U.S.-led international sanctions, beginning in December 2014, the first of four rounds, the final of which is under construction at the time of writing. As several interviewees emphasized, most often those critical of sanctions' usefulness, Congress's role complicated executive policymaking on Russia, since once applied, sanctions are difficult to remove. As one former ambassador noted, "What did the United States do? We resorted to a political response, and political response[s] are never very good when you're dealing with big-power politics."[128] The reason is that, with Congress, "it's always the most punitive approach possible because that plays well politically in town hall meetings.... In a town hall meeting, it's who can outdo the other."[129]

Yet critics of sanctions were in a marked minority after 2014. Some, like the small number of academic Russia engagers, many later signatories of the Graham letter, continued to rehash American mistakes. One of them commented,

> We created Putin, right? I mean, Putinism is an inevitable, very likely follow-on to Yeltsinism and the disaster of that relationship and the policies we've helped encourage. But there has been no rethinking whatsoever, even though the historical record—you probably know . . . the work of, you know, Mary Eloise Sarotte and others taking into [their calculations] the question of NATO expansion—that the record's pretty clear.... There was a promise made.[130]

More frequent among think tankers facing up to a new policy context, however, was an acceptance that "people in my broad camp would be those who think we need to find a more stable competition with Russia ... [while accepting] that there's no return to some sort of cooperative strategic partnership of the kind that people talked about before 2014."[131] As one academic explained,

> It was really 2014 that polarized viewpoints.... It came down to where you stood beside Ukraine, for example, and how you interpreted the Maidan revolution in Ukraine and Russia's involvement in the East. Did you see the conflict in Ukraine as merely Russian imperialism or . . . did local elements give

---

[127] Russia interview 040, 1 December 2020, via video call.
[128] Russia interview 044, 4 December 2020, via video call.
[129] Russia interview 044, 4 December 2020, via video call.
[130] Russia interview 015, 19 October 2020, via video call.
[131] Russia interview 010, 12 October 2020, via video call.

credence to the idea that the conflict was a civil war? ... Those were the extreme poles, and all sorts of people fell into the gray areas between them."[132]

Prophetically, this Russia engager proposed in late 2020 that "we haven't necessarily seen the worst yet."[133]

Russia Post-Trump

The 2016 election and its aftermath shattered the post–Cold War bipartisan consensus on Russia. As one Washington-based academic explained, "What the election interference in 2016 did was it changed the way the two parties approach Russia."[134] Where previously "the Republicans were tough on Russia and the Democrats were more ... 'We need to engage because of Putin's interference on behalf of Trump,' ... Republicans now viewed Russia more favorably than they did before ... [while] Democrats are angry."[135] As one former ambassador and state governor recalled, Russia (and China policy) was bipartisan, and then "you wake up to a world in which everything you do with Russia and China is polarized and it's red or blue, that it is Republican or Democrat. And you've got to adhere to the philosophical dictates of your camp."[136]

For one academic Russia-we-haver, therefore, "The 2016 election totally paralyzed any chance of meaningful agreement on Russia policy."[137] It became "similar to the Cold War. It became like any kind of serious engagement with Russia that didn't have an adequate level of criticism was tagged as pro-Russian."[138] But the reason was less about party politics pure and simple than the dynamics of Trump-era foreign policy. Unlike in the case of China, the election did not alter the principal camps within the Russia field, nor the relationship between the White House and the national security community. Struggling to staff his administration, Trump did not then hire Russia outsiders, as he had on China. Instead, his chief Russia position at the NSC went to Fiona Hill. Hill signed the Graham letter, but had a reputation prior to her appointment for holding robust views on Russia, and Putin in particular.[139] While "there is very little to be lost from saying we should take a harder line on Russia" under Trump, one think tanker

---

[132] Russia interview 036, 19 November 2020, via video call.
[133] Russia interview 010, 12 October 2020, via video call.
[134] Russia interview 006, 1 October 2020, via video call.
[135] Russia interview 006, 1 October 2020, via video call.
[136] Russia interview 043, 4 December 2020, via video call.
[137] Russia interview 011, 14 October 2020, via video call.
[138] Russia interview 036, 19 November 2020, via video call.
[139] Adam Entous, "What Fiona Hill Learned in the White House," *New Yorker*, 29 June 2020, https://www.newyorker.com/magazine/2020/06/29/what-fiona-hill-learned-in-the-white-house.

explained, it became much harder to say, "I'm not supporting the president, but we should engage with Russia. That's a much harder sell."[140]

As described in the previous chapter, the new Biden administration did not repeat its search for a new framing of China in the case of Russia. Instead, it fulfilled the prediction of one academic Russia watcher, for whom "once they have a Biden administration in power [the Democrats will] probably continue in autopilot to a certain [degree]. They'll probably try to engage Russia on ... the missile treaty [New START].... And I think they have political space to do that because Trump is the one that pulled out of it. They can frame it as an anti-Trump thing, but I don't expect anything dramatic or spectacular."[141]

New START duly came into effect in February 2021, due to expire in 2026, but was the only policy that might be described as pro-engagement with Russia. As in the case of China, the Biden administration appointees were not from the Russia-we-havers. NSC Russia director Andrea Kendall-Taylor had a reputation as middle of the road, a safe pair of hands for a relationship likely to be controversial and potentially crisis-prone—as it turned out.[142] Toria Nuland, appointed undersecretary of state for political affairs, had a long track record advocating for a more liberal, democratic Russia. With relations at a low point, autopilot was quickly overtaken by first private, then public, concern over Russian troop buildups ahead of what became the invasion of Ukraine.

Conclusion

By 2022, U.S. Russia policy, and the Russia expert field, was in stasis. As one Russia watcher noted, although involved in the formation of the Graham letter, he chose not to sign it, in part because "my problem with all of this is there's just no new thinking. It's like if you're familiar with [philosopher of science] Thomas Kuhn, ... *The Structure of Scientific Revolutions*. The problem right now, there's been no breakthrough out of this, you know, self-referential [debate], even or even among people that I agree with. There's no breakthrough. There's no new thinking."[143] The debates feature a limited array of meaningful events—the expansion of NATO, Putin's Munich speech, Crimea, people—George Kennan above all, and words—engage, détente, contain, Cold War. Policy options become limited: "Reset to normalcy, reset the normalcy. And it's like there's no

---

[140] Russia interview 004, 24 September 2020, via video call.
[141] Russia interview 036, 19 November 2020, via video call.
[142] Russia interview 050, 9 February 2022, via video call.
[143] Russia interview 036, 19 November 2020, via video call.

middle ground or there's no actual thinking of a way of engagement outside of that those spheres."[144]

Once again, the reason is that the policy debates depicted here are never just policy debates. They are, as in the case of U.S.-China relations, also always debates over legitimate expertise and the bearers of that expertise: the Russia-we-havers and the Russia-we-wanters.

---

[144] Russia interview 036, 19 November 2020, via video call.

7
The Politics of U.S. Russia Expertise

Professional status competition in the Russia-watching community shares important features with the China field. Putative experts police field boundaries, disagreeing both over what constitutes Russia expertise—language ability, time spent in country, academic prestige, government service—and whether Russia policy should be left to the specialists at all. Similarly, calls for and rejections of nuanced assessments align with distinct perspectives on relations with Moscow. How America's Russia experts see their object depends on where they see it from, as further analysis of the contending open letters of 2020 attests; different kinds of Russia experts believe different things about America's past connections to Russia and potential futures.

Juxtaposing the China and Russia cases highlights crucial differences, however. Absent the same kinds of divisions in the smaller and more unified Russia-watching community, it has not witnessed a paradigmatic turnover similar to China Engagement as frame and community. Salient here too are differences between China and Russia as objects of knowledge and the divergent, but connected, histories of China and Russia watching as institutionalized practices. In particular, where China watching steadily increased after the Cold War, the Russia field entered a steep decline, only arrested after 2014. Together, professional status competition among America's Russia watchers produced a narrower margin for innovation, exemplified by the post-2009 "reset." A new *policy* initiative, the reset is distinct from the paradigmatic turnover and fundamental re*framing* of China effected by the Trump administration.

Russia in the U.S. National Security Community's Professional Status Competition

The Russia field features "boundary work" typical of professional fields, including those beyond the sphere of national security.[1] As one early-career researcher at a major federally funded research and development center (FFRDC) in Washington explained, "I am by no means one of the sort of established, like

---

[1] Gieryn 1983.

real, no-kidding, full-on Russia expert[s]."[2] By contrast, someone like the Rand Corporation's Samuel Charap, "He's like a no-kidding Russia expert. This is his life. This is all he does. You're not going to find anybody more knowledgeable than he is, not in that age range."[3] For this analyst, there are different categories of Russia "experts." "[Charap and me], we're in different classes."[4]

Language ability again sits at the heart of boundary policing, with several experts confessing either their own or others' linguistic limitations. One former diplomat and State Department planner prefaced his reflections on the sociological dynamics of the field by saying, "I did not study Russia either in college or in graduate school. . . . I don't speak Russian. I don't read Russian. And I have no Russian friends or professional colleagues."[5] His expertise lies in diplomacy and policy planning. Others deployed language ability to cast doubt on prominent former policymakers, including Obama's chief Russia hand, Michael McFaul. "He speaks shitty Russian," one academic and Russia-we-haver noted.[6] Kurt Campbell, a former Russia expert turned China hand, "speaks neither Russian nor Chinese," and for one mid-career think tanker, the implications for Campbell's authority are evident.[7] As a longtime Russia hand warned,

> Be wary of China folks who don't speak the language. All of us [Russia experts] speak . . . the language and have lived there. And, you know, a lot of folks you talk about, Kurt Campbell and Ely [Ratner] and all these guys who I love and respect, they've never been there. I mean, they've never lived it, you know? . . . I think there's not a single person we've talked about here [as real Russia experts] . . . who hasn't lived there and spoken Russian.[8]

Other typical markers of expertise again include time spent in country and academic prestige. "In recent years I have not gone to Russia very often. I think [a leading Russia-we-haver] looks down on me because I have not been going to Russia very often."[9] In this well-respected political scientist's view, however, the relation between evidence and argument is more important than the source of that evidence, in Russia or beyond. "A good Russia watcher is somebody who is open to the evidence. And one of the ways that you can be open to the evidence is by talking with people. But another way you can be open to the evidence" is "by reading the [Russian] press."[10] Says another DC-based political scientist, "I do

---

[2] Russia interview 035, 5 November 2020, via telephone.
[3] Russia interview 035, 5 November 2020, via telephone.
[4] Russia interview 035, 5 November 2020, via telephone.
[5] Russia interview 011, 12 October 2020, via telephone.
[6] Russia interview 015, 19 October 2020, via video call.
[7] Russia interview 017, 20 October 2020, via video call.
[8] Russia interview 033, 16 November 2020, via video call.
[9] Russia interview 021, 26 October 2020, via video call.
[10] Russia interview 021, 26 October 2020, via video call.

not consider myself a Russia expert. For me the people that would fall into that category are scholars who've written books about Russia, who have language skills, who spent a lot of time there... [I'm] more of a national security generalist."[11] Harvard's Stephen Kotkin was a familiar reference, as comfortable at the top of the academic food chain as in White House briefing rooms.[12] So too was Thomas Graham, even for his opponents: "I would say [Tom] is the most important intellectual thinker on the realism side for Russia. I think he's wrong... [but] he's the most... serious thinker... and very compelling."[13]

Several interviewees doubted how intensely Russia experts policed the community's boundaries: "The boundary drawing or the gatekeeping is probably in my experience more pronounced for China than it is for Russia."[14] Indicatively, for them, family background in Russia and the Soviet Union has often served as sufficient warrant for expert recognition: "I feel that I personally benefit a great deal from [being] from the former Soviet Union.... I have the street cred."[15] Despite not working "on questions of defense ever, or Russian foreign policy ever, or having thought about Russia for five years... it didn't really bother anybody."[16] Russian heritage was enough, in others' view, to establish legitimacy as a Russia expert.

Other objective factors lower the salience of professional status competition in the U.S. Russia field. Many Russian official organs publish their policies and strategy statements in English, lowering the barrier to entry.[17] "[The Russians] desperately want to be talked about... and they want to be understood. Putting things in a language that everybody else reads certainly helps matters," one analyst noted.[18] Whereas the language barriers to analysis of China are significant, for Russia, "[Because] they have enough in English you don't really need the language skills to be able to... meaningfully answer questions."[19]

Other objective changes include the security environment in Russia, with obvious parallels to China. The above political scientist, criticized for infrequent research travel to Russia, replies, "I disagree [with critics because] with time I have gotten less and less out of going to Russia because people are saying less and less than they used to."[20]

---

[11] Russia interview 024, 31 October 2020, via video call.
[12] Russia interview 002, 21 September 2020, via video call.
[13] Russia interview 028 (first interview), 9 November 2020, via video call.
[14] Russia interview 026, 5 November 2020, via telephone.
[15] Russia interview 026, 5 November 2020, via telephone.
[16] Russia interview 026, 5 November 2020, via telephone.
[17] See http://government.ru/en/department/92/events/.
[18] Russia interview 026, 5 November 2020, via telephone.
[19] Russia interview 026, 5 November 2020, via telephone.
[20] Russia interview 021, 26 October 2020, via video call.

Because of the arrests that have been happening of American citizens, because I have been dealing with Russian defense-related topics . . . I have not been feeling safe in going, and when I have gone, which has been pretty rare, it's been at a conference where I get picked up by the conference organizers. I spend my time in the hotel. And then I get dropped off by people who are associated with the conference organizer. . . . It probably is not safe for me to go around wandering, doing the kinds of interviews that I did back when I used to go more often.[21]

In such an environment, other forms of expertise, particularly military "bombs and guns" knowledge, become more salient than deep country expertise based on linguistic ability. As one research analyst joked, "When I was a baby [at the Pentagon] after my master's, I spent a year working on China, and there were people showing up there who had been doing Soviet studies who had jumped in [to China studies], and my joke was, 'They're communist. They have nuclear weapons. How hard can this be?'"[22]

Finally, the longer-term origins of a security-oriented, and generally skeptical, view of Russia were frequently noted. "To study Russia is to hate it," one think tanker stated plainly.[23] Since "Russia watchers tend to become the equal and opposite of what they study, . . . they're generally a Russia hawk."[24] The view goes back to the Cold War, when America's "Sovietologists were more critical of the Soviet Union than China experts were of Mao's China, and much more inclined to be advocates of kind of tough policies."[25]

Skepticism about the reality of Russia expertise led some to reject Russia expertise entirely. Commented one London-based American Russia watcher, "I'm firmly of the view that, while specialists are helpful . . . [Russia policy] is too important to leave to the Russia specialists."[26] Specialist knowledge comes with professional biases, such as the tendency to think one's own issue is always the most salient, "which means if you left policy to area specialists [it would] always be a disaster."[27]

Yet few denied outright the importance of Russia expertise, as indicated notably in criticisms of overly ideological Russia watchers and so-called instant Russia experts. For one retired official and Russia-we-haver, "By and large, the liberal internationalists who were trying to drive [a tough Russia policy] were not experts on Russia, right. They were the people like Bob Kagan, his wife Toria

---

[21] Russia interview 021, 26 October 2020, via video call.
[22] Russia interview 017, 20 October 2020, via video call.
[23] Russia interview 012, 15 October 2020, via video call.
[24] Russia interview 012, 15 October 2020, via video call.
[25] Russia interview 044, 4 December 2020, via video call.
[26] Russia interview 012, 15 October 2020, via video call.
[27] Russia interview 012, 15 October 2020, via video call.

Nuland, Mike McFaul at Stanford."[28] By contrast, "People who really understand Russia, Russia's history, its national narratives and values, believe the attempt to impose our values and our concept of political order on Russia was completely untethered from reality."[29] Similarly, "People are definitely skeptical of commentary or contributions by people who nobody recognizes and you have no idea where they came from."[30] After the incursion into the Crimea and eastern Ukraine in 2014, "Everybody seemed to be surprised, and everybody started writing pieces . . . [asking] What is Russia doing? What are they after? What should we do about it, blah, blah, blah. Why didn't we foresee this? So you get quotes from people who are nobody's idea of a Russia expert, but because there was so much demand for commentary, everyone turned into a Russia expert overnight."[31]

Nuancing the Russia Debate

As in the China field, the notion of nuance acts as a line of division within the professional status competition among America's Russia watchers. Broadly put, Russia-we-havers place more emphasis on nuanced knowledge than their Russia-we-wanter counterparts. For the latter, the question of what Russia *is* is settled. No amount of nuanced knowledge of Russian culture and society will change the Putin regime. Once again, the division over nuance in the Russia community is arguably less stark than in the China field. Nonetheless, further investigation highlights important dynamics between the government and the knowledge produced by the China- and Russia-watching communities.

As a leading Russia-we-haver, based at a university in Washington, DC, explained, "What I'm often resistant to is the sort of less nuanced or less careful [assessments of Russia]," which can be "more misleading in the end than truly helpful."[32] Consequently, in his work he aims to "look as broadly as I can at Russia, and to look at Russian literature and to look at Russian culture to try to understand some of the sources within Russia."[33] Put differently, he aims to consider "Russia with a Russian accent, as opposed to looking at Russia with an American accent, which I do believe is something of an occupational hazard."[34] Another Russia watcher, this time employed at a Virginia-based research institute, says, "Part of my position is also trying to push back against what I take to

---

[28] Russia interview 009, 12 October 2020, via telephone.
[29] Russia interview 009, 12 October 2020, via telephone.
[30] Russia interview 026, 5 November 2020, via telephone.
[31] Russia interview 026, 5 November 2020, via telephone.
[32] Russia interview 008, 6 October 2020, via telephone.
[33] Russia interview 008, 6 October 2020, via telephone.
[34] Russia interview 008, 6 October 2020, via telephone.

be the dominant position, because you always want for the opposite side to get the best consideration possible, even if it loses out."[35] As one academic lamented, "We need to understand our adversaries, as well as our friends. We understand neither very well, these days."[36]

Likely because of my British accent and the ongoing fallout from Brexit throughout the reviewing period (2017–2023), interviewees frequently made the connection between knowing Russia and knowing the United Kingdom. "Does Boris Johnson equal Britain?" one academic Russia-we-haver asked pointedly. "No," I of course replied. Understanding the 2016 vote to leave the European Union, and the tumultuous years the UK government has spent trying to effect Brexit, cannot be limited to the personality of the country's leadership. The United Kingdom's culture, history, and political institutions all matter. Similarly, for my questioner, Russia was not just the regime, but a broader "cultural phenomenon."[37] Consequently, nuanced understanding of Russia was a necessary counterweight to assessments focused overly on the whims of the leadership in Moscow.

Often, views like these were incubated during the Cold War, when authoritarians and pluralists differed on the degree of control the Soviet regime exercised over Russian society, and the possibility for grassroots political action by civil society and ordinary Russians. One academic of long standing, now firmly a Russia-we-haver, worked during the pre-1989 period to provide "evidence that there's a lot of turmoil in society [contrary to what the authoritarians suggested].... Bringing this forward to today, that continues to inform my view, which is that whenever anybody says, 'It's all Putin,'... that's not the way societies work. Society is composed of very complicated interrelations, lots of people, lots of interests."[38] The problem, for this interviewee, however, is limitations imposed by social science: "We basically don't have as social scientists the sophistication to understand and describe [Russian society] very well. So we use shorthands, and those shorthands serve the purpose of simplifying the story, but they're not the... full story.... It's not a substitute for appreciating and constantly reiterating that we're only understanding the surface."[39]

Arguments for and against nuance in assessing Russian power and intentions are thus inseparable from those same analyses of Russian power, and what Russia represents as a U.S. national interest. "Russia has a lot of influence in the world, and it behooves us to find ways of working together with it," a Washington-based

---

[35] Russia interview 026, 5 November 2020, via telephone.
[36] Russia interview 014, 16 October 2020, via video call.
[37] Russia interview 022, 27 October 2020, via video call.
[38] Russia interview 022, 27 October 2020, via video call.
[39] Russia interview 022, 27 October 2020, via video call.

political scientist argued, after extolling the necessity of nuance.[40] For many others, typically those outside the Russia expert community, but some within it but on the more hawkish side, Russia is not powerful, and nuanced assessment is unnecessary. A common phrase in national security circles prior to the 2022 invasion of Ukraine was that "Russia is a gas station with nuclear weapons."[41] For one former National Security Council Russia hand,

> There is this business about how we have to understand ... a lot of what's happening in Russia as deeply rooted in national traditions ... that are taken seriously by elites and public alike. I don't like that myself ... because buried beneath that is an assumption ... that what drives Russian policy is really open to challenge. And that can lead you in a very wrong direction in trying to understand what American policy ought to be. ... I tend to think that we pay much too much attention to history and culture and thinking about Russia, not enough to political institutions.[42]

The virtues of nuance can be overstated.

Further assessment of the social bases of calls for nuance again ties them particularly to the ivory tower, highlighting that such claims are weakened by the practicalities of negotiating the government-academia boundary. As one academic explained, even if policymakers have country-specific knowledge and "studied China or India in college, ... now they have to deal with all of Southeast Asia, and India is background." Even more important, experts' advice has to "make sense" not only to the experts but also "to their boss, to the person they have to explain this to. So it gets pared down and pared down to two pages, then two sentences. And of course a huge amount of knowledge and nuance is lost, but that's the nature of ... government." At the "end of this process, no one is responsible for policy. No one. It is literally something that came about as a result of all of these people throwing some spice into this stuff. What happened to it? Nobody quite knows. They tasted it and nobody can understand how the stew tastes [as it does]."[43]

Pleas for nuance, once again, reflect an academic position, and *dis*position, in policy debates. As one Washington-based political scientist explained, he frequently gets asked to opine on current events in the U.S.-Russia relationship and is pressured to take

---

[40] Russia interview 045, 17 December 2020, via video call. https://www.armscontrol.org/factsheets/Nuclearweaponswhohaswhat. Russia has 6,255 nuclear weapons; China has 350.
[41] Russia interview 024, 31 October 2020, via video call.
[42] Russia interview 044, 4 December 2020, via video call.
[43] Russia interview 022, 27 October 2020, via video call.

a stand on this issue or something else, but that's not really the role that I see for academics in the narrow sense. It doesn't mean we shouldn't be out there with our opinions.... As far as taking [a] big, kind of concrete policy stance as an organization, I'm not sure that's productive. Part of my own reticence is that some ways of framing the questions [do not] seem to be a productive way.... Do you want to resist the bad things that Russia is doing? Yes. Should we try to engage Russia in a productive manner where possible to avoid risk of nuclear war? Yes.[44]

As one former policymaker commented, "I just remember being struck by how wide the gap was between academic views of NATO enlargement and the views that eventually persuaded the government.... It was like night and day."[45] Calls for nuance thus come from positions of structural weakness vis-à-vis decision-making. As one longtime historian of U.S.-Russia relations explained, the Russia-we-havers outside the Beltway "are not terribly influential. That's the problem.... They're mostly academics. And quite a few of those academics are not even academics at Ivy League kind of institutions with policy connections."[46] Another interviewee characterized those who do make decisions: "Inside the government, there are a lot of people whose job it is every day to do deterrence of Russia, and that ... obviously creates patterns of thoughts ... tens of thousands of people ... in one way or another.... For them, the Cold War never ended."[47] To them, nuance is an even more difficult sell. Referring to the decision to expand NATO in the mid-1990s, one former official and political scientist noted, "Once the national security advisor and the president go down a certain path, it's sort of over.... Once it looks like the train has left the station, you get on board or you leave."[48]

The aim here is not to identify fixed relationships between what different types of Russia watchers argue, whether for or against nuance, and their social location, in government, think tanks, or academia. Rather, it is to highlight how calls for nuance function in the Russia expert community, in contrast to the China field. The question raised is what type of individual can simultaneously be "nuanced" and policy oriented. As one FFRDC researcher noted, Georgetown University's Angela Stent is a good example of a person who wears both hats: "There are a few people who work at universities in DC who can be very easily connected to the policy community. And Angela's a very good example of that because she is an academic. She writes academic books. She also talks to all the policy people. And

---

[44] Russia interview 045, 17 December 2020, via video call.
[45] Russia interview 024, 31 October 2020, via video call.
[46] Russia interview 016, 19 October 2020, via telephone.
[47] Russia interview 010, 12 October 2020, via video call.
[48] Russia interview 024, 31 October 2020, via video call.

a lot of them are her students. And so I think there are some [who can do both]. But most people are either in one or the other [camp]."[49]

The Open Letters Revisited; or, Why the Different Camps See Russia as They Do

The polarization of Russia watchers in U.S. national security circles, separating the Russia-we-havers from Russia-we-wanters, is also a professional status distinction. As in the case of China policy, Russia-we-havers tend to adopt a more academic viewpoint and hold associated intellectual dispositions, in contrast to the more policy-oriented Russia-we-wanters. The result is that Russia-we-havers tend to distrust the bolder pronouncements of their more influence-oriented colleagues. Although less salient than in the China field, the result is a dividing line between calls for greater and lesser nuance, as views about policy bleed into disputes about expertise.

As one restraint-focused think tanker explained, "What's really notable in the Russian field is the extent to which the division [between Russia-we-wanters and Russia-we-havers] is actually an expert/nonexpert division. Not that the people that are nonexperts are not experts, but they're not *Russia* specialists for the most part."[50] Thus, this think tanker's "impression has been that a lot of the people making arguments about find[ing] ways to engage with Russia ('We need to not send more weapons to Ukraine'), ... those are the people that have been studying Russia for years."[51] The division is far from simple, not a "perfect split. But the people on the other side of that debate, people arguing, 'Let's send weapons to Ukraine, let's take a tougher line on Russia,' ... a lot of those are generalists. I find it quite an interesting division that is not within the field of Russia specialists."[52]

Further analysis of the open letters of 2020 offers a more fine-grained view of what type of Russia expert, or nonexpert, falls into each camp. One interviewee, a senior academic and former official, walked me through their reading of the letters: taking the "Graham letter" first, he noted that, of the 103 signees, "30 or 40 are arms controllers. Then come the foreign policy generalists, [who constitute around] 15 to 20 of the rest. Then senior business, energy and journalism, and some senior statesmen, like former California governor Jerry Brown[53] ["for Christ's sake," he added, evidently unconvinced of Brown's qualifications as a Russia expert]. Then 15 or so academics ... not as many as you might think."[54]

---

[49] Russia interview 034, 17 November 2020, via video call.
[50] Russia interview 004, 24 September 2020, via video call.
[51] Russia interview 004, 24 September 2020, via video call.
[52] Russia interview 004, 24 September 2020, via video call.
[53] 34th and 39th governors of California, 1975–1983 and 2011–2019.
[54] Russia interview 044, 4 December 2020, via video call.

The Russia-we-havers are thus not the same as the "China is not our enemy" crowd, largely on account of the overrepresentation of arms controllers in the Russia professional field: "We've had no tradition of arms control with China, and the nuclear issue hasn't loomed all that large in the relationship with China."[55] A significant factor in the writing of the letter, and the timing of its appearance, was thus "a kind of pushback, [an] angry pushback against the way in which the Trump administration ... disengaged from negotiated arms control agreements with the Russians. I think that's the biggest impetus here."[56]

For my interviewee, the expertise of arms controllers is not exactly Russia expertise. "I wouldn't really describe that many of them as real Russia experts ... or even people who dealt all that much with the Russians."[57] Something similar can be said of the foreign policy generalists who signed the letter. The foreign policy generalists are "somewhat informed about Russia" since, "if you're a foreign policy generalist, you've got to know a little bit about the great powers.... But none of those people would be described as Russia hands and I don't think ... would describe themselves that way."[58] The same applies to the next group, "your senior statesmen, Sam Nunn,[59] Gary Hart,[60] Jerry Brown,"[61] and a final "category, which is all of your former ambassadors. Eileen Malloy[62] and George Krol[63] ... These are all smart, knowledgeable people, but they're not academics either. And it's right to call them Russia experts and right to call them Russia hands since they spent a lot of time with hands-on dealing with the Russians."[64]

Once again, the Graham letter does not capture all of the Russia-we-have position, nor the Kramer letter the Russia-we-wanter view. Yet the former letter highlights how distinct groups coalesce around particular views, despite different starting points. For example, for this interviewee, "Depending on your purposes, you might want to put them [the senior statesmen, foreign policy generalists, and former ambassadors] in the same category as the academic specialists."[65] For the former group, the point is not to "get so worked up about [Russia]. We know how to handle the Russians, [to] defend our interests without being compromised by the process of dealing with them and certainly without

---

[55] Russia interview 044, 4 December 2020, via video call.
[56] Russia interview 044, 4 December 2020, via video call.
[57] Russia interview 044, 4 December 2020, via video call.
[58] Russia interview 044, 4 December 2020, via video call.
[59] Georgia Democratic senator (1972–1997). A powerful voice on foreign policy, Nunn was chair of the Senate Armed Services Committee between 1987 and 1995.
[60] Colorado Democratic senator (1975–1987).
[61] Russia interview 044, 4 December 2020, via video call.
[62] Ambassador to Kyrgyzstan (1994–1997) and subsequently deputy assistant secretary of state for European and Canadian affairs (1997–1999).
[63] Ambassador to Belarus (2003–2006), Uzbekistan (2011–2014), and Kazakhstan (2015–2018).
[64] Russia interview 044, 4 December 2020, via video call.
[65] Russia interview 044, 4 December 2020, via video call.

being suckered."⁶⁶ Although distinct, such a view has affinities to the "academic version of this, which is 'You people [i.e., strong Russia skeptics] don't understand much about Russian history, about culture, nationalism, traditions. And so you are improperly identifying the source of the trouble.'"⁶⁷ From distinct starting points, the signatories get to the same place, once again with connections to the call for nuance, which is to "say that you crude, vulgar, popular, public-pandering politicians don't get how to deal with a serious adversary. We know how to deal with Russia . . . in the text of a letter, you find a way to nod to the different constituency."⁶⁸ A final related view comes from the prominence of realism among Russia specialists and many foreign policy generalists. One interviewee commented, "I think Russia specialists tend to be more prone to realism as a school of international relations, just to start with, it's sort of a—it's just kind of a thing. They start out with . . . we all start [George] Kennan, and then it just goes from there."⁶⁹

Moving to the second letter, the Kramer letter, one academic and former policymaker stated plainly: "There is . . . literally nobody on that list who is a tenured professor. I hate to sound so parochial about this, but I don't think you got a tenured professor on that and that entire list, which isn't to say they're not experts, just that they have a different [set of credentials and associations]."⁷⁰ More often noted than the dearth of tenured academics was the prevalence of analysts and government officials, rather than former diplomats, among the Kramer letter's signatories. "Most of these groups [represented in the Kramer letter] are analysts," a former ambassador to Moscow told me. "They're not policymakers. . . . And I found there's a big difference. The analysts are essential to making good policy, but they know that when they're done, their analysis, their work is over. And policymakers depend heavily on good analysis, but good analysis links you into impossible choices often. You have to decide which arm and leg you're going to cut off to put the best position forward."⁷¹

For one academic Russia-we-haver, "The David Kramer response is all a combination of ideologues and former government officials and people with the East European background in some way that, in my opinion, biases and skews their perspective."⁷² For a think tanker of similar mind, the letters divide neatly between "people that have actually studied Russia versus you know, people who specialize in Eastern Europe, people that have more general strategic interests."⁷³

---

[66] Russia interview 044, 4 December 2020, via video call.
[67] Russia interview 044, 4 December 2020, via video call.
[68] Russia interview 044, 4 December 2020, via video call.
[69] Russia interview 004, 24 September 2020, via video call.
[70] Russia interview 044, 4 December 2020, via video call.
[71] Russia interview 042, 3 December 2020, via video call.
[72] Russia interview 011, 14 October 2020, via video call.
[73] Russia interview 004, 24 September 2020, via video call.

In the words of one former ambassador in central Asia, "There is a divide between the people who have been practicing diplomats, who have to deal with the day-to-day things with, do business with, these governments, whether you like them or not, [and others]."[74] "When you're an ambassador, you're an ambassador to that government, you're accredited to be able to work with that government effectively."[75] For them, the role runs counter to the Russia-we-want worldview. In response to the idea that democratization ... should be a key sort of mission ... we as diplomats tend to think, well, we're not really going to change these places too much. And so, you know, we've got business to do." What of ideas like Condoleezza Rice's "transformational diplomacy"?[76] "We all roll our eyes at this sort of stuff and thinking in places like Russia.... Russia is Russia."[77]

The same view, the need to treat Russia as it is, can thus take different forms, not necessarily emerging from liking Russia. Indeed, "Within the Foreign Service, you have those who have served in Russia ... and many of them have served when it was the Soviet Union. And they don't really think that, you know, Russia has been any different from what the Soviet Union was. And there is a certain deep animus, too, because of personal experiences they had, ... in the sense that you can never trust, you know, the Russians, period. They're like ... the Soviets whether they're Soviets or the Russian Federation—it's all the same."[78]

Yet not all former diplomats active in the Russia field are Russia-we-havers either. Some who have served in countries like Ukraine or Georgia "feel very deeply what the Russians have done. And they become extremely defensive of the Ukrainians and the Georgians based on their experience."[79] As a result, "If you look at that letter Kramer wrote, most people are associated with having been ambassadors of Ukraine and Georgia or the Baltic Republic and other places [like] that."[80] Diplomats call this "'clientitis,' where they've really bought into that these people can do no wrong. And it's the Russians. They're at fault in everything."[81] A critic might, of course, accuse diplomatic Russia-we-havers of the same vice of clientitis in the formation of their views, ignoring the abuses of the Russian government.

More important than accusations of clientitis are the social bases of the Russia-we-have and Russia-we-want positions—the affiliations, experiences, and professional statuses attached to more pro- and anti-Moscow views. The

---

[74] Russia interview 023, 29 October 2020, via telephone.
[75] Russia interview 023, 29 October 2020, via telephone.
[76] Secretary of State Condoleezza Rice, remarks at Georgetown University, 18 January 2006, https://2001-2009.state.gov/secretary/rm/2006/59306.htm.
[77] Russia interview 023, 29 October 2020, via telephone.
[78] Russia interview 023, 29 October 2020, via telephone.
[79] Russia interview 023, 29 October 2020, via telephone.
[80] Russia interview 023, 29 October 2020, via telephone.
[81] Russia interview 023, 29 October 2020, via telephone.

Russia-we-wanters, for example, often share affiliation with Eastern Europe–oriented organizations, such as the Atlantic Council and CEPA. The Russia-we-want perspective is thus close to the Eastern European view laid out in two letters that appeared in *Politico* in response to the Graham-Kramer exchange. From this perspective, America should not accept Russia as it is, since the democratic experience of the former Soviet states in Eastern Europe demonstrate the region wants and is capable of democracy, like the West.

As one noteworthy non-signatory of the Kramer letter noted, as a diplomat in Eastern Europe during the transition from communism, "I saw in Poland after the fall of communism how a communist country could build democracy and [a] free market system on the wounds of communism. . . . [The Poles] had a full generation of uninterrupted growth, democracy, rule of law, and basically a liberal spirit. And I compared that to the Russians. . . . And I thought, wait a minute, if the Poles can do it, it can be done."[82] After "working heavily on the original outreach to a more realistic but still hopeful relationship," this former official watched as it became clear Putin "wasn't the guy we thought he was and his terms for good relations were that we give him a free pass on autocracy at home and aggression now with his neighbors."[83]

Similarly, the diplomatic realist-inclined foreign policy generalist and the academic worldviews share crucial features: first, that Russia is an important, even existential issue, for America and for countries in the region. A former ambassador to Moscow asked, "Russia as an existential threat [on account of its nuclear arsenal] . . . where's the existential threat with China?"[84] As one former ambassador to central Asia noted, "In my own dealings with the neighboring countries . . . I recognized the importance of Russia. We thought the worst thing possible for them is when Russia and the United States are at loggerheads; [they] are caught in the middle and . . . forced to choose sides simply for existential reasons."[85]

Second, the foreign policy generalist and the academic share the view that the United States needs a clear understanding of what the Russians really want and how politics works in the country, especially in relation to why Russia's leaders are more popular than the Russia-we-wanters can fathom. As one recalled

> I remember when I was in Belarus and going to the NSC and . . . explaining why Lukashenko is popular. . . . It's not just repression, but his politics and the way he's a kind of a consummate populist politician who plays to the fears of people and the like. . . . And the reaction that [I got] from this person [who] didn't serve

---

[82] Russia interview 035, 18 November 2020, via video call.
[83] Russia interview 035, 18 November 2020, via video call.
[84] Russia interview 042, 3 December 2020, via video call.
[85] Russia interview 023, 29 October 2020, via telephone.

in the Foreign Service and came out of... the think tank world—he just looked at me and said, "Well, that's unacceptable."[86]

Third, the realist-inclined foreign policy generalists and the academics share a skepticism toward America's abilities to change Russia. As one of the Graham letter's signatories explained, "I once tried to conduct a review of our democracy development programs in Russia and ... to develop a set of tactics [for evaluating] how successful [they were]. Is this working? And there was tremendous resistance to even asking the question whether they were working or not or whether they weren't working, because that was heresy, to suggest that we shouldn't be doing these types of things."[87] By contrast, diplomacy, in their view, "is about working with your client... rather than trying to change it."[88]

Forgetting, and Unforgetting, Russia

Struggles among America's Russia experts over legitimate expertise—and those in the China knowledge community—are not only based on professional location in the field. What distinguishes different types of Russia experts and helps account for their views of U.S.-Russia relations, is more than whether they are former diplomats or analysts, think tankers or academics. Professional status competition is carried on among experts of varying ages and levels of experience, who entered the field on distinct timelines. Notable here is a significant gap that opened after the end of the Cold War in 1989 and the disintegration of the Soviet Union in 1991. Unlike the China field, which saw a steady expansion, an exodus from the Russia field, and a marked decrease in young experts entering the community, only reversed after 2014. The result is a large gap, frequently noted by interviewees, between Russia specialists in their thirties and those in their sixties and above, with very few in their late forties and fifties—when professionals take on key leadership roles inside or outside government. "There are very few individuals in this particular age cohort ... of Fiona Hill or Celeste [Wallander]."[89] While the precise impact on U.S. Russia policy is tough to gauge—views are hardly predicted by age—the Russia field features a notable bimodal structure and small numbers, offering a point of sharp comparison to the professional status competition among America's China watchers.

In the recollection of Russia experts, the end of the Cold War reshaped the U.S. national security community almost overnight. "The whole world of Soviet

---

[86] Russia interview 023, 29 October 2020, via telephone.
[87] Russia interview 030, 13 November 2020, via video call.
[88] Russia interview 030, 13 November 2020, via video call.
[89] Russia interview 039, 30 November 2020, via video call.

experts or Kremlinologists, or whatever, completely changes" after 1991, one explained. "By 1995, a Kremlinologist was about as useful as a Nazi economist ... they just weren't relevant."[90] The academic debates of the 1980s and before—which pitted the authoritarian and pluralist schools against one another—were rendered moribund, as the intellectual debate about whether reform was theoretically possible was replaced by the practical tasks of making connections in Russia, going to newly accessible archives, and designing aid and reconstruction programs.[91]

At the same time, however, as one former ambassador remarked, "The Soviet Union just wasn't seen as the big enemy anymore,"[92] and money dried up, both broadly within the Russian studies academic field, such as the American Councils for International Education, and within the Beltway. "In the academic world, the study of things about Eurasia, Russia collapsed, the funding for language study, the scholarship, and all this . . . simply was collapsing. As people went off into new directions, they weren't looking at the same stuff."[93] As a result, for one academic, "We just don't have people now who have gone through really any training in Russian studies to speak of, but certainly not the kind where you used to be able to go to a major university and have a history course, an anthropology course, and economics course all about Russia."[94]

Numerous younger interviews shared stories of having their career choice questioned. "When I was an undergraduate and I started studying Russian, people were like, 'Why on earth would you study Russia?'" one recalled. "Russia is a backwater," a declining power. Why waste your life studying it? A political scientist and Russia military blogger recalled, "[I was] at Harvard and there were two people working on Russia, started my year [in graduate school]. There were, I think, three the year before or four the year before that. [They used to take] two to four every year. And now it's like one every few years. Because the problem was for all these people is that the Soviet Union collapsed and Russia became less significant in the world and a lot of the jobs dried up. So you had to . . . get lucky or be brilliant or position yourself as a more general comparativist and go . . . to [a] politics kind of job."[95]

In Washington, "prior to 2014 nobody cared" about Russia, one mid-career analyst explained.[96] The effect was an effective halt on hiring new Russia experts at the major think tanks and research institutes. Only to the extent that "Russia figured in policy or operation questions . . . were [people] interested in it." But "it's

---

[90] Russia interview 013, 15 October 2020, via telephone.
[91] Russia interview 029, 12 November 2020, via video call.
[92] Russia interview 013, 15 October 2020, via telephone.
[93] Russia interview 013, 15 October 2020, via telephone.
[94] Russia interview 022, 27 October 2020, via video call.
[95] Russia interview 034, 17 November 2020, via video call.
[96] Russia interview 026, 5 November 2020, via telephone.

not like it warranted them having actual ... established experts on the field full time."[97] Interest in Russia from the Defense Department picked up after 2014, "at the expense of things like the Middle East and Islamic terrorism," leading to an increase in hiring. For this analyst, "It'd be fair to say that by about 2015," their research organization "suddenly found itself very heavy on the Middle East side and lagging on the Russia side."[98]

The discrepancy was most notable in relation to the study of Russian military capabilities. From the mid-1990s to 2014, "Nobody in the U.S. outside of government and under age 60 was working on the Russian military ... because it was seen as, you know, why would you waste your time on that?"[99] As one of the small number of specialists noted,

> In 2014, all thanks to Vladimir Vladimirovich [Putin], there were very few people around that knew much of anything about the Russian military. You had a fairly small community of experts that followed it ... and a lot of people whose last encounter was, like, Soviet studies. ... [I] have this joke analogy to it where you talk to those people and they have good insights. They're like, "Back in my day we had the longbow," and You're like, "Yeah, but this is the era of the gun. Do you know anything about the gun?" [They respond,] "I don't know much about the gun, but I do remember how we used to use the longbow really well." And so you'll say, "That's really fascinating and that will really inform the background of what we're writing. However, in the last 30 years in the Russian military has moved on from the crossbow." I love the eighties. I'm a child of the eighties. I love them, too. But we got to let them go.[100]

As another former ambassador explained, "People within the professional ranks, they make decisions based upon where they think their investment in language and regional studies is going to take them over [a] 20-, 30-, 40-year career."[101] During the 1990s, another observed, "the Russia account was not seen in ... the decade of the 2000s as really the place you want to make your future."[102] The importance of bilateral relationship at the time, however, is not the only relevant factor. Equally salient for many aspiring experts is prospect of making a difference. "[If] Russia is going to be a constant political dogfight, why do I want to invest in that? If China is going to be stalemated and become politicized, why do I want to do that?"[103]

---

[97] Russia interview 026, 5 November 2020, via telephone.
[98] Russia interview 026, 5 November 2020, via telephone.
[99] Russia interview 034, 17 November 2020, via video call.
[100] Russia interview 039, 30 November 2020, via video call.
[101] Russia interview 043, 4 December 2020, via video call.
[102] Russia interview 013, 15 October 2020, via telephone.
[103] Russia interview 043, 4 December 2020, via video call.

Nonetheless, "the throughput on the China side"—meaning the number of individuals coming into the field and reaching its upper ranks in the government—"is a lot more robust. Yeah. And covers a multiplicity of issues that have very, very high level." By contrast,

> The throughput in Russia is limited simply because there are aspects of that bilateral relationship that just have never matured. So you don't have any real economic expertise, for example, in U.S.-Russia relations, because we don't have a commercial relationship—with $25 billion in size—compared to $800 billion in the US-China relationship. On the China side, you'll have some ... China watchers and experts who are incredibly talented economists. And, you know, they step up and they're able to apply their expertise and work on it for decades.

The reason for the discrepancy is that "U.S. Russia policymaking is really focused less on the global stage, [whereas] U.S.-China is very much a global relationship."[104]

No hard-and-fast conclusions can be drawn as to the effect of the gap in knowledge of Russia that opened up in America during the 1990s and 2000s. Again, the question itself becomes one over which Russia experts themselves disagree.

As one former State Department officer commented, "The obvious question is, how has—I don't have any answer to [this]—the decline in Russian expertise affected the quality of us foreign policy toward Russia?"[105] As the phrase "decline in Russian expertise" suggests, in this interviewee's view, the gap represents a denigration in U.S. Russia knowledge, not neutral in its effects, in that "I think the debate of a Russia policy is a microcosm of a larger debate over what the organizing principle should be per U.S. foreign policy."[106] Should it be focused on diplomacy and engagement or a more military-driven liberal internationalism?

For others, the gap plays into a high degree of stasis in the Russia debate, especially at the senior level: Do we deal with the Russia-we-have or the Russia-we-want? For one astute observer, an analyst at an FFRDC close to the Beltway, the older generation is "all too old, and you're not going to convince them of anything.... So what's the point of writing anything for them? ... You're not going to convince Sandy Vershbow of anything. David [Kramer] decided everything long ago for himself. You're not going to convince them."[107] For them, a better strategy is to "shape the conversation for younger people in the field because lots of people got into Russia in the last six years.... And I don't want those people to look to Toria Nuland or Sandy [Vershbow] for the answers on Russia. I want

---

[104] Russia interview 043, 4 December 2020, via video call.
[105] Russia interview 009, 12 October 2020, via telephone.
[106] Russia interview 009, 12 October 2020, via telephone.
[107] Russia interview 039, 30 November 2020, via video call.

them to look to people like me. And so I'm writing all these articles actually for them."[108] As one journalist and watcher of the Russia watchers, observed, "The generational question is a very interesting one because you might think [new] generations [will think] 'We're going to come along to kind of, you know, correct the mistakes... of the elders.' And I think that's happening to a certain extent, but there's also a way in which... the ideas and people kind of reproduce themselves in the next generation."[109] Younger Russia experts are socialized into the debates by their seniors, despite the age gap, as "People have mentors that they come up under and [even with] a strong kind of personnel turnover, the ideas don't necessarily turn over."[110]

Despite the resurgence in demand for knowledge of Russia after 2014, especially after the invasion of Ukraine in 2022, Russia remains of lesser importance to China in the U.S. national security conversation. "As important as [Russia] is, it's not as important as China," one journalist noted.[111] "I'm just not sure Russia is a great power," a well-connected, Washington-based academic stated.[112] The community remains split between those in their late thirties—now early forties—"like me, Matt Rojansky, maybe a guy at Rand [Sam Charap]... who are now kind of the senior-most people in the Russia field when you really look at it, which is really comical... when you see how old are the people that are above us. ... We're in charge and those people are not like 45. ... They're not a few years older. ... They're like 65."[113]

Conclusion

Comparison between the professional status struggle in the China and Russia fields has uncovered similarities. The Russia field too features ongoing struggles over the nature of Russia-related expertise and disputed calls for nuance, especially given the recent proliferation of so-called instant Russia experts, after years of being ignored. Further analysis of the open letters of 2020 shows also how the arguments of Russia-we-havers and Russia-we-wanters are systematically connected to the social locations of the experts making them.

---

[108] Russia interview 039, 30 November 2020, via video call.
[109] Russia interview 002, 21 September 2020, via video call. These findings align with those of Keith Gessen in his analysis of America's Russia-watching community. See Gessen, "The Quiet Americans behind the U.S.-Russia Imbroglio," *New York Times Magazine*, 8 May 2018, https://www.nytimes.com/2018/05/08/magazine/the-quiet-americans-behind-the-us-russia-imbroglio.html.
[110] Russia interview 002, 21 September 2020, via video call.
[111] Russia interview 002, 21 September 2020, via video call.
[112] Russia interview 008, 6 October 2020, via telephone.
[113] Russia interview 039, 30 November 2020, via video call.

Juxtaposition of the two communities also highlighted marked divergences, however. Rapid expansion of the China community has brought military-security generalists to the fore at the expense of an older social type of "Engager." Congressionally mandated commissions, meanwhile, maintained a space for China skepticism within the field. By contrast, the Russia community saw a precipitous decline after 1989, as enterprising individuals chose alternative paths, only to return after 2014. In contrast to the China story, neither the Trump election—nor any prior or since—effected a turnover in the type of Russia watcher dominant within the U.S. government. A smaller and still relatively close-knit professional field, the Russia community has offered to successive administrations similar types of recognized expertise, resulting in a notable absence of sharp shifts in America's principal Russia frame.

8
Engagement with Russia Is Personal

The story of the rise and fall of engagement with Russia is also a personal tale. A smaller community than the China field, Russia experts describe their community as relatively collegial—although animosities exist. Individuals hold views that reflect their lives and careers, what Russia *is* to them, how and when they first encountered Russia, with such views held as a matter of faith as much as intellectual conviction.

Unlike the China "reckoning," however, post–Cold War U.S.-Russia relations have offered no personal vindication to America's Russia watchers. Where the China field saw paradigmatic turnover—a set of previous outsiders overturning the predominant framing and reshaping the government's relations with the China community, fracturing the Engager group—no similar insurgency took place on Russia. Instead, an inexorable decline in relations after Putin's rise to power was punctuated only with the attempt of a set of Russia community insiders—chiefly Michael McFaul and Celeste Wallander—to reset relations in an engagement direction. Following the return to the presidency of Putin and the failure of the reset—made concrete by the 2014 invasion of the Crimea, liberal integrationists like McFaul and Wallander moved to the side of the Russia skeptics, supported by Eastern European interest groups, consolidating the Russia-we-have and the Russia-we-want camps.

Lacking engagement as an overarching frame for Russia policy, and a clear pro-engagement community, America's Russia field features less intense struggle over careers and lives. Nonetheless, analysis of the failed appointment to a key position on Russia of Matthew Rojansky highlights the stakes when engagement gets personal. Consideration of the travails of Trump's top Russia hand, Fiona Hill, provides a counterpoint to Pottinger's success with China.

No Vindication to Be Had over Russia

The struggle for U.S. Russia policy since the Cold War is a story about real people, real personalities. Richard Holbrooke illustrates what a former ambassador to Central Asia described as the "personal dynamics that are on the whole how policies are made and come about."[1] As assistant secretary of state for European

---

[1] Russia interview 023, 29 October 2020, via telephone.

The End of Engagement. David M. McCourt, Oxford University Press. Oxford University Press 2024.
DOI: 10.1093/9780197765241.003.0009

and Canadian affairs (1994–1996), Holbrooke was a key player in U.S. policy toward Russia, including NATO expansion.[2] Holbrooke developed a bureaucratic "persona of being very hard ... [with] a way bullying of people ... so that the dynamic in any kind of a discussion ... [was that if] you know people's weaknesses you can kind of shut them down and bully them and ... you've dealt with that issue."[3] Biden's chief Russia hand, Toria Nuland, was another frequent reference. A strong personality and strident Russia-we-wanter, Nuland "served in Moscow as a junior officer" and "was there during the collapse of the Soviet Union.... But then she became very close to Strobe Talbott, who brought her out of Moscow. And then subsequently she became a power in her own right [with] an extremely important role because she had a great deal of influence on Talbott's thinking about Russia and NATO expansion."[4] "Some people can't stand her," one former official noted, but "we've been friends for 20 years."[5]

The Russia-we-have and Russia-we-want positions, captured in the 2020 open letters, thus reflect—imperfectly—personal experiences of a relatively small number of individuals. One analyst performed Daniel Fried's background in the first person: "I'm Dan Fried and I love Poland because it was my formative professional years, [the] 1980s in Poland," a period of social struggle against communism and the Soviet Union.[6] Fried has "a very kind of Polish perspective, ... feeling very sympathetic to the Poles and talking the Poles.... He's almost ideological about it. You just can't trust the Russians and you have to stick it to them every time. But he's had quite an influence on Russian policy."[7]

Prior to serving in Poland, Fried served on the Soviet desk in what was then Leningrad. As one former colleague noted,

> Apparently when he was in Leningrad (because I served there later and found out), he was kind of the person who covered the dissident community.... [Leningrad was] also a place where the KGB has its training center, and they would frequently use the U.S. Consulate as a kind of target for doing things like surveillance and things like that.... Apparently one evening Fried was coming back from something or he was accosted and beaten up.... [Fried] felt it ... was all planned to, you know, to teach him a lesson because he was ... hobnobbing with dissidents and the like. And I think that deeply affected him. And I think with any human being ... [who is] physically [assaulted] ... he's always had a very strong feeling about that.[8]

---

[2] Packer 2020.
[3] Russia interview 023, 29 October 2020, via telephone.
[4] Russia interview 023, 29 October 2020, via telephone.
[5] Russia interview 035, 18 November 2020, via video call.
[6] Russia interview 039. 30 November 2020, via video call.
[7] Russia interview 023, 29 October 2020, via telephone.
[8] Russia interview 023, 29 October 2020, via telephone.

Parallels here with Matthew Pottinger are worth highlighting. Pottinger was reportedly questioned and roughed up by the Chinese state security services while in China as a journalist for the *Wall Street Journal*.

The interviewee who characterized Fried also mentioned Michael Carpenter: "Or I'm Carpenter.[9] And I also love Poland. And I love Georgia."[10] Fried's ordeal notwithstanding, the result is *not* that Russia-we-wanters like Fried, Carpenter, Nuland, and McFaul *hate* Russia. "[Carpenter] doesn't hate Russia, doesn't speak Russian. He doesn't know much about Russia. He's not in Russia area studies . . . [his views come] from the fact that he is interested in Poland and Georgia."[11] Nuland and McFaul may strongly dislike Putin, but they do not hate Russia. In fact, most Russia-we-wanters in the policy community feel warmly toward the Russian *people*.

For Russia-we-wanters like David Kramer, "the whole promise of the 1990s was thwarted" by the return of authoritarianism in Russia, personified in Vladimir Putin. Kramer "really got to know all the dissidents and . . . intellectuals. David Kramer's super close friends with leadership."[12] One former colleague recalled a trip to Minsk: "We were walking across the square and [Kramer was] saying, 'Well, I guess this is where it's going to happen.' And I said, 'What [is going to happen]?' 'Well, you know . . . the revolution here . . . I feel it. I just feel it in my bones.'"[13]

Kramer's conviction that Belarus, like Russia, is ripe for liberal democratic revolution aptly demonstrates how the views held by America's Russia watchers—just like their China counterparts—are held as a matter of *faith* as much as cold reason. Policy debates are not only about facts, but convictions. As one research analyst explained, he sees no point arguing with the senior cadres of the Russia field because "[It's] like having a debate with your grandfather. . . . They decided everything a long time ago."[14]

People like Tom Graham, he went on, "are interested in Russia for Russian sake and they are interested in the U.S.-Russia relationship because they *believe* in one . . . [They believe that] a stable relationship between the U.S., Russia, the two main nuclear powers in the world, is essential for preventing war because Russia is the only country that can just destroy the United States in half an hour and that together the U.S. and Russia can solve big, important problems."[15]

---

[9] Carpenter served as special advisor for Europe and Eurasia to then Vice-President Biden, and Russia director on the National Security Council. Between 2015 and 2017 he was assistant secretary of defense for Russia, Ukraine, Eurasia and conventional arms control. Carpenter was nominated for the role of ambassador to the OSCE in June 2021, which he assumed in November 2021.
[10] Russia interview 039, 30 November 2020, via video call.
[11] Russia interview 039, 30 November 2020, via video call.
[12] Russia interview 025, 2 November 2020, via video call.
[13] Russia interview 023, 29 October 2020, via telephone.
[14] Russia interview 039, 30 November 2020, via video call.
[15] Russia interview 039, 30 November 2020, via video call. Emphasis added.

On the opposite side, Michael McFaul holds deep-seated convictions when it comes to Russia's democratic potential. "Let's talk about Michael McFaul, a former ambassador to Russia, Obama's number one Russia expert," one academic suggested. "I think he's an ideologue and highly emotional.... And I think he would be an embodiment of a highly ideological approach, right? I would say a missionary approach to Russia."[16] Another academic noted that he considers "McFaul ... an evangelical ... this idea that it's really about conversion.... It's a policy of conversion." For this Russia-we-haver, "If the Russians want to convert, then they should do that on their own. They don't. It's none of our business."[17]

As in the case of China, the personalized nature of the struggle over Russia policy extends beyond the top level of the government. Although difficult to measure, interviewees view their community as more close-knit, even friendlier, than the China field. For one central Russia-we-wanter, someone on the opposite side of the debate, like "Matt Rojansky of the Wilson Center," is nevertheless a "serious, knowledgeable person. He's very definitely wanted to put the American people [first]."[18] Similarly, another interviewee said, "I respect Tom Graham as a serious person," adding, "I didn't want to be part of an armed camp ... even though I'm usually pigeonholed anyway."[19]

The Russia "squabble," then, is "not an acrimonious squabble at all," a former ambassador and avowed Russia-we-wanter explained.[20] "I stay in touch with all these guys and we have all of these web conferences now and Tom [Graham] is on there. And David [Kramer].... Tom and I have worked together off and on over the last 30 years. It's great."[21] A former ambassador to Central Asia concurred: "I don't think [the debate is] viewed as personal. It's just kind of well, you know, 'I think you're wrong and you're barking up the wrong tree, but I'll still talk to you and shake your hand.'"[22] A strident Russia-we-wanter commented, "I run a Russia working group.... It meets monthly, it's off the record. And I invited Tom to speak to the group ... and he did. And [while] most of the people I invite to this working group are more in line with my thinking ... I also believe that if we just talk among ourselves that we're preaching to the converted.... We need to be challenged. And it was a very civil conversation."[23]

The congeniality of the smaller Russia sphere should not be exaggerated, however. "There were people who signed that letter [the Graham letter] whom

---

[16] Russia interview 011, 14 October 2020, via video call.
[17] Russia interview 036, 19 November 2020, via video call.
[18] Russia interview 035, 18 November 2020, via video call.
[19] Russia interview 031, 11 November 2020, via video call. Russia interview 035, 18 November 2020, via video call.
[20] Russia interview 041, 3 December 2020, via video call.
[21] Russia interview 041, 3 December 2020, via video call.
[22] Russia interview 023, 29 October 2020, via telephone.
[23] Russia interview 037, 20 November 2020, via video call.

I would want to have nothing to do with, [whom] I don't respect," one of the letter's leading critics said.[24] "I'm not going to name names since you probably know [who they are].... But I would say there may be one or two on that list who I might have suspicions about, to be perfectly blunt. And I'm sure they feel the same way about me."[25] Thus, "I would say that the Russian deal is quite polarized. ... I wouldn't want you to think that everything is ... hunky-dory.... There is some bad blood in the field."[26] "For some, it's pretty bitter," one analyst told me.[27]

Occasional bad blood is amplified the further into the public domain one travels, especially social media platforms, principally X—formerly Twitter. "I think social media played a really toxic role," one academic and Russia podcaster explained.[28] Many shy away from public engagement as a result, "because of all the shit that comes with it." The dynamic is especially noticeable on the Russia-we-want side of the debate, he went on. "If you call for any just basic diplomatic normalcy, you are pegged as, you know, sort of pro-Russia."[29] This included "anybody who engaged with the region seriously for years, you know, people ... not just like Stephen Cohen, who I think was one of the ones that received a lot of horrible response, but people like the head of the [Wilson Center's] Kennan Institute, Matt Rojansky."[30] Tellingly, this interviewee went on, "I do think it is important that ... the two camps should be talking to each other. I actually think that Fiona [Hill] and Rose [Gottemoeller] might even lean a little more toward our letter than the one they signed that the problem I think they had is it was a letter by committee."[31]

When Did You First Go to Russia? Generational Experiences and Russia-We-Have or Russia-We-Want

Like America's China experts, Russia watchers' formative experiences underpin their personal convictions. Some senior members of the field share formative experiences akin to the Committee for Concerned Asian Scholars as members of a select club of Americans to visit exotic lands in the 1970s. As one senior arms controller recalled, "I went to Russia under a particular circumstance ..., [as] an instrument of American propaganda."[32] "We used to have exhibits,

---

[24] Russia interview 037, 20 November 2020, via video call.
[25] Russia interview 037, 20 November 2020, via video call.
[26] Russia interview 037, 20 November 2020, via video call.
[27] Russia interview 039, 30 November 2020, via video call.
[28] Russia interview 036, 19 November 2020, via video call.
[29] Russia interview 036, 19 November 2020, via video call.
[30] Russia interview 036, 19 November 2020, via video call.
[31] Russia interview 037, 20 November 2020, via video call.
[32] Russia interview 027, 6 November 2020, via video call.

so-called 'cultural exchange exhibits.' The Soviet Union would send exhibits to the United States. We would send exhibits to the USSR. Nineteen seventy-six was my first trip to the Soviet Union."[33] The first exhibit followed from the famous 1956 "kitchen debate" between Nixon and Khrushchev, and the two sides would compete to show off the productivity of their respective systems.

> The exhibit I was on was called Photography USA ... [and was] supported by Kodak and Polaroid. I was there as an exhibit guide.... Our job was to stand on the exhibit floor eight hours a day and talk to the visitors about whatever they wanted to talk about. Usually they did not want to talk about the exhibit. They wanted to talk about how easy was it to buy jeans. How big was my apartment? What was the price of bread? ... Most of them had never seen an American before.[34]

Early American visitors to China's movements were tightly controlled, and the Russian authorities similarly "tried to keep us reined in, but young people would come to the exhibit and they'd say, 'Hey, come out with us tonight ... we'll get a bottle of vodka and go to the park.' And we ... practically everybody on the exhibit would go out and meet people at night and sit and just talk and talk and talk." Sharing the experience with other members of the self-styled "guide mafia," many of whom went into the U.S. government, this interviewee said, "I would say in general, we [developed an] affectionate [view of Russia]. And I would say it's a realistic point of view, recognizing that there are a lot of good people there ... [who are] not an evil member of the Putin regime.... There are many similarities between Americans and Russians, just in terms of our approach to humor."[35] The result, for this interviewee and likely others, was a "willingness to look for positives [about Russia] ... because we spent so much time on the [ground]."[36]

Tellingly, no interviews agreed with common saying in the Russia field that "to study Russia is to hate it." As one academic and former policymaker explained,

> I went there for the first time as a graduate student when I was doing my PhD ... and it was just fascinating to live there. My Russian was good enough that I could at least function, and then I just got kind of hooked on the subject. So, but I would say during the Cold War ... it was ... a sort of fascination and, to some extent, horror, some of the things that went on there, the way that people lived and the way they were treated. And then I would say when the Soviet Union collapsed it was—this was just almost unbelievable to someone who'd,

---

[33] Russia interview 027, 6 November 2020, via video call.
[34] Russia interview 027, 6 November 2020, via video call.
[35] Russia interview 027, 6 November 2020, via video call.
[36] Russia interview 027, 6 November 2020, via video call.

you know, having spent... time in the Soviet Union. So it was like a flourishing when the Soviet Union collapsed to have all of these people who've been critics who supported Gorbachev, and then this sort of sense of, you know, freedom of expression and endless possibilities. And so I'm probably like a number of people who thought things were really going to change. I mean, we didn't know, and you can always say anyone who studied Russian history should have been very wary of thinking that things were really going to change that rapidly, but I think we did have hope.[37]

A former ambassador agreed on the importance of the 1990s. In government circles, "It was a very heady time.... We were involved in reshaping the face of Europe ... working on things that were as much cooperative as they were competitive. [From] the early part of the mid-eighties through the beginning of the first half of the 2000s, ... that's period that the whole world of the Soviet experts or Kremlinologists or whatever completely changes."[38] In the academy, one historian recalled, "The collapse of the Soviet Union and the opening up of the archive just made possible things that were unimaginable before. And I did wonder then how on earth I had ever spent so many years reading *Pravda*. But then when things opened up, it became totally fascinating to go and talk to people and go places."[39]

Russia watchers' formative experiences are not, then, mere anecdotes. They are at the core of what explains the Russia-we-have and Russia-we-want structure of the Russia field up through 2022. "I understand where Mike [McFaul]'s coming from," a former ambassador noted.

We have them on the China side, too. And they were mostly from the academic community, [not] to begrudge the academic community, they're key in all of this. But I think there was an opening in Russia starting in about late 1990 going through 1991 and certainly through the breakup late summer of 1991 of their nation-state that led to the years of Yeltsin and the hopefulness of new institutions and a commitment to democracy and human rights and all of that.[40]

Another interview remembered, "They call it 'forward deployed' to the embassy [in Moscow].... In the nineties, they'd been really captivated by the place. I mean, you couldn't fail to be dazzled by watching this amazing process of transformation, even though it kind of went wrong."[41]

---

[37] Russia interview 015, 19 October 2020, via video call.
[38] Russia interview 013, 15 October 2020, via telephone.
[39] Russia interview 029, 12 November 2020, via video call.
[40] Russia interview 043, 4 December 2020, via video call.
[41] Russia interview 013, 15 October 2020, via video call.

Putin's rise to power and return in 2012 forestalled the vindication of the Russia-we-wanters' personal and professional hopes. For a longtime Russia hand, "I was on the street ... in 1991 and watched 250,000 Russians stand in the rain around their Russian White House wanting change."[42] This convinced her change is possible in Russia. It is what the Russian people want. For a Russia-we-haver like Graham, by contrast, "He was in the embassy during a period where oligarchism had really reinfected Yeltsin. And he felt like our policy [of democracy promotion] was enabling that."[43]

A cynical take on such personal convictions is, of course, possible. Tom Graham's connections to Kissinger Associates and consulting for firms investing in Russia is a case in point. "[He's] very close to Henry Kissinger," one academic noted.

> And so Henry Kissinger was always somebody who could be mainstream at home, but very much in favor of negotiations abroad. And my understanding of what Tom Graham's work is primarily about is using the situation for American businesses who still want to have contacts in Russia. And so one of the things that he does is, is he has to be very careful about what he says, because he has to make sure that nothing he says would have negative repercussions for the businesses that are he is advising.[44]

Other personal attachments mentioned include whether individuals were in the "diplomatic club" or had a hand in shaping U.S. policy, since "if not, you have a fundamentally different perspective to those that did. [They] are permanently defending their record."[45]

> I got into the club—the State Department likes to use that word, but, I mean, it's the Foreign Service. If you're going to be an expert on political or economic affairs, you really have to be a regional specialist and just because of your interest. But the way the personnel system ... works is that the regional bureaus and State are the ones who basically bring [you] to the personnel panel—you have to really become kind of a member of the club. Your club."[46]

Another interviewee noted the effect of personal and professional relationships: "For people like [former ambassador to Russia Thomas] Pickering, they're invested in in a set of relationships in government circles. That

---

[42] Russia interview 033, 16 November 2020, via video call.
[43] Russia interview 030, 13 November 2020, via video call.
[44] Russia interview 021, 26 October 2020, via video call.
[45] Russia interview 039, 30 November 2020, via video call.
[46] Russia interview 041, 3 December 2020, via video call.

just makes it inconceivable that you would harshly criticize U.S. government policies. You've been a representative of the United States government.... You're closely identified with the United States government policies."[47]

By contrast, for younger Russia hands, "It's not like I've spent decades advocating a position I have to stick to."[48] For another prominent, younger Russia-we-haver, the result is that

> I often find myself feeling very much like that there aren't many people on my side of the fence.... I never had the nineties euphoria... then... became disappointed in Russia. There were a lot of people had these very high hopes, like Mike McFaul's generation particularly, that experienced ninety-one sometimes firsthand and thought they were witnessing the birth of a democratic Russia and sort of couldn't get over that things didn't turn out that way.[49]

George Kennan and Russia: Rethinking Containment, Not Reliving the 1940s

Seventy-five years after the former diplomat's Long Telegram, Kennan is still everywhere in commentary on U.S.-Russia relations.[50] Putin's capture of Crimea in 2014 and the sanctions regime constructed in response urged Russia-we-haver Matt Rojansky in 2016 to revisit the lessons of Kennan and containment. "Containment was a mode of East-West relations that many presumed would be relegated to the dustbin of history at the end of the Cold War," Rojansky noted. "Yet the current period might accurately be dubbed the era of 'new containment,' with many urging the United States, NATO, and Europe to once again contain, constrain and counter what they view as Russia's expansionist policies and malign influence on the world stage."[51] Rojansky found in Kennan less a strict recommendation to limit Russia at every turn than the specific "recommendation that defeating the Soviet threat would require a robust Western capacity to understand Russia—a capacity that Kennan would judge to be sadly lacking today."[52]

Kennan's late-1940s recommendations upon which his legend was built have been arguably less powerful in recent debates than his post-1989 warnings about

---

[47] Russia interview 011, 14 October 2020, via video call.
[48] Russia interview 026, 5 November 2020, via telephone.
[49] Russia interview 010, 12 October 2020, via video call.
[50] See, among others, "What Would George Kennan Say about the Russia-Ukraine Conflict?," *Global Times*, 29 March 2002, https://www.globaltimes.cn/page/202203/1257094.shtml.
[51] Matthew Rojansky, "George F. Kennan, Containment, and the West's Current Russia Problem," *NATO Defense College Research Paper, No. 127*, 2.
[52] Rojansky, "George F. Kennan," 2.

U.S. policy toward Russia. In particular, Kennan's warnings against it NATO expansion have been deployed as an emphasis point for the "We should have known better" argument of both offensive realists, like John Mearsheimer, and restrainers, like Cato's Ted Galen Carpenter.[53] For the latter, "NATO's arrogant, tone-deaf policy toward Russia over the past quarter-century deserves a large share of the blame for the breakdown in relations and the war in Ukraine."[54] Citing ample evidence that America was warned of the likely Russian response to enlargement, by people from Boris Yeltsin to Strobe Talbott, Carpenter reserves a special place for Kennan:

> George Kennan, the intellectual father of America's containment policy during the Cold War, perceptively warned in a May 2, 1998 *New York Times* interview about what the Senate's ratification of NATO's first round of expansion would set in motion. "I think it is the beginning of a new cold war," Kennan stated. "I think the Russians will gradually react quite adversely and it will affect their policies. I think it is a tragic mistake. There was no reason for this whatsoever. No one was threatening anybody else."[55]

Similarly, Jordan Michael Smith in the *New Republic* traced the origins of the Ukraine invasion to the enlargement of NATO. Celebrating the "Cassandra-like prophecies" of "historians, diplomats, and political scientists"—like former director for European Affairs under President Clinton Charles Kupchan, who penned a *New York Times* op-ed in 1994 with a warning forecast: "An expanded NATO would lead Russia to reassert control over its former republics and to remilitarize." Smith again foregrounded Kennan. The warnings of Kupchan and others, Smith noted, "were bolstered in February 1997 by George Kennan, the legendary ambassador to the Soviet Union and Cold War theoretician. He wrote bluntly that NATO expansion was a historic error, one that might 'restore the atmosphere of the cold war to East-West relations, and impel Russian foreign policy in directions decidedly not to our liking.'"[56]

Perhaps paradoxically, therefore, Kennan's legacy is more contested in relation to Russia than the PRC. Neither the Russia-we-havers nor the Russia-we-wanters feel the need to invoke Kennan as part of a reliving of the 1940s, as do the Strategic Competitors with China. Kennan's name in the Russia debate

---

[53] George F. Kennan, "A Fateful Error," *New York Times*, 5 February 1997, https://www.nytimes.com/1997/02/05/opinion/a-fateful-error.html.
[54] See Ted Galen Carpenter, "Ignored Warnings: How NATO Expansion Led to the Current Ukraine Tragedy," https://www.cato.org/commentary/ignored-warnings-how-nato-expansion-led-current-ukraine-tragedy, February 24, 2022.
[55] See Carpenter, "Ignored Warnings."
[56] See https://newrepublic.com/article/165562/nato-critics-predicted-russia-putin-belligerence-ukraine.

appears mostly *not* as an advocate for containment—the approach he is credited as authoring in the late 1940s—but for a blend of competition and a view closer to engagement.

"Do You Go to Valdai?"

Critics of Engagement with China are suspicious of the relationship between Engagers and so-called barbarian handlers—the chaperones provided directly or indirectly by the CCP to high-ranking foreign visitors.[57] Chaperones ensure westerners remain naive about the communist regime and its governing practices, steering them away from sites and topics deemed unfit for foreign consumption. A corollary on the Russia side is the Valdai Discussion Club.[58] Founded in 2004 in Moscow through the collaboration of Russian international affairs organizations—including the Russian International Affairs Council and the Moscow State Institute of International Relations—Valdai styles itself a regular think tank. At the time of writing, programming includes "Norms and Values," "Asia and Eurasia," and "Modern Diplomacy." The question posed to America's Russia watchers is, to go to Valdai or not?

Valdai is not an American-style think tank.

> In 2004 the Russian government decided that it wanted to improve its image. And so it invited a group of foreign experts on Russia and in 2004 that were Americans, Europeans, . . . British journalists, Germans, French, Italians, a few Chinese and Japanese were flown to Moscow obviously then we went to the Valdai [which] was the name of one of Stalin's country homes. So we went then. But that was right in the middle of this hostage crisis, September of 2004 in Beslan. When these children were taken hostage, it was very badly handled. And in the end, you know, large numbers of people were killed. And so it was a very kind of raw time, but we started off having a dinner with food, which went on much longer than we thought it would.[59]

Valdai is organized along the lines of an Aspen Ideas Festival: "They have these big panels. It's all international. Now there's lots of Chinese this year; there are no Americans on the program. It's Chinese, Indian, you know, from all different parts of the world. And, I mean, we'll see Modi speak. . . . We'll see what he says, but it's all much more public now."[60]

[57] China interview 072, 19 February 2019, via video call.
[58] https://valdaiclub.com/.
[59] Russia interview 015, 19 October 2020, via video call.
[60] Russia interview 015, 19 October 2020, via video call.

One prominent DC academic and former official explained her decision to go:

> In 2004, I started going into the Valdai Discussion Club.... People who are very critical of Russia, they wouldn't go, and they've criticized those of us that go there because when you go you are the guests of the Russian government. And even though I don't come back and write articles saying everything that Putin does is wonderful, it's certainly very interesting to go and listen to what the policymakers say. So that's the value.[61]

Criticism has followed.

> I've been criticized by some of the Russia watchers here and in Russia and in Europe for being [a] useful idiot, et cetera, et cetera. But I personally found it very interesting, you know. You listen to what they want to tell you, ... this is a public message. [And] being able to meet people, obviously the Russians and others, that's been for me a very interesting experience, but one, as I say, it's not uncomfortable.[62]

Fiona Hill between the Russia-We-Have and the Russia-We-Want

Matthew Pottinger's Russia counterpart on Trump's NSC was think tanker Fiona Hill. Appointed special assistant to the president and senior director for European and Russian affairs, Hill lasted two years, leaving on 19 July 2019— normative for the White House, impressive given the turnover rate under Trump. Hill was subsequently swept up in impeachment proceedings, having been on the call during which Trump pressured Ukraine to remove U.S. ambassador to Kiev Marie Yovanovitch and open an investigation into former vice president Joe Biden and his son, Hunter, over their Ukraine business dealings. Hill's experiences while in office represent a useful mirror to the personal and personalized dynamics underpinning the reframing of U.S.-China relations under Trump. To compare Hill with Pottinger is not, of course, to equate them— any shift in Russia policy, especially toward small-*e* engagement, faced significant obstacles—not least a Congress strongly critical of Moscow and the highly politicized nature of Russia in U.S. domestic politics following allegations of election interference. Nonetheless, Hill's experiences highlight the personal and personalized factors shaping a possible paradigmatic shift on Russia—again, the signal achievement of Pottinger and his team.

---

[61] Russia interview 015, 19 October 2020, via video call.
[62] Russia interview 015, 19 October 2020, via video call.

Prior to her appointment, Hill was known for hawkish but "realist" views on Russia but was also on record as supporting the sort of stable relations sought by some in the administration, including Trump himself. Hill might, hypothetically, have sought a new paradigm for relations with Russia—complete with a new frame and new community. That she did not tells us much, especially about the degree of polarization of the U.S. Russia space, and the distance between the Russia-we-wanters and the Russia-we-havers.

Like Pottinger, Hill is a well-respected and experienced Russia expert, who marries mainstream credentials and affiliations with a degree of outsider status not uncommon among Trump's appointees. Born in northern England, with a still-strong accent, Hill was not the typical Trump appointee. Hill "hailed from the Brookings Institution, the epitome of the D.C. establishment Trump had pointedly rejected,"[63] but enjoyed mostly mainstream credentials, including a Harvard PhD, consulting experience at the Eurasia Group, and time advising previous presidents Obama and Bush Jr. on intelligence relating to Russia. Hill also checked the traditional boxes for language competence and time spent in-country, having studied in Moscow while an undergraduate at St. Andrews University prior to moving to America. Hill also had good connections, from former advisors Graham Allison and Robert Legvold to eminent Russia specialists like Strobe Talbott and Trump appointees like McFarland, who each urged her to serve.[64]

Hill was advised against joining the Trump administration by others, however, including "never Trumper" Eliot Cohen and NSC predecessor Celeste Wallander.[65] But like Pottinger, a sense of duty and the hope of playing the role of the "adult in the room" persuaded Hill to "go in," telling Wallander, "when your house is on fire, you've got to go in and save something."[66] As Hill later recalled, "I did not join Donald Trump's National Security Council for the glamour or thrill of working at the White House. I wanted to serve my country, and I felt that I had something to offer, given my educational training and long experience of dealing with Russia, including during my previous stint in government at the National Intelligence Council."[67]

Unlike Pottinger, however, Hill came to office with neither the dispositions, the desire, nor the ability to effect a paradigmatic turnover in America's approach to Russia. In particular, Hill was not in the position to reframe U.S. Russia

---

[63] Natasha Bertrand, "The Russia Hawk in the White House," *Politico*, 30 September 2019, https://www.politico.com/magazine/story/2019/09/30/fiona-hill-russia-trump-adviser-228758/.
[64] Hill 2021: 193; Adam Entous, "What Fiona Hill Learned in the White House," *New Yorker*, 29 June 2020, https://www.newyorker.com/magazine/2020/06/29/what-fiona-hill-learned-in-the-white-house.
[65] Entous, "What Fiona Hill Learned."
[66] Entous, "What Fiona Hill Learned."
[67] Hill 2021: 191.

policy as a way to express and justify the policy views of a distinct set of Russia watchers—as had been the case with the China Engagers. As described in previous chapters, the Russia field was both smaller and less polarized. While the Russia-we-havers and Russia-we-wanters disagreed on *policy*, they largely saw the challenge from Putin's Russia in similar ways.

In the shifting terrain of America's Russia watchers, Hill sat uneasily between the Russia-we-havers and the Russia-we-wanters. Several of Hill's op-ed contributions to public debate positioned her closer to the Russia-we-have position. In the aftermath of the attack on Beslan in September 2004, Hill urged policymakers to listen to Putin.[68] More recently, she has cautioned against provision of heavy weapons to Ukraine, for fear of escalating the then-limited conflict in the East.[69] But within the Russia field, Hill was not seen as aligned with the Tom Graham realist position. Her book with Clifford Gaddy was unflinching in its portrayal of Putin. Moreover, like Pottinger's run-in with the Chinese Ministry of State Security, Hill had been on the receiving end of retribution from the Russian security services—suffering a suspected poisoning after a meeting with Chechen dissidents.[70] Hill was thus more of a hawk than the Russia-we-havers, and less focused on shaping Russia's internal politics than the Russia-we-wanters.

Adam Entous, Hill's *New Yorker* profiler, explained how Hill "soon became what her friends and colleagues describe as a Russia 'realist.'"[71] In 2013, nearly a decade after urging the West to try to work with Putin and roughly a year before Russia forcibly annexed Crimea from Ukraine, Hill wrote that Putin "has never seen the West as a model for Russia. Now, he is not even interested in joining it as a partner."[72] Hill was therefore not inclined to try to forge a new paradigm for U.S.-Russia relations, based on a new narrative framing. Of the previous attempt, the Russia reset, Hill had been supportive but skeptical. "The reality is this: There are no big deals to be had with Putin," she wrote along with coauthor Cliff Gaddy. "Outside the traditional U.S.-Russian bilateral realm of arms control, there is no great opportunity for the Obama administration in Russia."[73] Hill recognized that, given the power and legitimacy of the Russia-we-want position in the United States national security conversation on Russia, there was no space for a grand agreement: "The only quid pro quo Putin would likely strike with the United States is one no administration could (or would) contemplate—where

---

[68] Entous, "What Fiona Hill Learned."
[69] Entous, "What Fiona Hill Learned."
[70] Natasha Bertrand, "The Russia Hawk in the White House," *Politico*, 30 September 2019, https://www.politico.com/magazine/story/2019/09/30/fiona-hill-russia-trump-adviser-228758/
[71] Entous, "What Fiona Hill Learned."
[72] Entous, "What Fiona Hill Learned."
[73] Bertrand, "The Russia Hawk."

Moscow agrees not to make life too difficult for Washington, as long as the U.S. ignores Russian domestic developments and human rights abuses."[74]

Even had Hill had the disposition to try to effect a reframing of the U.S.-Russia relationship, she lacked any affordance to do so—meaning her ability to navigate the bureaucracy under the specific context of the Trump administration. As she herself recognized, "Joining the administration would be a tough and controversial assignment, but with the encouragement of Brookings colleagues and longtime mentors ... I resolved to see what I could do to help tackle the Russian intelligence services' attack on American democracy."[75] Unlike Pottinger, who in April 2017 was dusting off "Bill's Paper" and settling into reframing China in official U.S. strategy documents, Hill "wasn't sitting around ... debating what policies to implement," said a former NSC official who's worked with Hill. "Damage control [was] really her purview. In the Trump era, that's hardly a minor role."[76] Her main job on Russia was to steady the relationship, to try to get her boss to understand something of Putin's personality and diplomatic modus operandi—of which she was skeptical, like the Russia-we-wanters. A realist like the Russia-we-havers, however, Hill was not interested in forging a new framing of Russia, or a new diplomatic reset. That had been tried and had failed.

Unlike Pottinger, Hill had to contend with the factional struggles inside the Trump administration. China was part of the issue. The China-skeptical Steve Bannon had read her book on Putin and considered her a "consummate professional" on Russia. But he tried to block her appointment anyway because he concluded she wouldn't be on board with getting Putin to side with the United States against China, urging Flynn to "find someone a little bit more malleable on Russia."[77] The result was that even among possible supporters, Hill was viewed with suspicion.

Hill was vulnerable from the outset, having previously worked with former British intelligence operative Christopher Steele, who had produced prior to the 2016 election a dossier of intelligence for an attorney associated with the Hillary Clinton campaign, which suggested Russia had compromising information about Trump. Hill also came under fire for agreeing to a meeting with leading Russia-we-wanter Michael McFaul, after Russian security services sought to question McFaul after Trump had agreed to a proposed plan with Putin for reciprocal access for police to question Americans and Russians of interest. State had rejected the proposal, but on 17 July 2017, Russia's prosecutor general's office put in a request to speak to 11 Americans, including McFaul. McFaul asked to see Hill, who said yes to the meeting. One of John Bolton's deputies at NSC accused

---

[74] Bertrand, "The Russia Hawk."
[75] Hill 2021: 193.
[76] Bertrand, "The Russia Hawk."
[77] Entous, "What Fiona Hill Learned."

her of disloyalty.[78] By September 2017, Hill was the subject of a concerted effort to discredit her, with an anonymous *Times* op-ed naming someone "working diligently" in the administration to frustrate Trump's agenda. Rick Grenell, ambassador to Germany at the time, was spreading the rumor it was Hill.[79] When Hill raised concerns about a possible meeting with far-right Hungarian leader Viktor Orbán, conservative Republican Connie Mack made public the funding the Brookings Institution received from George Soros, allowing Mack to proclaim that Hill was "doing Soros's bidding" in the White House.[80]

Hill was not without allies. K. T. McFarland was an early supporter, Hill having been "first approached to join the Trump administration by K. T. McFarland, a Fox News program host who, like me, was a member of the Council on Foreign Relations (CFR). We had frequently discussed U.S.-Russian relations on the margins of CFR events."[81] McFarland told Hill pointedly she did not give Flynn rumors much credence, and said she wasn't convinced by the Steele dossier in any case.[82] McMaster also took her seriously, uninterested in the claims, and became an important ally. As *Politico* reported, "A former NSC official recalled an episode in which Russia's national security adviser, Nikolai Patrushev, wanted to meet with McMaster but faced enormous pushback by the State Department and Pentagon. 'Fiona, on the other hand, was very supportive of McMaster maintaining that channel,' the former official said. 'She understands the role that Patrushev plays, and that he's more important in the Russian hierarchy than, say, Foreign Minister Lavrov. So that's also why she encouraged that dialogue.'"[83]

The palace intrigue neither caused nor hastened the end of Hill's tenure, but Hill later expressed surprise at the degree of factionalism in the Trump White House, which she described as "a motley crew of people with few ties to each other and some with no prior government experience whatsoever, all jockeying for influence—and often launching political assaults to oust perceived enemies from their positions."[84] As Hill admitted, "I knew the intrigue in Russia better than the intrigue at home,"[85] and "I was naive about U.S. politics and how much it was possible—or not possible to get done in such a highly charged environment after the 2016 election."[86] She tried to treat her time in the White House as "a social anthropological study . . . turning the lens around on the United States and noting the parallels with upheavals I had seen and experienced elsewhere.

---

[78] Entous, "What Fiona Hill Learned."
[79] Entous, "What Fiona Hill Learned."
[80] Entous, "What Fiona Hill Learned."
[81] Hill 2021: 192.
[82] Bertrand, "The Russia Hawk."
[83] Bertrand, "The Russia Hawk."
[84] Hill 2021: 194.
[85] Entous, "What Fiona Hill Learned."
[86] Hill 2021: 191.

256 ENDING ENGAGEMENT WITH RUSSIA

The political machinations around the Trump White House turned out to be as dirty and filled with intrigue as the Kremlin's."[87]

Not surprisingly, Hill found that being a woman in Trump's White House significantly shaped what was and was not possible. "As far as President Trump was concerned," Hill has recalled, "my academic and professional credentials and expertise were irrelevant. For all intents and purposes, as a woman and an outsider, I was not part of his team."[88] Called by staffers of White House chief of staff Reince Priebus "that Russia bitch," Hill quickly became aware that fashion standards were high, driven largely by First Daughter Ivanka, and that the accident of wearing sneakers worn during her first meeting with the president in the Oval Office must not be repeated. Hill was later mistaken for a secretary and asked to type up a 2 May 2017 press release about a call between Trump and Putin—"it wasn't the first or the last time that I would be mistaken for the secretary—it was a long-standing occupational hazard."[89]

Hill's stories about the gendered dynamics of the Trump White House would be mere anecdotes except that they materially shaped what was and was not possible. As she noted, "It very quickly became apparent that I was never going to have any kind of sit-down with Donald Trump to talk about Vladimir Putin or Russia, or pretty much anything else in my portfolio. One of the major reasons was that I was a woman."[90] Initially at least, Russia was Secretary of State Rex Tillerson's domain. When McMaster introduced Hill to Trump by saying she'd written "the best book on Putin," Trump replied, "'Rex is doing Russia. . . . He's done billion-dollar energy deals with Putin.' . . . Trump is fixated on arms control." Hill comments, "Who's he going to listen to, Rex or some woman?"[91] The result was a further push toward the technical and away from any sort of big thinking on Russia.

> I figured after my early encounters with the president that I would focus my efforts elsewhere. I would make sure that my boss, the national security adviser . . . and all my colleagues at the NSC got the best information, insight, and advice I could offer on Putin, Russia, and everything else in my portfolio. I would concentrate on forging good relations with the other officials working on Europe and Russia across the U.S. government as well as my counterparts in foreign governments.[92]

---

[87] Hill 2021: 192.
[88] Hill 2021: 194.
[89] Hill 2021: 204.
[90] Hill 2021: 194.
[91] Hill 2021: 197.
[92] Hill 2021: 206.

This comparison between Hill and Pottinger—two respected but not entirely conventional country experts—should not be taken too far. Where Pottinger had a well-thought-out plan to reframe China in the U.S. national security conversation, and a community of anti-Engagers to draw intellectual and personal support from, Hill had little confidence any movement was possible with Moscow—whether policy should be more or less engaged. Yet Hill's experience shines a light by their absence on the conditions under which Pottinger could operate, skillful bureaucratic fighter he clearly was. Both operated below the level of Trump and were thus "nonplayers in his world,"[93] but Hill was unable to find solid ground to do more than survive.

The Case of Matthew Rojansky

The case of Matthew Rojansky represents a comparative case in the community, with Rojansky blocked from taking a position on Biden administration's National Security Council due to his pro-engagement views. Again, cases like Rojansky's are where the rubber of knowledge communities' impact hits the road of U.S. policymaking.

President and CEO of the U.S. Russia Foundation—a 501(c)3 founded to support civil society, private enterprise, and rule of law in Russia—and fellow at the Kennan Institute of the Wilson Center, Rojansky's resume clearly signals membership in the "Russia-we-have" camp. With former ambassador and Russia-we-haver James Collins, for example, Rojansky in 2011 wrote in support of the two-year anniversary of the founding of the U.S.-Russia Bilateral Presidential Commission (BPC), for them "the best mechanism to ensure continued success in managing U.S.-Russian relations is to endow the BPC with the structure and resources it needs to become an enduring foundation for intergovernmental and societal cooperation."[94]

Writing nine years later, in a less optimistic context, Rojansky and Michael Kimmage advocated viewing Russia as neither friend nor foe, but a neighbor: "Neighbors are rarely strangers to the irritations of proximity, which can include bristling resentment at perceived violations as well as hot and cold varieties of conflict. They are prone to complain about one another and to bicker over shared spaces and resources. Neighbors also know one another, and benefit from that knowledge. Although some neighborhoods are conflict zones, all

---

[93] Entous, "What Fiona Hill Learned."
[94] James Collins and Matthew Rojansky, *An Enduring Approach to U.S.-Russia Cooperation*, Carnegie Endowment for International Peace, 27 July 2011, https://carnegieendowment.org/2011/07/27/enduring-approach-to-u.s.-russian-cooperation-pub-45189.

neighbors have a vested interest in having their neighborhood not be a conflict zone—and in having their neighborhood prosper."[95]

Such signaling is subtle. In a June 2021 opinion in *Politico*, Rojansky struck a decidedly strident tone, supporting Biden's declaration of America's "tough" approach toward Putin. The signaling came in the form of nuance: Rojansky clarified the meaning of toughness as making the United States' red lines clear, and then defending them, in contrast to the Obama administration's approach to the use of chemical weapons in Syria. Similarly, in June 2020 Rojansky teamed up with Abraham Denmark, deputy assistant secretary of defense for East Asia in the second Obama administration to argue that America's success abroad begins with sound policymaking at home—a key theme of left- and progressive-leaning foreign policy discourse, think of Richard Haass's *Foreign Policy Begins at Home*. Not surprisingly, Kennan's name was prominent. For Denmark and Rojansky, "Kennan ... abhorred wasteful expenditure of financial and military resources, and he cautioned against excesses of bravado toward allies and adversaries alike. Yet he also recognized the essential linkage among foreign policy success, a compelling national idea, and the ability to inspire others by solving problems at home."[96]

In each case, Rojansky unmistakably signaled how, while not naive about Russia, "enmeshing the relationship in process" plus clear diplomatic engagement is the best basis for relations with Moscow. The following year, writing with Dmitri Alperovitch, Rojansky suggested Biden had an opportunity to learn from his predecessors' mistakes in their dealings with Putin.[97] Noting that "Biden has his own history with Putin, whom he has previously characterized as a killer without a soul," the authors praise his desire for "a more "stable and predictable" relationship with Russia, and with good reason: Russia's nuclear and conventional forces remain threats to the United States and its allies, while Russian aggression against its neighbors, interference in American and European politics, and disruptive cyberattacks have struck blows against the rules-based international order that Biden seeks to shore up."[98]

Beyond his writing, Rojansky's association with the Russia-we-have camp is also tied to his executive chairmanship of the Dartmouth Conference, a series of Track Two dialogues held between two Russian and American leaders since

---

[95] Matthew Rojansky and Michael Kimmage, "The Third Neighbor: Can America Live with Putin's Russia," *National Interest*, 3 July 2020, https://nationalinterest.org/feature/third-neighbor-can-america-live-putins-russia-163806.

[96] Abraham Denmark and Matthew Rojansky, "American Success Abroad Is Anchored to Problem-Solving at Home," *War on the Rocks*, 25 June 2020, https://warontherocks.com/2020/06/american-success-abroad-is-anchored-to-problem-solving-at-home/.

[97] Dmitri Alperovitch and Matthew Rojansky, "Putin Has Bedeviled American Presidents. Biden Can Learn from Their Mistakes," *Washington Post*, 14 June 2021, https://www.washingtonpost.com/outlook/2021/06/14/biden-putin-presidents-cybercrime/.

[98] Alperovitch and Rojansky, "Putin Has Bedeviled American Presidents."

1960. The Dartmouth Dialogues embody the sort of deep engagement Rojansky advocates. As a recent review notes, "Dartmouth doesn't have an American voice or a Russian voice; it has a blended voice all of its own."[99] Despite the demise of engagement, participants see the dialogues as an opportunity for constructive collaboration—from managing the relationship to exchanges to combating shared threats and prompting exchanges—"while at the same time opposing Russian policies and actions contrary to our core values and interests."[100]

The result, one interviewee explained, is that "Matt Rojansky . . . sometimes is vilified by some of the harder-liner members of the Kramer and John Herbst camp."[101] The criticism comes from "peer pressure," particularly from organizations like the "Atlantic Council [which] does have a kind of monolithic view. . . . That's why they focus so heavily on Ukraine."[102] As someone with "a foot in each camp, or maybe one foot in the hard-liner camp and at least a half a foot" in Rojansky's camp, "I think maybe sometimes it's a little overdone."[103]

Typical of the Russia- and China-watching communities, such personal criticism would be inconsequential if it did not affect the practical issue of who does, and does not, enter government service. Rojansky was passed over for the Biden NSC. As one anonymous source told *Politico*, "Several current and former senior officials warned the White House against hiring Rojansky, arguing that appointing him would signal a conciliatory U.S. policy toward Moscow."[104] Opponents included Russian dissidents like Garry Kasparov and activist Bill Browder. Tellingly, an anonymous colleague spoke in support of Rojansky, calling him a "'nuanced analyst' with a 'strategic and realist' view about how to engage with Moscow."[105]

The upshot is not that Rojansky's pro-engagement views nixed his appointment, but rather that controversy trumps nuance in Washington's revolving door. The post was filled by the less controversial choice of the Center for a New American Security's Andrea Kendall-Taylor. Rojansky's chance may come again with a future democratic administration, but it seems unlikely.

---

[99] Mathews 2021: v.
[100] Stewart 2021: 93.
[101] Russia interview 038, 30 November 2020, via video call.
[102] Russia interview 038, 30 November 2020, via video call.
[103] Russia interview 038, 30 November 2020, via video call.
[104] Natasha Bertrand, "Biden Won't Bring on Board Controversial Russia Expert," *Politico*, 19 April 2021, https://www.politico.com/news/2021/04/19/biden-russia-expert-483000.
[105] Bertrand, "Biden Won't Bring on Board."

Conclusion: After Engagement

Engagement with China and Russia is dead. Engagement with China's demise was evident before NSC Indo-Pacific coordinator Kurt Campbell proclaimed it deceased in the spring of 2021.[1] The furor surrounding House Speaker Nancy Pelosi's August 2022 trip to Taiwan, and China's large-scale infractions of Taiwanese airspace in response, is only one example of the new reality: Washington and Beijing are locked in a global competition that promises to dominate the 21st century.[2] As the October 2022 Biden-Harris NSS confirmed, "The People's Republic of China harbors the intention and increasingly the capacity to reshape the international order in favor of one that tilts the global playing field to its benefit."[3] More unmistakably, the 2022 Ukraine invasion signaled the end of engagement with Russia, as U.S. support forged a de facto if not de jure alliance between Washington and Kiev. "Russia's brutal and unprovoked war on its neighbor Ukraine has shattered peace in Europe and impacted stability everywhere,"[4] NSS 2022 stated.

Could engagement with one or both countries re-emerge in the future? Some hope so, especially in relation to China. For America's biggest firms, especially those on Wall Street, there is still money to be made.[5] Academics hope to return to China for research, and many scientists wish to continue collaboration with their Chinese counterparts.[6] At the highest levels of the government, "The United States remains committed to managing the competition between our countries responsibly," President Biden affirmed in NSS 2022.[7]

---

[1] The transcript of Campbell's commentators, speaking alongside deputy Laura Rosenberger at Stanford University on 27 May 2021, is available at https://aparc.fsi.stanford.edu/news/white-house-top-asia-policy-officials-discuss-us-china-strategy-aparc%E2%80%99s-oksenberg-conference.

[2] "Nancy Pelosi Visits Taiwan Despite Chinese Warnings," *Washington Post*, 2 August 2022, https://www.washingtonpost.com/world/2022/08/02/nancy-pelosi-taiwan-visit/; "Pelosi's Taiwan Visit Ushers in New Phase of China's Pressure Campaign," *Washington Post*, 3 August 2022, https://www.washingtonpost.com/world/2022/08/03/pelosi-taiwan-visit-china-response-military/.

[3] *National Security Strategy*, October 2022, https://www.whitehouse.gov/wp-content/uploads/2022/10/Biden-Harris-Administrations-National-Security-Strategy-10.2022.pdf, foreword.

[4] *National Security Strategy*, October 2022, foreword.

[5] Thomas Hale, Harriet Agnew, Michael Mackenzie, and Demetri Sevastopulo, "Wall Street's New Love Affair with China," *Financial Times*, 28 May 2021, https://www.ft.com/content/d5e09db3-549e-4a0b-8dbf-e499d0606df4.

[6] See Dan Murphy, "Like It Or Not, America Needs Chinese Scientists," *New York Times*, 25 May 2023, https://www.nytimes.com/2023/05/25/opinion/china-usa-scientists-technology.html.

[7] *National Security Strategy*, October 2022, foreword.

Even if engagement returns, however, it will be a phenomenon qualitatively different from what we termed above Engagement 1.0 or 2.0: a new approach for a changed world. The China of the early 2000s is gone forever, not to mention the 1980s and 1990s. An economic and military peer of the United States, any renewed engagement would be based on cold realpolitik, not optimism about what the future might bring. No U.S. policymaker could honestly claim that engagement with Beijing will promote liberalization in China. Conversely, at the time of writing a post-Ukraine war Russia looks likely to be even further diminished. Absent regime change in Moscow, an extended period of frozen relations appears inevitable. The post–Cold War period of engagement is over; the post-post–Cold War era is here.

This concluding chapter recaps the book's argument before assessing what it all means for U.S. foreign policy in a post-engagement world. Readers happy in their grasp of the book's case can move past the following section, which revisits the debate over engagement's ending before the next draws out the most salient features of the China-Russia comparison. The chapter then assesses where U.S. China and Russia policy, and America's China and Russia watchers, go from here. I note modes of convergence and divergence, as U.S. China policy stalemates, and begins to look more like Russia policy, including the replacement of the Engagers and anti-Engagers with what looks more like a set of "China-we-havers" contesting the "China-we-want" consensus.[8] Despite U.S. involvement in Ukraine, China remains capable of greater mobilization in national security discussions in Washington, suggesting a period of sustained tensions. Finally, a third part draws back from the specific cases under review to assess analytical and normative questions raised by the book's focus on knowledge communities in the making of U.S. foreign policy. What is, and should be, such knowledge communities' role in national security policy?

The Failure of Engagement, Again

The power of the common-sense view that engagement's failure followed changes in China and Russia cannot be overstated. As one interviewee noted simply, "Once China was no longer reforming in the direction that we expected it to, Engagement became more difficult."[9] Similarly, who could deny that after 1999 Vladimir Putin took Russia in a direction that made cooperation impossible? Although it took America longer to realize it, who could contest the notion

---

[8] See, for example, China expert Robert Zoellick's call for U.S. leaders to "accept China as it is." Bob Davis, "Q&A: Robert Zoellick on Accepting China as It Is," *Wire China*, 5 August 2022, https://www.thewirechina.com/2022/08/05/robert-zoellick-on-accepting-china-as-it-is/.

[9] China interview 077, 24 May 2021, via video call.

that Xi Jinping has led China in a direction that renders engagement naive at best, treasonous at worst? Engagement died, it seems, because China and Russia changed, and not for the better.

China and Russia *have* changed. Readers should not confuse the argument made in this book for a denial of the fact. Russia and China are not the same type of objects for U.S. policymakers as they were at the Cold War's end.

Between 1990 and 2020, China's GDP increased from some $300bn to almost $15tn, while its population grew by some 300m (from 1.1bn to 1.4bn). The fabric of Chinese society changed dramatically over the period too. These changes were reflected after the global financial crisis and the successful 2008 Beijing Olympics in a newly confident and assertive outlook in its foreign relations, culminating in the rejection of Deng's maxim "Bide your time, hide your strength," and a renewed authoritarianism at home. In erstwhile Engager Susan Shirk's words, China has "overreached," derailing its peaceful rise.[10] For stronger critics, China is years—perhaps decades—into a plan to control not only China's domestic society, but the world.[11] U.S. policymakers, therefore, have responded to very real changes inside China and in its dealings with the wider world.

Demographic developments in Russia have trended in the opposite direction, with a decrease in population (148m in 1990 to 144m in 2020) and stagnant growth in GDP ($517bn to $1.48bn over the same period). This contraction in Russian power, however, has provided the reverse stimulus for the same outcome: a desire to remain relevant at the top table of international politics, after a decade of perceived ignorance on the part of the United States, leading to bellicose Russian behavior domestically and internationally. Once again, U.S. policymakers tried to get along with Putin but were ultimately frustrated.

Yet, while China and Russia have changed, it does not follow that engagement failed *because* China and Russia changed. Put differently, while a persuasive *political* argument, the stylized story that China and Russia changed is a poor *analytical* account of the trajectory of U.S. policymaking toward Beijing and Moscow. Again, certain sectors of the U.S. economy and society did very well from engagement with PRC, as America's own GDP expanded from $5.9tn to $20.9tn. Not all growth is attributable to expanded trade with China, the U.S. economy as a whole did well from engagement. Conversely, Russia's own demise after the Cold War, including the dissolution of the Soviet Union in 1991, strengthened America by leaving it the world's only superpower.

What "China and Russia changed" means, therefore, is that Chinese and Russian *behavior* changed. This too is undeniable. In the mid-2010s China began to flex its military and economic might, through the Belt and Road Initiative

---

[10] Shirk 2022.
[11] For example, Chin and Lin 2022; Joske 2022.

and so-called Wolf Warrior diplomacy.[12] Russia meddled in the domestic politics of Western countries, poisoned political opponents on the streets of the United Kingdom and Germany, and invaded Ukraine. New revelations emerge daily about China and Russia's misdeeds, from mass killings in eastern Ukraine to Chinese diplomats beating up pro-democracy protestors in Manchester, England, in full view of the public.[13] Who can deny, in such circumstances, that China and Russia have changed so much that neither is now a trustworthy interlocutor? Even China Engagers, more optimistic than their Russia counterparts, accept that the debate in Washington has moved on. The train of Strategic Competition has left the station.

But this subtle shift of emphasis from the broader systemic changes to actions and decisions raises the question of what *specific* initiatives on the part of Beijing and Moscow led to what—equally specific—responses by which constituencies in the United States. As Jessica Chen Weiss notes, the change in Beijing's behavior "is certainly part of the story, and it is as much a product of China's growing clout as of Xi's way of using that clout. But a complete account must also acknowledge changes in U.S. politics and policy as the United States has reacted to developments in China."[14] The same could be said of U.S. Russia policy.

In short, while a useful device in the political arena, as scholarship the narrative that engagement failed because Russia and China changed represents an inaccurate account of the rise and fall of engagement with Moscow and Beijing. Such an account requires attention to the messier reality of U.S. foreign policymaking, and its past, present, and potential future authors: the American national security community and its sub-segments—the China and Russia experts.

Knowledge Communities and U.S. Foreign Policy: The Argument

Addressing engagement's end from the perspective of America's China and Russia expert communities remains an unusual tack to take. Foreign policymakers, certainly, but experts? Experts typically have limited input into foreign policy when considered alongside the military and intelligence services, and the activities of

---

[12] Martin 2021.
[13] "At Mass Grave Site in Ukraine's Northeast, a Sign of Occupation's Toll," *New York Times*, 16 September 2022, https://www.nytimes.com/2022/09/16/world/europe/ukraine-graves-russia.html; "Protester Is Dragged into a Chinese Consulate in England and Beaten," *New York Times*, 17 October 2022, https://www.nytimes.com/2022/10/17/world/asia/manchester-china-consulate-beating.html.
[14] Jessica Chen Weiss, "The China Trap: U.S. Foreign Policy and the Perilous Logic of Zero-Sum Competition," *Foreign Affairs*, September–October 2022, https://www.foreignaffairs.com/china/china-trap-us-foreign-policy-zero-sum-competition.

lobbyists and business associations.[15] They simply do not matter enough to take center analytical stage.

In the case of China especially, consequently, none of the three major ways of explaining engagement's downfall centers the China field. To recap, the first explanation focuses on engagement's policy failings. For critics Kurt Campbell and Ely Ratner, the PRC "defied American expectations," exposing as fanciful U.S. policymakers' hopes of influencing Chinese development.[16] A second explanation centers the shifting balance of global power coupled with a new authoritarianism in Beijing.[17] From this viewpoint, the PRC's rise follows a historical pattern—the "Thucydides Trap"—wherein rising and declining leading states enter a spiral of mistrust that frequently ends in conflict.[18] A final explanation for the shift away from engagement stresses the policy preferences of President Donald J. Trump.

Yet the reason America's China and Russia expert communities are sidelined is not that they do not matter, it is that they fall outside the gaze of academics, on the one hand, and those in the policy community, on the other. Academics adopt what we might call a scholarly gaze drawn to structural explanations for policy outcomes, like the balance of power. The gaze is a consequence of the scholars' detached social location, often too far from the day-to-day of Washington to track with much accuracy the ins and outs of day-to-day political, professional, and personal struggles over policy in the way I have attempted here.

Those in the policy community, meanwhile, adopt the opposite gaze, facing outward—to China and Russia in this case—and directed toward influencing predominant opinions in Washington, and from their U.S. policy. The policy gaze sees the political, professional, and personal struggle, but *from the inside*. Not only is it rude to name names and throw around labels, therefore, doing so gets in the way of addressing arguments made for policy: Did engagement fail? How can the United States defend the rules-based international order (RBIO)? Again, asking prior questions—as someone like Alastair Iain Johnston tends to do—of the nature of Engagement or the RBIO might be interesting but is a waste of time. In a very real sense, therefore, America's China and Russia experts fall in the oft-noted gap between the ivory tower and the Beltway.

The perspective I have adopted here has consequently sought to avoid the distortions of the scholarly and policy gazes. Rather than take engagement at face value, either as a detached scholar or invested participant, I have distinguished between Engagement with a capital *E*, as a frame for U.S. relations specifically with the PRC, and engagement with a lowercase *e*, denoting the practical

---

[15] Jacobs and Page 2005.
[16] Campbell and Ratner 2018.
[17] Mearsheimer 2019.
[18] Allison 2017.

processes and policy manifestations of engaging Moscow and Beijing. I then disaggregated engagement into its three principal aspects—policy, frame, and community—which helped identify what China Engagement's demise really entailed: Engagement's replacement with a new set of policies aimed at managing U.S. interactions with the PRC; justified using a new framing narrative of China's rise; and carried on by new members and coalitions of China experts. I then identify three distinct processes that facilitated Engagement with China's demise, using the case of engagement with Russia as a comparative foil: *polarization, professional status competition*, and *personalization*.

The End of Engagement with China

Polarization is the formation of distinct groups taking opposite sides on China policy and the most appropriate framing of U.S.-China relations, within the China professional community and its relations with the U.S. government. Polarization is not limited to partisan affiliation. Although partisanship is common in the national security community, only rarely does it determine a person's views on a given issue. Indeed, foreign policy—and China policy specifically—is one of the few areas resistant to the polarizing tendencies of contemporary U.S. politics.[19] Polarization here has referred instead to the emergence of camps within the China expert community sharing broad positions, beyond the common, but equally misleading, notion of "hawks" and "doves." I have labeled these groups the "Engagers" and the "anti-Engagers."

The aim of tracing Engagement's polarization was to identify the relationship between membership of such groups and the way Engagers and anti-Engagers see the world. When and how did China policy become a polarized issue? By what processes do policymakers and experts identify as members of one group or another, or seek to avoid such positioning? What are the institutional bases of the two camps? What was the role of successive presidents in either pushing or seeking to limit polarization around Engagement?

Polarization was not a new feature of U.S. China policy under Trump. China skeptics—particularly in the area of human rights—had long maintained a strong presence in the China field, with particular influence in Congress. Nevertheless, the Trump election was a critical juncture. Tough rhetoric and the development of an alternative China policy, framed as Strategic Competition, solidified the Engagers and anti-Engagers as distinct social groups within the mainstream

---

[19] "Why China Might Be the Last Bipartisan Issue Left in Washington," 21 March 2021, *NBC News*, https://www.nbcnews.com/politics/congress/why-china-may-be-last-bipartisan-issue-left-washington-n1261407.

China segment of the U.S. national security community. Trump's election then provided anti-Engagers opportunities previously denied them to leverage their distinct epistemic and professional capital. Trump's victory led to a new and distinct set of China experts controlling the levers of frame- and policymaking power. At the same time, the rhetoric, framing, and policymaking of the Trump administration posed a challenge to the American China policy community and the China epistemic community more broadly: to either adapt to the new way of depicting China—as a competitor for global power rather than a collaborator in defending the international order—or identify with, and accurately stake out, another perspective, whether labeled "Engagement" or something else beside. In this way, Trump's election forced Engagers onto the intellectual and political defensive, weakening the Engager position by fragmenting it between those willing to adapt to the new reality of Strategic Competition and those rejecting the foundations of the approach.

Realists in IR will recognize polarization as a primary social dynamic. But here polarization is a feature not of states but of knowledge communities. A sociological perspective thus adds sensitivity to the specific modes in which struggle is carried on. In the case of China policy, the polarized struggle for policymaking control is inseparable from broader professional and personal contests. Crucially, such contests have distinct stakes, rules of engagement, and rewards. In *professional status competition*, participants struggle for cultural rewards such as status and prestige, rather than political rewards like power or the economic reward of wealth. The primary division in the China field separates the holders of intellectual prestige and credibility from those without such status, outsiders nevertheless seeking to influence the conversation. Professional struggles are thus inseparable from political struggles but are related only orthogonally. Here the fate of "nuance" in ongoing attempts to influence the formation of a post-Engagement frame is illustrative of broader dynamics. Nuance is the embodiment of the intellectual social position in the politicized struggle over China policy. Yet nuanced knowledge of China is not required when the nature of China—as a threat—has been determined, weakening arguments for a partial return to Engagement.

The end of Engagement with the PRC was the outcome of polarized contestation and professional status struggle in America's China expert community. The account would be incomplete, however, without sensitivity to a final, *personalized*, form of contestation. While large and growing, the top level of the China field forms a relatively small group of people, many of whom have known each other personally for many years. Beyond polarized contestation and professional struggle, therefore, Engagement as policy, frame, and community was tied to the particular perspectives and careers of specific individuals. No account of the end of Engagement is complete without attention to the often-intense emotional and affective ties people have to certain policies, positions, and decisions.

The End of Engagement with Russia

The Russia case presented a distinct object for comparison. In reference to Russia, "engagement" is not a framing of U.S.-Russia relations, or a distinct community within the Russia professional field—as it is in the China field—but a set of policy manifestations only. A matter of deep contestation among China watchers, unlikely to be settled definitively, Engagement was deployed infrequently during the 1990s to refer to China's integration into the global economy, and was subsequently drawn upon heavily (and negatively) to justify the shift under Trump to a new approach, Strategic Competition. Neither was required in the case of Russia. Engagement was the operative mode of U.S.-Russia relations into the new millennium. No one was arguing in the 1990s that the United States should stop engaging; disagreements were over *how* to engage—especially over NATO enlargement. The 2009 "reset" was, in effect, an engaged policy development, a commitment by the Obama administration to engage again, with a new interlocutor in the Kremlin. After its failure, and especially after the occupation of the Crimea and Russian actions in Ukraine from 2014, no organized call for a new "engagement" frame was forthcoming.

Instead, a group of realists, predominantly from the worlds of arms control and diplomacy, coalesced around a policy call: to deal with Russia as it is, not as America would like it to be. Encapsulated by the 2020 open letter to the *Washington Post* penned by Tom Graham, Fiona Hill, Rose Gottemoeller, and Thomas Pickering, the Russia-we-havers warned of the combined consequences of an ever-tightening U.S. sanctions regime and a lack of America attention, especially to the control of Russia's nuclear arsenal. Under Graham's intellectual leadership, Russia-we-havers came to see Russia as a great power with interests opposed to the West's first, a kleptocratic autocracy second. Sober in the face of the challenge of dealing with Putin, and the conflict in eastern Ukraine, Russia-we-havers nevertheless therefore advocated a reinvigoration of diplomatic ties with the Kremlin, including reassessing the efficacy of U.S. sanctions.

The Russia-we-have group emerged in opposition to an even more diverse set of what I term Russia-we-wanters. Russia-we-wanters rejected their colleagues' call for engagement with a regime in Moscow many deemed illegitimate. As one of the most prominent Russia-we-wanters explained,

> I do call it a regime. . . . I gave a talk at what was then still called the Nixon Center. . . . And the Russian ambassador at the time, the famous or infamous

Sergei Kislyak, was there and took strong exception to my referring it to as a regime rather than the government. And I told him it was entirely deliberate on my part. It wasn't a slip. I don't view it as legitimate. And that, too, I think, colors my views of how to deal with this because they basically destroy the opposition and make sure that elections are decided before people actually go and cast their votes. So, you know, all that certainly influences my views on how to deal with this problem.[20]

Comprising former officials, especially connected in some ways to Eastern Europe, those supporting democracy promotion in Russia and support for Russian exiles and dissidents, the Russia-we-wanters reject calls for concessions on America's part, including suspension of parts of the international sanctions regime.

Like the China Engagers and anti-Engagers, neither the Russia-we-havers nor Russia-we-wanters are a cohesive group, much less a corporate body. No one formal or informal organization houses all of either group. Indeed, there is a large overlap on what interviewees' called the "Venn diagram" of America's Russia-watching community, as evidenced especially by those who declined to sign either of the letters in 2020, as being too far from their views. The Russia field is smaller than the China field and arguably more collegial. Nevertheless, the politicization of U.S. Russia policy was evident after the reset, highlighting through its absence the sort of expert turnover seen on the China side under the Trump administration. While Trump appointed Fiona Hill to the senior Russia director position at the NSC, it was not because Hill was a Russia-we-haver. While the reasoning behind any such appointment is secret, Hill had a reputation especially as an incisive and critical analyst of Vladimir Putin.[21]

On its face a similar tale, the rise and fall of a U.S. strategy, the end of engagement with Russia is a different type of process to the downfall of Engagement with China. In the Russia case too, however, politicization does not exhaust the factors behind U.S. policymaking. The split between the Russia-we-havers and the Russia-we-wanters is also a division between distinct modalities when it comes to Russia expertise. Broadly speaking, the Russia-we-havers are arms controllers, former diplomats, and Russia-focused—as opposed to Eastern Europe–focused—think tankers and academics. Again, calls for "nuanced" understanding of Russia, rather than equation of the country with the ruling apparatus in Moscow, are not only policy prescriptions, but also reflections of the Russia-we-havers' diplomatic or academic dispositions functioning in the

---

[20] Russia interview 037, 20 November 2020, via video call.
[21] Adam Entous, "What Fiona Hill Learned in the White House," *New Yorker*, 29 June 2020, https://www.newyorker.com/magazine/2020/06/29/what-fiona-hill-learned-in-the-white-house.

political realm. For distinct reasons, each see black-and-white reasoning as unhelpful in finding a modus vivendi with Russia. On the other side are Eastern Europe specialists, democracy-promoters, and former officials, deploying distinct epistemic authority and asserting the sort of conviction about the regime in Moscow Russia-we-havers seek to nuance.

With conviction come disagreements, and like the end of Engagement with China, the course of U.S. policymaking toward Russia is inexplicable without grasping its personalized nature. Where the anti-Engagers saw a paradigmatic turnover in America's framing of China as a vindication of sometimes decades spent opposing U.S. policy, the Engagement frame, and the Engagers, no such vindication has occurred in the Russia field. All Russia watchers are frustrated with the direction Putin has taken the country, especially since assuming the presidency for the second time in 2012. But while bitter personal disputes are relatively infrequent in the Russia field, the case of Russia-we-haver Matthew Rojansky's blocked candidacy in 2020 for the Biden NSC shows once again that in a small world, one's face still has to fit when it comes to the door into and out of the top levels of the government.

Engaging China without Engagers?

The transformation of relations between the government and the American China field under Trump comes after Engagement with China as frame, policy, and community. Is a new frame for China in development? (Hint: no, it isn't.) Are the Engagers—either individually or collectively—likely to retake the reigns of U.S. policymaking? (Hint: no, they aren't.)

As a framing label, Engagement remains firmly off the table at the time of writing (August 2023). Anti-Engagers hate the term. Responding to diplomatic initiatives toward Beijing, Wisconsin congressman Mike Gallagher criticized the Biden team's "zombie engagement." "President Biden foresees a 'thaw' in relations," Gallagher explained, and "Treasury Secretary Janet Yellen suggests that we needn't fret about our economic dependence on China, as the costs of decoupling would prove 'disastrous.'"[22] But "we've seen this movie before."[23] In terms almost identical to those of the May 2020 *United States Strategic Approach to the People's Republic of China*, Gallagher concluded, "For more than 30 years, Washington has pursued economic engagement with communist China on the theory that economic growth would lead to political liberalization. We now

---

[22] Mike Gallagher, "Zombie Engagement with Beijing," *Wall Street Journal*, 14 June 2023, https://gallagher.house.gov/media/columns/zombie-engagement-beijing.
[23] Gallagher, "Zombie Engagement with Beijing."

know that prosperity has served only to embolden Mr. Xi's worst authoritarian instincts."[24] For anti-Engagers, the word "engagement" should remain in the dustbin of history.

Alternative frames face problems, however. What, for example, does "competition" mean? The sports analogy suggests competition with China is something the United States can win, which may be misleading in an international politics context. Yet synonyms are in short supply. A simple thesaurus search comes up with no suitable alternatives: involvement, association, or interaction are all too vague; cooperation or integration are even worse from a China skeptic's perspective. Perhaps "engagement" is usefully innocuous after all, especially since some measure of engagement with the PRC will be necessary—whether "partial" engagement in the economic sphere, or military cooperation in matters such as securing North Korean nuclear weapons in the event of regime collapse.[25] As Engagers are keen to point out, even at the height of the Cold War, Washington maintained lines of communication and some minimal diplomatic engagement with Moscow. Given China's deep enmeshment in the international economy and global governance architecture—and, of course, its nuclear arsenal—the sort of decoupling some New Cold Warriors would prefer is not a viable option.[26]

That China is too large to be isolated from the international system is the conclusion reached by Gallagher's targets inside the Biden administration. Meetings with Chinese counterparts by Blinken and Sullivan reflected the desire to reforge top-level diplomatic ties with Beijing, the worrying lack of which was made apparent by the discovery of Chinese spy balloons over the United States in January 2023.[27] The possible return of Engagement was even more apparent in the language used and symbolism of economic secretaries Janet Yellen at the Treasury and Gina Raimondo at Commerce.[28] In a speech at Johns Hopkins SAIS on the U.S.-China economic relationship, Yellen made clear that she and Biden

---

[24] Gallagher, "Zombie Engagement with Beijing."

[25] Respectively, Charles Boustany and Aaron Friedberg, "Partial Disengagement: A New U.S. Strategy for Economic Competition with China," *National Bureau of Asian Research Special Report* no. 82; and Mastro 2018.

[26] See also Roach 2022 for a fuller discussion.

[27] "Blinken Meets with Xi as China and China Try to Rein in Tensions," *New York Times*, 18 June 2023, https://www.nytimes.com/2023/06/18/world/asia/blinken-china-xi-diplomacy.html; "Readout of National Security Advisor Jake Sullivan's Meeting with Chinese Communist Party Politburo Member and Director of the Office of the Foreign Affairs Commission Wang Yi, Vienna," 11 May 2023, https://www.whitehouse.gov/briefing-room/statements-releases/2023/05/11/readout-of-national-security-advisor-jake-sullivans-meeting-with-chinese-communist-party-politburo-member-and-director-of-the-office-of-the-foreign-affairs-commission-wang-yi/; John K. Culver, "The Balloon Crisis Was a Drill. Here's How the U.S. and China Can Prepare for a Real Crisis," 22 February 2023, https://www.atlanticcouncil.org/blogs/new-atlanticist/the-balloon-drama-was-a-drill-heres-how-the-us-and-china-can-prepare-for-a-real-crisis/.

[28] For anti-Engager Josh Rogin, "Biden's Economic Diplomacy Push with China Is High Risk, Low Reward," *Washington Post*, 26 April 2023, https://www.washingtonpost.com/opinions/2023/04/27/china-us-economic-talks-national-security-biden/.

do not "see the relationship between the U.S. and China through the frame of great power conflict." Explicitly using the E-word, Yellen noted that "negotiating the contours of engagement between great powers is difficult.... But we can find a way forward if China is also willing to play its part."[29] Shortly after, Yellen met with the U.S.-China Business Council's board of directors in June 2023—symbolically on account of its longtime support for Engagement. Yellen affirmed "the importance of trade and investment with China, given deep integration between the two economies."[30] Raimondo pointedly stated in November 2022 that "we are not seeking the decoupling of our economy from that of China's."[31]

These initiatives reflect less the return of Engagement as policy than a fear that competition with China might give way to actual conflict. U.S. policy toward Beijing remains firmly competitive. At the time of writing, the Biden administration was planning to expand export controls to China on advanced computers and semiconductors initially placed in late 2022,[32] and barred Hong Kong chief executive John Lee from the Asia-Pacific Economic Cooperation meeting in San Francisco in November 2023.[33]

Actions like these that are both sure to anger China's leaders and popular in Washington suggest the center of gravity among the U.S. China field remains with Strategic Competition, rendering Engagers outside the government unlikely to see high office. In part the issue is credibility and the practicalities of congressional approval. Could an avowed Engager get through the sort of grilling navigated by Ely Ratner, confirmed as assistant secretary of state for Indo-Pacific security affairs? Asked, for example, for his "interpretation of the meaning of 'expanding the competitive space'" and "how ... it impacts U.S. competition with China?" Ratner could confidently respond that it "means leveraging all elements of its U.S. power, including economic, diplomatic, intelligence, cultural, and military tools, in a whole-of-government effort to address the multi-domain challenges posed by China."[34] Could someone with pro-Engagement sympathies say as much?

---

[29] "Remarks by Secretary of the Treasury Janet S. Yellen on the U.S.-China Economic Relationship at Johns Hopkins School of Advanced International Studies," 20 April 2023, https://home.treasury.gov/news/press-releases/jy1425.
[30] "Readout: Secretary of the Treasury Janet L. Yellen's Meeting with U.S. China Business Council's Board of Directors," 8 June 2023, https://home.treasury.gov/news/press-releases/jy1528.
[31] "Remarks by Secretary of Commerce Gina Raimondo on U.S. Competitiveness and the China Challenge," 30 November 2022, https://www.commerce.gov/news/speeches/2022/11/remarks-us-secretary-commerce-gina-raimondo-us-competitiveness-and-china.
[32] "Biden Plans to Sign Order Curbing US Tech Investments in China by Mid-August, Bloomberg Reports," *Reuters*, 28 July 2023, https://www.reuters.com/technology/biden-plans-sign-order-curbing-us-tech-investments-china-by-mid-august-bloomberg-2023-07-28/.
[33] "Biden, Testing Xi, Will Bar Hong Kong's Leader from Economic Summit," *Washington Post*, 27 July 2023, https://www.washingtonpost.com/national-security/2023/07/27/hong-kong-john-lee-apec/.
[34] Transcript available at https://www.armed-services.senate.gov/imo/media/doc/Ratner%20APQ%20Responses.pdf.

The failed Senate ratification of State Department official Susan Thornton in 2018 is indicative of what a future appointee tainted with Engagement might face—particularly should the Republicans return to office. For Engagers, as a career State Department official and Mandarin speaker, Thornton had the sort of expert credentials interviewees considered imperative for anyone holding high office in relation to China.[35] For critics, Thornton association with Engagement rendered her unacceptable. Thornton was opposed by Senator Marco Rubio in particular, who has staked a reputation as a strong critic of China as a member of the Senate Foreign Relations Committee and the CECC. On 17 May 2018, Rubio tweeted that he would "do all I can do to prevent Susan Thornton from ever being confirmed as Ass[istant] Secretary of State for E. Asian and Pacific Affairs," claiming that Thornton was at that moment in Tokyo undermining the president by advocating for only a partial surrender of nuclear weapons by North Korea.[36] In the background was Rubio's view that Thornton was an Engager. Among her supporters were Daniel Russel, senior director for Asian Affairs on President Obama's National Security Council.[37] Thornton's ratification also became entangled with the palace wars within the Trump White House, namely that between advisor Steve Bannon and Secretary of State Rex Tillerson. Tillerson had strongly supported Thornton to assume the assistant secretaryship on a permanent basis, being impressed by Thornton's knowledge of East Asia and cognizant of the need to maintain morale among career Foreign Service officers in the department.[38] Bannon considered Thornton weak on China and made clear his intention to get "hawks" in and "Thornton out."[39] Thornton retired in August 2018.

More likely than any sort of return to Engagement-as-community is the oscillation of control over China policy between Democratic and Republican Strategic Competitors. The former will be more concerned with crisis management and finding useful modifiers for competition; the latter more strident in their criticisms of Beijing. Yet both will seek to push forward competition as policy. Going forward, Strategic Competition—like Engagement before it—is likely to become simply the conduct of U.S.-China relations, and getting on with it will be the name of the (policy) game.

---

[35] China interview 072, 19 February 2019, via video call.
[36] https://twitter.com/marcorubio/status/997120123164135424.
[37] See Carol Morello, "Tillerson Scores a Personal Win, as Top East Asia Adviser Is Nominated," 24 December 2017, https://www.washingtonpost.com/world/national-security/tillerson-scores-a-personnel-win-as-top-east-asia-adviser-is-nominated/2017/12/24/fd1bd20a-e743-11e7-a65d-1ac0fd7f097e_story.html?undefined=&wpisrc=nl_headlines&wpmm=1.
[38] See Morello, "Tillerson Scores a Personal Win."
[39] https://www.washingtonpost.com/news/josh-rogin/wp/2018/03/15/without-rex-tillersons-protection-a-top-state-department-nominee-is-in-trouble/. See also https://prospect.org/power/steve-bannon-unrepentant.

Engaging Russia after the War in Ukraine

The onset in February 2022 of Russia's "special operation" in Ukraine vindicated the Russia-we-wanter position and the Russia-we-wanters as a group. In so doing, the war all but eliminated the space for calls for engagement, raising questions about the credibility of Russia-we-havers as potential appointees. Russia-we-havers hoping to remain relevant to public debate and open to future government service were limited to offering nuanced explanations of Putin's intentions, urging a negotiated end to the conflict, and—counterintuitively—emphasizing exactly how worried the West should be, especially vis-à-vis possible use of nuclear weapons.

Russia critics urged Biden to adopt a tough line, from a possible NATO no-fly zone to supporting Ukraine's swift accession to the alliance. Russia-we-wanter Michael McFaul, for example, argued for full U.S. support for Kiev.[40] "President Volodymyr Zelensky, his Ukrainian warriors and his courageous people fight on," he wrote in April 2022 after the successful defense of the Ukrainian capital, but "They still need help from the West."[41] Calling Putin's bluff on escalating the war, America should provide the Ukrainians everything from bullets and helmets to heavy weapons and air defense systems.[42] Writing alongside chess grandmaster and dissident Garry Kasparov, McFaul urged "the democratic world [to] impose additional import restrictions on technologies such as aircraft parts, sonar systems . . . and oil-field equipment. Russia should be completely unable to obtain any high-tech imports [that] helps Putin kill more Ukrainians."[43] The West should also, McFaul urged, support Russian exiles, like Dmitry Gudkov, "a young, charismatic rising star in the Russian parliament [who] opposed many of the Kremlin's favorite moves, such as the annexation of Crimea." McFaul stressed the practical obstacles to Gudkov's exile, from opening a bank account to residency. "The democratic world has not done enough."[44]

---

[40] See also, among many others, Max Boot, "Putin Is Reeling: Now Is the Time to Help Ukraine Win," *Washington Post*, 20 September 2022, https://www.washingtonpost.com/opinions/2022/09/20/ukraine-allies-defeat-putin/; Josh Rogin, "Putin Is Trying to Build a New Axis of Autocrats," *Washington Post*, 8 September 2022, https://www.washingtonpost.com/opinions/2022/09/08/russia-china-iran-alliance-dictators/.

[41] Michael McFaul, "The West Shouldn't Back Down in the Face of Russia's Threats," *Washington Post*, 13 April 2022, https://www.washingtonpost.com/opinions/2022/04/13/west-help-ukraine-win-next-phase-russia/.

[42] McFaul, "The West Shouldn't Back Down."

[43] Garry Kasparov and Michael McFaul, "The Sanctions against Russia Still Have Holes: Here's How to Plug Them," *Washington Post*, 8 September 2022, https://www.washingtonpost.com/opinions/2022/09/08/garry-kasparov-michael-mcfaul-russia-sanctions/.

[44] Michael McFaul, "Want to Undermine Putin? Help Russians Who Are Opposed to the War," *Washington Post*, 1 June 2022, https://www.washingtonpost.com/opinions/2022/06/01/west-help-antiwar-russians-exile/.

On 8 March, some 27 Russia specialists signed an open letter in *Politico* asking NATO to impose a limited no-fly zone over eastern Ukraine.[45] The signatories overlapped with the Kramer letter, emerging firmly from the Russia-we-want camp, and included Daniel Fried; Evelyn Farkas, former deputy assistant secretary of defense for Russia, Ukraine, and Eurasia; and former ambassador John Herbst. The letter drew a rapid and sharply negative response, however. Rich Lowry of the *National Review* called it a "calamitously bad idea."[46] Ukraine's bravery in the face of Russia aggression, Lowry concluded, "is something to behold. But we can't ignore our own national security interests." Olga Oliker and Brian Finucane, of the Brussels-based International Crisis Group, concurred, calling NATO's and Biden administration's refusal to impose a no-fly zone the right thing to do.[47] Similarly, a remark by Biden in a speech in Warsaw on 26 March that Putin "cannot remain in power" drew a swift walk-back from his advisors, worried the president had just committed the country to regime change in Moscow.[48]

Yet, short of direct military involvement, the Russia-we-want position dominated after the invasion. Pointing the finger squarely at Putin, Biden implicitly rejected engagement as a policy as long as the Russian leader remains in power: "In the lead-up to the current crisis, the United States and NATO worked for months to engage Russia to avert a war. I met with him in person and talked to him many times on the phone.... But Russia was bent on violence from the start."[49]

The result was the constriction of the space from which to make arguments that either are, or might be construed, as pro-engagement with Moscow. At issue here is the *credibility* of individual Russia-we-havers as regional experts if they express views too sympathetic toward Moscow in content and tone. Sam Charap of Rand and Jeremy Shapiro from the European Council on Foreign Relations, for example, made a strong call in June 2022 for the United States and Russia to "start talking before it's too late"—repeating what was essentially the same call they had made in January 2020.[50] But tellingly, few others from the

---

[45] https://www.politico.com/f/?id=0000017f-6668-ddc5-a17f-f66d48630000.
[46] Rich Lowry, "A No-Fly Zone Is a Calamitously Bad Idea," *Politico*, 17 March 2022, https://www.politico.com/news/magazine/2022/03/17/no-fly-zone-bad-idea-zelenskyy-00018290.
[47] Brian Finucane and Olga Oliker, "Zelensky Wants a No-Fly Zone. NATO Is Right to Say No," *New York Times*, 25 March 2022, https://www.nytimes.com/2022/03/25/opinion/no-fly-zone-ukraine-nati-russia.html.
[48] See "Remarks by President Biden on the United Efforts of the Free World to Support the People of Ukraine," 26 March 2022. https://www.whitehouse.gov/briefing-room/speeches-remarks/2022/03/26/remarks-by-president-biden-on-the-united-efforts-of-the-free-world-to-support-the-people-of-ukraine/, and Jennifer Rubin, "Putin Shouldn't Remain in Power. Biden's Advisers Blew It," *Washington Post*, 28 March 2022.
[49] "Remarks by President Biden on the United Efforts."
[50] Samuel Charap and Jeremy Shapiro, "The U.S. and Russia Need to Start Talking before It's Too Late," *New York Times*, 27 June 2022, https://www.nytimes.com/2022/07/27/opinion/ukra

Russia-we-have camp attempted a call for engagement, instead adopting one of two rhetorical strategies to remain in the conversation.

First, Russia-we-havers have adopted what might be called a "warning" stance: using their in-depth and nuanced knowledge of Russia to raise the alarm in Washington against complacency. Charap, for example, suggested in March 2022 that Putin considered himself to be in an existential struggle with the West.[51] Three months later, when the war was going badly for Ukraine, he argued in *Foreign Affairs* that Ukrainian neutrality could bring peace and security and might by Kiev's last chance.[52] The tactic of warning is also available for strong critics of Russia. On 11 February, for example, Evelyn Farkas opined in the *New York Times*, as the title of her op-ed put it, "We Underestimated Putin Once. We Can't Make That Mistake Again."[53] But the approach has been more marked from the Russia-we-havers. Tom Graham warned early on of the potential for conflict to spread beyond Ukraine.[54] Andrea Kendall-Taylor and Michael Kofman cautioned in June that while the Russian army's inability to secure its initial war aims showed that "Russia was down," it was "not out" and should not be underestimated.[55]

A second rhetorical mode is less surprising: that of explaining the nuances of the situation, typically in dispassionate tones. Angela Stent and Fiona Hill, for example, penned an in-depth assessment of Putin's understanding of the war in historical context. Neither is squarely in the Graham camp, and they are sometimes seen as more closely aligned to the Russia-we-have position. For Hill and Stent, Putin's view is that *the* Ukraine is part of Greater Russia, a view he published in 2021 in an essay "On the Historical Unity of Russians and Ukrainians."[56] On Putin's reading, the period after 1991 is just another brief interlude between the periods of connection of Russia and Ukraine, one in which

---

ine-russia-us-diplomacy.html; Samuel Charap and Jeremy Shapiro, "Why We Must Talk to Russia," 2 January 2020, https://www.atlanticcouncil.org/blogs/ukrainealert/why-we-must-talk-to-russia/.

[51] "Samuel Charap Considers How Russia's War in Ukraine Could Escalate," *The Economist*, 10 March 2022, https://www.economist.com/by-invitation/2022/03/10/samuel-charap-considers-how-russias-war-in-ukraine-could-escalate.

[52] Samuel Charap, "Ukraine's Best Chance for Peace: How Neutrality Can Bring Security—and Satisfy Both Russia and the West," *Foreign Affairs*, 10 March 2022, https://www.foreignaffairs.com/articles/ukraine/2022-06-01/ukraines-best-chance-peace.

[53] Evelyn Farkas, "We Underestimated Putin Once. We Can't Make That Mistake Again," *New York Times*, 11 February 2022, https://www.nytimes.com/2022/02/11/opinion/putin-russia-biden-ukraine.html.

[54] Thomas Graham, "Preventing a Wider European Conflict," Council on Foreign Relations, 8 March 2022, https://www.cfr.org/report/preventing-wider-european-conflict.

[55] Andrea Kendall-Taylor and Michael Kofman, "Russia Is Down. But It's Not Out," *New York Times*, 2 June 2022, https://www.nytimes.com/2022/06/02/opinion/russia-ukraine-war-nato.html.

[56] Hill and Stent 2022.

the West has "used Ukraine as a platform to threaten Russia, and it has supported the rise of 'neo-Nazis' there."[57]

Strident opposition to support for Ukraine thus only came from those outside the Russia community, from generalists and commentators less concerned with their legitimacy as country experts. IR theorist John Mearsheimer doubled down on his claim that America is to blame for the war in Ukraine due to having ignored Russia in the 1990s and 2000s.[58] Others sought to make clear that the extent of U.S. support meant that Washington is essentially at war with Russia,[59] or cautioned the United States and its allies not to "bleed Russia," instead to couple aid with rhetorical resources for an end to the war short of Russia's total defeat.[60] The *Washington Post*'s Katrina vanden Heuvel—widow of strong Russia-we-haver Stephen Cohen—argued strongly for a real debate about the Ukraine War. As the United States doubled down on support for Ukraine, with little objection in Congress, vanden Heuvel urged, "Climate action is being sidelined as reliance on fossil fuels increases; food scarcity and other resource demands are pushing prices upward and causing widespread global hunger; and the worldwide refugee crisis... poses a massive challenge."[61]

A final constituency was those within Republican ranks either supportive of Putin or so critical of Biden that politics did not stop at the traditional water's edge. Republicans such as Paul Gosar, Thomas Massie, Matt Rosendale, and Marjorie Taylor-Greene have tried to tie support for Ukraine to action on immigration, proposing a parity of U.S. troops in Europe to those stationed at the Mexico border.[62] For Max Boot, so-called MAGA Republicans are not isolationists or America firsters, but actively pro-Putin and anti-Democratic.[63]

---

[57] Hill and Stent 2022: 109.

[58] John J. Mearsheimer, "Why the Ukraine Crisis Is the West's Fault: The Liberal Delusions That Provoked Putin," *Foreign Affairs*, September–October 2014, https://www.mearsheimer.com/wp-content/uploads/2019/06/Why-the-Ukraine-Crisis-Is.pdf; "John Mearsheimer on Why the West Is Principally Responsible for the Ukraine Crisis," *The Economist*, 19 March 2022, https://www.economist.com/by-invitation/2022/03/11/john-mearsheimer-on-why-the-west-is-principally-responsible-for-the-ukrainian-crisis; Christopher Caldwell, "The War in Ukraine May Be Impossible to Stop. And the U.S. Deserves Much of the Blame," *New York Times*, 31 May 2022, https://www.nytimes.com/2022/05/31/opinion/us-ukraine-putin-war.html.

[59] Bonnie Kristian, "Are We Sure America Is Not at War in Ukraine?," *New York Times*, 6 June 2022, https://www.nytimes.com/2022/06/20/opinion/international-world/ukraine-war-america.html.

[60] Tom Stevenson, "America and Its Allies Want to Bleed Russia. They Really Shouldn't," *New York Times*, 11 May 2022, https://www.nytimes.com/2022/05/11/opinion/russia-ukraine-war-america.html.

[61] Katrina vanden Heuvel, "We Need a Real Debate about the Ukraine War," *Washington Post*, 24 May 2022, https://www.washingtonpost.com/opinions/2022/05/24/ukraine-russia-war-biden-strategy-debate/.

[62] Max Boot, "MAGA Republicans Aren't Isolationist. They're Pro-Putin," *Washington Post*, 24 May 2022, https://www.washingtonpost.com/opinions/2022/05/24/republican-gop-pro-russia-pro-putin-ukraine-war-isolationism/.

[63] Boot, "MAGA Republicans Aren't Isolationist."

They are, to be sure, more opposed to the occupant of the White House than the Kremlin.[64]

Crucially, such criticisms of U.S. support for Ukraine were muted, isolated, and not made by credible Russia experts. As the case of Matthew Rojansky discussed in the previous chapter demonstrates—deemed unsuitable for the role of chief Russia hand in Biden's NSC amid accusations of being soft on Moscow—it seems unlikely any Russia-we-havers will be appointed to key positions in future administrations, Democrat or Republican. At the time of writing, strong Russia critic Toria Nuland's promotion to acting deputy secretary of state upon the retirement of predecessor Wendy Sherman in July 2023 signaled the direction of U.S. policymaking.[65]

Foreign Policy Expertise in Polarized Times: Final Reflections

The end of engagement illustrates what happens when struggles over policy among members of America's knowledge communities become entangled with personalized contestation over professional status as experts. The need for greater collegiality in hope of greater insight and more effective policymaking might seem a possible conclusion. Yet such a call rings hollow in today's hyperpolarized times. America's China and Russia experts will even disagree about whether polarization brings insight or blinders. For anti-engagers on both sides, the end of engagement was overdue: the rejection of a failed policy and its proponents, and the maintenance of a realistic strategy toward Moscow. For the Engagers and Russia-we-havers, Engagement's polarization has opened the door to the overly combative approach of the Strategic Competitors, and the dominance of the Russia-we-wanters has resulted to policy stasis on containment of Russia.

As an outside observer, I am in no position to adjudicate who is right and who is wrong in that debate. *What normative conclusions follow about polarization's effects, therefore, when the experts disagree on whether the effects are good or bad?* At stake, I believe, is nothing less than the role of experts in democratic politics. Are the two not, in some sense at least, at odds? If America's China and Russia

---

[64] Dana Milbank, "Republicans Are So Eager to See Biden Fail They'd Let Putin Succeed," *Washington Post*, 1 March 2022, https://www.washingtonpost.com/opinions/2022/03/01/republicans-biden-fail-putin-succeed/.

[65] Anthony Blinken, "On the Retirement of Deputy Secretary Sherman," Press Statement, 24 July 2023, https://www.state.gov/on-the-retirement-of-deputy-secretary-sherman/. See also Connor Echols, "Über Russia-Hawk Victoria Nuland Rises to Acting Deputy Secretary of State," *Responsible Statecraft*, 25 July 2023, https://responsiblestatecraft.org/2023/07/25/uber-russia-hawk-victoria-nuland-rises-to-acting-deputy-secretary-of-state/.

experts disagree on the U.S. national interest, is the knowledge they offer *as China and Russia experts* not compromised?

The debate over the role of experts in democratic life goes back at least to that between Walter Lippmann and John Dewey at the turn of the 20th century.[66] The former defended the role of elites as uniquely situated to uncover the public interest. Dewey, by contrast, worried about elite capture, and instead emphasized the role of experts in identifying publics through which the people can be truly represented. The debate has re-emerged in recent years alongside fears of the death of expertise, as populist leaders around the world—with Donald Trump a key example—have been fed by and in turn fueled—a rejection of experts.[67] As noted at the outset, the concept of expertise on China and Russia is a curious phenomenon. Even the most knowledgeable individual—steeped in the language, culture, history, and economic and social trends—can only offer partial insight. Does the United States *need* China and Russia experts? Given the role of foreign policy generalists in the shift from Engagement to Strategic Competition and the instant experts on Russia that popped up after the invasion of Ukraine, could the United States do without country experts in its strategy-making toward Moscow and Beijing?

Sociologist Gil Eyal has questioned whether we are witnessing the decline of expertise, or rather its apogee, as society becomes more divided into specialized areas, making us more, not less, reliant on experts.[68] Eyal's conclusion suggests that the United States is likely to need more expertise on China and Russia, not less, going forward, which does seem to be borne out by the continually expanding China- and Russia-watching communities. Few would deny that the American government needs experts on both countries—individuals able to understand their counterparts, to pick up on subtleties of meaning in diplomatic exchange, to "get" the nuances of cultural references and symbolism. If Eyal is correct, and I think he is, America's knowledge communities are not going anywhere. The China and Russia communities will increase in size and population, as new organizations are formed—from think tanks and consulting firms to academic centers. The U.S. government, finally, will still rely on highly skilled and motivated members to "go in" to the government when called upon. America's China and Russia watchers will remain a vital national resource for thinking Washington's way through this new post–Cold War era.

Most experts agree that U.S. policy toward its rivals swings too far between unrealistic optimism and overly dark pessimism. Rather than make a utopian call for greater collegiality, therefore, the normative conclusions that flow from

---

[66] See Lippmann 1922, 1927; Dewey 1927.
[67] Nichols 2017.
[68] Eyal 2019.

the book center on identifying times and places where America's knowledge communities have managed to contain the inevitable processes of polarization, professional status competition, and personalization, and how they might do so again. We might look to other countries where expert polarization is lesser.[69] America's China and Russia experts might reflect on the history of their fields, when their predecessors formed camps, competed vigorously for honors and status markers, and disagreed strongly with each other, all while remaining open to competing visions of America's national interest. Either way, we should recognize America's knowledge communities—and their polarization, professional status competitions, and personalization—as central rather than marginal features of the making and remaking of U.S. foreign policy in this new post-post–Cold War era.

---

[69] Like Australia and the United Kingdom. See McCourt 2021.

Methodological Appendix
Watching the China and Russia Watchers

The book draws on a range of primary and secondary data. The main source is a set of 170 interviews with U.S.-based China (117) and Russia (53) analysts, scholars, and former policymakers, conducted between late 2016 and spring 2023.[1] The interviews served two functions. First, they represent an original set of first-person perspectives used to trace the shifting opinions of America's China and Russia experts on U.S. policy. Second, the interviews also provide a guide to the Russia and China segments of the American national security establishment—their idioms, acronyms, shared reference points, and common senses, which to the outsider can be bewildering, to say the least.

Knowledge and information are in many ways the currency of the national security world. There is therefore no shortage of publicly available primary and secondary data—from official policy-documents, speeches, and testimony to articles, op-eds, commentaries, interviews, and podcasts. Data access is less the problem than what we might call signal-to-noise ratio. While I still do not claim mastery of America's China and Russia fields, speaking to participants myself has allowed me to better parse the data, heightening my sensitivity to key developments, dynamics, events, and personalities in America's China and Russia expert communities.

The first question faced was how to identify interviewees. Who *counts* as a China or Russia expert? Given the contested nature of China and Russia expertise—as I emphasize throughout the book—I did not impose my own judgment on who is, and is not, a *real* expert. Instead, I followed interviewees' suggestions on "who I must talk to," turning over the decision of who is or is not included in the category expert to the China and Russia watchers themselves. This makes sense since, as I describe in chapter 3, defining who counts as an expert and who has a valuable perspective—and perhaps also the credentials and ability to make U.S. policy—is at least as much of what America's China and Russia watchers spend their days doing as is providing knowledge of their object. A small number of interviewees were thus professionally located outside or at the margins of the field. Examples include a non-China political scientist whose work on cybersecurity the interviewee into the China space, or an IR scholar whose early work focused on U.S.-Soviet relations but who has since moved in a more theoretical direction but nonetheless maintains some connections.[2] On the outside looking in, these interviewees offered some of the most insightful observations about the major dynamics of the China and Russia fields.

---

[1] Further information about the interviews is in the author's possession. The University of California's Institutional Review Board granted permission to conduct the interviews under protocol no. 1036710.

[2] Part of a broader project on the production of knowledge of China in the United States, I excluded material from 35 interviews where the content of the discussion, and the interviewee, were deemed too distant from policymaking.

Interviewing in each community began with personal connection—a friend-of-a-friend research analyst at a major think tank in Arlington in the case of China, an academic in the case of Russia. I then asked for suggestions for further interviews, and where possible, a note of introduction. As a strategy, this is known as snowball sampling. But a better way to describe my approach perhaps is that I have endeavored to talk to as many people as possible, pausing to allow time to analyze my findings, write, and conclude when interviews began to cover familiar ground or reach "exhaustion." Because the potential pool is composed of people who are comfortable being asked their opinions—on a topic of immediate relevance—the take-rate for interviews was high. The vast majority of individuals I approached agreed to speak to me, from journalists, consultants, and researchers representing the whole political spectrum of DC-based think tanks, to academics from across the social sciences, humanities, and law.

My aim was to achieve balanced coverage of the China and Russia fields—demographically, politically, and professionally—while not overcorrecting for their particularities in any direction. Balance in terms of age and experience was straightforward, with interviewees ranging from former diplomats, including former ambassadors to Beijing (two) and Moscow (six), through prominent academics and think tankers, to junior and aspiring experts. Like the national security community itself,[3] the interviews display a marked imbalance in terms of gender—with 13 of 53 female experts in the case of Russia, 22 of 117 in the case of China—and ethnicity, with the majority of interviewees of Caucasian descent, with notable numbers of experts of East Asian and Russian / Eastern European family heritage.

National security experts frequently wear many hats, complicating efforts to categorize interviewees by profession. Think tankers are often former or potential future policymakers; several "went in" at some point during the interviewing period or will almost certainly do so in the future. Think tankers also maintain academic affiliations, however, by adjunct lecturing and publishing in recognized academic outlets. Nonetheless, some descriptive statistics give a sense of the professional basis of the interviewees. First, interviews centered on think tankers: 31 in the case of China, 21 for the Russia field. Second, I spoke to eight individuals on the China side who at some point during the interviewing period worked in government, whether at the National Security Council, State Department, Department of Defense, or National Intelligence. Seventeen China interviewees had formerly been employed in those roles. The comparative figures on the Russia side are one current and 20 former officials. Second, 36 of the China interviews were with academics, 16 in the case of the Russia field. Finally, I spoke to 10 China-related journalists and 11 employed in business or consulting, two each in the case of Russia. Other interviewees included congressional staffers, consultants, and human rights professionals.

The data therefore skews in ways that should be acknowledged and perhaps also explained, since it offers clues as to the makeup of the China and Russia fields. Academic interviews are skewed toward political scientists (22 for China, 13 for Russia), with historians the second most common (seven and three respectively), which speaks to the academic division of labor when it comes to national security. So too does the unique perspective, not mirrored on the Russia side, of the five interviews with scholars of Chinese

---

[3] As feminist scholars have made clear, national security is a male-dominated and masculinized profession (Cohn 1987 remains in my view the classic text). I sought therefore to acknowledge this without oversampling in response.

law, given the importance of U.S.-China legal exchanges since the 1980s. The China interviews are more evenly balanced between current and former policymakers and experts situated beyond the Beltway, with the Russia interviews centered more squarely on policy, with 21 of 53 either former or current policymakers. Finally, the data is skewed toward mainstream think tanks such as the Center for Strategic and International Studies (seven), Brookings (three), Rand (five), and the Carnegie Endowment for International Peace (five), over conservative establishments such as the Heritage Foundation, the American Enterprise Institute, and Hudson Institute, which together provided only one interview.[4] I have sought to correct for these imbalances in the interviews with data gained from publicly available sources.

The project was initially focused solely on the China field, with interviewing beginning in Washington, DC, in the fall of 2016 in the midst of the early rumblings of what would be the momentous shift in American opinion described in this book. Those China experts paying close attention would have been aware of planning inside the Pentagon looking beyond the war on terror and the Islamic State to the return of great power competition, not to mention presidential candidate Donald J. Trump's fiery rhetoric directed at Beijing. But others less plugged in—including myself at the time—would not have been, with the broader public awakening to U.S.-China tensions still ongoing in many ways. Further and deeper interviews were conducted in fall of 2017 and the spring and fall of 2018. The interviewing period has hardly been short on drama, therefore. When I began, Engagement with China was under strain, but was still the operative mode of the U.S. government. As chronicled here, the edifice of Engagement with China began to topple from January 2017, crumbling rapidly. The topic of my interviews duly changed, as Engagement's failings became a topic of intense interest between 2017 and 2019 or so, and then an increasingly historical debate from 2020 onward.

On the suggestion of several colleagues, in early 2020 I widened the project to include the Russia expert community as a comparative case. Aided by the onset of Covid and the normalization of video conferencing, the majority of the Russia interviewees were conducted in a busy fall of 2020. The openness of the Russia community to scholarly interest was striking. Before the Russian invasion of February 2022, Russia experts were clearly more at a loose end than their China counterparts. Where it took me three years to interview a high-ranking China diplomat, within two weeks in September 2020 I moved from well-known if peripheral academics to six of the 10 U.S. ambassadors to Moscow since the dissolution of the Soviet Union.

Interviews were semi-structured in format. They typically began with a biographical account of the interviewees' trajectory into the China and Russia professional communities and route upward. Discussion then moved to the main dynamics of the field from the interviewees' viewpoint—such as principal social divisions in the field, key personalities, and core issues of contention. The aim was to position the interviewee in the community, illuminating important aspects of the community at the same time. The discussion then moved to recent U.S. policy—a topic that shifted over the course of the interviewing period.

---

[4] My lower take-rate with these organizations may reflect different organizational cultures related to engaging academics and journalists, as well as assumptions about the (leftist and likely pro-engagement) political leanings of sociology, easily gained from a web search for my professional biography.

Interview data was professionally transcribed and coded by hand, using what is best described as an abductive process.[5] Neither deductive nor purely inductive, the research moved back and forth between empirical observation and theoretical or conceptual development as I sought to build an interpretation. Coding of topics discussed quickly uncovered the three topics used to structure this book: (1) dispute over how best to deal with a changing China, including debate over the fundamental drivers of U.S. policy in previous years and current events; (2) disagreement over the types of expertise best suited to making U.S. policy, and reflections on the China and Russia fields themselves; and (3) discussions about particularly individuals and groups, and the merits and demerits of their initiatives, decisions, and analysis.

Such an abductive process highlighted processes by which individuals come to agree more with "Engagers" than "anti-Engagers," or the "Russia-we-havers" than the "Russia-we-wanters." But at no point should such generalizations be considered set in stone. The views of the book's subjects are changing, as individuals face the question whether and how to react—publicly and privately—to developments like the war in Ukraine, and the shooting down of a Chinese spy balloon in February 2023.[6] As I emphasize in chapter 4 especially, the top levels of the China and Russia fields are relatively small, highly personalized spaces. While generalizations emerge, so too do exceptions. For example, I note in the book that those holding traditional forms of China expertise—mainly academic and bureaucratic—tend toward a more sympathetic view of Engagement. But there are exceptions, such as Biden's NSC director for China Rush Doshi and Trump's deputy national security advisor, Matthew Pottinger, both of whom possess traditional China professional credentials. Throughout, then, I endeavor to justify the generalizations I draw about America's China and Russia watchers.

I have refrained from identifying interviewees by name. While this choice introduces a degree of clunkiness into the writing, maintaining confidentiality enabled more open conversations than would otherwise have been the case. I use numbers to identify distinct interviews, seeking to contextualize comments as far as possible by situating interviewees' position in the community of China experts, as well as using publicly available interviews wherever possible.

As much a gateway into the China- and Russia-watching communities as a source of data, the information gained from the interviews is augmented with several other sources. The first is a set of reflections gained from attendance at several in-person China-watching events, from book talks to panel discussions, both in Washington, DC, during research trips in November 2016, November 2017, March and November 2018, October 2021, October 2022, and May 2023, and elsewhere, including the University of California, San Diego (December 2018) and meetings of the Association for Asian Studies in Washington, DC (March 2018) and Denver (March 2019). Due to the Covid pandemic, such in-person observation of the Russia community was impossible.

Although Covid interrupted the research in some respects, in others it facilitated at-a-distance observation by shifting the activities of national security experts in think tanks, academic researchers, and the media online. I have attempted to sample this inexhaustible range of online panels, talks, and hearings, with which China and Russia could easily

---

[5] Tavory and Timmermans 2014.
[6] "Downing of Chinese Spy Balloon Ends Chapter in Diplomatic Crisis," *New York Times*, 4 February 2024, https://www.nytimes.com/2023/02/04/us/politics/chinese-spy-balloon-shot-down.html.

fill every moment of every day. The ubiquitous X/Twitter has provided a final source, to be handled with care.

Together, these sources of data underpin the book's close account view of the decline and fall of Engagement with China since 1989, set in relief by comparison with U.S. policy toward Russia over the same period.

Bibliography

Abbott, Andrew. 1988. *The System of Professions*. Chicago: University of Chicago Press.
Abbott, Andrew. 2001. *The Chaos of Disciplines*. Chicago: University of Chicago Press.
Acheson, Dean. 1969. *Present at the Creation: My Years in the State Department*. New York: W.W. Norton.
Adler, Emanuel, and Michael Barnett, eds. 1998. *Security Communities*. Cambridge: Cambridge University Press.
Allen, Bethany. 2023. *Beijing Rules: How China Weaponized Its Economy to Confront the World*. New York: Harper.
Allison, Graham. 2017. *Destined for War: Can America and China Escape Thucydides' Trap?* New York: Houghton Mifflin Harcourt.
Ash, Robert, David Shambaugh, and Seiichiro Takagi, eds. 2007. *China Watching*. New York: Routledge.
Austin, Anthony, and Robert Clurman. 1969. *The China Watchers*. New York: Pyramid Books.
Beckley, Michael. 2018. *Unrivalled: Why America Will Remain the World's Sole Superpower*. Ithaca: Cornell University Press.
Beckley, Michael. 2023. The Peril of Peaking Powers: Economic Slowdowns and the Implications for China's Next Decade. *International Security* 48 (1): 7–46.
Bernstein, Richard. 2015. *China 1945: Mao's Revolution and America's Fateful Choice*. New York: Vintage.
Bernstein, Richard, and Ross H. Munro. 1997. *The Coming Conflict with China*. New York: Knopf.
Bessner, Daniel. 2018. *Democracy in Exile*. Ithaca: Cornell University Press.
Blackwill, Robert, and Ashley Tellis. 2015. *Revising Grand Strategy toward China*. New York: Council on Foreign Relations. https://www.cfr.org/report/revising-us-grand-strategy-toward-china.
Bradley, James. 2015. *The China Mirage: The Hidden History of American Disaster in Asia*. Boston: Little, Brown.
Brands, Hal. 2022. *The Twilight Struggle: What the Cold War Teaches Us about Great-Power Rivalry Today*. New Haven: Yale University Press.
Brands, Hal, and Michael Beckley. 2022. *Danger Zone: The Coming Conflict with China*. New York: W.W. Norton.
Brands, Hal, and John Lewis Gaddis. 2021. The New Cold War: America, China, and the Echoes of History. *Foreign Affairs*, November–December. https://www.foreignaffairs.com/articles/united-states/2021-10-19/new-cold-war.
Brophy, David. 2021. *China Panic: Australia's Alternative to Paranoia and Pandering*. Melbourne: La Trobe University Press.
Brose, Christian. 2020. *The Kill Chain: Defending America in the Future of High-Tech Warfare*. New York: Hachette.
Brown, Kerry. 2017. *CEO, China: The Rise of Xi Jinping*. London: I. B. Tauris.
Brown, Kerry. 2020. *China*. Cambridge: Polity.
Brown, Kerry. 2022. *Xi Jinping: A Study in Power*. New York: Icon Books.
Campbell, Kurt M. 2016. *The Pivot: The Future of American Statecraft in Asia*. New York: Twelve.
Campbell, Kurt M., and Ely Ratner. 2018. The China Reckoning. *Foreign Affairs* 97 (2): 60–70.

Canfield, Roger. 2002. *Stealth Invasion: Red Chinese Operations in North America*. Fairfax, VA: United States Intelligence Council.

Chang, Gordon. 2001. *The Coming Collapse of China*. New York: Random House.

Chin, Josh, and Liza Lin. 2022. *Surveillance State: Inside China's Quest to Launch a New Era of Social Control*. New York: St. Martin's.

Chiu, Joanna. 2021. *China Unbound: A New World Disorder*. Toronto: House of Anansi Press.

Chollet, Derek. 2016. *The Long Game: How Obama Defied Washington and Redefined America's Role in the World*. New York: PublicAffairs.

Christensen, Thomas. 2015. *The China Challenge: Shaping the Choices of a Rising Power*. New York: W.W. Norton.

Cohn, Carol. 1987. Sex and Death in the Rational World of Defense Intellectuals. *Signs* 12 (4): 687–718.

Colby, Elbridge. 2021. *The Strategy of Denial: American Defense in an Age of Great Power Conflict*. New Haven: Yale University Press.

Collins, Harry, and Robert Evans. 2007. *Rethinking Expertise*. Chicago: University of Chicago Press.

Colton, Timothy, Timothy Frye, and Robert Legvold, eds. 2010. *The Policy World Meets Academia: Designing U.S. Policy toward Russia*. Cambridge, MA: American Academy of Arts and Sciences. https://www.amacad.org/sites/default/files/publication/downloads/policyTowardRussia.pdf.

Committee of Concerned Asian Scholars. 1972. *China! Inside the People's Republic*. New York: Bantam.

Cross, Maï'a K. Davis. 2013. Rethinking Epistemic Communities Twenty Years Later. *Review of International Studies* 39 (1): 137–60.

Cumings, Bruce. 1999. *Parallax Visions: Making Sense of American-East Asian Relations at the End of the Century*. Durham: Duke University Press.

Curran, James. 2022. *Australia's China Odyssey: From Euphoria to Fear*. Sydney: NewSouth Publishing.

Davies, John Paton, Jr. 2012. *China Hand: An Autobiography*. Philadelphia: University of Pennsylvania Press.

Davis, Bob, and Lingling Wei. 2020. *Superpower Showdown: How the Battle between Trump and Xi Threatens a New Cold War*. New York: Harper Business.

Decker, Brett M., and William C. Triplett II. 2011. *Bowing to Beijing: How Barack Obama Is Hastening America's Decline and Ushering a Century of Chinese Domination*. Washington, DC: Regnery.

Denmark, Abraham. 2020. *U.S. Strategy in the Asian Century: Empowering Allies and Partners*. New York: Columbia University Press.

Desch, Michael. 2019. *Cult of the Irrelevant: The Waning Influence of Social Science on National Security*. Princeton: Princeton University Press.

Dewey, John. 1927. *The Public and Its Problems*. Denver: Alan Swallow Press.

Doshi, Rushi. 2021. *The Long Game: China's Grand Strategy to Displace American Order*. New York: Oxford University Press.

Drezner, Daniel. 2017. *The Ideas Industry: How Pessimists, Partisans, and Plutocrats Are Transforming the Marketplace of Ideas*. New York: Oxford University Press.

Easton, Ian. 2019. *The Chinese Invasion Threat: Taiwan's Defense and American Strategy in Asia*. Manchester: Eastbridge.

Easton, Ian. 2022. *The Final Struggle: Inside China's Global Strategy*. Manchester: Eastbridge.

Economy, Elizabeth C. 2019. *The Third Revolution: Xi Jinping and the New Chinese State*. New York: Oxford University Press.

Economy, Elizabeth C. 2022a. Is Engagement Still the Best US Policy for China? In Maria Adele Carrai, Jennifer Rudolph, and Michael Szonyi, eds., *The China Questions 2: Critical Insights into US-China Relations*. Cambridge, MA: Harvard University Press, 31–37.

Economy, Elizabeth C. 2022b. *The World according to China*. Cambridge: Polity.

Economy, Elizabeth C. 2022c. "Xi Jinping's New World Order: Can China Remake the International System?" *Foreign Affairs* 101 (1): 52–67. https://www.foreignaffairs.com/articles/china/2021-12-09/xi-jinpings-new-world-order.

Engerman, David. 2009. *Know Your Enemy: The Rise and Fall of America's Soviet Experts.* New York: Oxford University Press.

Eyal, Gil. 2013. For a Sociology of Expertise: The Social Origins of the Autism Epidemic. *American Journal of Sociology* 118 (4): 863–907.

Eyal, Gil. 2019. *The Crisis of Expertise.* Cambridge: Polity.

Eyal, Gil, and Larissa Buchholz. 2010. From the Sociology of Intellectuals to the Sociology of Interventions. *Annual Review of Sociology* 36: 117–37.

Feldman, Noah. 2015. *Cool War: The United States, China, and the Future of Global Competition.* New York: Random House.

Ferguson, Niall, and Moritz Schularick. 2007. "Chimerica" and the Global Asset Market Boom. *International Finance* 10 (3): 215–39.

Fish, Isaac Stone. 2022. *American Second: How America's Elites Are Making China Stronger.* New York: Knopf.

Flibbert, Andrew. 2006. The Road to Baghdad: Ideas and Intellectuals in Explanations for the Iraq War. *Security Studies* 15 (2): 310–52.

Friedberg, Aaron. 2022. *Getting China Wrong.* New York: Polity.

Fukuyama, Francis. 1992. *The End of History and the Last Man.* New York: Free Press.

Gates, Robert M. 1974. Soviet Sinology: An Untapped Source for Kremlin Views and Disputes Related to Contemporary Events in China. PhD dissertation. Georgetown University.

Gentile, Gian, Michael Shurkin, Alexander T. Evans, Michelle Grisé, Mark Hvizda, and Rebecca Jensen. 2020. A History of the Third Offset Strategy, 2014–2018. Santa Monica: Rand Corporation.

Gertz, Bill. 2000. *The China Threat: How the People's Republic Targets America.* Washington, DC: Regnery.

Gertz, Bill. 2008. *The Failure Factory: How Unelected Bureaucrats, Liberal Democrats, and Big Government Republicans Are Undermining America's Security and Leading Us to War.* New York: Crown Forum.

Gertz, Bill. 2019. *Deceiving the Sky: Inside Communist China's Drive for Global Supremacy.* New York: Encounter.

Gewirtz, Julian. 2017. *Unlikely Partners: Chinese Reformers, Western Economists, and the Making of Global China.* Cambridge, MA: Harvard University Press.

Gieryn, Thomas. 1983. Boundary-Work and the Differentiation of Science from Non-science. *American Sociological Review* 48 (6): 781–95.

Gill, Bates. 2007. *Rising Star: China's New Security Diplomacy.* Washington, DC: Brookings.

Gingrich, Newt. 2019. *Trump vs. China.* New York: Center Press.

Goldgeier, James, and Michael McFaul. 2003. *Power and Purpose: U.S. Policy toward Russia after the Cold War.* Washington, DC: Brookings Institution Press.

Goldstein, Lyle. 2015. *Meeting China Halfway: How to Defuse the Emerging US-China Rivalry.* Washington, DC: Georgetown University Press.

Gordon, Jill. 1997. John Stuart Mill and the "Marketplace of Ideas." *Social Theory and Practice* 23 (2): 235–49.

Haas, Peter. 1992. Epistemic Communities and International Policy Coordination. *International Organization* 46 (1): 1–35.

Haass, Richard. 2014. *Foreign Policy Begins at Home.* New York: Basic Books.

Hamilton, Clive. 2018. *Silent Invasion.* Sydney: Hardie Grant.

Harding, Harry. 1992. *A Fragile Relationship: The United States and China since 1972.* Washington, DC: Brookings Institution Press.

Harding, Harry. 2023. The United States and China: From Partners to Competitors in America's Eyes. In Evan Madeiros, ed., *Cold Rivals: The New Era of US-China Strategic Competition.* Washington, DC: Georgetown University Press, 66–89.

Hartcher, Peter. 2021. *Red Zone: China's Challenge and Australia's Future*. Carlton: Black.
Hass, Ryan. 2021. *Stronger: Adapting America's China Strategy in an Age of Competitive Interdependence*. New Haven: Yale University Press.
Hayton, Bill. 2015. *The South China Sea: The Struggle for Power in Asia*. New Haven: Yale University Press.
Herken, Greg. 2015. *The Georgetown Set: Friends and Rivals in Cold War Washington*. New York: Knopf.
Hill, Fiona. 2021. *There Is Nothing for You Here*. New York: Mariner Books.
Hill, Fiona, and Clifford G. Gaddy. 2015. *Mr. Putin: Operative in the Kremlin*. Washington, DC: Brookings Institution Press.
Hill, Fiona, and Angela Stent. 2022. The World Putin Wants: How Distortions about the Past Feed Delusions about the Future. Foreign Affairs 101 (5): 108–22.
Hirschman, Daniel, and Elizabeth Berman. 2014. Do Economists Make Policies? On the Political Effects of Economics, *Socio-economic Review* 12 (4): 779–811.
Hopf, Ted. 2012. *Reconstructing the Cold War: The Early Years, 1945–1958*. New York: Oxford University Press.
Hung, Ho-Fung. 2015. *China Boom: Why China Will Not Rule the World*. New York: Columbia University Press.
Hung, Ho-Fung. 2021. The Periphery in the Making of Globalization: The China Lobby and the Reversal of Clinton's Trade Policy, 1993–1994. *Review of International Political Economy* 28 (4): 1004–27.
Hutton, Will. 2007. *Writing on the Wall: China and the West in the 21st Century*. New York: Little, Brown.
Jacobs, Lawrence, and Benjamin Page. 2005. Who Influences U.S. Foreign Policy? *American Political Science Review* 99 (1): 107–23.
Jacques, Martin. 2009. *When China Rules the World: The End of the Western World and the Birth of a New Global Order*. New York: Penguin.
Janis, Irving. 1972. *Victims of Groupthink*. Boston: Houghton Mifflin.
Jervis, Robert. 1976. *Perception and Misperception in International Politics*. Princeton: Princeton University Press.
Johnston, Alastair Iain. 2003. Is China a Status Quo Power? *International Security* 27 (4): 5–56.
Johnston, Alastair Iain. 2019. The Failure of the "Failure of Engagement." *Washington Quarterly* 42 (2): 99–114.
Jones, Peter. 2015. *Track Two Diplomacy in Theory and Practice*. Stanford: Stanford University Press.
Joske, Alex. 2022. *Spies and Lies: How China's Greatest Covert Operations Fooled the World*. Melbourne: Hardie Grant.
Kagan, Robert. 2019. *The Jungle Grows Back: America and Our Imperiled World*. New York: Vintage.
Kaplan, Robert D. 2014. *Asia's Cauldron: The South China Sea and the End of a Stable Pacific*. New York: Random House.
Kimmage, Michael, and Matthew Rojansky, eds. 2019. *A Kennan for Our Times: Revisiting America's Greatest Diplomat in the 20th Century*. Washington, DC: Wilson Center.
Kissinger, Henry. 2011. *On China*. New York: Penguin.
Kuhn, Thomas. 1962. *The Structure of Scientific Revolutions*. Chicago: University of Chicago Press.
Kuklick, Bruce. 2007. *Blind Oracles*. Ithaca: Cornell University Press.
Lampton, David, Joyce A. Madancy, and Kristen M. Williams. 1986. *A Relationship Restored: Trends in U.S.-China Educational Exchanges, 1978–1984*. Washington, DC: National Academy Press.
Lanza, Fabio. 2017. *The End of Concern: Maoist China, Activism, and Asian Studies*. Durham: Duke University Press.

Layne, Christopher. 2012. This Time It's Real: The End of Unipolarity and the *Pax Americana*. *International Studies Quarterly* 56 (1): 203–13.
Lee, Kai-Fu. 2018. *AI Superpowers: China, Silicon Valley, and the New World Order*. New York: Harper Business.
Leslie, Stuart W. 1994. *The Cold War and American Science: The Military-Industrial-Academic Complex at MIT and Stanford*. New York: Columbia University Press.
Li, Cheng, eds. 2005. *Bridging Minds across the Pacific: U.S.-China Educational Exchanges, 1978–2003*. Boulder: Rowman and Littlefield.
Lieberthal, Kenneth, and Susan Thornton. 2021. Forty-Plus Years of U.S.-China Diplomacy: Realities and Recommendations. In Anne F. Thurston, ed., *Engaging China: Fifty Years of Sino-American Relations*. New York: Columbia University Press, 365–90.
Lippmann, Walter. 1922. *Public Opinion*. New York: Harcourt, Brace.
Lippmann, Walter. 1927. *The Phantom Public*. New York: Macmillan.
Madsen, Richard. 1995. *China and the American Dream: A Moral Inquiry*. Berkeley: University of California Press.
Martin, Peter. 2021. *China's Civilian Army: The Making of Wolf Warrior Diplomacy*. New York: Oxford University Press.
Mastro, Oriana Skylar. 2018. Conflict and Chaos on the Korean Peninsula. *International Security* 43 (2): 84–116.
Mathews, David. 2021. Dartmouth: Looking Forward. In Philip D. Stewart, *Six Decades of U.S.-Russia Citizen Dialogue: Past Lessons, Future Hopes*. Dayton: Kettering Foundation Press, v–vi.
Mearsheimer, John J. 2019. Bound to Fail: The Rise and Fall of the Liberal International Order. *International Security* 43 (4): 7–50.
Medvetz, Thomas. 2013. *Think Tanks in America*. Chicago: University of Chicago Press.
Menges, Constantine C. 2005. *China: The Gathering Threat*. Nashville: Thomas Nelson.
Mertha, Andrew. 2021. The Study of China and the Role of the China Scholar Community. In Anne F. Thurston, ed., *Engaging China: Fifty Years of Sino-American Relations*. New York: Columbia University Press, 89–119.
Mann, James. 1998. *About Face: A History of China's Curious Relationship with China, from Nixon to Clinton*. New York: Vintage.
Mann, James. 2004. *Rise of the Vulcans: The History of Bush's War Cabinet*. New York: Penguin.
Mattis, Peter. 2018. From Engagement to Rivalry: Tools to Compete with China. *Texas National Security Review* 1 (45): 80–94. https://tnsr.org/2018/08/from-engagement-to-rivalry-tools-to-compete-with-china/.
McCourt, David M. 2021. Framing China's Rise in the United States, Australia, and the United Kingdom. *International Affairs* 97 (3): 643–65.
McCourt, David M., and Stephanie L. Mudge. 2022. Anything but Inevitable: How the Marshall Plan Became Possible. *Politics & Society* 51 (4): 463–92. https://journals.sagepub.com/doi/full/10.1177/00323292221094084.
McCourt, David M., and Garrett Ruley. 2023. How Is the American Foreign Policy Establishment Structured? A Multiple Correspondence Analysis of the U.S. China Field. *Foreign Policy Analysis* 19 (2). https://doi.org/10.1093/fpa/orad002.
McFaul, Michael. 2018. *From Cold War to Hot Peace: An American Ambassador in Putin's Russia*. Boston: Houghton Mifflin Harcourt.
Mearsheimer, John J. 2001. *The Tragedy of Great Power Politics*. New York: W.W. Norton.
Mearsheimer, John J. 2019. Bound to Fail: The Rise and Fall of the Liberal International Order. *International Security* 43 (4): 7–50.
Meredith, Robyn. 2007. *The Elephant and the Dragon: The Rise of India and China and What It Means for All of Us*. New York: W.W. Norton.
Medcalf, Rory. 2019b. Australia and China: Understanding the Reality Check. *Australian Journal of International Affairs* 73 (2): 109–18.

Medcalf, Rory. 2022. *Contest for the Indo-Pacific: Why China Won't Map the Future*. Melbourne: La Trobe University Press.
Minzner, Carl. 2018. *End of an Era: How China's Authoritarian Revival Is Undermining Its Rise*. New York: Oxford University Press.
Montgomery, Evan Braden. 2016. *In the Hegemon's Shadow*. Ithaca: Cornell University Press.
Mosher, Steven W. 2017. *Bully of Asia: Why China's Dream Is the New Threat to the World*. Washington, DC: Regnery.
Mudge, Stephanie L. 2008. What Is Neoliberalism? *Socio-economic Review* 6 (4): 703–31.
Mudge, Stephanie L. 2018. *Leftism Reinvented: Western Parties from Socialism to Neoliberalism*. Cambridge, MA: Harvard University Press.
Navarro, Peter. 2008. *The Coming China Wars*. Upper Saddle River, NJ: FT Press.
Navarro, Peter, and Greg Autry. 2011. *Death by China: Confronting the Dragon*. Upper Saddle River, NJ: Pearson.
Newman, Robert P. 1992. *Owen Lattimore and the "Loss" of China*. Berkeley: University of California Press.
Neumann, Iver B., and Ole Jacob Sending. 2010. *Governing the Global Polity: Practice, Mentality, Rationality*. Ann Arbor: University of Michigan Press.
Nichols, Thomas M. 2017. *The Death of Expertise: The Campaign against Established Knowledge and Why It Matters*. New York: Oxford University Press.
Nye, Joseph. 2015. *Is the American Century Over?* New York: Polity.
O'Brien, Kevin J. 2011. Studying Chinese Politics in an Age of Specialization. *Journal of Contemporary China* 20 (71): 535–41.
Oren, Ido. 2003. *Our Enemies and Us: America's Rivalries and the Making of Political Science*. Ithaca: Cornell University Press.
Organski, A. F. K. 1958. *World Politics*. New York: Alfred Knopf.
Packer, George. 2020. *Our Man: Richard Holbrooke and the End of the American Century*. New York: Vintage.
Paulson, Henry. 2016. *Dealing with China*. Washington, DC: Twelve.
Pifer, Steven. 2010. Formulating U.S. Policy toward Russia. In Colton, Timothy, Timothy Frye, and Robert Legvold, eds. *The Policy World Meets Academia: Designing U.S. Policy toward Russia*. Cambridge, MA: American Academy of Arts and Sciences, 92–95.
Pillsbury, Michael. 2015. *Hundred-Year Marathon: China's Secret Strategy to Replace America as the Global Superpower*. New York: Henry Holt.
Platt, Nicholas. 2010. *China Boys: How U.S. Relations with the PRC Began and Grew*. Washington, DC: New Academia Publishing.
Poling, Gregory B. 2022. *On Dangerous Ground: America's Century in the South China Sea*. New York: Oxford University Press.
Pomfret, John. 2017. *The Beautiful Country and the Middle Kingdom: America and China, 1776 to the Present*. New York: Picador.
Pompeo, Mike. 2023. *Never Give an Inch: Fighting for the America I Love*. New York: Broadside.
Porter, Patrick. 2018. Why America's Grand Strategy Has Not Changed: Power, Habit, and the U.S. Foreign Policy Establishment. *International Security* 42 (4): 9–46.
Pouliot, Vincent. 2010. *International Security in Practice: The Politics of NATO-Russia Diplomacy*. Cambridge: Cambridge University Press.
Rachman, Gideon. 2017. *Easternization*. New York: Other Press.
Risse-Kappen, Thomas. 1994. Ideas Do Not Float Freely: Transnational Coalitions, Domestic Structures, and the End of the Cold War. *International Organization* 48 (2): 185–214.
Roach, Stephen. 2022. *Accidental Conflict: America, China, and the Clash of False Narratives*. New Haven: Yale University Press.
Roberts, Margaret. 2018. *Censored: Distraction and Diversion inside China's Great Firewall*. Princeton: Princeton University Press.
Roberts, Priscilla. 1992. "All the Right People": The Historiography of the American Foreign Policy Establishment. *Journal of American Studies* 26 (3): 409–34.

Rogin, Josh. 2021. *Chaos under Heaven: Trump, Xi, and the Battle for the Twenty-First Century.* New York: Mariner.
Rohde, Joy. 2013. *Armed with Expertise.* Ithaca: Cornell University Press.
Roy, J. Stapleton. 2018. Engagement Works. *Foreign Affairs* 97 (July–August): 185–86. https://www.foreignaffairs.com/articles/china/2018-06-14/did-america-get-china-wrong.
Rozman, Gilbert. 1983. Moscow's China Watchers in the Post-Mao Era: The Response to a Changing China. *China Quarterly* 94 (June): 215–41.
Rozman, Gilbert, ed. 1984. Soviet Studies of Communist China: Assessments of Recent Scholarship. PhD dissertation. University of Michigan.
Sandles, Gretchen Ann. 1981. Soviet Images of the People's Republic, 1949–1979. PhD dissertation. University of Michigan.
Sapolsky, Harvey M., Eugene Gholz, and Caitlin Talmadge. 2017. *US Defense Politics: The Origins of Defense Policy.* Abingdon: Taylor & Francis.
Sarotte, M. E. 2021. *Not One Inch: America, Russia, and the Making of the Post–Cold War Stalemate.* New Haven: Yale University Press.
Schell, Orville. 1989. *Discos and Democracy: China in the Throes of Reform.* New York: Anchor.
Schwartz, Morton. 1978. Soviet Perceptions of the United States. PhD dissertation. University of California, Berkeley.
Schweizer, Peter. 2022. *Red Handed: How American Elites Get Rich Helping China.* New York: Harper.
Shambaugh, David. 1991. *Beautiful Imperialist: China Perceives America, 1972–1990.* Princeton: Princeton University Press.
Shambaugh, David, ed. 2012. *Tangled Titans: The United States and China.* Lanham: Rowman and Littlefield.
Shambaugh, David. 2014. *China Goes Global: The Partial Power.* New York: Oxford University Press.
Shambaugh, David, ed. 2020. *China and the World.* New York: Oxford University Press.
Shambaug, David. 2023. The Evolution of American Contemporary China Studies: Coming Full Circle? *Journal of Contemporary China* 33 (146): 314–331.
Shifrinson, Joshua. 2018. *Rising Titans, Falling Giants.* Ithaca: Cornell University Press.
Shirk, Susan L. 2022. *Overreach: How China Derailed Its Peaceful Rise.* New York: Oxford University Press.
Short, Philip. 2022. *Putin.* New York: Henry Holt.
Shum, Desmond. 2021. *Red Roulette: An Insider's Story of Wealth, Power, Corruption and Vengeance in Today's China.* New York: Scribner.
Silove, Nina. 2016. The Pivot Before the Pivot: U.S. Strategy to Preserve the Power Balance in Asia. *International Security* 40 (4): 45–88.
Smith, Tony. 2007. *A Pact with the Devil: Washington's Bid for World Supremacy and the Betrayal of the American Promise.* New York: Routledge.
Smolla, Rodney. 2019. The Meaning of the "Marketplace of Ideas" in First Amendment Law. *Communication Law and Policy* 24 (4): 437–75.
Snyder, Timothy. 2022. *The Road to Unfreedom: Russia, Europe, America.* New York: Crown.
Spalding, Robert. 2019. *Stealth War: How China Took Over while America's Elite Slept.* New York: Portfolio Press.
Spalding, Robert. 2022. *War without Rules: China's Playbook for Global Domination.* New York: Sentinel.
Steinberg, James B. 2019–2020. "What Went Wrong? U.S.-China Relations from Tiananmen to Trump." *Texas National Security Review* 3 (1). https://tnsr.org/2020/01/what-went-wrong-u-s-china-relations-from-tiananmen-to-trump/.
Steinberg, James B., and Michael E. O'Hanlon. 2014. *Strategic Reassurance and Resolve: U.S.-China Relations in the Twenty-First Century.* Princeton: Princeton University Press.
Stent, Angela. 2014. *The Limits of Partnership: U.S.-Russian Relations in the Twenty-First Century.* Princeton: Princeton University Press.

Stewart, Philip D. 2021. *Six Decades of U.S.-Russia Citizen Dialogue: Past Lessons, Future Hopes*. Dayton: Kettering Foundation Press.

Stone Fish, Isaac. 2022. *America 2nd: How America's Elites Are Making China Stronger*. New York: Alfred A. Knopf.

Suettinger, Robert L. 2003. *Beyond Tiananmen: The Politics of U.S.-China Relations, 1989–2000*. Washington, DC: Brookings Institution Press.

Tammen, Ronald L. 2008. The Organski Legacy: A Fifty-Year Research Program. *International Interactions* 34 (4): 314–32.

Tavory, Iddo, and Stefan Timmermans. 2014. *Abductive Analysis: Theorizing Qualitative Research*. Chicago: University of Chicago Press.

Thurston, Anne F., ed. 2021. *Engaging China: Fifty Years of Sino-American Relations*. New York: Columbia University Press.

Timperlake, Edward, and William C. Triplett II. 1998. *Year of the Rat: How Bill Clinton Compromised U.S. Security for Chinese Cash*. Washington, DC: Regnery.

Trump, Donald J. 2015. *Crippled America: How to Make America Great Again*. New York: Threshold Editions.

Tuchman, Barbara W. 1971. *Stilwell and the American Experience in China, 1911–45*. New York: Macmillan.

Tsygankov, Andrei P. 2009. *Russophobia: Anti-Russian Lobby and American Foreign Policy*. New York: Palgrave Macmillan.

Van Apeldoorn, Bastiaan, and Naná de Graaff. 2016. *American Grand Strategy and Corporate Elite Networks: The Open Door since the End of the Cold War*. London: Routledge.

Vogel, Ezra, ed. 1997. *Living with China: U.S.-China Relations in the Twenty-First Century*. New York: W.W. Norton.

Walt, Stephen. 2018. *The Hell of Good Intentions: America's Foreign Policy Elite and the Decline of U.S. Primacy*. New York: Farrar, Straus, and Giroux.

Wang, Dennis. 2020. *Reigning the Future: AI, 5G, Huawei, and the Next 30 Years of US-China Rivalry*. Potomac: New Degree Press.

Ward, Jonathan D. 2019. *China's Vision of Victory*. Fayetteville: Atlas.

Wertheim, Stephen. 2020. *Tomorrow the World: The Birth of U.S. Global Supremacy*. Cambridge, MA: Belknap Press.

Westad, Odd Arne. 2019. The Sources of China Conduct: Are Washington and Beijing Fighting a New Cold War? *Foreign Affairs* 98 (5): 86–95. https://www.foreignaffairs.com/articles/china/2019-08-12/sources-chinese-conduct.

Winchester, Simon. 2009. *The Man Who Loved China*. New York: HarperPerennial.

X [George F. Kennan]. 1947. The Sources of Soviet Conduct. *Foreign Affairs* 25: 566–82.

Zakaria, Fareed. 2012. *The Post-American World: Release 2.0*. New York: W.W. Norton.

Zarakol, Ayşe. 2011. *After Defeat: How the East Learned to Live with the West*. Cambridge: Cambridge University Press.

Index

For the benefit of digital users, indexed terms that span two pages (e.g., 52–53) may, on occasion, appear on only one of those pages.

Allen, Craig, 118–19, 143–44
Allison, Graham, 158, 252
American Enterprise Institute (AEI), 6–7, 77, 127, 134–35, 282–83
Ashford, Emma, 1, 195
Atlantic Council, 21, 175, 195, 203, 204, 205, 259
AUKUS, 1–2, 103–4

Bader, Jeffrey, 118–19, 137, 143–44
Bannon, Steve, 51–52, 83, 84, 128, 272
Barr, Bill, 36, 69
Berger, Sandy, 50
Berris, Jan, 64, 143–44
"Bill's Paper", 63–64, 80, 177
Blackwill, Robert, 34–35, 77, 213–14
Blinken, Anthony, 32, 92, 94, 96, 97–100, 104–5, 270–71
Blue Team, the, 26, 52, 84, 116–17, 128, 132–33, 137–38, 144–45, 164–65, 169–74
Bolton, John, 77–78, 254–55
Brands, Hal, 124, 145–46, 157–58
Brookings Institution, The, 10–11, 39–40, 65, 108, 118–19, 120–21, 124, 142, 157–58, 252, 254–55, 282–83
Burns, William, 54–55, 103–4, 106
Bush, George H. W., 9, 10, 20, 45, 48, 53–54, 62–63, 120, 137
Bush, George W., 9, 10, 76–77, 80, 84, 115–16, 136, 154, 160, 173, 212–13, 252

Campbell, Kurt, 32, 34, 35, 37–38, 39–40, 41, 43–44, 48, 50–51, 52, 92–95, 96, 115, 123–24, 135, 136, 137, 163, 182–83, 185–86, 188, 222, 260, 264
Carter, Ashton ("Ash"), 50–51, 67–68, 145
Center for European Policy Analysis (CEPA), 6–7, 21, 232–33
Center for a New American Security (CNAS), 96, 123–24
Center for Strategic and Budgetary Assessments (CSBA), 6–7, 52, 159, 161

Center for Strategic and International Studies (CSIS), 101, 118–19, 124
Chang, Gordon, 14–15, 133, 144–45, 146
Charap, Samuel, 221–22, 238, 274–75
Christensen, Thomas, 39–40, 118–19, 141–42, 160
Clinton, Hillary, 34, 54–55, 62, 90–91, 254–55
Clinton, William ("Bill"), 40–41, 47, 54, 62–63, 136
Coalition for a Prosperous America (CPA), 79
Cohen, Eliot, 76–77, 83–84, 252
Cohen, Jerome, 124, 142–43, 163–64
Cohen, Stephen, 207–8, 209–10, 244, 276
Colby, Elbridge ("Bridge"), 115–16, 124, 145, 157–58, 188
Committee of Concerned Asian Scholars (CCAS), 129–31, 132, 207–8
Committee on the Present Danger-China (CPD-China), 83, 128, 173–74
Congressional-Executive Commission on China (CECC), 159–60, 161, 272
Cotton, Tom, 84, 148
Council on Foreign Relations (CFR), 6–7, 57–58, 95, 99–100, 124, 152–53, 158–59, 185–86, 213, 214–15, 255, 274–75
Cox, Christopher, 132–33, 171–72

Daly, Robert, 142, 169–70
Davies, John Paton, 7–8, 129
Doshi, Rush, 12, 70, 93, 96, 171–72, 284

Easton, Ian, 126–27, 144–45
Economy, Elizabeth, 8, 95, 125, 141–42

Fanell, James ("Kimo"), 128, 157–58, 188
Flynn, Michael, 108–9, 180–81, 254, 255
Fravel, M. Taylor, 118–19, 168
Freeman, Charles ("Chas"), 39, 118–19, 150–51
Fried, Daniel, 199, 216, 241, 274
Friedberg, Aaron, 41–42, 60, 70, 77, 93, 172

Gallagher, Mary, 118–19, 142–43, 168

Gallagher, Mike, 182–83, 269–71
Garnaut, John, 82–83
Gertz, Bill, 79–80, 127, 144–45, 170
Gingrich, Newt, 14–15, 83, 127
Gottemoeller, Rose, 194–95, 244, 267
Graham, Thomas, 34–35, 57, 194–96, 198–200, 201, 202, 216, 217, 218–20, 223, 229, 230–31, 232–33, 234, 242, 243–44, 247, 253, 267, 275–76

Hadley, Stephen 118–19, 131–32
Hass, Ryan, 120–21, 122, 159
Heritage Foundation, 6–7, 77, 172, 282–83
Hill, Fiona, 26–27, 108, 194–95, 197–98, 213, 218–19, 234, 240, 244, 251, 252–56, 257, 267, 268, 275–76
Holbrooke, Richard, 240–41
Huawei, 49–50, 89, 90, 181–82
Hudson Institute, 35, 64–65, 66, 71, 72, 75–76, 90, 282–83

Indo-Pacific, the, 13–14, 63–64, 70–71, 94–95, 96, 97, 102, 103, 175, 177, 179
Indo-Pacific Strategic Framework, undated, 80

Jinping, Xi, 2, 8–9, 12, 17, 35, 37, 61, 72, 74, 86, 88, 90–91, 93, 104–5, 119, 125, 126–27, 136, 148, 169, 179–80, 181, 182–83, 184–85, 261–62
Jintao, Hu, 119, 136, 169
Johnston, Alistair Iain 39–40, 41, 152, 172, 264

Kagan, Robert, 1, 83, 224–25
Kasparov, Gary, 259, 273
Kendall-Taylor, Andrea, 219, 259, 275
Kennan, George, 163, 164–65, 174–77, 197, 205, 206, 219–20, 230–31, 244, 248–50, 257, 258
Kerry, John, 91, 96
Kimmage, Michael, 197, 257–58
Kissinger, Henry, 21–22, 148–49, 163, 164, 247
Kramer, David, 144, 193, 199, 200, 202–3, 231, 232, 233, 237–38, 242, 243, 258–59, 274
Kuhn, Thomas, 58–59, 219–20
Kuo, Kaiser 120–21, 163–64
Kushner, Jared, 76, 79, 183

Lampton, David ("Mike"), 35, 137, 142
Lattimore, Owen, 7–8, 129
Li, Cheng, 118–19, 142
Lieberthal, Kenneth, 31, 50–51, 62–63, 118–19, 143–44, 156–57

Lighthizer, Robert, 14–16, 51–52, 76–77, 78–79, 87, 88–89
Link, Perry, 129–31, 168
Lord, Winston, 31, 124, 137, 141–42

Mattis, Peter, 127, 177–78
McCarthyism, 7–8, 131, 154–55
McFarland, K. T., 77–78, 180–81, 236, 255
McFaul, Michael, 15, 54, 57–58, 146, 203, 210, 213, 215–16, 222, 224–25, 240, 242, 243, 246, 248, 254–55, 273
McMaster, H. R., 51–52, 77–78, 79–80, 97, 179–80, 255, 256
Mearsheimer, John J., 16–17, 123, 146, 198–99, 248–49, 276
Medvedev, Dmitry, 15, 54–55, 57–58, 214–15, 216
Mnuchin, Steven, 51–52, 76, 86–87, 179–80

National Defense Strategy (NDS) summary 2018, 68, 81, 99–100, 179
National Security Strategy (NSS) 2017, 1–3, 56, 67, 69–70, 71, 72, 98–99
National Security Strategy (NSS) 2022, 1, 31, 98–99, 110
Navarro, Peter, 14–16, 51–52, 76, 77–79, 83, 84, 88–89, 128, 138
"Never Trump" letter, The, 77, 83–84, 252
New START, 54–55, 110, 216–17, 219
Nixon, Richard, 19, 36, 39, 43–44, 136, 164, 168, 244–45, 267–68
North Atlantic Treaty Organization (NATO), 4, 9–10, 11, 13–14, 15, 24, 25, 58, 198–99, 204, 206, 209–10, 212, 217, 219–20, 228, 240–41, 248–49, 267, 273, 274
Nuance, claims to, 5, 25–26, 140, 146, 150–52, 181, 188, 221, 225–27, 228–29, 230–31, 258, 259, 266, 268–69, 273, 275–76, 278
Nuland, Toria, 110, 219, 224–25, 237–38, 240–41, 242, 277

O'Brien, Kevin, 142–43, 155–56
O'Brien, Robert, 36, 51–52, 65–66, 72, 90, 110–11
Office of Net Assessment (ONA), 52, 132–33, 161, 172–73
Oksenberg, Michel, 40, 50–51, 118–19

Paal, Douglas, 137, 142
Partnership for Peace, The, 14, 42
Pelosi, Nancy, 105, 132, 260
Pence, Michael, 35, 64–65, 68, 71, 73–74, 75–76, 80

Pillsbury, Michael, 8, 14–15, 52, 74–75, 93, 170, 177–78
Pompeo, Michael, 36, 37, 49–50, 51–52, 65, 66, 69, 72, 74, 75–76, 77–78, 85, 86–87, 107, 125–27, 176–79
Pottinger, Matthew, 26–27, 51–52, 63–65, 77–78, 79–80, 81, 85, 90, 97, 108, 123–24, 137–38, 147, 149, 164–65, 177, 179–86, 240, 242, 251, 252–53, 254, 257, 284
Project 2049, 52, 88, 123–24, 126–27, 144–45, 161
Putin, Vladimir, 3, 4, 8–10, 12, 13, 15, 17, 19, 26–27, 32, 54, 58, 76–77, 108–9, 110, 182–83, 194–96, 197–200, 201, 203, 211–13, 214–17, 218–20, 225, 226, 233, 236, 240, 242, 245, 247, 248, 251, 252–55, 256, 258, 261–62, 267, 268, 269, 273, 274, 275–78

Ratner, Ely, 13, 34, 35, 37–38, 39–40, 41–42, 92, 94–95, 96, 103–4, 115, 123–24, 135, 145, 182–83, 222, 264, 271
Reagan, Ronald, 40, 78, 94, 136, 201
Reset, the Russia, 3, 4, 10, 15–16, 46, 53–55, 56, 57–58, 59, 200–2, 203, 211–12, 215–17, 219–20, 221, 240, 253–54, 267, 268
Rice, Susan, 91, 118–19
Rogin, Josh, 63–64, 75, 76, 78–79, 80, 90–91, 127, 158–59, 175–78, 182
Rojansky, Matthew, 26–27, 34–35, 57, 195, 197, 201, 238, 242, 243, 244, 248, 257–59, 269, 277
Rosenberger, Laura, 32, 92–93, 193
Roy, J. Stapleton ("Stape"), 7–8, 31, 38, 39, 118–19, 131–32, 136, 137, 150–51
Rubio, Marco, 84, 148, 182, 272
Rules Based International Order (RBIO), the, 69–71, 97–98, 264

Sarotte, Mary Eloise, 9–10, 14, 42, 217
Schell, Orville, 31, 124, 141–42
Schriver, Randall ("Randy"), 77, 79–80, 123–24
Shambaugh, David, 124, 141–42

Shirk, Susan, 50–51, 118–19, 141–42, 156–57, 169–70, 262
Steinberg, James, 43, 143–44, 161
Stent, Angela, 57, 228–29, 275–76
Stokes, Mark, 126–27, 144–45
Sullivan, Jake, 93–94, 99, 106, 270–71
Swaine, Michael, 118–19, 137, 144–45, 159

Taiwan, 2, 16–17, 32, 47–48, 83–84, 90, 91–92, 105, 126–27, 132–33, 151, 167, 170, 172–73, 184, 260
Talbott, Strobe, 204, 240–41, 248–49, 252
Third Offset Strategy, 10–11, 67–68, 81–82
Thornton, Susan, 8, 62–63, 164–65, 188, 272
Thucydides' Trap, 16, 158, 164, 264
TikTok, 49–50, 101–2
Trade War, the U.S.-China, 14–15, 51–52, 79, 85, 87–89, 120, 133–34, 137–38

Unites States-China Economic and Security Review Commission (USCC), 159–60, 161, 173
United States Strategic Approach to the People's Republic of China (May 2020), 35–36, 41–42, 43, 65, 69–70, 72–75, 177, 269–70

Valdai Discussion Club, 250, 251

Wallander, Celeste, 15, 43–44, 215–16, 234–35, 240, 252
WeChat, 49–50, 101–2
Weiss, Jessica Chen, 164–65, 185–87, 188, 263
Work, Robert, 67–68, 81
Wray, Christopher, 36, 90

Xiaoping, Deng, 13, 38, 119, 168–69, 262

Yellen, Janet, 95, 269–71
Yeltsin, Boris, 9–10, 13, 54, 209–10, 212, 217, 246, 247, 248–49
Yu, Miles, 125–26

Zoellick, Robert, 11, 48